W9-BRB-714

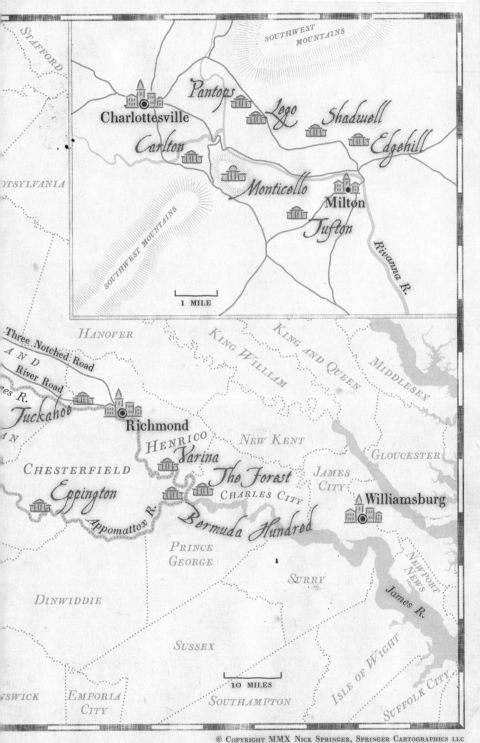

SOUTHWEST MOUNTAINS

Charlottesville

Pantops

Lego

Shadwell

Carlton

Edgehill

Monticello

Milton

Tufton

SOUTHWEST MOUNTAINS

STAFFORD

OTSYLVANIA

Rivanna R.

1 MILE

HANOVER

Three Notched Road

AND

River Road

KING WILLIAM

KING AND QUEEN

MIDDLESEX

es R.

Tuckahoe

AN

Richmond

HENRICO

Varina

NEW KENT

GLOUCESTER

CHESTERFIELD

Eppington

The Forest

JAMES CITY

CHARLES CITY

Williamsburg

Appomattox R.

Bermuda Hundred

PRINCE GEORGE

NEWPORT NEWS

DINWIDDIE

SURRY

James R.

SUSSEX

ISLE OF WIGHT

SUFFOLK CITY

10 MILES

SOUTHAMPTON

NSWICK

EMPORIA CITY

© COPYRIGHT MMX NICK SPRINGER, SPRINGER CARTOGRAPHICS LLC

Additional Praise for
THE WOMEN JEFFERSON LOVED

"The author brings out each of the women's importance in Jefferson's life and, along the way, looks at what life was like in America for women of their various social stations. . . . Scharff illuminates her impressive research, and she effectively contextualizes each of these women's stories, using them to illustrate the times and traditions in which they lived. A focused, fresh spin on Jeffersonian biography."

—*Kirkus Reviews*

"Scharff weaves a fascinating tale, enriched by the insights of the best contemporary scholarship, and seamlessly constructed from family lore, letters, garden and account books, and Martha Jefferson's housekeeping journal. This is a terrific read!"

—Barbara Oberg, General Editor,
The Papers of Thomas Jefferson, Princeton University

"If you think there's nothing new to learn about Thomas Jefferson, think again—and read this original, shrewd, and, above all, compassionate book. Virginia Scharff introduces us to the remarkable women who, as much as Jefferson himself, illuminate their time, through their lives and their strength of character."

—Elliott West, author of
The Last Indian War: The Nez Perce Story

THE WOMEN
JEFFERSON
LOVED

THE WOMEN
JEFFERSON
LOVED

VIRGINIA
SCHARFF

HARPER

An Imprint of HarperCollins*Publishers*
www.harpercollins.com

THE WOMEN JEFFERSON LOVED. Copyright © 2010 by Virginia Scharff. All rights reserved. Printed in the United States of America. No part of this book may be used or reproduced in any manner whatsoever without written permission except in the case of brief quotations embodied in critical articles and reviews. For information, address HarperCollins Publishers, 10 East 53rd Street, New York, NY 10022.

HarperCollins books may be purchased for educational, business, or sales promotional use. For information, please write: Special Markets Department, HarperCollins Publishers, 10 East 53rd Street, New York, NY 10022.

Page 451 constitutes an extension of this copyright page.

FIRST EDITION

Library of Congress Cataloging-in-Publication Data

Scharff, Virginia.
    The women Jefferson loved / Virginia Scharff.—1st ed.
      p. cm.
    Includes bibliographical references and index.
    ISBN 978-0-06-122707-3
    1. Jefferson, Thomas, 1743–1826—Relations with women. 2. Jefferson, Thomas, 1743–1826—Family. 3. Jefferson family. 4. Presidents—United States—Biography. I. Title.
    E332.2.S33 2010
    973.4'6092—dc22

                                         2010005717

10 11 12 13 14 OV/QF 10 9 8 7 6 5 4 3 2 1

TO

CHRIS

who understands the claims

of the head and the heart

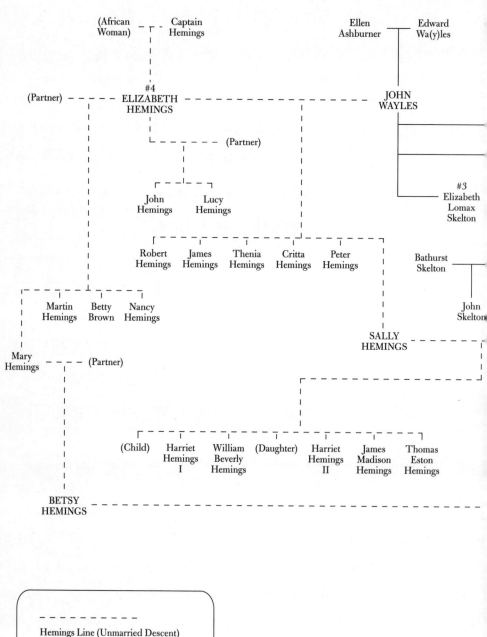

(African Woman) — Captain Hemings

Ellen Ashburner — Edward Wa(y)les

(Partner) — #4 ELIZABETH HEMINGS — JOHN WAYLES

(Partner)

John Hemings   Lucy Hemings

#3 Elizabeth Lomax Skelton

Robert Hemings   James Hemings   Thenia Hemings   Critta Hemings   Peter Hemings

Bathurst Skelton

Martin Hemings   Betty Brown   Nancy Hemings

John Skelton

Mary Hemings — (Partner)

SALLY HEMINGS

(Child)   Harriet Hemings I   William Beverly Hemings   (Daughter)   Harriet Hemings II   James Madison Hemings   Thomas Eston Hemings

BETSY HEMINGS

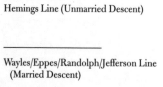

- - - - - - - - - -
Hemings Line (Unmarried Descent)

————————
Wayles/Eppes/Randolph/Jefferson Line (Married Descent)

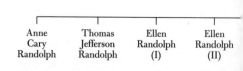

Anne Cary Randolph   Thomas Jefferson Randolph   Ellen Randolph (I)   Ellen Randolph (II)

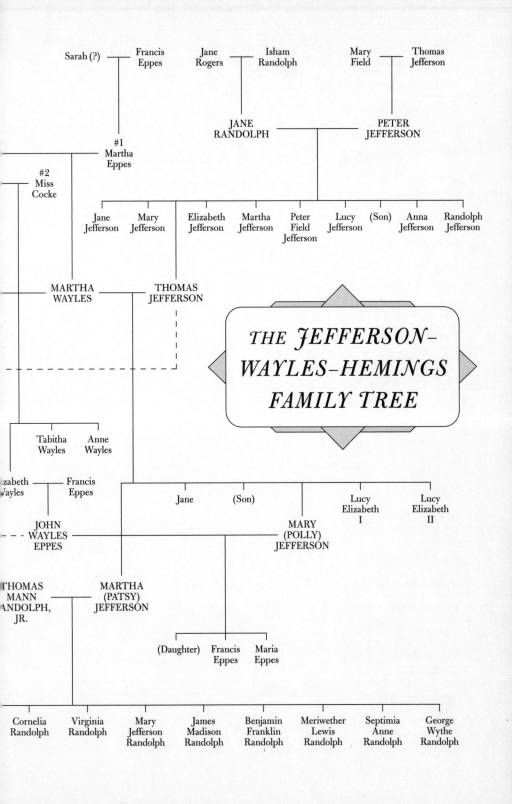

THE JEFFERSON–
WAYLES–HEMINGS
FAMILY TREE

Nobody cares for him who cares for nobody.

—THOMAS JEFFERSON, 1786

Contents

III. SALLY

IV. PATSY AND POLLY

V. A HOUSE DIVIDED

A Few Words on
Nomenclature and Genealogy

IN THIS BOOK, at the risk of appearing to lack respect for my subjects, I will often refer to people by their first names and even by nicknames, rather than by their full names or last names. I do so to avoid confusion among relatives with names so bewilderingly similar that even the most dogged reader would be flattened by the effort of trying to make sense of all the Janes and Marthas and Marys, Jeffersons and Randolphs, Johns and Thomases. I hope that by referring to Sarah Hemings as Sally and to Martha Jefferson Randolph as Patsy, I enable my readers to keep these women in plain sight. I refer to Martha Wayles Skelton Jefferson, Thomas Jefferson's wife, by her formal first name, and not her nickname (which was Patty), in order to avoid confusion between her and her long-lived daughter, Patsy Jefferson Randolph. For consistency, I also use the spelling "Hemings" for all members of the Hemings family, though some members (notably, John Hemings and Betsy Hemings) spelled their surname with two *m*'s.

Anyone who enters the world of Thomas Jefferson must also grapple with the problem of genealogy. Americans' current enthusiasm for the subject reflects our history as a nation of immigrants, a fascination with finding out from whom, and from where, we came. That passion is particularly deep-rooted in Virginia, where a cult of founding families has produced the acronym FFV, shorthand for First Families of Virginia, a three-letter soubriquet that packs a gigantic load of meaning. But genealogies, which seem to mark the orderly procession of births and marriages, the cementing of harmonious ties, hide as much complexity and conflict as they reveal. The Randolph family, for example, one of the most storied of the FFVs, has a genealogy that one wag said resembled "a tangle of fish hooks." Thomas Jefferson knew from decades of experience that genealogy was no guarantee of virtue, wisdom, loyalty, or even sanity.

Genealogies also tend to be stultifyingly repetitive and confusing, none more so than those of the Virginia families who appear here. But they are also indispensable to histories of people related by blood. I want to show the ways in which the Wayles, Hemings, Jefferson, and Eppes families came together and shadowed one another through three generations. So that readers may know the players, I offer a program, a family tree in the front, and a Dramatis Personae at the back of this book. Unlike most genealogical charts, this one includes lines that cross, which some readers may find puzzling, or even troubling. That is probably as it should be.

Introduction

CORNELIA JEFFERSON RANDOLPH, a spinster at twenty-seven, contemplated her family's ruin with more optimism than she had any right to feel. Her dear grandfather, Thomas Jefferson, had died five months before, on the fiftieth anniversary of his Declaration of Independence. His passing had left Cornelia's mother, Martha Jefferson Randolph, homeless, destitute, depressed, and exhausted. The family was making do as best it could, crowded together in makeshift households, scrimping on coffee and sugar and firewood, depending mostly on Cornelia's harried brother, Thomas Jefferson Randolph, to house them and feed them and fend off the creditors and the scavengers.

On that dreary December day of the hardest Virginia winter she had ever known, Cornelia wrote to her sister Ellen, who had escaped the worst by marrying a Yankee and moving to Boston. Cornelia confided that she hated "dependance particularly dependance on brother Jeff." Noble as he was, Jeff annoyed his sisters Cornelia, Mary, and Virginia with his nagging and penny-pinching, his second-guessing of their housekeeping, his aversion to music. Cornelia was determined to find her way to independence, inspired by her grandfather's example. "We are his children," she declared, "and the energy he has shewn in public affairs, is in our blood & we will shew it in our private affairs. we will never despair, we will never be cast down by difficulties, we will bear ourselves bravely & be cheerful in the midst of misfortunes, & if we are thrown upon our own resources we will find them in ourselves." Cornelia had seen her grandfather's perseverance. When his crippled right hand hurt too much to go on, he picked up the pen and wrote with the left.

At that very trying moment, Cornelia Randolph felt particularly close to Thomas Jefferson. She was immersed in copying his papers, perhaps the most precious thing he had left behind. Priceless as they were to his family, they were also a badly needed financial asset, soon to be sold to the Library of Congress, that great institution her grandfather had founded. Jeff Randolph served as official executor of the papers, but his sisters had the job of making legible copies of the manuscripts. As they scratched away with frozen fingers, huddled close to a meager fire, they may also have carried on another family tradition: feeding the flames with anything that felt too private or caused too much pain, anything that could not be comfortably explained or ignored.

Nearly all his adult life, Thomas Jefferson had methodically filed the letters he received, and made his own copies of the ones he wrote. But many of those letters have never been found. Like the twinned black inkblots in a Rorschach test, the missing letters sometimes form meaningful patterns, hinting at a suggestive shadow literature of their own, a record of the things Jefferson and his descendants did not care to pass down to posterity. Jefferson himself, and his daughters and granddaughters as well, sometimes ended personal letters by urging the recipient to "throw this in the fire." The burning was as creative as it was destructive. Just as Thomas Jefferson's slaves "burned" bricks to construct the walls of his magnificent house, he and his descendants burned letters to construct an imaginary but seemingly impenetrable wall between his public legacy and his private life.

As much "pulling down and putting up" went into fashioning Thomas Jefferson's correspondence for public consumption as there was in the many makings of Monticello. The voluminous corpus that remains for public perusal seems a complete collection, just as the mansion we see today appears a timeless masterpiece. But both were products of changing times and close editing, artifacts of careful storytelling, history handmade by Thomas Jefferson, his loving family, his preservers and defenders.

THOMAS JEFFERSON MEANT to make his own history. But he could not do so just as he pleased. Even as he worked to preserve the wall between his public and private lives, he insisted that everything he did and said and worked for in public, all the remarkable achievements that have made him the most beloved and vexing of the Founding Fathers, he did out of love for his family and home. His love for those closest to him, and the sacred bonds of affection, inspired his immortal embrace of life, liberty, and the pursuit of happiness. No wonder the American public has been fascinated with his private life. We agree with James Parton, the Jefferson biographer who wrote in 1874, "If Jefferson was wrong, America is wrong." We see in him America's greatness and meanness, its generosity and arrogant possessiveness, its good intentions and bad habits, its magnificent achievements and tragic shortcomings. We want to know what made him tick, to see the beating heart of him.

What Jefferson tried hardest to hide, we suspect holds the key. As it turns out, his most closely guarded secrets, most fiercely maintained silences, nearly all had to do with the women he loved. This book is about those women, about what love meant to him and to them, and about what it cost them all. Their ways of loving were different from ours, but love was a powerful force in their lives, nonetheless. We see proof of the power of love in scores of carefully preserved, fascinating letters, exchanged among Jefferson and his daughters and grand-daughters. But some of the women Jefferson loved most are hardest to know.

There may, of course, be remnants of these mysterious women hidden in private collections, keepsakes of a family history deemed too precious or too potentially embarrassing to share with the public. But as far as we know, not a scrap of paper between Jefferson and his mother survives. He, or someone else, burned every last exchange with his wife, and nearly every letter that might have mentioned his slave and concubine, Sally Hemings. After he died, his grandchildren charged themselves with keeping his secrets and preserving his legacy. They suppressed some stories and told others. They did a fine job, but they did not always tell the truth. Now we have new tools to restore what flame destroyed, what careful forgetting tried to wipe out, new ways to approach the stories passed down and repeated, denied and bitterly contested.

For decades—centuries, even—those who told the official story of Thomas Jefferson's life concealed what Jefferson wanted hidden. They tended to be white Victorian women and southern gentlemen who defended Jefferson's honor according to the code of white supremacy and racial segregation. They believed, as is written in stone at the Library of Congress, that THE HISTORY OF THE WORLD IS THE BIOGRAPHY OF GREAT MEN. Writing about the heroic Jefferson, they worked to preserve a way of life that excluded or at least diminished the importance of those people not deemed great—black people and women of any color, for example—suggesting that perhaps they were not worthwhile subjects for history at all.

But Thomas Jefferson lived out his long life embedded in a multi-generational web of biological, social, and emotional connections between his cherished white family and the family of his slave, Sally Hemings. His father-in-law, John Wayles, was father not only to Jefferson's wife, Martha Wayles Skelton Jefferson, but also to Sally Hemings and five of her sisters and brothers, making Martha and Sally half-sisters. Martha grew up with the Hemingses, brought them with her to Monticello, gathered them around her as she lay dying. Jefferson, in turn, was father to Martha's six children, and also to Sally's seven children. The Hemingses were half-cousins to Martha's daughters; they were also half-sisters and half-brothers. Jefferson's son-in-law, John Wayles Eppes, would carry on the family tradition with Sally Hemings's niece, Betsy. The two families were linked, intimately and genetically, for three generations. They have shadowed one another through history.

To this day, many who revere Thomas Jefferson see it as their duty to erase, ignore, obscure, dismiss, and angrily dispute the fact that Jefferson inhabited a house divided, one half of his family designated as white and free, the other half denigrated as black and enslaved. When Fawn M. Brodie acknowledged and investigated that kinship in her bestselling 1974 biography of Jefferson, the "Jefferson Establishment," including Julian Boyd, the editor of the definitive (and ongoing) edition of Jefferson's papers, Dumas Malone, author of the magisterial multivolume biography, and Merrill Peterson, distinguished historian of Jefferson's legacy, could no longer ignore the story. So they determined to ruin Brodie professionally, accusing her of sloppy research, falsification of data, and not least, of womanly weakness.

Much has changed since Brodie's time. Over the past dozen years or so, historians at Monticello, led by Lucia Stanton, the Shannon Senior Historian, have begun the monumental task of reuniting what had been so painstakingly kept apart, and restoring Thomas Jefferson to the complicated world in which he lived. The pathbreaking 1997 study of the evidence for Jefferson's paternity of Sally Hemings's children, by law professor and historian Annette Gordon-Reed, revealed the racism at the heart of the argument for denial and made a powerful case that Jefferson had indeed fathered Sally Hemings's children. A year later, a DNA study by Dr. Eugene Foster and others established that a Jefferson male had fathered Eston Hemings, the youngest of those children. Fraser D. Neiman, director of archaeology at Monticello, added the weight of a rigorous statistical analysis and the application of Occam's famous razor: of all Jefferson males, Thomas was far and away the likeliest father not only of Sally Hemings's youngest son, but of all her children. Gordon-Reed's highly acclaimed family history, *The Hemingses of Monticello*, stands as triumphant proof of the past it is possible to know when we stop acting as if some people never lived, or if they did, never mattered.

It is time to stop pretending that history never happened. Once we see Jefferson in his own world, the shell of the sphinx cracks, crumbles, falls away. Beneath the veneer, we find a man vulnerable and knowable, a man who makes sense, a man who belongs to all of us. In this book, I enter the world that Brodie and Stanton and Gordon-Reed and others have illuminated, to see in one place the divided family that lived so intimately together, people whose histories have been wrenched apart by the habits of intellectual apartheid. They shared a physical intimacy lasting three generations—several lifetimes of trust and betrayal, hope and disappointment, caring and resentment, obligation and desire. They were not simply Jeffersons and Hemingses; their veins also ran with the blood of Randolphs and Wayleses and Eppeses. They were linked by the power of paternity, and the blood and the pain and the love of women.

Some will object that these stories do not belong together. American slavery divided the Jeffersons and Wayleses and Eppeses and Randolphs from the Hemingses, the white families from the black, erecting a wall of tyranny that no amount of intimacy could breach. Likewise, many will point out that the habit of thinking in black and white was so deeply ingrained in all the people I write about here, that to imagine intimacy across the color line misses the larger matter of violent oppression.

The fissures of race and caste cut so deep that they wound our nation to this day. Those chasms have been kept open by force and hatred and physical brutality, including sexual violence. But it is time to relinquish the burden of segregationist histories and to imagine the possibility of reconciliation. In this book, readers will see not only the divisions, but the connections; not just the estrangements, but the (always troubled) intimacies, and not simply the prurient aspects of those intimacies, but the everyday bonds of tension and affection. Masters and slaves, men and women, did not have equal access to power or property or fame, or even to control over their own bodies. But they depended upon one another, from one generation to the next, to the point of life and death.

MY TITLE, *The Women Jefferson Loved,* invites the winking observation, "Oh, I bet there were *lots* of them!" Everybody wants to know about Jefferson's sex life. Everybody always has, ever since the days in which he had one. But I have not written this book as an inquiry into the history of Thomas Jefferson's progenerative body parts. I will disappoint some readers when they discover that I am more interested in what he did with his head and his heart. I want to know how he loved women, how he thought about and practiced his deep love of women—his mother, Jane Randolph Jefferson; his wife, Martha Wayles Skelton Jefferson; his enslaved mistress, Sally Hemings; his diverse daughters, Martha Jefferson Randolph, Mary Jefferson Eppes, and Harriet Hemings; and his Randolph granddaughters, Anne, Ellen, Cornelia, Mary, Virginia, and Septimia.

I contend that he loved them all—a controversial enough claim in its own right. Fawn Brodie and others suggested that he hated his mother. Many historians deny that he had any real feelings for Sally

Hemings. And some have seen in him a sexist reactionary pure and simple, a notable misogynist even for his own time. I see Jefferson as a possessive patriarch, as sure of his right to rule his domain as any of the kings he despised, but also as a man who loved women. Love is not a simple or predictable or necessarily helpful thing, and it is certainly not in any sense "pure." Love hurts as much as it heals, and even when love is trying its hardest to be a force for good, it makes people do small, sometimes benighted things that have great consequences. Please see the works of Shakespeare or Faulkner for examples.

AND WHAT OF the women themselves, the women Jefferson loved? Why have I chosen to focus on the women of his family? Jefferson had a number of close female friends, including, for a time, Abigail Adams, one of the great figures in American history. He formed a deep attachment to the Anglo-Italian artist Maria Cosway during their time together in Paris, and corresponded with her for the rest of his life. We have letters, quite a few letters, that attest to his regard for those formidable persons.

Abigail Adams and Maria Cosway played important parts in Jefferson's life, and readers will meet them in this book. And for a time, of course, Thomas Jefferson was *in love* with Maria Cosway. But real love between men and women was, for him, something deeper, a sacred bond that imposed on both parties a lifetime of reciprocal duties and obligations. His connections to the women in this book showed him that love was more than infatuation or companionship or a stroll through a lovely garden. Remarkable as Adams and Cosway were, they learned, to their frustration, that Thomas Jefferson sailed through his life on his own terms, and his great regard for them had no bearing on his course. The women of his family, by contrast, were the stars by which he plotted the voyage. His love for them shaped his vision for the nation, his most monumental achievements, his ongoing legacy. It is time we got to know them better.

STILL, YOU MAY say: books about Thomas Jefferson are about as rare as Tuesdays. Why this one?

The time is ripe. We have newly available materials, from the brilliantly annotated editions of Jefferson's memorandum books, to the online collections of his papers and his family's letters, to the archaeological excavations at Shadwell and Monticello. These sources make it possible to know a great deal about women who have long been considered ciphers, particularly his mother, Jane, his wife, Martha, and his slave mistress, Sally Hemings. His daughters' and granddaughters' letters are now available to anyone with an Internet connection.

Some of these women were pampered children of privilege, commanding fine houses, riding blooded horses, setting their tables with imported linen and china and silver. Some were condemned to be bondservants to their relatives, under the constant threat of sale. All of them lived in a harsh and volatile world. They were scarred by fire and flood, by slavery and war and motherhood. They had friends and relatives and acquaintances who had committed murder, and others who died by violence. Some of them were fragile, but they were not innocent. They knew kidnapping and domestic abuse and the organized viciousness of the slave trade. If nothing else, the toll of childbearing taught them about life and death.

The women Jefferson loved knew how to give orders and take them, how to make soap and bottle cider, how to make over a made-over dress. Some loved flowers and some drank beer. Some hated housekeeping, but they knew what it took to slaughter a hog, mix up a pudding, or prepare a body for burial. Some sailed across the ocean.

Some could speak French, or even Spanish and Italian, and some could read the classics in the original Latin. One could render architectural drawings with a fine hand. One saw to it that her children would go free. Not one of them could hope to attend college or cast a vote in an election.

For the most part, they relied on the weapons of the weak: indirection and manipulation. We should not look to them as perfect role models for our daughters. They were flawed humans with fascinating stories, and they mattered. Their lives, their Revolutions, their vulnerabilities shaped the choices Jefferson made, from the selection of words and ideas in his Declaration, to the endless building of his mountaintop mansion, to the vision of a great agrarian nation that powered his Louisiana Purchase. So far, the histories of these women have appeared to us as fragments of separate stories, divided by generation and, more drastically, by race. But that was not how they lived. Their fortunes and their honor were bound up with, and often at odds with, one another.

Thomas Jefferson did not live his whole life according to the things he read in the books in his library. He learned about love between men and women from his parents, and grew into a curious and exuberant young man, dreaming and planning, in a family full of sisters, in his mother's plantation house. He adored his wife and never got over the anguish of believing that he had killed her not only with his desire, but with his ambition. He cherished his daughters and tried to mold them into paragons of womanhood, looking forward to the day he could retire to Monticello and revel in the happiness of his extended family. When he entered into a liaison with the enslaved half-sister of his late wife, he vowed to do right by Sally Hemings and their children.

His notion of domestic utopia was his most tenacious and most foolish fantasy. In an ideal world, he would preside over an extended household, where they all lived together in harmony and plenty. No one will be surprised to learn that everyday difficulties and life-changing tragedies got in the way of his dream. But setbacks and crises seemed always to take him by surprise. Asking each of the women he loved to honor his commitment to the others, to suppress their warring interests, jealousies, and anger, he imposed upon them a regime of silence and tension we can barely fathom.

Jefferson struggled all his life to fulfill the promises he made to the women of his family, to honor the love they bore him, each in her own fashion, which he returned, in his. He pledged his devotion in the midst of political upheaval, invasion, and war, at heady moments of liberation and amid the mundane cruelties of slavery, in the fertile exuberance of a Monticello spring and the crushing torment of a new mother's deathbed. His promises differed just as much as there are different ways a son loves his exasperating mother, a husband his mortal wife, a father his devoted daughters, a master his solicitous mistress and slave, a grandfather his adoring granddaughters.

Jefferson talked about love all the time, but we have either not listened very carefully to what he was saying, or have refused to take him at his word. In the heat of his greatest political challenges—writing the Declaration, dealing with Cornwallis's invading army, fomenting revolution in France, awaiting the outcome of the election of 1800—he longed to be home, surrounded by peace and harmony and attentive women and charming children. He never gave up that romantic vision, and he never stopped trying to make it a reality. For Jefferson, love was indestructible and lifelong, a self-evident truth and a sacred obligation. Love was loyal and generous beyond limit. But it was not equal.

As strongly as he argued that men must have individual liberty, he believed just as deeply that women were fitted by nature to depend on men. He embraced that natural order as a fundamental condition for happiness, in large matters as well as small: the personal was the political. Jefferson thought men should protect and provide for the women they loved. He labored his whole life to fulfill that sacred trust. But he was also idealistic and nostalgic, sentimental and self-justifying. He could be nearly delusional in his optimism, insisting that he would take care of everyone and everything, that things would turn out all right. And when he failed, it broke his heart.

THE WOMEN
JEFFERSON
LOVED

Part I

JANE

1

The Planter's Daughter

BEFORE SHE REACHED the age of six, Jane Randolph took the most momentous step of her life. She walked up the gangplank of a ship bound from England, across the ocean to the Chesapeake. Jane, of course, had no choice in the matter. Her father, Captain Isham Randolph, had decided to return to the land of his birth. The Randolph clan was fast becoming one of the richest and most influential families in Virginia, and Isham's parents had bequeathed substantial colonial estates to all their sons. It was time to take up planting in earnest.

Isham had called London home for years. He had gone to sea as a young man and in 1710, at the age of twenty-five, had assumed command of his first vessel, the *Henrietta*. He took up residence in England, and seven years later married an Englishwoman, Jane Lilburne Rogers, who hailed from the parish of Shadwell, a precinct at the edge of London that was just beginning to attract the chaotic custom of seafaring men. Captain and Mrs. Randolph entertained visitors from near and far. One such guest, a young Virginia gentleman by the name of John Carter, found Isham lively company and described his young bride as "a pretty sort of woman."

Isham Randolph prospered, commanding ships and selling tobacco for his fellow Virginians, buying and shipping British goods. But the tobacco trade was shifting from London to Glasgow, Liverpool, and Bristol. He had a choice to make. His brother, Edward, moved to Bristol with his English wife, who was said to despise slavery so much that she flatly refused to consider living in Virginia. Isham charted a different course and wagered his prospects on Virginia and tobacco and slavery. His first two children had been born in England, but his future offspring would be native to the New World. He would raise them all to take their places as plantation masters and mistresses.

THE RANDOLPH FAMILY sailed to America sometime between August 1724 and October 1725. As a small child, Jane could not have understood the perils she faced. Passengers heading westward in those days typically bade their farewells with no small measure of fear. Some were literally bound for the New World, forced to go as indentured servants, or under the lash of enslavement. Many were lost at sea, and those who survived might never again see the loved ones they had left behind.

In times of war, ships traveled in immense convoys extending into the hundreds of vessels. Captains like Isham Randolph hated the delays, the discipline, and the perils of knocking into other boats, or the equally daunting danger of lagging behind or blowing off course and into the hands of the enemy, or the clutches of pirates. But happily, England was at peace, and Isham Randolph was no neophyte. Mrs. Randolph and her daughter and small son could feel confident on the voyage.

Of course, a transatlantic voyage was no easy thing. They would be on the water at least six weeks with fair winds, and longer in bad weather. Even if they made good time, they had to endure the close and crowded quarters, the pitching and rolling of small wooden vessels, the perils of wind and choppy seas, the foul drinking water.

Little water could be spared for washing. Many ships had problems with rats and worm-infested, spoiled, or scarce provisions. Passengers who did not suffer from seasickness could not escape from those who did, and ships were ideal and infamous containers for deadly contagions including smallpox.

Even on voyages where stores were abundant, passengers and crew ate mostly ship's biscuit, salted meat, peas, and cheese. If they wanted anything further, fresh meat, for example, someone would have to slaughter a sheep or a pig on deck. Passengers ate what and where they could, often balancing their dinners on their laps, sometimes sharing one bowl among several people, passing a spoon from hand to hand. It was enough to drive people to drink even more than they did on land. The combination of poor sanitation and rolling waves made the crossings interludes of nastiness, misery, and even death, for too many travelers. Captain Randolph's English wife knew the dangers all too well. The year before their journey, an acquaintance of her husband's, a twenty-three-year-old Virginian named Thomas Jefferson, had died aboard Isham Randolph's ship, the *Williamsburg.*

But whether the journey was long and difficult, or blessedly short and calm, or something in between, both Mrs. Randolph and little Jane and her baby brother proved equal to the crossing. They were pampered passengers, assuredly not among those obliged to slit an animal's throat and clean up the blood and entrails, or even to cook the bacon. Captain Randolph's wife and children were accustomed to being waited on by servants, some of them perhaps Africans the Randolphs held in slavery. Isham's business interests included trafficking in slaves, a hideous commerce England had opened to private merchants in 1712. Scarcely sixty years earlier, the Virginia legislature had passed a law declaring that such people taken from Africa would be obliged to serve their masters all their lives, and that their slavery would be hereditary. Some or all of those servants would have accompanied the family on board, to ease the discomforts of passage for the white man and woman and their children. They would not have been left behind, because slaves were valuable property. From the moment they disembarked in Virginia, the Randolphs' African servants and all their progeny would be considered not people, but chattel.

Before Captain Randolph's family ever sailed, little Jane had already assumed some of the privileges she would enjoy as the eldest daughter of a slaveholding Virginia family. But Jane could not have begun to imagine what she would find upon her arrival in a new world of amazing possibility and massive brutality.

AS THE SHIP sailed into Chesapeake Bay, into the mouth of the James River, the heavily wooded shoreline, broken here and there by plantation landings and small settlements, was a wondrous, daunting sight to English eyes accustomed to the tamed and cutover aspect of their native land. But there was family aplenty to welcome them. While their own home was being readied, the Randolphs found shelter in Williamsburg, and with Isham's father, William, at Turkey Island plantation, at the juncture of the Appomattox and the James. By 1730, young Jane Randolph and her parents, brother, and two small sisters found their way to their new home; they ferried up and across the rivers and creeks of water-scored country to Dungeness plantation in Goochland County, on the north bank of the James.

Isham Randolph traded the ocean for the land, planted vast fields of tobacco, and took his place in local politics. As he did his duty with the colonial militia, stood for the House of Burgesses, and exchanged the title of "captain" for "colonel," he built a fortune on high tobacco prices and erected a house said to be among the most lavish in the colony.

Which was, let it be said, pretty lavish. In a world of Virginia to-bacco gentry dedicated to keeping up with English fashions in learn-ing, living, and consuming, Isham and Jane Randolph set the bar high. A portrait of Isham, painted not long before he left England, re-veals a stout fellow in a curled white wig, frock coat, vest, and spotless linen cravat, gazing calmly at the viewer, a portfolio under his arm. His Dungeness estate was a stunning place, with a coach house, mill house, henhouse, horses and chariot for riding, and vast gardens se-questered behind brick walls. The household was stocked with the very latest in European furnishings, food, and drink, and was tended by a hundred enslaved people. Family portraits hung on the walls. In London, Isham had kept company with wealthy merchants like Philadelphia's Peter Collinson, a devotee of the science of botany, and members of the Royal Society, including Hans Sloane, founder of the British Museum. In Virginia, he maintained his reputation as a stylish, generous host and a cultivated man. When Collinson's friend and protégé, Pennsylvania botanist William Bartram, began to make plans for a tour of Virginia, Collinson urged Bartram to seek out Isham Randolph. "No one," Collinson told Bartram, "will make thee more welcome."

Randolph's hospitality came with expectations. Virginia tobacco lords and ladies dressed in satins and lace in the latest style. They wore elaborate wigs and hats and elegant shoes and silk stockings (al-though, truth be told, bathing was not generally among their daily habits). Bartram, a farmer by trade and a Quaker by faith, affected plain speech and modest clothing. Peter Collinson urged his protégé to dress to impress, or at least not to embarrass. "One thing I must desire of thee," Collinson wrote Bartram: do "not appear to disgrace thyself or me; for though I should not esteem thee less to come to me in what dress thou will, yet these Virginians are a very gentle, well-dressed people, and look, perhaps, more at a man's outside than his inside. For these and other reasons, pray go very clean, neat, and handsomely dressed, in Virginia."

An opulent establishment like Dungeness required a mistress who knew how to manage legions of people and immense quantities of food, drink, and furnishings. Jane's mother had to entertain guests with witty conversation and amusing activities, planning each day as if a horde of unexpected visitors might arrive at any minute. The mistress needed to perform her duties, and compel others to do theirs, in sickness and in health, a tall order. Disease, infection, accident, and, not least, the manifold dangers of pregnancy and childbirth killed Virginia women early and often. In fact, in colonial Virginia, as in many other places and times in the world's history, there were two kinds of women: those lucky enough to be fitted for carrying and bearing children, and those for whom maternity was deadly. Isham Randolph had made a fortunate choice in his wife. Jane Rogers Randolph would be the first of her line in Virginia to prove a great breeder.

Daughter Jane was the eldest of the nine of Jane Rogers Randolph's children who survived to adulthood, six of them female, five born at Dungeness. Such a brood must have rattled the walls of even a very large mansion, and a growing girl in a crowded house knew something about the rigors of pregnancy and childbirth, as her mother loomed heavy and large, again and again, as each labor began and as the pains wore on. Someone would be called to help, a relative, a slave "auntie," a neighborhood midwife, entrusted to oversee the proceedings. Everyone might treat the lying-in times as matters of course, going mostly about their business, but surely sometimes the household grew hushed and fearful, listening anxiously to groans or screams until the crisis was past, the newest Randolph suckling or sleeping. Was young Jane allowed into the room, to hold a hand, or fetch water, or just be a comfortingly healthy sight? Perhaps she was curious and eager to learn about women's duties and destinies. Or maybe she was querulous or timid or fretful or angry, best kept out of the way?

Whether or not she was deliberately brought to witness her mother's trials, Jane doubtless acquired some knowledge of the mysteries of childbirth, just as surely as she learned to inventory the hams hanging in the smokehouse, count up the silver spoons, and keep track of the wine goblets. She also watched her elders demonstrate how to give orders, and learned to practice that art at a very early age. Planters' daughters like Jane had slave girls near their own age as maids to iron their linens and carry their slops. Jane was raised to be a lady. She was taught to read and write, by her mother or perhaps by a tutor hired primarily to give lessons to her brothers. She learned to dance and play and sing from the dancing masters and music teachers who came to Dungeness to instruct the master's children. She was being prepared for the marriage market.

AT THE AGE of nineteen, Jane was more than old enough to marry, and she needed to do so. Dungeness, and Isham Randolph's other holdings, did not belong to Jane. Her three brothers would inherit the lands, furnishings, and people that her father left behind. The six Randolph daughters were promised so-called marriage portions of two hundred pounds each, but Jane and her sisters had to find their own fortunes in husbands, preferably reliable men with good prospects.

Jane may well have welcomed the chance to get married and have a house of her own, away from a mother hardened by duty. According to family tradition, recalled decades later by Jane's great-granddaughter, Jane's mother was "a stern, strict lady of the old school, much feared and little loved by her children." Jane had accepted the commands of her father, the disciplines imposed by her mother, and now she would have the duty to obey her husband. She would keep a tidy, comfortable, orderly house, instruct her children, and submit to her husband's will and wishes. If the man she married lived up to expectations, he in turn would provide financial security and protect her, as far as he could, from physical harm. But even as a husband should be lord and master, a planter's wife had privileges and responsibilities of her own.

Jane Randolph was something of a pioneer, the first among a new generation of women in her family raised from childhood to run plantations and command slaves. Her mother had come to Virginia as an adult and a foreigner. When she arrived in the Chesapeake, this Englishwoman from the outskirts of London had to learn new tasks and habits, how to use or avoid the unfamiliar plants and animals that surrounded her, how to instill obedience in people whose loyalty could not be assured. Simply to get from one place to another in Virginia, Isham Randolph's wife had to navigate a watery landscape of far-flung households linked by creeks and rivers. Spring "freshets," the Virginian term for floods, occurred with regularity. In 1724, one famous freshet wrecked houses and destroyed most of the tobacco along the James River, and even drove boats ashore. When Jane grew up and had her own place on the Rivanna, recurring freshets carried off boats and outbuildings and destroyed a painstakingly built mill dam.

Jane Randolph's mother had to learn the lay of the land and the movements of water, and she had to master the peculiarities of slaveholding, to find her place among the people of Virginia. The rigors of such a life transformed Isham Randolph's wife from the "pretty sort of woman" of London into the "stern, strict lady . . . much feared and little loved" of Virginia. Mrs. Randolph, like her daughter Jane, learned how to live in Virginia from a man who had made his living commanding ships and growing and trading tobacco and slaves.

Neither sea captains nor plantation masters were renowned for their tender mercies.

IF HIS TREATMENT of other people's human property offers any clue to how he ruled his own slaves, Isham Randolph was a harsh master. Like most elite Virginia men, he served his time as a justice of the peace and commander of militia, and rose to the rank of adjutant general of the colony. And like most planters and magistrates, Randolph dealt harshly with any sign of unrest among the enslaved. When he was judge in the trial of "some Negroes charged with murder," Randolph saw no reason for clemency, even toward three of the accused who were his own brother's slaves. According to Randolph family chronicler Jonathan Daniels, Isham Randolph

> . . . approved the sometimes savage punishments which prevailed. As a justice he joined several other such officials in the trial of some Negroes charged with murder. Since three of the slaves on trial belonged to his brother William he might have excused himself. Still he agreed in the judgment that two convicted slaves not only be hanged but that their bodies be dismembered and that the heads and quarters be displayed on poles in various parts of the county. The decorative society in which Isham lived could be a harsh one too . . . well described by [William] Byrd who had slaves whipped and then gave them a bottle of rum: "they had a fiddle and danced while I walked in the garden."

Dismemberments and gardens, whippings and fiddles and rum. Young Jane Randolph grew up in a world of savage contradictions, where gayety and cruelty, fear and privilege sat uneasily side by side. She learned to be a woman amid a hundred enslaved people hoeing tobacco and holding horses, gathering eggs and butchering pigs, hauling water and carrying dishes to table. Slaves waited on the denizens and guests of Dungeness plantation and did the everyday work of farming and feeding and clothing and cleaning. They coped with itinerant botanists and mounted banquets and balls and weddings and funerals. They labored out of fatalism or loyalty, out of habit or an inability to envision alternatives, and always under the threat of punishment. Their work might bring some pleasure, some joy even, but in the end they were compelled, at the snap of the lash, to do what their masters wanted them to do.

For all their power, the masters feared their slaves. Rumors of slave conspiracies, and the actuality of punishments for rebellion, swirled like a poisonous fog around Jane Randolph's early days and brought swift retribution upon discovery. A 1722 plot had landed seven enslaved men in the Williamsburg jail, awaiting a trial in which three of the leaders would be sentenced to be sold and transported out of the colony for "conspiring among themselves and with the said other slaves to kill murder & destroy very many." These conspirators, like seven men convicted not long after in a similar scheme, were sold and exiled rather than executed, since judges did not want to have to reimburse masters out of the public treasury. But exile, for the enslaved, likely meant a trip to the sugar plantations, tantamount to a sentence of death.

Insurrection scares and real plots led the Virginia legislature in 1723 to clamp down on enslaved people in a series of harsh measures. Slaves' ability to travel, assemble, attend church or go to funerals, or possess weapons was severely curtailed. The law also made it hard for masters to free their slaves. In young Jane's world, owners who had misgivings about the institution of slavery kept their thoughts to themselves. They worked hard to maintain control, suspecting that some slaves would turn to violence to escape their chains, if they could.

In 1730, when Jane was ten, a larger plot was uncovered. A rumor had spread that the king had issued an order freeing all Christian slaves, but that Virginia's Governor William Gooch had suppressed the king's proclamation. Slaves fired with the holy spirit of Christian evangelism determined that their salvation in the next world should entitle them to their freedom in this one. The rebellion spread to as many as five Virginia counties. Four ringleaders were executed, and the rest were severely punished. Governor Gooch called up white militias to patrol two or three nights a week to prevent secret meetings, and even required militiamen to bring their guns to church on Sundays.

What did such alarms mean for the Randolphs of Dungeness, the home of so many enslaved Africans and their American-born descendants? Our glimpses of Isham Randolph's draconian judicial record suggest that the genial, gracious master of Dungeness, "a Gentleman well known and universally loved" according to the terms of his appointment as adjutant general of Virginia, ran his realm with a belief in the efficacy of terror.

A YOUNG VIRGINIA gentlewoman of the 1730s might have looked uneasily to her future, anxious for a husband who could provide for her needs and, with any luck, treat her with at least a little respect and affection as he increased the family's fortunes. For Jane Randolph, Peter Jefferson appeared a solid bet. He was thirteen years older than Jane, a giant, some said, big and powerful enough to tip up a thousand-pound hogshead of tobacco with each hand. When he went off on long surveying trips in the wilderness, they said, Peter "could tire out his assistants, and tire out his mules; then eat his mules, and still press on, sleeping alone by night in a hollow tree, to the howling of the wolves."

This early American Paul Bunyan must have towered over his future wife. As for her temperament, her great-great-granddaughter avowed that Jane Randolph was "a woman of a clear and strong understanding, and, in every respect, worthy of the love of such a man as Peter Jefferson." She was said to possess that "cheerful and hopeful temper and disposition" so characteristic of her eldest son, Thomas. Henry Randall, the man Thomas Jefferson's grandchildren chose to write the first grand Jefferson biography, deemed Jane

> an agreeable, intelligent woman, as well educated as the other Virginia ladies of the day, . . . but that by no means implying any very profound acquirements—and like most of the daughters of the Ancient Dominion, of every rank, in the olden time, she was a notable housekeeper. She possessed a most amiable and affectionate disposition, a lively, cheerful temper, and a great fund of humor. She was fond of writing, particularly letters, and wrote readily and well.

Unaccountably, some later Jefferson biographers took a dimmer view of the great man's mother. Randolph family chronicler H. J. Eckenrode offered an unflattering portrait based solely on her age at the time of her marriage to Peter Jefferson:

> Possibly the Dungeness family was glad to get such a level-headed young chap as a husband for the girl. It is even probable that she was not good-looking and, consequently, was not much pursued by the young gentlemen of the vicinity. She was nineteen years old when married, a ripe age for marriage in a period when, because of the urge for population, girls married at sixteen, fifteen, or even earlier.

In fact, white women of Jane's time and place typically married in their late teens or early twenties, so she was hardly "on the shelf" when she wed Peter Jefferson. Her father promised her husband a dowry of two hundred pounds sterling, no more than he offered for his other daughters. Such an amount, while substantial, was well within the means of a man engaged in the big business of the day: tobacco and slaves. The year that Jane married Peter Jefferson, Isham Randolph shared a consignment of 380 persons, captured from Africa to be brought to Virginia and sold into slavery. Isham might even have offered Jane a marriage portion including slaves, as many slaveholding fathers did. But if there were human beings among Jane Randolph's wedding presents, no marriage settlement recorded the gifts. Whatever Isham Randolph's intentions, the dowry pledge was eventually paid out of his estate. Isham Randolph died four years after Jane and Peter Jefferson's marriage. By that time the couple had headed west, to grow up with the country.

2

The Planter's Wife

PETER JEFFERSON WAS a man of substance, with complicated and far-flung affairs to tend. As an expert surveyor and mapmaker, he trekked off to remote corners of Virginia for weeks and months at a time. He sought and won public office, as justice of the peace, then sheriff of the county, and like his father-in-law, he was commissioned colonel in the colonial militia. He had dozens of slaves and hundreds of acres of real estate. He wanted more land and would acquire more human property. When Peter was absent, Jane had to see to the farm and deal with anyone who came to buy or sell, to collect debts, to make demands. There must have been days she dreaded, times when she wondered and worried.

Peter did what he could to give his family comfort and prosperity. Men who meant to rise by planting tobacco looked for land on the water so they could ship their crop to market. He had inherited from his father a place on Fine Creek, some fifteen miles distant from Dungeness on the other side of the James. But he wanted to move west. He had some land up on the Rivanna River, just east of the Blue Ridge Mountains, where he hoped to build a permanent home. The best place for a house, however, was on an adjoining tract owned by Jane's cousin William Randolph, a rich and almost too convivial young man. William and Peter were great friends, and a Jefferson family story related the casual way in which Peter Jefferson came to possess his Albemarle County plantation. When he let William Randolph know he wanted the land for his house, Randolph offered to trade the land for a bowl of arrack punch. Peter called the new place Shadwell, in homage to Jane's birthplace, a gesture designed to help her imagine this farm in the forest as a new home, however removed from her family and friends. Peter may have moved to Shadwell as early as 1737, and when they married in 1739, Jane joined him there. The first child born to Jane at Shadwell, in 1740, was a daughter, named Jane after her mother and grandmother.

In eighteenth-century Virginia, having babies was the most dangerous thing a person could do, more lethal than hunting or going to battle or drinking a bowl of arrack punch and then getting on a horse to ride home. We may wonder how Jane Jefferson prepared for what was then called her "confinement" in a country where white settlers were still few and houses were far apart. Her sister, Mary Lewis, lived nearby, and they probably summoned a neighborhood midwife, as they did for slave women at Shadwell. And what of Peter? Was he at home when the babies were born, or would it have taken some time, even been impossible, merely to get word to him, off in the fields or forests or tending to remote business, that Jane's time had come? Whatever the company or the circumstances, Jane Jefferson was fitted for childbearing. She had a second daughter, Mary, in 1741, and was pregnant with her third child when her father, Isham Randolph, died in 1742. Thomas Jefferson, born at Shadwell in 1743, never knew the grandfather who had planted his family in Virginia, nor did his sister Elizabeth, born a year and a half after her brother.

At the moment Thomas Jefferson was introduced to the world, Shadwell was a work in progress. It took a long time to cut down trees and pull up stumps, to frame and roof and finish even a modest house, in that era of hand-hewn joints and hand-forged nails. Peter probably did some of the building himself, but he also hired free workers and used slave labor. Shadwell was a place still being torn out of a country of densely wooded steep hillsides, cut by rivers that could swell and rage, miles from the cluster of plantations along the James that Jane Randolph Jefferson knew best. But Shadwell was also the beautiful place where she would live out her life. Maybe Jane loved it from the first, when it was still wild, and loved it still more as work and time brought order and prosperity. The Jeffersons would ultimately have a fine house there, a center of hospitality fully equipped with everything a prominent Virginia family might need or want.

In the early years, with four children and an enterprising, fast-moving husband, Jane had plenty to do to make Shadwell feel like home. We may wonder how she managed the trick. Did she sing as she stewed apples or beat a carpet? Did she have a guitar or a fiddle, was she partial to hymns or country tunes or lullabies, did she read music, as so many well-born Virginia girls did? Surely bearing four children in less than five years took a toll on her spirits as well as her body. Doubtless she longed for company and comfort. Amid her tangle of kin and friends at Dungeness, Peter Jefferson had been an up-and-comer in a well-established community. Out at the edge of settlement, he was a leading man in a new world. As his wife, Jane had to deal with visitors as well as children and servants. The planter's wife had dozens of daily duties: clothes to be made and mended, meals planned and prepared, a cow to feed and milk, chickens and eggs, a garden to tend, beer to be brewed. Pigs were useful—fat to render into lard for cooking or mix with ashes and lye for soap, meat to be butchered and smoked, bristles for brushes. Jane left the heaviest and dirtiest jobs to others—to slaves, by and large, but also to hired help. As mistress of an increasingly grand establishment, Jane delegated to others many of those things that humbler housewives did themselves. For one thing, it seems that she did not nurse her babies. She probably handed that task over to a slave mother who cared for the little Jeffersons along with her own children.

Now Jane had a place of her own after growing up amid the hubbub of so many sisters and brothers and cousins and friends. But if she was sometimes overworked and homesick, fate provided a tragic cure for the malady. William Randolph, the cousin who had deeded Shadwell to Peter Jefferson for a bowl of punch, died in 1745. Randolph had been a widower, and he left three young children and a fine plantation house at Tuckahoe, scarcely ten miles from Dungeness. Facing his death, Randolph had asked Peter to move to Tuckahoe and take care of his orphaned children. Peter and Jane, their four children, and some of their slaves packed up and headed back to Goochland County, where they would remain for nearly eight years.

Most people have a hard time remembering events of their lives before the age of three, but in the quality of his memory, as in so many other things, Thomas Jefferson proved a prodigy. His earliest recollection was of the journey to Tuckahoe, when he was scarcely two years old, being carried on a pillow by a slave on horseback. We do not know whether Jane rode a horse or traveled in a carriage, but she may have been pregnant, again, when she made the trip.

Whatever Jane's reservations about leaving her home, there were advantages to moving to Tuckahoe. The house, an H-shaped brick and frame structure with two tall chimneys, was grander than the Jeffersons' Shadwell place, and Tuckahoe was much nearer to her family and friends. There Jane would bear four more children, a daughter, Martha, in 1746; Peter Field, born in 1748, who survived only a month; an unnamed son, born in 1750, who lived but a day; and Lucy, born in 1752.

At Tuckahoe, Peter Jefferson took on the management of a large house, enormous landholdings, and scores of enslaved people in addition to his own properties. At least seven Tuckahoe overseers supervised the growing of far more tobacco than Peter grew at Shadwell and his other Albemarle County plantations. This was also the time in their marriage when Peter launched his greatest adventures as a surveyor. In 1746 and again in 1749, he led ambitious mapmaking expeditions commissioned by crown and colony. He headed off into the dense forests and rough terrain, to face rotten weather, wild animals, unruly crews, and hunger bordering sometimes on starvation. On these dangerous excursions he was far out of touch. He left the management of the land and field workers to overseers while Jane looked after her six surviving children and the three young Randolphs, in a household larger than any she had commanded before.

Tuckahoe was not precisely hers to command. She was the wife rather than the husband, and she was not fully the lady of the house. The Jeffersons and their Randolph charges could live in the double-winged mansion almost as two families, with the Jeffersons as resident plantation stewards and caretakers of the Randolph heir-in-waiting and his sisters. Jane had to impose her will on the enslaved people who carried out her commands, some of them brought from Shadwell, others destined to become the property of young master Thomas Mann Randolph, still others newly hired or purchased. Keeping order, preventing or dealing with open defiance, could not have been easy. Or pretty.

BACK HOME AT Shadwell, slaves and hired managers saw to things while the Jeffersons were gone. They moved back permanently to Shadwell in the summer of 1753. The Jeffersons' newly expanded story-and-a-half house had four large rooms and a hall passage on the ground floor, with two bedrooms upstairs, encompassing some 1,600 square feet of living space, along with a large brick cellar below.

The house faced the Rivanna on the south, and the "Three-Notched Road," the county's main east-west thoroughfare, to the north. There was a kitchen outbuilding and a house for an enslaved cook and her family, along with quarters for thirty or more slaves. There were fences and gates and vegetable and flower gardens laid out in numbered beds, each row designated by a letter. Peter erected a sundial to track the hours of the day. Shadwell was a busy, orderly, beautiful place. Jane and her children planted hyacinths and narcissus, carnations and marigolds, lilacs and Spanish broom. In the woods, violets and dwarf irises and wild honeysuckle bloomed.

Jane had grown up in a family that owned the latest imported luxuries—French silk and English china and dainty glassware, walnut and cherry furniture and silver flatware, spices for cooking, wine and leather-bound books. The Jeffersons too had such things, entertaining their guests with coffee and tea, punch and wine, rum, Madeira, and cider, and eating their meals on well-set tables spread with damask cloths. Jane's son Thomas would, in later years, become famous for his love of gourmet cuisine and fine wine, of fragrant flowers and fresh vegetables. He learned early and well the delights of the first peas and asparagus and cucumbers of the season, served in refined style at his mother's table.

The Jeffersons sated their appetites with fancy imported goods, but they raised and made and processed all kinds of things on the plantation. The people at Shadwell consumed massive amounts of beef, corn, pork, and wheat, and needed light as well as heat, clothing as well as food. Jane, or her daughters and slaves, brewed beer, and someone at Shadwell made candles, a process that began with the slaughtering of animals and the rendering of fat. There were sheep at Shadwell, and both there and later at Monticello, slave women spun and wove. When Thomas Jefferson moved to Monticello, he sent his mother unwashed wool and picked cotton, so somebody in her household must have been washing and carding and spinning before the time came for knitting stockings or weaving cloth or cutting out clothes.

Jane's daughters took on some of that work. Jane Jr. and Mary were thirteen and twelve when they moved back to Shadwell, easily old enough to work a spinning wheel and handle a pair of knitting needles, and both girls eventually owned wheels of their own. Elizabeth, at eight, would already have shown signs of the mental retardation that kept her a child the rest of her life. Martha, at six, was just beginning to help her mother around the house, though Lucy, still a baby, would have been years away from taking on even small tasks. There would be extra work for the girls in 1755, when their mother gave birth to twins, Anna Scott and Randolph, both of whom may also have suffered brain damage at birth. But Jane also paid small sums to neighbor women for "knitting stockings for the children" and making "negroes clothes." Jane spent her own time on other pursuits.

As the Jefferson children were growing up, Shadwell was on a main east-west route through Virginia. Friends and family lived close enough to visit, but often too far away to go home at night. Entertaining visitors meant feeding and sheltering not only the human guests and the slaves who attended them, but also the horses that brought them and drew their carriages. Thomas Jefferson, later celebrated for his lavish generosity, learned about hospitality from watching his mother welcome people to Shadwell. Generation after generation of Randolph and Jefferson women taught their daughters the occupations of plantation housekeeping and entertaining, and they were not always happy housewives. In fact, Jane's great-granddaughters vocally detested the job, even as they accepted their duty.

Running a plantation house was not simply a matter of making sure the soup was salted and the bed linens aired. Jane, like Randolph and Jefferson women before and after, also showed her daughters how to see themselves as mistresses of enslaved people. She modeled for them the deep habits of distance, haughtiness, and taken-for-granted contempt that made it possible for them to command people they knew intimately—knew, in some cases, all their lives, people whose parents and children they also knew well. To Randolph and Jefferson daughters, the power to command slaves had to seem as natural as the duty to obey their fathers, to defer to their brothers, and ultimately, to rely on their sons.

Jane Jefferson's daughters also learned to read and write, and some of them learned to sing and play instruments, and all of them learned to dance. Thomas and his sister Jane were particularly fond of music, and they played together, he on the violin, she on a spinet. Much later, Jefferson recalled that "I suppose that during at least a dozen years of my life, I played no less than three hours a day." Their literate mother likely took it upon herself to show her children their ABCs, and she and Peter plainly expected that their children would be educated. At Tuckahoe young Thomas Jefferson, and perhaps the girls, had lessons in a one-room house close to the main residence. After the move back to Shadwell, Jane hired a tutor named Benjamin Snead to teach her daughters as well as her younger son, Randolph, though neither he nor his twin sister, Anna, ever progressed much beyond basic literacy. Her elder son, Thomas, of course was another story. Surely he was a curious, quick, remarkably focused little boy. That famously passionate learner was sent out to board with clergymen schoolmasters, starting when he was nine years old. Both Thomas and Randolph had more formal schooling than their sisters, but the Jefferson women were unusually well educated for their time.

Peter and Jane Jefferson were married for eighteen years. While no one can ever really know the inside of a marriage except the two parties to the relation, it seems that they shared a sense of duty, respect for learning, and enjoyment of the fine things of life. Peter's "tastes approached to the elegant, in his own household," wrote Jefferson biographer Henry Randall. "After the wearisome and often stirring events of a day of border life were passed, he spent the evening in reading historians, essayists, and even poets. Addison, Swift and Pope were prime favorites with him—but Shakespeare was his great favorite!"

Together they brought the trappings of gentility to a frontier town, raised a family, commanded slaves and ran a plantation, and established their place as Virginia gentry. Peter might be often absent but Jane could be confident he would do all he could to provide for her and the children. She, in turn, tried to make Peter's home a welcoming place, where children knew their duty and their manners and the wife did all she could to please him.

PETER WAS FIFTY years old, and Jane was thirty-seven, when he died on August 17, 1757, of some unknown illness. He had written his will a month earlier, and appointed a high-powered team of executors. He was buried at Shadwell; preaching the funeral sermon was the Reverend James Maury, who was an Episcopal clergyman and Thomas Jefferson's tutor. Peter had been a pillar of his community, a vestryman and public officeholder, planter and surveyor, slaveholder and family man. His death was an event not only for his family, but for all the people who worked for and with him, for myriad friends and acquaintances and allies, people who owed him money and some sixty people whom he himself owned. But the person most affected was the woman with whom he also shared the blessing of affection. Peter's will referred to Jane as his "Dear & Well beloved Wife," and he did everything he could to provide for her after his death.

We can only begin to imagine the distress and confusion that beset Jane Jefferson when her husband died. During their years of marriage, Peter kept the books and ran the farms and managed their business dealings, from transactions with neighbors to transatlantic commerce. Jane took care of the household and children. While he and Jane were certainly partners in running a successful plantation and raising a family, neither of them expected Jane to deal with financial matters. Peter chose his friends and neighbors, Dr. Thomas Walker and John Harvie, as his executors. They assumed the management of his estate for seven years, until Thomas, his firstborn son and principal heir, turned twenty-one.

Some widows of Jane's time and place welcomed the challenge of running their own affairs and flourished as they took control over people, land, and intricate questions of business. Jane's own father, Isham Randolph, had trusted his widow enough to make her the executor of his estate. But Jane Jefferson had never had much to do with her husband's business. There is not one scratch of her handwriting in her husband's account book, not a line penned to her son Thomas about business affairs when he finally took over, assuming responsibility for his younger siblings as well as his mother. Instead, with eight children between the ages of two and seventeen and a complicated household to run, Jane left the management of thousands of acres and dozens of people to her late husband's executors. She assumed that they would be honest and competent, manage her lands and slaves, and pay the bills she ran up with local merchants. Eventually she would apply not to John Harvie or Thomas Walker for her pocket money, but would instead rely on her eldest son to make sure that her credit with shopkeepers was good.

In many regards, she was a lucky woman. Peter Jefferson had left her with a prosperous and beautiful place to live, without the worry of pressing debt, and with children mature and loving enough to offer her some support. But losing her husband left her brokenhearted. We can hear a whisper of Jane's grief in a letter written nearly fifty years after the death of Peter Jefferson, by Thomas Jefferson. His volatile son-in-law, Thomas Mann Randolph, Jr., was quarreling with his even more unstable cousin, John Randolph of Roanoke, and Jefferson feared that a duel was imminent. Terrified that his daughter Patsy might be left a widow, the aging Thomas Jefferson tried to talk some sense into her hotheaded husband. Jefferson's letter to Tom Randolph echoed Jane's deep sorrow and helplessness, and Thomas Jefferson's own earliest pain. The son had revered his father's strength, his regard for learning, his devotion to his farm and family. He too was crushed by the loss, but his words, so many years later, carried loving echoes of his mother's devastation, and of the effect of her loss on her children, as he compared his son-in-law's situation to that of the bachelor John Randolph:

> How different is the stake which you two would bring into the field! On his side, unentangled in the affections of the world, a single life, of no value to himself or others, on yours, yourself, a wife, and a family of children, all depending for their happiness and protection in this world on you alone. Should they lose you, my care for them, a poor substitute at my time, could continue, by the course of nature, but for a short time. Seven children, all under the age of discretion and down to infancy could then be left without guide or guardian but a poor broken-hearted woman, doomed herself to misery the rest of her life. And should her frail frame sink under it, what is then to become of them? Is it possible that your duties to these dear objects can weigh more lightly than those to a gladiator?

If Jane Jefferson was "a poor broken-hearted woman, doomed herself to misery the rest of her life," she was fortunate that Peter had left his affairs in good order. At the time of his death, he was one of the wealthiest men in Albemarle County, the second-largest slaveholder in the county. Unlike many Virginia planters, he left no debt. Thus Jane was spared the fate of so many widows who were plunged into poverty by their husbands' unpaid obligations, or cheated by unscrupulous trustees, or left destitute by their sons' profligate ways. There was money enough to see to her sons' education, boarding with schoolmasters and then at the College of William and Mary. There were funds for furniture and household supplies, gloves and jewelry and silk corsets for the girls, dancing lessons for all the children. The widow Jefferson's life of hosting kin and friends, commanding her servants, looking after her children, shopping and paying visits of her own, continued amid joy and pain. This woman who had crossed an ocean and lived in half a dozen houses, borne ten children, buried two of her babies, cared for a mentally disabled daughter, and managed two households and dozens of people had remarkable power to endure. But in the years to come it must have seemed to Jane Jefferson that for every life that came into her world, someone she loved was torn away.

3

The Widow Jefferson

THE DEATH OF a father can shatter a family. Under the best of circumstances, the survivors, like planets searching for a new sun, shift in their orbits, exerting the pull of gravity on one another, searching for a new solar center. In the wake of Peter's death, Jane had to maintain stability at Shadwell without actually taking command. As a new widow she was entitled to inherit one-third of the people her husband had owned. She had hard and fateful choices to make. Even if she wanted to keep enslaved parents and children together, Peter Jefferson's will bequeathed certain slave children to the Jefferson children. Jane's family was entwined with the families of the slaves she chose.

Jane owned a woman named Sall, whose children served the Jefferson children. Ever since Thomas had been a small child, he had been attended by Sall's son, Jupiter, a boy his own age. One of Sall's daughters was assigned to wait on Thomas's older sister, Mary. Jane decided to claim thirty-five-year-old Sall herself, along with her son, Caesar, and two of her other daughters, Lucinda and "Little Salley," who would look after Jane's mentally challenged daughter, Elizabeth Jefferson. Jane also claimed a number of other people, including a baby named Fanny, though she did not claim Fanny's mother, a twenty-five-year-old woman named Myrtilla, who took care of the younger Jefferson children. Myrtilla would be inherited by Thomas Jefferson when he came of age, and she may have been the first person Thomas Jefferson ever sold.

HOWEVER SHE GRIEVED, the widowed Jane Jefferson ran a household bursting with daughters and sons and relatives and guests. In time the place was once again alive with music and warm with the aromas of good food. Jane and her children enjoyed a quality of life impossible without the work of enslaved people who did everything from cultivating tobacco to churning butter, from scrubbing out chamber pots to dressing her daughters' hair. Jane likewise visited family and friends on other plantations, traveling in a carriage or by horseback, enjoying the hospitality that the Virginia gentry took for granted. She did what she could to re-create the comfort in which she had grown up at Dungeness, even if on a less grandiose scale.

On April 13, 1764, when Thomas Jefferson turned twenty-one, he assumed command of everything at Shadwell and Peter Jefferson's other properties. Thomas was then studying the law in Williamsburg, where he had spent much of his time since he'd enrolled at William and Mary in 1760. He would be frequently at the colonial capital, or on the road, practicing his profession. But busy as he was, he began to take over the family accounts from trustee John Harvie, to manage his mother's and sisters' spending, and to pay attention to goings-on at Shadwell. He made a point of being home often enough to notice when the flowers in the woods began to bloom. He took time to plant his garden and enjoy its bounty.

Thomas Jefferson recorded his delight in his mother's home in the earliest jottings in the "garden book" that he would keep for more than half a century. He wrote the famously exuberant first line of that book, "Purple hyacinth begins to bloom," not at Monticello, but at Shadwell, in 1766. He and his sisters helped out in their mother's garden, as slaves like young Caesar no doubt also did, and there they grew a wondrous variety of vegetables and fruits for the table: peas and asparagus, celery and onions, radishes, lettuce, broccoli and cauliflower, cucumbers, gooseberries, and tiny luscious strawberries (Thomas noted, "100 fill half a pint"). The Shadwell garden produced a profusion of fragrant and showy flowers: narcissus and various "flags" (irises), carnations, Indian pinks, marigolds, globe amaranth, Dutch violets, lunaria, sweet William, hollyhocks, larkspurs, snapdragons, poppies, lychnis, and "a flower like the Prince's feather, Lathyrus."

As Jane tended her garden and rebuilt her life among her children and in the midst of her families of slaves, the Jefferson children began hiving off. They would be lucky to have as good a marriage as their parents had, solid as oak, respectable as a family portrait, and with enough warmth to produce children who danced and sang. Judging from the few of his early letters that remain, Thomas Jefferson, as a boy and a young man, was as high-spirited as he was scholarly, as sociable as he was brilliant, thrilled by the fascinating variety of the world. Sorrow and betrayal would layer reserve and caution over that youthful buoyancy, but nearly to the end of his life he never lost the capacity for delight. That gift sustained him through setbacks and heartbreaks, and no one has it late in life if it is not nurtured early.

Jane's children learned to look to marriage as a source of happiness. But not all were destined to enjoy wedded bliss. Three years after Peter's death, Jane's second daughter, eighteen-year-old Mary, wed John Bolling, a planter and gentleman and a very likely prospect. The Bolling family, long-standing friends of Jane's parents, had lands near Dungeness in Goochland County, and Mary and her husband set up housekeeping at Fairfields, halfway between Richmond and Charlottesville. Peter Jefferson bequeathed Mary a marriage "fortune" of two hundred pounds and an enslaved woman named Nan. In 1766, Jane would separate Myrtilla from her daughter Fanny, a girl of perhaps six years of age, giving the child to Mary Bolling "In & of consideration of the Natural love & affection which I have and so bear unto my Daughter." Mary Jefferson Bolling kept in close touch with her mother and sisters. She returned when she could to Shadwell to visit. She and her husband buried a child there and planted cedars by the grave. After Jane's death, Mary's little sister, Anna Scott Jefferson (nicknamed Nancy), went to live with the Bollings in the years before her own marriage.

The Bollings' forty years of marriage yielded nine children, but also considerable misery for Mary. She endured the deaths of children, and John sank ever deeper into alcoholism. For a time they were separated, and in her increasing unhappiness, Mary relied on her family and friends, her brothers and sisters and their children, and took a keen interest in their lives.

By contrast, Martha, the second of Jane's daughters to marry, did indeed find harmony with her husband, making a match that delighted her family. On July 20, 1765, nineteen-year-old Martha married Dabney Carr, Thomas Jefferson's best friend, a promising lawyer soon to be elected to the Virginia House of Burgesses. Biographer Henry Randall offered a highly sentimental portrait of the attachment between the two young men, "inseparable companions, [who] read, studied, took their exercise, practiced their music, and formed their plans together. They daily repaired to an oak near the summit of the Monticello . . . where they had constructed themselves a rustic seat, and here, in the deep woods, far away from the sight and hearing of man, they together pored over Bracton, Coke, and Matthew Bacon; read their miscellaneous reading; discussed the present, and painted the glowing visions of the future."

Dabney and Martha Carr moved to a modest house at Spring

Forest in Goochland County, where Martha followed in the footsteps of her prodigious mother and grandmother, bearing six children in eight years. When Thomas Jefferson visited the Carrs in 1770, he found them in humble but cheerful circumstances, writing to his friend John Page, "This friend of ours, Page, in a very small house, with a table, half a dozen chairs, and one or two servants, is the happiest man in the universe."

With the household at Shadwell now reduced by two daughters, tragedy soon took a third. Thomas's older sister Jane, age twenty-five, died on October 1, 1765. We know nothing of the circumstances of her death. This young woman, revered in family lore as "the pride and ornament of her house," was remembered as "her brother's constant companion when at home, and the confidant of all his youthful feelings." She lived long in Thomas Jefferson's memory. He told his grandchildren that he had regarded his sister Jane as "fully his own equal in understanding, and there was a depth, earnestness, purity and simplicity in her high nature which made an impression on his mind which was never effaced." According to Randall:

> More than half a century afterwards he continued to occasionally speak of her to his grand-daughters in terms of as warm admiration and love as if the grave had just closed on her. It was listening to church music that oftenest struck the chord of these memories. She had been a singer of uncommon skill and sweetness, and both were particularly fond of the solemn music used by the Church of England in the Psalms. . . . His sister Jane excelled in this description of music, to the execution of which she brought the fervor of a deep religious devotion; and many a winter evening, round the family fireside, and many a soft summer twilight, on the wooded banks of the Rivanna, heard their voices, accompanied by the notes of his violin, thus ascending together.

Young Jane Jefferson left behind an impressive estate for a woman, including three slaves, furniture and bedding, a saddle and riding chair, trunks, a spinning wheel, a fashionable wardrobe, jewelry, and books. Still unmarried at the time of her death, she remained forever a daughter and a sister, never a wife. Her family missed her. In December 1771, Thomas made plans for the picturesque cemetery he envisioned at Monticello, a landscape "among antient and venerable oaks, intersperse some gloomy evergreens," with a small Gothic temple at the center of a spiral path, and "in the middle of the temple an altar, the sides of turf, the top a plain stone. Very little light, perhaps none at all save only the feeble ray of an half extinguished lamp." He was considering having her body disinterred from the burial ground at his mother's home and moved to a new resting place, and he wrote an epitaph for her tombstone: "Jane Jefferson. Ah, Joanna, best of girls. Ah, torn away from the bloom of vigorous age. May the earth be light upon you. Farewell, forever and ever."

A fourth Jefferson daughter left the household in 1769. Lucy, then sixteen, married her first cousin, Charles Lilburn Lewis, son of Jane's sister Mary and her husband, Charles Lewis. The couple moved to Buck Island, Lewis's plantation a few miles from Shadwell. While Jane surely approved of her new son-in-law's breeding, Charles Lewis proved a bad businessman. When he fell deep into debt, the Lewises moved to Kentucky in search of better luck.

Young Virginia gentlemen, like their English counterparts, commonly left home early to go to school, and Thomas Jefferson had been sent away to board with his tutor at the age of nine. The experience put him at some emotional as well as physical distance from Shadwell, but the boy who loved the deep woods and the sight and smell of his mother's gardens, who revered his father and sang with his sister, was surely sometimes lonely and homesick. Jane too must have missed her absent children. The only Jeffersons remaining at

Shadwell by the beginning of 1770 were Jane herself, her twenty-five-year-old, developmentally disabled daughter, Elizabeth, and fifteen-year-old twins Randolph and Anna Scott. Still, the other children returned often, for days or weeks at a time. On one of Thomas's visits home, the world Jane had so painstakingly nurtured at Shadwell went up in smoke.

NO ONE KNOWS how the fire started. Thomas Jefferson and his mother were away from home, "on a visit to a neighbor," Thomas wrote. It was February, and there would have been need for many fires, islands of warmth against winter's deep chill. Cooking fires, heating fires, the fires of everyday life could burst, in a flash, into fires of tragedy. Such things were common in those days—a stray spark from a neglected hearth, a chimney not cleaned, carelessness, or happenstance.

Or malice. Every master or mistress knew the lurking danger. Even those slaveholders who tried to avoid violence, who hoped to manage their houses and fields with humanity and persuasion, relied in the end on the whip. The weak had their weapons, from sulking to sabotage, spoiled porridge to poison, costly accident to careful destruction. Jane Jefferson had grown up with the ever-present fear of conspiracies and revolts. Every planter prayed the day would never come when smoldering resentment would burst into flaming rebellion.

Nobody suggested that the fire that destroyed Jane Jefferson's house at Shadwell plantation on February 1, 1770, was set deliberately. Those who left the written records were not there to witness the first flames. One account, set down many years later, blamed "the alarm and confusion of the slaves" for the great destruction. Some of the slaves did what they could to save a bed here, a few books there. An enslaved man rescued Thomas Jefferson's violin and presented the instrument with poignant pride to the young master. The house and nearly everything in it was burned, so whatever was salvaged must have held special significance, then and thereafter. Perhaps saving the violin came with a reward, and that was why, on that day, twenty-six-year-old Thomas paid three shillings and sixpence to a man named "old Toby," a member of the Shadwell household since before the death of Peter Jefferson, Thomas's father, in 1757.

One other longtime member of the household at Shadwell made an appearance in Thomas Jefferson's accounts for that terrible week, but not to claim a reward. Myrtilla had been a Jefferson slave since his father's time. Four days after the fire, on February 5, Thomas Jefferson quietly sold Myrtilla to Benjamin Moore, a man who appeared in Jefferson's voluminous financial memoranda only this once, in connection with the purchase of this woman. We know nothing else about Benjamin Moore: who he was, where he lived, why he wanted to buy Myrtilla, why Thomas Jefferson saw fit to sell her. As far as the records tell us, no other person serving in the house at Shadwell had ever been sold by Thomas Jefferson.

Thomas mourned the loss of his papers and his precious law books. He had plans to build his own place, three miles distant, across the river, on a mountaintop, and now he wanted to get a house built as soon as possible. He left no hint of his feelings toward the crushing loss borne by his mother, or the fate or emotions of the siblings still at home under Jane's care. The Shadwell fire was the crucible of Thomas Jefferson's passage into manhood, the disaster that gave his Monticello project an urgency beyond hopes and dreams. That same event was a catastrophe for those who remained to sort through the ashes.

Jane lost the gracious home she'd created with her husband, Peter, the house in which she'd raised her children and welcomed family, neighbors, friends, and connections, the center and the compass of her life and world for nearly twenty years. There she had journeyed as a bride, birthed babies, commanded dozens of servants, fed and sheltered multitudes of guests and relations. A week before her fiftieth birthday, she was homeless, with three of her ten children still to care for and dozens of slaves still under her supervision.

The fire also threatened the security of Shadwell slaves. Peter Jefferson, and later his executors and heir, had run Peter's plantations on a sound financial basis. But the institution of slavery guaranteed neither ease nor safety for those in its thrall. After the fire, or perhaps shortly before, a slave woman named Hannah left the Shadwell household. Like Myrtilla, Hannah had a daughter named Fan. They had all belonged to Peter Jefferson at the time of his death, and they may have been related by blood. Hannah and her daughter were sent from Shadwell to Snowdon, a plantation on the Fluvanna River set aside as an inheritance for Randolph Jefferson, only fourteen years old at the time and far from ready to take control of his legacy.

Sometime in 1770, a man named Isaac Bates was hired as overseer at Snowdon, and early in his tenure there he beat a slave named Hannah to death. We can't be certain whether the Hannah who left Shadwell for Snowdon and the woman murdered by Isaac Bates were one and the same, but everyone on the Jefferson holdings, slave and free, would have known about this terrible event.

All we have are the cold traces of business that followed this murder, in Thomas Jefferson's words, "by a cruel whipping." Thomas, acting on behalf of his minor brother, sought Bates's arrest and sued the murderer for compensation for Randolph's financial loss. Jane Jefferson also did what she could to make up for Hannah's death. In the wake of the murder, Jane gave Randolph a two-year-old girl named Rachel, daughter of the woman who took care of Elizabeth Jefferson. Jane showed her affection for her own children by separating the mothers and children who worked as her slaves.

*   *   *

WHILE THE SITE of the Shadwell house was cleared of charred debris and prepared for the building of a new, smaller dwelling for Jane and her children, the mistress made do. Randolph could be sent off to live with relatives until he left for the College of William and Mary in October 1771. Jane and Elizabeth and Anna, and the slave women who attended them, took refuge in an overseer's house. They could visit cousins or go to stay with Jane's married daughters at their homes not far away. Her son Thomas, closest at hand of all her children, was just a couple of miles away and across the river, building his house, planting his gardens, and courting a widow while also assuming command of the family's farms and business affairs.

Jane no longer needed as many slaves to see to the needs of her children, and just as the fire destroyed walls and timbers, furniture and linens and books and countless letters and cherished keepsakes, so it may have gutted her desire to keep house in the grand manner. To re-create the capacious Shadwell household would take an enormous effort on her part, not to mention the help of children who were busy with plantations and families of their own. Perhaps that was why she began to send off the women who had served in her house, why little Fanny, Myrtilla's child, was sent to the Bollings at Fairfields, why Thomas removed Hannah and Fan to the horror at Snowdon, why Myrtilla was sold while the embers of Shadwell still smoldered. With Thomas moving up onto the mountain, Jane remained responsible for Elizabeth, still a child at age twenty-six, and the twins, still minors. But her life at the center of a social universe was slipping into the mist of memory.

4

The Revolutionary's Mother

ON A SEPTEMBER day in 1772, Jane Randolph Jefferson took up a handsome Bible, probably a replacement for a cherished book lost in the great fire, and began to set down her family history. On the page facing the title page, she wrote "Jane Jefferson Her Booke" and the date. Then she noted the dates and locations of the births of each of her children with Peter Jefferson, the deaths of two of those children, along with the date of Peter's death, "Wednesday 17th Aug: 1757." In this careful, spare inscription, the only known vestige of her handwriting apart from her will, Jane rebuilt her world; she ordered and memorialized the family that was her life.

Jane had spent more than thirty years making a home for her family. But now the center of that family was shifting across the river and up the mountain, to a place only just cleared and planted, only just becoming the site of a small brick house, the seat of a plantation grandly and romantically called Monticello. Thomas had courted a young widow, Martha Wayles Skelton, daughter of a rich lawyer-planter in Charles City County and already the mother of a young son. Thomas and Martha had married on New Year's Day, 1772, at Martha's father's house. Now she would occupy Thomas Jefferson's heart and his home, even as his public life, and momentous events of the day, began to claim more and more of his time, his talent, and his genius. Martha would soon inherit a fortune in land and slaves, along with a mountain of debt, and she and Thomas would begin to build their own family. Perhaps it was the impending birth of their first child, daughter Martha, born on September 27, 1772, that inspired Jane to write down her own family's history.

But if Jane Jefferson began to feel marginal in her children's lives, they still returned home to visit and continued to rely on her in their own times of need. In May 1773, Jane's daughter Martha Jefferson Carr came back to Shadwell to give birth to her sixth child in the small house built for Jane on the site of the home she had lost. Martha's husband, Dabney, had been elected to the Virginia House of Burgesses, and since he was expected back in Williamsburg, it seemed best that his wife go to her mother's place to have her baby. Only a month before, Dabney Carr had launched his career in Virginia politics with a triumphant speech in the House of Burgesses, introducing resolutions that established Virginia's Committee of Correspondence. At a time when Virginia politicians were joining their Massachusetts brethren in stirring up the growing unrest in the colonies, it looked as if Dabney Carr, not yet thirty years old, would take a leading role.

Martha had her baby, a son named Dabney Jr. The baby's father stayed at Shadwell for the birth, then set out on horseback to return to Williamsburg. Not far from Shadwell, Carr was suddenly stricken with "a bilious fever," possibly typhoid. He was brought back to Shadwell, where Dr. George Gilmer, favorite physician of the family at Shadwell, did what he could to save him. But to no avail. On May 16, after a short, violent illness, Dabney Carr, Sr., died.

In her later years, as a cherished aunt to Thomas Jefferson's children and grandchildren, Martha Jefferson Carr impressed at least one young relative as "a woman of vigorous understanding and earnest warmth of heart." But weak and sick after giving birth, and now newly widowed, Martha Carr, family legend had it, nearly went crazy. According to Henry Randall,

> Carr's sudden death fell with stunning force on his wife. She was ill, from recent confinement, when her husband set out on his last journey, and her mind was perhaps therefore filled with the most gloomy presentiments concerning him. After her last farewell, she again raised herself on her sick couch, to catch a parting glimpse of him as he rode past her window; but she saw merely his moving hat. This object took strong hold of an imagination rendered morbid by disease, and soon to be fearfully excited by an almost despairing grief. For weeks and months, whether in the blaze of noon-day or in the darkness of night, the moving, phantomy hat was ever passing before her eye. For a period, reason tottered on its throne.

With Thomas away in Williamsburg, dividing his time between the legislature and his own mortally ill father-in-law, Jane Jefferson was left to cope with birth, death, her daughter's wild bereavement, her own loss, and not least, her six Carr grandchildren. The steamy heat of a Virginia summer was already coming on; as Thomas Jefferson noted, a week later in his Garden Book, "this spring is remarkably forward." Given the weather and the virulence of Carr's final illness, Jane had good reason to worry that whatever had killed him might spread like fire among the people at Shadwell. And so those who mourned him settled on a quick funeral. Dabney Carr was laid to rest in the Shadwell burying ground.

Thomas's return to Albemarle County brought a fresh round of frantic grief as he claimed the power and the status of the family patriarch, possessor of the right to determine not only the fate of the living, but also the disposition of the dead. Thomas insisted that his brother-in-law's body be dug up and moved, to be reburied up on the mountain, under the oaks where he and Dabney had so often read and talked. Jefferson distanced himself from his sorrow, and that of his mother and widowed sister, in a way that would become a hallmark of his character. He turned an emotional event into a mathematics problem: "2 hands grubbed the Grave yard 80 f. sq. = 1/7 of an acre in 3 ½ hours, so that one would have done it in 7. hours, and would grub an acre in 49 hours = 4 days." Thomas made his notes as he watched two enslaved men laboring in the spring heat to clear his Monticello cemetery. Neither he nor anyone else left a record of his mother's or his sister's reaction to his appropriation of Dabney Carr's body, or for that matter, any hint of the thoughts or feelings of the men who dug Carr's second grave. This was the first burial in the new Monticello cemetery.

Thomas Jefferson composed an epitaph for his brother-in-law that reflected Dabney Carr's immersion in the Shadwell family as much as it recorded Thomas's own desolation:

HERE LIE THE REMAINS OF
DABNEY CARR
Son of John and Jane Carr, of Louisa County,
Who was born—, 1744.
Intermarried with Martha Jefferson, daughter of Peter
And Jane Jefferson, 1765;
And died at Charlottesville, May 16, 1773,
Leaving six small children.
To his Virtue, Good Sense, Learning and Friendship
This stone is dedicated by Thomas Jefferson, who, of all men living,
loved him most.

Perhaps the death of Dabney Carr precipitated Jane's fears about her own mortality. Or maybe those thoughts were merely the product of an aging body and the health problems that pile up as time passes. Sometime in 1772 or 1773, Jane wrote her will, making bequests to her unmarried children: slaves for Anna and Randolph, and for Elizabeth a bed and some of Jane's clothes. By this time Jane had come to rely utterly on Thomas's stewardship of her affairs. Dr. Gilmer paid dozens of visits to Shadwell, and Jefferson paid the doctor's fees and settled her accounts of all kinds. Local storekeepers applied to him when she charged things, and he handled matters when she wanted to buy or sell animals. Thomas kept careful track of his expenses on her behalf, and as the years passed, it became clearer and clearer that she had no way to repay him. So in September 1773, in return for his assumption of all her debts, she handed over to him her only property of value, the deeds to her remaining slaves.

The Reverend Charles Clay, Episcopal minister, ardent patriot, and lifelong friend of Thomas Jefferson, had preached Dabney Carr's funeral service, and was paid forty shillings (two pounds) for his efforts. The following year, the Reverend Clay would perform another sad office for Jane Jefferson's family. On February 21, 1774, at 2:11 in the afternoon, the first recorded earthquake in Virginia history "shook the houses so sensibly that every body run out of doors." Two aftershocks followed. Sometime shortly after the tremors, Elizabeth Jefferson and her maid, Little Sall, who was sister to Thomas's slave Jupiter, attempted to cross the Rivanna in a skiff, trying to get to Thomas's place on the other shore. The river was running high; by March 6, the Rivanna would be in flood, eighteen inches "higher than the one which carried N. Lewis's bridge away . . . the highest ever known except the great fresh in May 1771."

On March 1, Thomas wrote sorrowfully, "My sister Elizabeth was found last Thursday being Feb. 24." Elizabeth and Little Sall had drowned in the Rivanna. Thomas made no mention of the death of the enslaved woman he had known for most of his life, sister of the man who attended to his daily needs and cared for his horses and drove his carriage, the woman who looked after the Jefferson sister who could not take care of herself. Neither Elizabeth nor Sall was buried at Monticello, so we may assume that their bodies were taken back to Shadwell, to be buried by their grieving mothers and remaining brothers and sisters. Jane Jefferson had now outlived her husband and four of her children.

THE FINAL YEARS of Jane's life were anything but peaceful. As she coped with the changes and losses in her family, a larger revolution gathered. Her son eagerly joined and then led the insurgency in Virginia, on his way up the ladder of risk and fame and notoriety and greatness. When Thomas Jefferson and Dabney Carr had plotted to establish Virginia's Committee of Correspondence in 1773, the royal governor, John Murray, Fourth Earl of Dunmore, responded by proroguing the House of Burgesses—in essence, suspending the assembly, which did not meet again until May 1774. By that time some Bostonians had made their famous protest against the tea tax, and the British had declared the port of Boston closed. Thirty-one-year-old Thomas Jefferson wasn't much for making speeches, but he labored behind the scenes and began to establish himself as a clear, bold, and inspiring writer on behalf of the patriot cause.

Amid rising political tensions, life at Shadwell and Monticello went on pretty much as usual. Thomas continued to manage his family's affairs, now including his sisters' estates and his wife's inheritance. But he was becoming ever more involved in political controversy. Lord Dunmore refused to permit the House of Burgesses to meet, but the rebellious Virginians determined to assemble anyway. Thomas Jefferson headed off to Williamsburg to attend that meeting, but on the way suffered an attack of dysentery and was forced to turn back. He nonetheless sent to Williamsburg, probably in the hands of Jupiter, his draft of resolutions he hoped the Virginia delegates would present in Philadelphia. That document would shortly be published as a pamphlet, *A Summary View of the Rights of British America,* setting out some of the ideas he would present in the Declaration of Independence and catapulting Thomas Jefferson to the forefront of philosophers and propagandists of the revolutionary cause.

What was a mother to think, as her son and his compatriots tacked toward treason? Jane Randolph Jefferson had been born in England and reared among British gentry in Virginia. She valued the fine things connected with the mother country. She still had family in England, and even those who agitated for change in the colonies' status considered themselves, as the title of Thomas's pamphlet suggested, British Americans. Jane was long accustomed to the men of her family taking leading roles in public life; her father and husband, her son and sons-in-law all sat in the House of Burgesses. In ordinary times her men might hold any number of bold ideas or unconventional philosophical leanings, but such notions would have fewer real consequences.

These were extraordinary times. British colonies that had once dealt with one another chiefly through the mother country had begun to communicate, and to plot their responses to British policies. Now Thomas Jefferson was elected a delegate from Virginia to a Second Continental Congress. As he set out for Philadelphia in June 1775, to take up an office that kept him far distant from his family for months on end in a fetid and unhealthy city, he courted the fury of an empire.

Jane Jefferson may never have sensed greatness in her elder son. She knew, early on, that Thomas was uncommonly bright, devoted to his books and his music with a rare discipline. She saw his passionate curiosity, his ardor for planning and calculating, planting and building. Certainly she could see the vast differences between Thomas and her younger son, Randolph, who had scraped by at William and Mary for a year and a half before returning to Albemarle, to take up life as a Piedmont planter, a man of humble accomplishments, rudimentary learning, and little ambition. In the course of his life Randolph would be a man who stayed close to home, tending his tobacco, hunting with his dogs, living down a road he could never get around to repairing, failing even to make it to his sister's funeral at Monticello, twenty miles away. Even during Jane's lifetime, Thomas was a different story. She knew well her eldest son's devotion to family duty, the daily responsibilities he recorded in meticulously detailed memorandum books. But Jane's father, Isham Randolph, and her husband, Peter Jefferson, had likewise been learned, civic-minded, family men and community leaders, eminent Virginians in their time.

There was something different about Thomas Jefferson. He and his colleagues, propelled by the greatest political crisis in the history of the British colonies in North America, were committing sedition and contemplating revolution. If Jane was proud of Thomas's achievements, surely she was also terrified at the thought of seeing her son with a noose around his neck.

The wrath of the English authorities was not the only force to be feared. All over Virginia, people wondered whether so much talk of liberty would incite the enslaved to rise up and seize their own freedom. Now, as white Virginians began to gather up arms and organize militias, Lord Dunmore considered encouraging slaves to rebel against their masters. In November 1775, Dunmore issued a proclamation declaring the colony to be in a state of rebellion. He instituted martial law and offered freedom to all slaves willing to take up arms and fight for the British.

Thomas Jefferson, then in Philadelphia, heard of Dunmore's

actions from Robert Carter Nicholas, who had written a letter to
Virginia's delegates in Congress. Nicholas captured the terror that
Dunmore's order struck in the hearts of slaveholding Virginians:

A few Days since was handed to us from Norfolk Ld. D's [Dun-
more's] infamous Proclamation, declaring the Law martial in
force throughout this Colony and offering Freedom to such of
our Slaves, as would join him . . . great Number's have flocked to
L.D's Standard. The Tories of Norfolk are said to be the Ringleaders; many of our Natives it is said have been intimidated and
compeld to join them and great Numbers of Slaves from different
Quarters have graced their Corps. The Tenders are plying up
the Rivers, plundering Plantations and using every art to seduce
the Negroes. The Person of no Man in the Colony is safe, when
marked out as an Object of their Vengeance; unless he is immediately under the Protection of our little Army. They have many
Prisoners of different Classes; . . . No Country ever required
greater Exertions of Wisdom than ours does at present. . . .

The Jefferson family endeavored to make at least some effort to
keep slave families together, to provide decent food and clothing and
medical treatment. But the murder of Hannah at Snowdon unmasked
the bloody force underlying domestic tranquility on the Jeffersons'
lands. Slaves and slaveholders alike knew that not far beneath the surface of plantation life lurked resentment at enforced labor, the dull
and menacing hum of simmering violence. Across the South, severe
slave codes testified to the planters' fears. The widow Jane Jefferson
had grown up, come of age, and grown old amid the brutalities of
slavery: the petty indignities, mundane mortifications, and extreme
cruelties, from her father's execution of her uncle's slaves to her son's
overseer's vicious killing of a slave woman. Jane would not live to see

a crime even more horrendous. In 1811, Jane's grandsons, Isham and Lilburne Lewis, "literally chopped a Negro slave to pieces."

How loyal were the Jefferson family slaves to their owners? We will never know for certain why Myrtilla, a longtime member of Jane's household, was sold so soon after the Shadwell fire. Two years earlier, Thomas Jefferson had trusted Myrtilla enough to have given her and a farm laborer named Harry, possibly Myrtilla's husband, an "order on R. Harvie for goods to 16/6." Six years later, in 1781, the year in which Governor Thomas Jefferson would see British soldiers rampaging across Virginia and occupying his very home, more than thirty of the people he owned left to join the British. Among them would be Harry, who had been a Jefferson slave for at least twenty-four years.

JANE JEFFERSON LIVED out her last months amid the building fear and carnage of war, though she would not survive to see the creation of a new nation. She died on March 31, 1776. She may have been in failing health for some time, since Thomas made many payments to doctors on her behalf, and he and Martha may have brought his aging mother up to Monticello for nursing. Still, the end came more suddenly than anyone expected. As Thomas wrote to his mother's brother, William Randolph, Jane had died "after an illness of not more than an hour," after what Jefferson called an apoplexy—a stroke. According to the inscription on her tombstone, she died at Monticello and was buried there. Jane was survived by four daughters and two sons, numerous grandchildren, dozens of enslaved people, and a wide community of family, friends, and acquaintances in Albemarle County, across Virginia, across the ocean in England. Once again the Reverend Charles Clay preached a funeral service for the Jefferson family, the third in three years. Following her death, Thomas Jefferson suffered a migraine headache that lasted some six weeks.

Relationships between parents and children are never simple, and the warmest attachments have their chilly moments. Even among those who remain in intimate circumstances, grown children's feelings toward their parents are seldom easy. From all we can tell, Jane Jefferson had stayed close to her children, though she had sent her precocious oldest boy away for his schooling at an early age. We should certainly assume that as in all families, there were edgy times. Whatever the conflicts, Jane's children relied on her, just as she depended upon them. Mary buried a child at Shadwell; Martha returned there to bear a son and mourn a husband; Lucy married Jane's sister's son, and Randolph would eventually marry a daughter of that same sister. If Thomas was often away from Shadwell, he nonetheless lived in his mother's house longer than any of his siblings except the afflicted Elizabeth. He built his dream estate on lands that adjoined his mother's place, though he could have chosen more distant properties he had inherited, or for that matter, could have moved to one of the lovely and productive plantations his wife had inherited from her father. Duty bound the Jefferson family together, and the love between Jane Jefferson and her children was deeply rooted in their mutual pledges, of parental care and filial loyalty. There was as much affection as obligation in the mix, as the family's memory of her, preserved by her great-granddaughter Ellen Randolph Coolidge, and her great-great-granddaughter, Sarah Nicholas Randolph, suggest.

We have no letters between Jane and her children to help us understand what passed between mother and children, how they felt about her or she about them. The Shadwell fire of 1770 consumed nearly everything that might give us a glimpse inside those relationships. If family lore that she was a great letter writer holds any truth at all, we may assume that she wrote to her daughters when they were away, sometimes only a few miles away at their own houses, or slightly farther, visiting friends and relations. Jane likely sent letters to her son while he was in Williamsburg and possibly in Philadelphia, and if Thomas's later performance as a letter writer for the ages is any indication, he wrote back. In the years after 1770, their letters may have been less frequent, partly because they lived in proximity much of the time, but also because Thomas Jefferson would marry and focus more on his wife than his mother.

One way or another, no trace of correspondence between them remains, lost through careless or deliberate destruction by one or the other party, perhaps in the throes of grief. Or maybe, at least in the 1770s, there was just not much there in the first place.

Some historians have made a leap of logic from the absence of documents to insist that the most famous of Jane Jefferson's children did not write to her, or chose to destroy his letters, out of a desire to obliterate her influence on his life. They have concluded that the ever-scribbling Thomas Jefferson disliked his mother. Vaulting beyond Sherlock Holmes, who deduced the solution to the mystery by noticing the dog that didn't bark, these scholars presume that the lack of surviving letters implies a want of affection between Jane and her celebrated son. If that were true, we ought to have dozens and dozens of letters between Jefferson and his adored wife, Martha Wayles Skelton Jefferson. But we don't. Neither, for that matter, do we have letters between Thomas Jefferson and his closest male friend, Dabney Carr.

Historians have ignored the absence of letters between Jefferson and Carr, and have assumed that Jefferson burned his correspondence with his mother, as well as his wife, reducing those precious documents to ash as cold and silent as the remains of his childhood home. But why identify the lack of letters to or from Jane as proof that she and Thomas were on strained terms? The similar absence of correspondence in the cases of Dabney Carr and Martha Jefferson has been held as either insignificant (in Carr's case) or as a token of Jefferson's undying love and devotion (in Martha's). Why assume that documentary silence means one thing in the case of the mother, precisely the opposite in the case of the wife, and nothing at all in the matter of his bosom friend?

Perhaps some of Thomas Jefferson's biographers have let their own sentiments color their readings of Thomas Jefferson's feelings about Jane Randolph Jefferson. As the historian Susan Kern has pointed out, "Jane suffered greatly during the twentieth century at the hands of the Momists, psychohistorians, psychosexual historians, and worshipers of the patriarchy . . . [she] stands as the often-maligned mother with whom her son Thomas could just not relate. . . . Yet the family remembrances of Jane and the nineteenth-century biographers of Thomas Jefferson who relied on those remembrances present Jane in glowing terms, suggesting that in her own time, she was revered."

Why the about-face? Those who argue that Thomas Jefferson disliked his mother have pointed to the seven years between the death of Peter Jefferson and Thomas's attainment of his majority, a time when the son was purportedly chafing under the control of a domineering mother. They also point to the vicious misogyny evident in Thomas Jefferson's commonplace book, a collection of literary quotations he copied out as a young man. But the traces of Jane Jefferson in the Shadwell accounts and in archaeological remains offer no evidence that the widow stepped up to manage her husband's estate while her son seethed at having to wait his turn. Instead, it seems, Jane was content to let the trustees handle business, having plenty to do just caring for her children, running her household, pursuing her social duties, and dealing with the enslaved people whose work and attentions made the Jeffersons' comfortable life possible.

As for the anti-woman quotes in Thomas's commonplace book, it seems too great a stretch to insist that those generic words were aimed directly at his mother. We should recall that Thomas Jefferson came of age in an era in which open misogyny was as common as dirt, and that he grew up in a house full of sisters, two of them older than himself. Commonplace books of the sort kept by the young Thomas Jefferson functioned in somewhat the same way that teenagers' diaries do, as places to vent the loves and hates and wishes and rages that beset us at our stormiest point in life. What is so notable about the boy who is furious with his mother, or his sisters, or for that matter, the girls who fail to return his ardor? And what more likely place for that anger to surface than in the private book reserved for outbursts not fit for public expression?

Those who have dismissed Jane Jefferson as a cipher or a despised burden in her son's life rest their case even more heavily on the fact that he seldom mentioned her (a fact Dumas Malone reasonably attributed to "his characteristic reticence about the women of his family"). Apart from that silence, they cite only two fragments of evidence: the letter written to Jane's brother, William Randolph, nine years younger than Jane, sometime in the late spring or early summer of 1776, and a passing reference in the autobiography Thomas Jefferson began to write at the age of sixty-six, upon retirement from the presidency, but never finished. In the latter, the aging Jefferson remarked archly that his mother "was the daughter of Isham Randolph, one of the seven sons of that name and family settled in Dungeness, in Goochland. They trace their pedigree far back in England and Scotland, to which let every one ascribe the faith and merit he chooses." Jefferson had, by 1809, pursued a long political course largely in opposition to the British, studded with achievements as stellar as the Declaration of Independence and as ill-conceived as the Embargo of 1807. He had also lived for more than six decades among the many descendants of Isham Randolph and his six brothers, from his unstable, hard-pressed son-in-law, Thomas Mann Randolph, Jr., to his explosive cousin, John Randolph of Roanoke, to the many cousins, nephews, nieces, and other relatives who went broke, stole, cheated, betrayed their kin, went crazy, and even committed murder.

When Jane Jefferson wrote her family history in her Bible, she transcribed not the names of her ancestors, but those of her children. It was her husband, Peter, who had written down a fragment of Jane's own Randolph family history, the birthplaces and dates of Jane and her brothers and sisters. For all we know, Jane may have taken pride in her Randolph pedigree; we have no strong evidence either way on that question. Jefferson's daughters and granddaughters had a habit of referring to eccentric, touchy, or stubborn behavior in any family member as a showing of "the Randolph." Jefferson, at sixty-six, had many more reasons other than particular shortcomings evinced by his mother to question his English heritage and mock Randolph family claims to inherited superiority.

So what of the letter written to his uncle, William Randolph, so soon after his mother's death? Some observers have found Thomas Jefferson's language cold to the point of antipathy: "The death of my mother you have probably not heard of. This happened on the last day of March after an illness of not more than an hour. We suppose it to have been apoplectic. Be pleased to tender my affectionate wishes to Mrs. Randolph and my unknown cousins. . . ."

Once again we need to put these words in context. William Randolph was the heir to Dungeness plantation, Jane's childhood home. But he had moved to England, joining other Randolphs there, not simply on the other side of the ocean from his property, but on the opposite side of the cause that would very shortly rip Virginia away from the mother country to join the new nation. William had written to his sister's son to ask if he would collect the rent due on William's Virginia properties, complaining about the inconveniences he was experiencing due to the boycott of British trade by the rebellious colonies.

Thomas's reply invoked the ties of familial affection, but it also carried clear undertones of his anger at a relative who had abandoned his farm and home in search of wealth, a relative who had chosen the wrong side of the cause to which Thomas Jefferson had decided to pledge his life, his fortune, and his sacred honor. This same relative had deserted a sister he would never see again. Thomas Jefferson was capable of anger toward his mother and sisters, and forgiveness toward an estranged relative. But Jefferson was, more importantly, a man whose whole life testified to a deep belief in the duty of sons and brothers to protect and provide for mothers and sisters who had no husbands to take care of them. Jefferson was no egalitarian when it came to the sexes. He believed that men and women were essentially different, in strengths and weaknesses, in temperament, talent, and possibilities. They owed one another not equal duty, but reciprocal responsibility. Throughout his life he felt a sense of obligation toward women who depended upon him, a trust that lay at the heart of his way of loving women. Women, in turn, owed men their unquestioning obedience and loyalty and nurturance, and even their silent submission. That kind of love was, for Jefferson, rooted in the laws of nature. It was sacred and absolutely essential to a just and good society.

Jefferson began his letter to William Randolph disingenuously, by assuring his uncle that "I am extremely concerned at the difficulties under which you are thrown by the stoppage of trade," but also pointing out that "I heartily join with you in wishing you had chosen a residence among us." In his earlier letter, William Randolph had expressed concern about the safety of Virginia, and Jefferson responded with assurances that carried a note of sneering fury, contrasting the virtuous lot of the farmer (himself) with the insecure greed of the merchant (William Randolph):

> Our interior situation is to me most agreeable, as withdrawing me in great measure from the noise and busle of the world. It's remoteness from the seat of war, which you mention as conferring security, we do not however consider in that point of view. Our idea is that every place is secure except those which lie immediately on the water edge; and these we are prepared to give up. But I can easily conceive the situation of a farmer, depending on none but the soil and seasons, preferable to the precarious tho' more enlarged prospects of trade.

He followed immediately with the news of his mother's death, as if to say, "And oh. By the way. If you care at all, my mother—your sister— is dead." He finished with a testimonial to family ties that could not have sounded more wounded, or have concluded more equivocally:

> I hope no dissentions between the bodies politic of which we happen to be members will ever interfere with the ties of relation. Tho' most heartily engaged in the quarrel on my part from a sense of the most unprovoked injuries, I retain the same affection for individuals which nature or knowledge of their merit calls for.

We have long known that Thomas Jefferson's opposition to the British in 1776 involved both economic interest and high principle. But what this letter reveals is the intensely personal dimension of that rebellion, the connection, in his heart, with the loss of his mother, her abandonment by a Tory brother, his own determination to redress "unprovoked injuries" at the hands of England, if not specifically of

William Randolph. This letter, indeed, goes far toward explaining a strikingly passionate section of Thomas Jefferson's Declaration of Independence written not long after the letter, later excised by Congress. In this passage, Jefferson reflected on the willingness of "our British brethren" to permit their king to usurp American rights, and to send foreign mercenaries to prey on their American kin:

> These facts have given the last stab to agonizing affection, and manly spirit bids us to renounce for ever these unfeeling brethren. We must endeavor to forget our former love for them, and to hold them as we hold the rest of mankind enemies in war, in peace friends. We might have been a free and a great people together; but a communication of grandeur and of freedom it seems is below their dignity. Be it so, since they will have it. The road to happiness and to glory is open to us too. We will tread it apart from them.

Historian Joseph Ellis has observed, "What strikes the modern reader is not the timidity of the Continental Congress for excising the passage so much as the melodramatic sentimentalism of Jefferson in composing it." But when we realize that at the time Thomas Jefferson wrote those words, he was deep in mourning for the mother he had lost, the woman whose death he had flung in the face of just such an unfeeling English brother, the language seems not so much melodramatic or sentimental as shockingly personal; too personal, indeed, for such public declaration.

JANE RANDOLPH JEFFERSON was not the target of Thomas Jefferson's sarcasm in either his autobiography or his letter to his uncle. But those historians who insist that he never wrote about her anywhere else, and by inference, never gave her another warm thought, are wrong about that, too. On October 7, 1791, a day Thomas Jefferson was at home at Monticello, cleaning up old business, he responded to a letter from a Mr. James Lyle, written nearly a year before. Lyle had written as an agent of the merchant firm of Kippen and Company, requesting payment from Jane Jefferson's estate of a debt to a local merchant amounting to £126.9.5 from "before the beginning of the war." Sixteen years after Jane's death, Jefferson described his perpetual attention to his mother's debts, but also his efforts to ensure that she did not worry about money while she was alive. He told Lyle, "I have greatly overpaid the assets of that estate which have come to my hands, even counting at their full value negroes on which the testatrice had only a life estate. Yet as I paid all demands against her during her life, and believe that on view of that she had credit & quiet from the merchants with whom she dealt, I am willing to assume this debt also to be paid with interest." This was the voice of an exasperated son, dealing with a mother who seems to have had so little gift for keeping track of her expenses. But here we also find the tenderness of a man who hoped to lift her burden of worry, even as Jane Jefferson's debts added to the crushing weight that bore ever more heavily down upon her son over the course of his life.

Duty and devotion spurred his actions, but Jefferson made his choices as a slaveholder. In this effort to finish paying off debts including those of his mother, he wrote to his brother-in-law, John Bolling, "I find myself obliged this winter to make a very considerable sale of negroes in addition to the sale of land I have already made and shall further make." Though he did not, in that instance, actually sell people, he, like Jane, showed his devotion to his white family by his willingness to break up the families of his slaves.

And then, of course, there was her Bible. This most bookish of Jane Jefferson's children was the person who had the means and the persistence to find a replacement for a cherished Bible lost to the flames in 1770, a gift of tender kindness. After her death, Thomas Jefferson preserved that relic with more than usual care. The book would be passed down to his daughter, Martha, and in turn to her youngest daughter, Septimia. Sometime in the late eighteenth century, he had Jane's Bible rebound into a volume that also included Thomas's own Book of Common Prayer, a London concordance, and the page on which Peter Jefferson had recorded the birth dates and places of Jane and her Randolph siblings. Thomas added his own notations in that volume, as did his daughter Martha and granddaughter Septimia.

Thomas Jefferson cared for his mother no less than he attempted to protect and provide for all the people who depended on him, and upon whom he would find himself dependent—his wife, his daughters, his grandchildren, and his slaves. What had started as the filial attachment of the son became obligation to stand in for his father in protecting his mother. That patriarchal responsibility was more than a duty, more than a promise; it was, for him, a sacred trust, his part of a bargain grounded in nature and sealed in mutual affection, nurturing, loyalty, and comfort. He had learned to believe in that fundamental exchange early, and with fervor, in the home of his parents, Peter and Jane Jefferson. He lived up to his part of the bargain where his mother was concerned, and we have no reason to doubt that she in turn lived up to hers. His devotion and duty to the women he loved would guide him in matters great and small for the rest of his life.

Part II

MARTHA

5

The Debt Collector's Daughter

JOHN WAYLES OF Virginia, a planter and a lawyer, was a man of business and charm. Born in Lancaster, England, in 1715, he grew up poor, but with talent and ambition. Sometime in the 1730s, he crossed the Atlantic as a "Servant Boy," and within ten years he had acquired a thriving law practice and thousands of acres of land. He dealt in real estate and tobacco and in human beings by the hundreds. As slavery thrust millions into misery, it lifted John Wayles higher.

Wayles moved among the lordly ladies and gentlemen of Virginia's famous families, cultivating fine manners and a winning personality. Yet he perpetually walked the line between coldhearted commerce and the customs of the country, between the English merchants he often represented and the Virginia gentlemen who were his friends, and soon to be his relations. He stood just a little outside their ranks, not simply because he was a self-made man, but also because he'd chosen one path to fortune that put him at odds with those he sought to please. John Wayles was a debt collector.

The most opulent plantation mansions, the finest horses and coaches, the most elegant gardens and verdant fields of Virginia were built not simply on the brute foundation of forced labor, but also on the slithering silt of ever-mounting debt. Wayles's future son-in-law, Thomas Jefferson, once observed that Virginia planters were "a species of property annexed to certain mercantile houses in London." When John Wayles came to visit, he might expect a gentleman's welcome, but all too often the host greeted him with dread. Some found reason to be absent when they learned he intended to call.

As the agent for Farell and Jones, the Bristol, England, tobacco merchants who shipped so much of Virginia's signature crop, Wayles had to squeeze his neighbors on behalf of their distant creditors, to figure out who was likely to pay, and how much, and when. The debtors were a wily bunch, and they tried every stratagem to put him off. Some offered bonds given them by friends and family, basically secondhand IOUs. "When I came to inquire after the people [who had first signed the bonds]," Wayles discovered, "they mostly lived on the Borders of Carolina. It would probably take 7 Years to Collect them." Others used their family connections to evade payment. Of one Nathaniel Harrison, Wayles observed, "I have wrote more Letters, & made more Personal Applications for so small a Sum, then I ever did to any other Gentlemen. This family is somehow or other so connected with your other Friends, that, where the debt is not in danger, indulgencies are unavoidable." In Virginia, of course, family connections were the coin of the realm. A Mr. Syme, said Wayles, "cannot be worth less than 15 or 20 thousand pounds." Syme had "married an heiress possessed of the Lands about New Castle where he lives & other Estate to a considerable Value."

For all the awkward moments demanded by his position, Wayles still managed to ingratiate himself with the prominent and the powerful. He was, according to Thomas Jefferson, "a lawyer of much practice, to which he was introduced more by his great industry, punctuality and practical readiness, than to eminence in the science of his profession. He was a most agreeable companion, full of pleasantry and good humor, and welcomed in every society." John Wayles studied the habits of the Virginia aristocracy, and he knew how to succeed among them. Like the solvent Mr. Symes, John Wayles married an heiress. In fact he would marry three daughters of Virginia's first families, two of them heiresses of no small means.

The first was the widow Martha Eppes Eppes, a real catch. She was born in 1721 at Bermuda Hundred, her father's plantation at the confluence of the James and Appomattox rivers in Chesterfield County, not far from Wayles's place, "the Forest," in Charles City County near Williamsburg. The Eppeses loved hunting and horse racing and high living. When she married John Wayles in May 1746, Martha Eppes had property inherited from her late husband (an Eppes cousin), as well as a substantial legacy from her father and from a deceased older brother. She owned 1,200 acres of land, feather beds and silver spoons, a horse, a saddle, furniture, and nine enslaved people.

According to the English law of coverture, a woman's property passed to her husband upon marriage. The law assumed that husbands would protect and provide for the wives and children who depended upon them. But Martha Eppes, a second-time bride, shared a pragmatic outlook with her prospective husband. She made a somewhat different arrangement with John Wayles. According to the couple's marriage indenture, a contract signed a few days before the wedding, John Wayles would be entitled only to the use of his wife's property during his lifetime. If he died before she did, Martha would resume control over her estate, "notwithstanding her Coverture." Her property was not his to dispose of as he saw fit. If Martha died before her husband, according to their contract, her assets would pass to her own children, and not to any children Wayles might have with anyone else.

There certainly was reason for Martha Eppes to be concerned. In colonial Virginia, " 'til death do us part" could be a near-term proposition. She had already lost one husband, and even among the most privileged Virginians, wives had a tendency to die young, leaving their children at the mercy of future stepmothers. Childbirth was then, as now, a bloody business, but in Virginia in the middle of the eighteenth century, having a baby was far too often a lethal experience for the mother, the child, or both.

Seven and a half months after they married, Martha Eppes Wayles gave birth, prematurely, to twins, a boy and a girl. Her daughter was born dead. Her son lived only a few hours. A year later, she was again pregnant, and this time the baby survived, but the ordeal killed the mother. She delivered a daughter on October 31, 1748, lay dying for five days, and then she was gone, dead at the age of twenty-seven. The baby, named Martha after her mother and called Patty by her family, never knew the woman who gave her life at the cost of her own. The father quickly sought a new wife to raise his small daughter and run his household. John Wayles married a woman of the Cocke family, yet another prominent Virginia planter clan. The second Mrs. Wayles gave him four more daughters, three of whom—Elizabeth, Tabitha, and Anne—lived to adulthood. But Wayles's second wife died, leaving him a widower yet again.

By January 1760, Wayles had found himself a third wife, yet another stepmother for his daughters. This time he chose the widow Elizabeth Lomax Skelton, who had inherited property from her late husband, Reuben Skelton. Scarcely more than a year after the wedding, she too was dead. Wedding, bedding, and burying a third wife was enough for John Wayles. He never married again.

WE KNOW ALL these things about the Wayles family from a single document: a memorandum written by Thomas Jefferson, who had a well-known penchant for recording statistics, vital and otherwise, and for cataloging the names of things. The man who eventually married Martha Wayles took care to mark the births, marriages, and deaths of his wife's immediate family members, information he must have learned from Martha herself. But Jefferson entered no given names for either of Martha's stepmothers. Martha, it seems, did not speak of those women often enough for their names to lodge in the mind of a devoted husband with a legendary memory. Given her later desperate terror of stepmothers, Martha's silence may have been a way to quell the bad memories of a motherless child. Those things we actively refuse to speak about echo in the mind and scorch the heart.

John Wayles, thrice wifeless, did not live out his days alone; he took a concubine. He turned to a woman who had lived in his household longer than any of his wives. Elizabeth "Betty" Hemings was the daughter of an English sea captain and an enslaved African woman. She had come to the Forest at about the age of thirteen, as Martha Eppes's slave. Over eleven years, Betty Hemings bore twelve children. John Wayles was the father of six of them, three boys and three girls: Robert, James, Thenia, Critta, Peter, and Sally. Their half-sisters, Martha, Elizabeth, Tabitha, and Anne, bore their father's last name of Wayles, but Betty's six children would bear the surname Hemings and be held as slaves by their father. Their half-sister, Martha Wayles, would inherit them all, according to the terms of her mother's marriage contract.

John Wayles, wrote Annette Gordon-Reed, "grew rich himself off of Africans. He used them as items of trade, held them in bondage, and mixed his blood with theirs."

The Wayles sisters surely knew that six of the Hemingses were their half-siblings. Betty Hemings had known the Wayles girls from birth—knew them as Patty, Betsy, Tibby, and Nancy. She may have assisted in bringing them into the world, and she had outlasted all their mothers as the most constant fixture in their household. She would have had a hand in raising all four, and Martha, the daughter of her late mistress, most of all.

When Betty Hemings began her liaison with John Wayles, she already had four children. By the time she gave birth to Robert, known in the neighborhood to have been John Wayles's child, Martha Wayles was thirteen years old, old enough, according to Virginia law, to marry in her own right. If her sisters were at that moment too young to suspect what had arisen between their father and his slave, the arrival of five more mixed-race babies, the last born in 1773, must have made the case plain.

We cannot know how the Wayles girls talked about the matter among themselves, whether their father ever said anything to them, whether they ever asked. Perhaps there was no need. The Forest was a substantial house, but it was not a great mansion, not a place where the comings and goings of some inhabitants would escape the notice of others. Children see more than their parents think they do, even when they learn not to talk about what they know. White people might pretend to know nothing of interracial sex, but public silence was no bar to private action. Indeed, where sex across the color line was commonplace, maintaining public silence required family acquiescence.

Martha Wayles learned her place in a world of open secrets. As a well-to-do white woman, she was born to direct, but also to obey. In order to command her kin as servants, she had to master distance, to learn not to see what was in front of her eyes, to play a deadly serious game of genealogical make-believe. Some of John Wayles's children took his name and claimed his race. Others would be known as black or negro or colored, and go by the name of Hemings. Hemingses would be enslaved for life, made to serve their Wayles relatives, hidden in plain sight, in houses where women skated along the bloody bodily edge of race and bondage.

*   *   *

THE WAYLES HALF-SISTERS grew up privileged, though not strictly secure. Their father made a fortune but in the process fell into the debt he deplored in his neighbors. Risk, after all, was inherent to the kind of business he did. Still, there were huge profits to be made from high prices for tobacco and slaves bought and sold on credit. Martha and her sisters moved in the most elevated circles, visiting and hosting friends and relations, Eppeses and Skeltons, Bollings and Harrises and Cockes. They took along slaves to light their fires and carry their water, iron their linens, fetch their tea, rub down their horses. They had fancy goods as well as skilled attendants: pattern books and fine fabrics, stays and stockings and slippers and boots, hair powder and cloaks and jewels.

Familiar as he was with the avalanche of debt that threatened to bury some of his friends and relations, their father was leery of extravagance for its own sake. Wayles had seen planters borrow more and more from British merchants. He observed in 1766 that in his younger years, a planter's debt of one thousand English pounds "due to a Merchant was looked upon as a Sum imense and never to be got over." But times had changed.

Ten times that sum is now spoke of with Indifference & thought no great burthen on some Estates. . . . Luxury & expensive living have gone hand in hand with the increase of wealth. In 1740 I don't remember to have seen such a thing as a turkey Carpet in the Country except a small thing in a bed chamber. Now nothing are so common as Turkey or Wilton Carpets, the whole Furniture of the Roomes Elegant & every appearance of Opulence. All this is in great measure owing to the Credit which the Planters have had from England . . . tho many are ignorant of the true Cause.

Martha Wayles was taught from an early age to prize thrift and beware reckless spending, as she prepared to take on the myriad tasks of an industrious plantation wife. At barely the age of fourteen, motherless again, she assumed the duties of woman of the house. While her slaves performed the hardest and worst jobs, she learned the ways of butchering hogs, cattle, and fowl, rendering lard to mix with lye and ashes for soap, brewing beer, counting out the linens and spoons, and dispensing clothing and food to slaves. She saw to these duties at the Forest and took part in running John Wayles's other plantations. As Martha stood in for her mother and stepmothers, she completed her training in housewifery under the eyes of Elizabeth Hemings.

Whatever Betty Hemings could teach Martha Wayles about housekeeping, she could not train Martha in everything she needed to know. Other women, female relations and friends, initiated Martha into the niceties and treacheries of white plantation society, the arts of mingling politeness and poison in genteel conversation, or setting tiny stitches in fancy sewing. Her father likely taught her to keep household accounts, and someone showed her how to sit a horse. Teachers and tutors came to the Forest to instruct the young ladies in music and dancing and drawing. Martha was known for her musical gifts, her skill on the spinet and harpsichord and her sweet singing voice.

By the age of seventeen, Martha began to look for a husband among the young men she met in plantation drawing rooms, in the ballrooms and parlors of Richmond and Williamsburg. She would have been as good a match as her mother had been, or even better: her rich father, having no male heir, would settle his property on his daughters. But Martha possessed attractions of her own. According to family tradition, which doubtless painted her in the rosiest tones, Martha was a beautiful young woman, auburn-haired and hazel-eyed, "with a lithe and exquisitely formed figure, . . . a model of graceful and queenlike carriage." While Isaac Jefferson, who spent most of his life as a slave at Monticello, described Martha as "small" and "low," others recalled that she had been somewhat above medium height for a woman.

She had, it seems, a sparkle about her. Her sister Tabitha's husband, Robert Skipwith, knew her well and praised Martha as possessor of "the greatest fund of good nature [and] sprightliness and sensibility." Her granddaughter, Ellen Randolph Coolidge, celebrated "her wit, her vivacity and her agreeable person and manners," while her great-granddaughter, Sarah Nicholas Randolph, added that Martha was "a person of great intelligence and strength of character," with "a mind of no ordinary caliber. She was well-educated for her day, and a constant reader; she inherited from her father his method and industry."

This paragon of white southern womanhood was not, however, all sweetness, as even her most devoted descendants admitted. "My grandmother Jefferson," wrote Ellen Randolph Coolidge, drawing on her own mother's memories, "had a vivacity of temper which might sometimes border on tartness." We should not be surprised that John Wayles's daughter sometimes expressed herself in blunt, even acid terms.

Tart-tongued or not, Martha had her share of suitors, even though she entered the marriage market at a time of family turmoil. In the summer of 1766, her father had taken the case of a man named John Chiswell, a heavily indebted planter accused of murdering a merchant named Robert Routledge in a Williamsburg tavern. The murder happened amid conflict between Virginia planters and the English merchants they owed, a tension that contributed mightily to the coming confrontation with the British government. John Wayles found himself to be a man in the middle. When he agreed to serve as Chiswell's lawyer, he surprised his merchant allies. And when he managed to get his client released on bail, Routledge's friends were furious, charging that the court had given the accused special deference due to his rank in society. If John Wayles had not seen the nasty side of courtliness before that point, the Chiswell affair gave him a lesson in the spectacle of the Virginia gentleman in full snarling attack. William Rind, publisher of the *Virginia Gazette,* made John Wayles the target of written tirades. That he was attacked as a "Judas" suggests that some of his critics saw him as a traitor to his own interests.

Martha and her sisters may have chosen not to read the scurrilous stuff in Rind's paper, the bad satiric poetry ridiculing their father's good manners and calling him "ill-bred," the essays accusing him of lying and claiming that he'd long had a bad reputation, although Rind demurred from specifying the nature of Wayles's offenses. But the Wayles girls could not have been unaware of the attacks, or the fact that their father was representing the very sort of debtor that he usually pursued. Wayles tried to refute what had been said and written, but simply by engaging his assailants publicly he fed the fire of controversy. The outcry died down when John Chiswell, Wayles's client, committed suicide while awaiting trial. Before that ugly denouement, and surely after, the Wayles girls must have heard whispers, perhaps even open slights, when they went out into society, a hard thing for young women in any age. The gossip seemingly strayed into the territory of John Wayles's peculiar domestic arrangements, and bad blood between Martha's kin and the Rind family would, as it turned out, be passed on for another generation.

If the Chiswell matter caused discomfort in the Wayles household, far worse lay in store. In the same summer, Martha's first cousin, Richard Henry Eppes, was murdered at Bermuda Hundred, the plantation where her own mother had grown up. According to a story published in the *New-York Mercury* and datelined "Williamsburg, in Virginia, June 20":

On Thursday last Week, the following melancholy Affair happened in Chesterfield County: A Negro Girl carried Mrs. Epps's

Son to the River Side with a Pretence to divert him, but when he got there, she struck him several Times on the Head with a Stave, until he was stunn'd, and then flung him into the Water; but recovering a little, he made shift to get out; upon which, with the Help of a Negro Boy, she again beat him until he appeared to be dead, and flung him into the River, and then made off; but a Boat coming by immediately after, discover'd him, and carried him home, where he had not been long before he recovered so far as to give the above Account, but died soon after.

The teenage Richard Henry Eppes had lived with his mother and his older half-brother, Francis, at Bermuda Hundred. Local authorities wasted no time bringing his attackers to justice. On June 21, the day after the dateline of the story in the *New-York Mercury* and nine days after the incident, two enslaved people belonging to Mrs. Eppes, Sukey and Will, were tried for the murder. Will, the alleged accomplice, was found not guilty. According to family history, Sukey was convicted and hanged.

This story, which traveled like lightning all the way to New York, gives us an inkling of the terror the event occasioned in Virginia, let alone in the neighborhood, not to mention among the family. A young slave woman had planned with care a brutal assault on a planter's son and had involved an accomplice. For slave owners, the fear of violence against masters might be repressed, but it never ceased to bubble beneath the surface of everyday life. Sukey's (and Will's) fury tapped the slaveholders' deepest anxiety, like a dentist's drill hitting a nerve.

Why would a slave girl, a person with no rights of any kind, risk everything to kill the young master? She must have been either crazy or desperately provoked. Masters, after all, enjoyed the legal right to starve, to beat, to sexually assault and exploit, to use in any way, even to kill those they enslaved, for any reason, or no reason at all. Richard

Henry Eppes was not legally Sukey's owner (she belonged to the boy's mother), but as a son of the house, who stood to inherit Sukey and the rest of his mother's property, he was, for all purposes, her master.

The killing of Richard Henry Eppes was not some distant event for people at the Forest, Wayleses and Hemingses alike. The Wayles sisters were very much at home at Bermuda Hundred, a neighboring plantation. The victim's father had signed John Wayles and Martha Eppes's marriage indenture. Elizabeth Hemings had been raised at Bermuda Hundred and knew the Eppes family well. Three years later, Elizabeth Wayles, the sister closest to Martha, married the murdered boy's older brother, Francis Eppes. In the Wayles household, where the wall between master and slave had been so repeatedly breached, the news of murder so close at hand set off screaming alarms.

6

Bride and Widow

IN THE SHADOW of suicide and scandal and murder, eighteen-year-old Martha Wayles became a bride. She married twenty-two-year-old Bathurst Skelton on November 20, 1766. They had known one another for years. In the convoluted manner of Virginia planter families, Martha's new husband was by way of being her step-uncle: the youngest brother of her stepmother's first husband, Reuben Skelton. Martha had property of her own, but no marriage indenture was recorded for Martha and Bathurst Skelton. Instead John Wayles relied on the contract he had made with Martha's mother twenty years earlier, reinforced in his own will, which guaranteed that his eldest daughter would inherit money and land and people, including Betty Hemings and her children. One way or another, the law would transfer her property to her young husband, who would promise to protect and provide for her, as she in turn would pledge to honor and obey him, so long as they both lived.

Bathurst Skelton was just two years out of the College of William and Mary when he married Martha Wayles. The small library he would leave behind offers an inkling of his aptitudes, or at least of the college curriculum, including volumes on mathematics and algebra, mechanics, astronomy, French, and geography. He owned two translations of Virgil, Addison and Steele's *Spectator,* and a good smattering of the essentials in English literature: Milton's *Paradise Lost,* eight volumes of Swift and ten of Pope, Smollett's *Roderick Random*, and Dr. Johnson's Dictionary. Young Skelton may or may not have read these books with any care, or at all, and his wife may or may not have ever given them a glance. But Martha did marry two men who possessed books, one of them a passionate reader and collector, and on her deathbed, she would struggle to trace out beloved lines from Laurence Sterne.

The Skeltons set up housekeeping at Elk Hill, a Goochland County plantation that John Wayles had purchased in 1746, a beautiful place both of them knew well. They occupied a bluff-top brick house overlooking Byrd Creek at the confluence of the James. The newlyweds could gaze out over the lush bottomland of Elk Island, where Bathurst Skelton owned a thousand-acre plantation and John Wayles leased land and grew tobacco. Elk Hill must have seemed an obvious place for the young couple to make their home. Here they had a comfortable house with a gorgeous view, offering an abundance of game and access to the Elk Island plantation. They hosted hunting parties and family gatherings as the warm and vivacious Martha began her life as Mrs. Bathurst Skelton.

Of course, a Virginia plantation wife's principal duty was to provide her husband with an heir. Martha fulfilled that expectation without delay. On November 7, 1767, not quite a year after their wedding, Martha gave birth to their first and only child, a boy they named John, after his grandfather Wayles.

Whatever joy they felt at the birth of their son would be cut short. Ten months later, on September 30, 1768, Bathurst Skelton died suddenly. He made his will on his deathbed, too weak to sign the document himself. In extremis, Skelton was aware of his wife's legacy from her mother, the foundation of her fortune, currently in his hands. But knowing that Martha was likely to remarry, he made sure to provide for his son in the chief form of wealth he possessed: enslaved people. "Whereas my wife Martha will be entitled to sundry slaves at the death of her father, by virtue of a marriage settlement made betwixt him and her mother, all which slaves I give to her and her heirs forever in case my son dies under age, or unmarried," his will read. "But if he attains to lawful age or marriage, then the said slaves to be equally divided betwixt them, my wife and son." Skelton named Martha and John Wayles as guardians for little John, and as his own executors, and added a note bequeathing his phaeton, a light, doorless, two-wheeled carriage with a seat for two, and horses to Martha.

Thus Martha, at the age of nineteen, found herself a widow and the mother of a child who had not yet reached his first birthday. She left Elk Hill behind, though years later she found a way to reclaim her first bridal home. She went home to the Forest, where her father—and Elizabeth Hemings—could care for her and her son.

Not yet twenty, Martha Wayles Skelton had endured loss after loss. How did she cope? Many people seek solace in faith, but whether religion provided some comfort, we cannot say. Her father was a church-going man after the fashion of elite Virginians of the time, more given to the social than spiritual aspects of their observances. He was an active member of his Episcopal church, but not precisely a pious pillar of devotion. Maria Byrd, wife of William Byrd III, had written to her husband that Wayles was working to recruit speakers for the congregation, including one "Parson Duglish, he says to make us laugh."

Perhaps that capacity to laugh sustained his daughter, too. Despite so many blows, she somehow managed to retain the spark that those who knew her best remarked on so often. Her ability to move forward with grace and purpose, to seek and find joy, bespeaks an impressive inner strength. That strength would be more than tested in the years to come.

WHEN MARTHA RETURNED to the Forest, late in 1768, she found a household full of Hemingses. Elizabeth Hemings had borne John Wayles two sons and a daughter: Robert (born 1762), James (born 1765), and Thenia, born the same year as their half-nephew, little John Skelton. Hemings's four eldest children—Mary (fifteen), Martin (thirteen), Betty (nine), and Nancy (seven)—were old enough to take on household duties. Martha's enslaved half-brothers and half-sisters were still too young to work, though Robert, now six, might have been enlisted, alongside the older children, to carry water and make fires, to help mind his little brothers and sisters and John Skelton. While Martha lived as a widow in her father's house, Betty Hemings gave birth to two more half-siblings, Critta, in 1769, and Peter, in 1770.

John Wayles and Elizabeth Hemings had the kind of relationship that everyone knew about and many denied. But their connection endured more than a decade, lasted until his death, and stubbornly survived in the memory of their descendants and neighbors. Whatever Martha felt about her father's liaison, about her slave brothers and sisters, about their mother, the enslaved matriarch of the Hemings clan and the young widow Skelton were raising little children in the same household, even as they regarded one another across the abyss of race and caste. What Annette Gordon-Reed has called "the catechism of white supremacy—one of those things people live by, even though they know they're not true"—kept that chasm from closing. It corroded Martha's vision of their kinship as surely as a bottle of vitriol thrown in the eyes. And it forced the Hemingses to pretend ignorance of what they knew to be true. The law gave Martha Wayles Skelton a right to own property, though like all women, she ceded that right to any man she married. The law viewed Elizabeth Hemings *as* property. She had no authority over her own children, no right even to her own body.

The shock and pain of Bathurst Skelton's death inevitably ebbed, and Martha looked ahead. She began to enjoy society again, and it seems, to entertain suitors. One such admirer arrived at the Forest for a brief visit in early October 1770. Twenty-seven-year-old Thomas Jefferson—lawyer, planter, and member of the Virginia House of Burgesses—came on horseback, or perhaps in his phaeton, accompanied by Jupiter, his body servant. He was so determined to get there that he persisted through some mishap—a thrown horseshoe, a broken spring. Martha encouraged his attentions, and she must have been much on his mind, since he soon returned.

Thomas Jefferson was a busy man, shuttling back and forth between Williamsburg and Charlottesville in the wake of the terrible Shadwell fire, occupied too with a law practice that obliged him to ride around to plantations and county courthouses and the General Court in Williamsburg. As a member of the House of Burgesses, he was increasingly consumed by the growing conflict between the British government and the colonial legislatures. And he was working frantically to get a house built at Monticello. But he still managed to find the time to go to see Martha.

At some point Jefferson emerged as the leading contender among Martha's numerous suitors. Some five years her senior, six feet two inches tall, brilliant and agreeable, he had charms of his own. Biographer Henry Randall offered an appealing picture of the young man:

> Mr Jefferson was generally . . . rather a favorite with the other sex, and not without reason. His appearance was engaging. His face, though angular, and far from beautiful, beamed with intelligence, with benevolence, and with the cheerful vivacity of a happy, hopeful spirit. . . . He was an expert musician, a fine

dancer, a dashing rider. . . . There was a frankness, earnestness, and cordiality in his tone—a deep sympathy with humanity—a confidence in man, and a sanguine hopefulness in his destiny.

Martha Skelton and Thomas Jefferson shared the gift of music. He was devoted to his violin, she to her spinet, and they both loved to sing. They rejoiced in playing together. For many years after, their descendants preserved a favorite story of their courtship. It seems that two of Martha's other suitors, still holding out hope, arrived at the Forest one day and met accidentally in the hall. Just as they prepared to enter the drawing room, they heard Thomas and Martha singing together. They exchanged a knowing look, put on their hats, and left.

What, apart from music, drew Thomas Jefferson and Martha Wayles Skelton together? They were of similar rank in society, both related to important families through their mothers, with fathers who had succeeded in business by working hard, by cultivating friendships with powerful people, and by marrying well. Each was left with only one parent. They were both products of plantation life, had both been raised to take for granted their right to command and own slaves. They were accustomed to wealth, to fine imported goods, even as the House of Burgesses was struggling with the British government over taxes on luxury items.

But they also had similar ideas about the pursuit of happiness. Both were devoted to the novels of Laurence Sterne, a writer who celebrated sentiment. They also discussed the poetry of Ossian (a supposedly ancient Scottish poet, purportedly translated by the eighteenth-century writer James Macpherson). Martha had an eminently pragmatic father, but she embraced the sentimentalism then popular in the cultured classes of Europe and the colonies. Thomas Jefferson, for all that he would soon emerge as the most famous disciple of reason in American history, never underestimated the claims of the heart. One of his early biographers, James Parton, hyperbolically observed that "the mightiest capacity which this man possessed was the capacity to love. In every other quality and grace of human nature he has been often equalled, sometimes excelled; but where has there ever been a *lover* so tender, so warm, so constant, as he?"

We cannot estimate with any precision the rank of Thomas Jefferson among the great lovers in history, but throughout his life he proved to be a man who loved deeply, and whose actions and ideas were shaped by that love. His passion for the woman who would become his only wife was fervent, lifelong, and consequential.

By the beginning of 1771, Thomas Jefferson had made his intentions clear, though Martha Skelton had not quite accepted his proposal. He wrote to his friend James Ogilvie on February 20 with news of a mutual friend who "is wishing to take himself a wife; and nothing obstructs it but the unfeeling temper of a parent who delays, perhaps refuses to approve her daughter's choice." Like the friend, Jefferson hoped to marry soon. But he was forced to wait, he insisted, not because of parental disapproval, but due to the fire that had destroyed Shadwell a year earlier, robbing him of a proper house to which to bring a bride:

> I too am in that way [of hoping to marry]; and have still greater difficulties to encounter not from the forwardness [*sic*] of parents, nor perhaps want of feeling in the fair one, but from other causes as unpliable to my wishes as these. Since you left us I was unlucky enough to lose the house in which we lived, and in which all its contents were consumed. A very few books, two or three beds &c. were with difficulty saved from the flames. I have lately removed to the mountain from whence this is dated, and with which you are not unacquainted. I have here but one

room, which, like the cobler's, serves me for parlour for kitchen and hall. I may add, for bed chamber and study too. My friends sometimes take a temperate dinner with me and then retire to look for beds elsewhere. I have hopes however of getting more elbow room this summer.

Jefferson envisioned a summer wedding, though he still had to convince Martha to marry him. They did manage to see each other, sometimes in the capital, and their friends hoped he would succeed. A Quaker woman he knew from Williamsburg urged him, "persever thou, good Young Man, persevere.—She has good Sence, and good Nature, and I hope will not refuse (the Blessing shal' I say) why not as I think it,—of Yr. Hand, if her Hearts, not ingaged already. . . . And belive me, that I most sincerly wish You, the full completion, of all Yr. Wishes, both as to the Lady and every thing else."

Why did Martha hesitate? Perhaps she thought it was seemly to do so. Maybe she was considering other offers. Possibly she was afraid to commit herself again, having lost one husband so young. And while Jefferson's letter to James Ogilvie suggested that neither his mother nor her father opposed the match, Jefferson had supported the Virginia Burgesses' nonimportation agreements in response to the Townshend Acts, and John Wayles was the agent for British merchants; in 1766, Wayles had declared the uproar over the Stamp Act a "great Licentiousness." Still, Wayles was a friend to the Randolph clan and doubtless knew Jane Jefferson as well as her son. He must have seen pleasing prospects in the match.

By the beginning of June, Thomas Jefferson had won over his prospective bride. And why did Martha say yes? She had reason enough to choose a husband carefully. As Henry Randall observed, "With rank and wealth (if the last can be supposed to have had any influence on the men of the olden time!) it is not wonderful that Mrs. Skelton was a favorite with the other sex—that her hand was sought by wooers far and near." She stood to inherit more than Jefferson possessed, so she was not marrying for money. As a daughter of the Eppes line, she did not need to marry for social advantage. She might have remained an unmarried widow, as her future sister-in-law, Martha Carr, would do, under the far more difficult circumstance of raising six children, and as another future sister-in-law, the childless Anna Jefferson Marks, would do much later. Jefferson's two sisters, left vulnerable by their husbands' deaths, fell back on their brother as provider and protector, and Martha had no brother. But she did have a fortune of her own, and if she needed a man to administer her affairs, her father could certainly arrange with his friends to serve as trustees. So, why?

Martha Skelton accepted Thomas Jefferson's proposal, it would seem, not out of necessity, but on account of desire. She wanted more children, but she could have had those with a richer, more important man. She chose Jefferson because she wanted *him*. In 1771 no one could have predicted where the course of life would take him. He was a Virginia planter with good prospects to be a leading man in the colony, but who could have imagined more? That, assuredly, was enough for Martha at the time she agreed to become his wife. And it was almost surely not his greatest asset, in her eyes. We have to conclude, in the end, that she decided to marry Thomas Jefferson because of a mutual attraction, an emotional and physical chemistry between them that meant a great deal to both of them. Many people they knew married without such connections or expectations, seeing sustenance, security, and status as good enough causes to make a match. Many were content with less, but Martha wanted more. As we would say now, she loved him, and accepted his proposal because of that, and because he loved her.

* * *

AS JEFFERSON LOOKED forward to setting up housekeeping with Martha at Monticello, he indulged in one of his favorite pastimes: he shopped. And in doing so, he failed, or at least skirted, a political test. As American resistance to England spread, colonial legislatures passed laws against the importing of British goods. Jefferson wanted to honor the boycott but he nonetheless wrote to London merchant Thomas Adams requesting a large order of expensive goods, as soon as possible. He was an exacting customer. In a previous letter he had ordered a clavichord, but now he allowed as how "I have since seen a Forte-piano and am charmed with it. Send me this instrument then instead of the Clavichord. Let the case be of fine mahogany, solid, not vineered. The compass from Double G. To F. In alt. A plenty of spare strings; and the workmanship of the whole very handsome, and worthy the acceptance of a lady for whom I intend it." He was, indeed, "very impatient" to have the pianoforte and urged Adams to send it forthwith.

Music, love, luxury, and indebtedness suffused the marriage between Martha Wayles Skelton and Thomas Jefferson. "By this change of the Clavichord into a Forte-piano and addition of the other things," Jefferson acknowledged to his merchant correspondent, "I shall be brought in debt to you." But that did not bother him, and indeed, he asked Thomas Adams to send him not just goods, but also "an architect . . . as soon as you can." To pay what he owed, he proposed an arrangement familiar to all Virginia planters and all English merchants: "To discharge [the debt] I will ship you of the first tobaccos I get to the warehouse in the fall."

Martha too had high hopes as the snows of winter melted and the trees budded, as the crocuses and wood violets of spring gave way to flowering dogwood and lilac and honeysuckle. She looked forward to life with a scintillating and adoring husband, brothers and sisters for

John, and the promise of a beautiful house on a mountaintop. Jefferson, for his part, prepared to take on a wife and stepson, setting up an account for little John Skelton in his fee book. But that spring brought new suffering and sorrow. On May 26, a terrible flood on the James—"the greatest flood ever known in Virginia," as Jefferson wrote in his Garden Book—washed away the Jefferson mill at Shadwell and wrecked John Wayles's tobacco crop at Elk Island. Martha's own dower lands on the island were doubtless inundated, though we have no record of those losses. Leaving the cleanup at Shadwell in others' hands, Jefferson made his way to the Forest, where tragedy awaited. We don't know if little John Skelton was a sickly child from the first, or whether some childhood disease or tragic accident took him. But in June 1771 he died at the age of three and a half.

Coping with devastation both emotional and physical, they postponed the wedding. Thomas had to parcel out his days between Williamsburg and Monticello, Shadwell and the Forest, spending as much time as he could with Martha. He was determined to get Monticello ready for his bride, but the place was a construction site on which one brick outbuilding, twenty by twenty feet, had served as Jefferson's bachelor quarters. The grand house to come was then nothing more than a Palladian dream, years of commotion and chaos away. Still, Martha and Thomas were both optimists. How else, amid a landscape littered with the wreckage the raging James River had left behind, in the wake of a child's death, can we explain a famous exchange of letters between Jefferson and his prospective brother-in-law, Robert Skipwith, who was soon to marry Martha's sister Tabitha?

Robert Skipwith had written to Jefferson to ask for advice about books. Jefferson, who had quickly refurnished his own library after the Shadwell fire, was only too glad to comply. In a gesture that would prove characteristic in him over the years, he imagined convincing his friend and soon to be brother-in-law to move to Albemarle and become his neighbor. Sitting in his one-room house at Monticello, amid the din and smoke as enslaved men and boys moulded bricks and hauled them to the kiln to be "burned," Jefferson shared with Skipwith an effusive fantasy of a life together, married to Wayles sisters:

Come to the new Rowanty, from which you may reach your hand to a library formed on a more extensive plan. Separated from each other but a few paces, the possessions of each would be open to the other. A spring, centrally situated, might be the scene of every evening's joy. There we should talk over the lessons of the day, or lose them in Musick, Chess, or the merriments of our family companions. The heart thus lightened, our pillows would be soft, and health and long life would attend the happy scene. Come then and bring our dear Tibby with you; the first in your affections, and second in mine. Offer prayers for me too at that shrine to which, tho' absent, I pay continual devotion. In every scheme of happiness she is placed in the foreground of the picture, as the principal figure. Take that away, and it is no picture for me.

Skipwith's delighted reply gives us a hint that by September, despite her mourning, Martha was finding her way back to imagining future happiness with Thomas Jefferson:

Your invitation to the New Rowanty with the pleasing plan for a happy life but above all the affectionate manner in which you speak of my dearest Tibby are so flattering that were it not ruinous to my small fortune I would at all events be neighbours to a couple so well calculated and disposed to communicate knowledge and pleasure. My sister Skelton, Jefferson I wish it were, with the greatest fund of good nature has all that sprightliness and sensibility which promises to ensure you the greatest happiness mortals are capable of enjoying. May business and play musick and the merriments of your family companions lighten your hearts, soften your pillows and procure you health long life and every human felicity! Adieu!

The pretty vision they shared would never come to pass. Sometime between this letter and February 1773, Tabitha Wayles Skipwith died. We know nothing of the cause of that untimely death, but if Jefferson's reference to "our dear Tibby" reflected his bride-to-be's affection for her younger sister, here was another crushing loss. Martha could not get past one source of grief before another swooped down.

7

Mr. and Mrs. Jefferson

THROUGHOUT THE FALL of 1771, Thomas Jefferson worked at his law practice and pushed ahead at Monticello, directing free and enslaved workers as they made thousands of bricks, cleared stumps, and dug out and graded the first of his roundabout roads and a turnaround for carriages. In a sweet moment amid all the heavy work, he noted the small delight of harvesting his first peaches on the mountaintop, at the late date of October 8.

Finally, after all the delays, the wedding between Jefferson and Martha Skelton was set for January 1, 1772, at the Forest. Francis Eppes, who was married to Martha's sister Elizabeth, signed the marriage bond, and Jefferson paid forty shillings for the license. The guest list included the bride's father and the Eppeses, who were then building their house at Eppington in Chesterfield County. Her other sisters, Anne and Tabitha, and the men who would be their husbands, brothers Henry and Robert Skipwith, probably also attended. Jane Jefferson, if her health permitted, would have wanted to be present at the wedding of her eldest son and to bring along her daughters Elizabeth and Anna and son Randolph. Jefferson's sister Mary and brother-in-law John Bolling, friends of the Wayles family, would also be invited. We cannot say whether Martha and Dabney Carr would have been in attendance, given their fast-growing family. But their house at Spring Forest was in Goochland County, and Martha had lived nearby during her marriage to Bathurst Skelton. Surely Jefferson wanted his brother-in-law and best friend, and the sister who had become his closest sibling, to see his joy. There was music and feasting, judging by the liberal tips Jefferson gave to "a fidler" and various enslaved people at the Forest (including Betty Hemings and her son, Martin) for tending to the guests, their slaves, and their horses. The Reverend William Coutts officiated, although the minister for the parish, William Davis, was also present, and Jefferson paid each man five pounds, five times what the law demanded.

MARTHA WAYLES SKELTON and Thomas Jefferson made their vows according to the rites of the Church of England, as embodied in "The Form of Solemnization of Matrimony" in the Book of Common Prayer. The ceremony began with the three "causes for which matrimony is ordained," the first being for "the procreation of children, to be brought up in the fear and nurture of the Lord, and to the praise of His holy name"; the second, as "a remedy against sin, and to avoid fornication"; and the third, "for the mutual society, help and comfort, that the one ought to have of the other, both in prosperity and adversity." Thomas Jefferson promised to "love her, honor her, comfort her and keep her in sickness and in health." Martha Skelton swore to "obey him, serve him, love, honor and keep him in sickness and in health." John Wayles stepped forward to give his daughter to Jefferson, as he had done once before to Bathurst Skelton. Both vowed to love and cherish one another, and Martha again promised to obey her husband. Prayers followed: that the couple be blessed with children, and live long enough to give those children a Christian upbringing; that in the marriage, representing "the spiritual marriage and unity between Christ and his church," Thomas would love his wife, and Martha would "be loving and amiable, faithful and obedient to her husband, and in all quietness, sobriety and peace, be a follower of holy and godly matrons." Reverend Coutts reminded the couple of Saints Paul and Peter's advice on the duties of husbands and wives, enjoining Jefferson to love his wife even as himself, weaker vessel that she was; and reminding Martha to "submit to your husband as unto the Lord, for the husband is the head of the wife, even as Christ is the head of the church," to be in subjection and obey with a meek and quiet spirit, "as Sarah obeyed Abraham, calling him Lord."

Thomas and Martha Jefferson loved one another deeply. For them love was not what many of us today think it should be. It was not a bond between equals. But neither was marriage what it had been for their parents' generation, when there had been no question about who was in charge, and not much sentiment about arrangements made primarily as alliances of family and property. By the time Martha and Thomas came together, elite Virginians had begun to believe that husbands and wives should share "mutual affections." These feelings were different for each; they were reciprocal obligations and emotions. Thomas and Martha both embraced what the age called "sensibility," a "development of sensitivity toward others, particularly one's inferiors—the poor and the weak, including females and children." They still expected different things from one another.

Thomas Jefferson was a devoted partisan of "domestic tranquility," an ideal that depended on a wife's willingness to put the goal of pleasing her husband above every other need or desire. He took pride in keeping his own temper in check, in presenting a mild face to the world, though he intended to be in charge. He assumed that Martha would play her part as a sweet and sunny helpmeet who would defer to his wishes and judgments. "Gentle and sympathetic people always attracted him most, and clearly she was that sort," wrote Dumas

Malone, Jefferson's great biographer, conceding that "she may have had her fiery moments before childbearing wore her out."

How would they maintain such tranquility? Thomas Jefferson believed that men must control themselves, reining in their anger and ruling their households with a firm but loving hand. Women, he thought, had a sacred duty to please their husbands in all regards, to make themselves attractive and keep a clean, welcoming, and abundant home. They should never object to their husbands' decisions, and should repress even the urge to quibble or complain. The historian Kathleen Brown has written that men like Jefferson may have embraced the notion of domestic tranquility in their effort "to maintain the upper hand against women who often brought significant economic resources to the marriage." Martha, as her friends and family knew her, was a spirited, popular, sometimes sharp-tongued woman, a widow who had lost a son. She was no longer a girl, and she brought the power of her future inheritance to their union.

Martha pledged to obey as well as love and honor her new husband, to tailor her wishes to his desires and determinations. But she worked to manipulate what she could not control. Thomas had promised, for his part, to provide for and protect her, a taller order than either of them could know. As before, she made no prenuptial agreement in this marriage, left no trace of writing to signify her claims. She preferred to get what she wanted using other means.

THE NEWLYWEDS STAYED for a time at the Forest and made a visit to Tuckahoe before heading off to Monticello. The trip would become the stuff of family legend, and a favorite tale of Jefferson biographers. Their daughter Martha Jefferson Randolph recounted her father's story of a honeymoon journey in a snowstorm. Thomas and Martha Jefferson set out in the phaeton, but as the snow piled higher and higher, they left the vehicle at a neighbor's house, continuing up the mountain on horseback through snow growing ever deeper. By the time they arrived, it was long past dark. Since they had not sent word that they were coming, no one on the mountain had prepared for their arrival. Who, after all, would travel in such weather? As Jefferson would record in his Garden Book, "the deepest snow we have ever seen. In Albemarle it was 3. f. deep."

The place was dark, the hearth cold, and Martha, her daughter would attest, "shivered at the horrible dreariness of such a house." The slaves who lived on the mountain were asleep in their own cabins. According to Henry Randall, "Part of a bottle of wine, found on a shelf behind some books, had to serve the new-married couple both for fire and supper. Tempers too sunny to be ruffled by many ten times as serious annoyances in after life, now found sources of diversion in these ludicrous *contre-temps*, and the 'horrible dreariness' was lit up with song, and merriment, and laughter!" James Parton found even more romance in the scene. "Who could wish a better place for a honeymoon than a snug brick cottage, lifted five hundred and eighty feet above the world, with half a dozen counties in sight, and three feet of snow blocking out all intruders? What readings of Ossian there must have been! I hope she enjoyed them as well as he."

Linger here a moment, at the very instant in which Jefferson biographers have led us to imagine the first flowering of a Monticello idyll, of what Thomas Jefferson would depict as "ten years in unchequered happiness" with Martha Wayles Skelton Jefferson, his beloved and only wife. Here is a picture of them lighting up the dark in a frigid brick cottage, singing and sipping and sporting to the rhythms of a fraudulent Celtic poet, a poet Dr. Samuel Johnson believed so bad, indeed, that when someone asked Johnson whether he believed that any man could have written the poems of Ossian, he was said to have replied, "Yes. Many men, many women, and many children."

* * *

JOHNSON, OF COURSE, may have been too hard on Ossian, as he was on any number of people. But if the poetry was of debatable provenance, what of the idyll? Consider the cold comfort of Martha's first encounter with Monticello, a place, we are told, she and the deliriously happy Jefferson soon warmed with their joy in each other, in a bed he had recently bought for the substantial sum of nearly eight pounds. Martha Jefferson, gentlewoman, slaveholder, and daughter of a slave trader, expected to be cared for and catered to. Both she and Thomas generally traveled with servants, in Martha's case probably fourteen-year-old Betty Brown, Betty Hemings's daughter, while Thomas usually rode with Jupiter. When the newlyweds set out in the phaeton, they likely sent their baggage in a wagon, and if the story of their arrival alone at the mountaintop is true, at some point in the snowy journey they must have left their slaves and the luggage behind. Otherwise Jefferson surely would have sent Jupiter ahead to announce their arrival and begin to make preparations, as he did on many other occasions. Possibly there were four, not two people slogging their way up the mountain that night, and Jefferson's reminiscences merely reflect the slaveholder's habitual erasure of the presence of the enslaved.

But perhaps the couple decided they cared more about privacy than comfort at Jefferson's little house. Maybe they preferred not to share the one room, or to spend time making sleeping arrangements for two other people. One way or another, Martha proved a confident horsewoman, riding sidesaddle in wet skirts, to put herself through such a trip.

As the miles wore on and the snow drifted and blew, deeper and deeper, Thomas and Martha surely hoped that someone at Monticello had prepared to make them comfortable. The story, told so often and meant to inspire laughter, still bespeaks their disappointment at finding the place dark and cold. No one had laid a fire or even left dry wood, prepared a hot meal, or just set out cold bread and cheese. But why should things have been otherwise? The master had only moved into the house in a provisional way. Since first taking up residence, Thomas Jefferson had been absent more than he'd been home—off to Williamsburg, riding around tending his law practice, visiting his bride-to-be. He'd been gone for weeks, since long before the wedding and nearly a month after. This epic winter journey was not, as Jefferson scholars have suggested, the freezing but merry beginning of Martha and Thomas Jefferson's housekeeping at their legendary home. It was, instead, a brief, memorable episode in a journey that would take Thomas back to his work in Williamsburg, and Martha back to her own home places.

Martha might reasonably have felt dismay, disappointment, or anger at finding herself cold and hungry after such a hard trip, in a place doubtless oversold by her enthusiastic and romantic husband. Here was a first, excellent lesson in how to create domestic tranquility: by looking on the bright side. No doubt she was relieved to get off the horse, and in any case she adored her new husband. He believed it was a woman's duty to shrug off minor inconveniences and even major disappointments, and nothing she could do would change his mind. So Martha cheered up as best she could, and as she would do again and again over ten years scored with trauma after trauma. After her death, Jefferson would remember her as the embodiment of gentleness, warmth, and forbearance. Putting a good face on things, whenever possible, helped Martha get what she wanted, though at a cost she would later find hard to pay.

The diversions of rustic seclusion had a short shelf life. And the snow began to melt. By February 2, they had relinquished the rough pleasures of Monticello for the comfort of Elk Hill, the house Martha had shared with Bathurst Skelton. Martha determined to claim that residence as her own, and returned there again and again. Meanwhile, because of business obligations, Thomas spent much of their first year of marriage living in rented rooms in Williamsburg. Martha was not with him. She went not to Monticello, but back to her family.

MARTHA AND THOMAS Jefferson returned to Monticello at the end of June. She had once again proven herself a fertile bride, with the baby due in the fall. She may have had some trouble with the pregnancy, or perhaps she was simply acting on a previous problem with breastfeeding, since Thomas purchased breast pipes, blown glass instruments used to elongate inverted nipples, in Williamsburg. To use those pipes, someone had to suck through a glass tube attached to a bowl. The fact that Thomas Jefferson bought such devices for his wife suggests he was intimately involved in seeking to relieve the uncomfortable aspects of her pregnancy.

Martha set about her housekeeping with energy as soon as they returned to Monticello. She borrowed an account book in which Thomas was keeping some legal notations, and began keeping track of her household activities. That journal of daily endeavor at Monticello, one of the few surviving documents in Martha's hand, offers a kind of counterpoint to Thomas Jefferson's famous garden and farm books. Historians have delighted in the entry that opened the Garden Book in 1766—"Purple hyacinth begins to bloom"—just as they have contemplated the coldly dispassionate way Jefferson tallied his human property in the Farm Book. Martha's book—or part of a book, a sheaf of borrowed pages—began in a homelier and more pragmatic way, echoing Thomas's Garden Book through a misspelling. On February 10, 1772, she wrote, "opened a barrel of col. Harrisons flower."

Many of the entries for that year dealt with slaughter: "a mutton killed" on February 13 and again on March 20; turkeys and pullets and ducks and geese, shoats and pigs slaughtered. She wrote down when she broke open loaves of sugar, and recorded the hard and soft soap she made from the rendered fat of the butchered sheep. She bought eighty pounds of butter and no small quantity of beef. She was downright devoted to the brewing of beer, mainly "small beer" with low alcohol content. Over the course of the year, Martha brewed no less than fourteen casks of beer at Monticello.

As hard as they worked for their masters, enslaved people sometimes managed to raise a little cash by gardening, gathering, raising poultry, and trapping small game. In the summer of 1772, Martha paid slaves for eggs, peas, ducks, watermelons, and nearly a hundred chickens! Thomas saw to the ongoing house construction and road building and paid a man for cleaning the well. The Monticello well was unreliable and even dried up from time to time. Jefferson had chosen to build his dream house at the top of a mountain, a site calculated more to provide a view than to ensure a steady supply of fresh water. In drought years, slave wagoners hauled barrels of water up the mountain from springs below. In 1773 and again in 1777, the well was completely dry, and Martha had to manage a large and complex household, not to mention having babies and keeping them healthy, without ready access to clean water.

Their daughter Martha, nicknamed Patsy, was born September 27, 1772, just shy of nine months after the wedding (the Jeffersons, it seems, had answered the first of the Episcopalian causes for holy matrimony, if not necessarily the second). For all the trouble Martha would later have with pregnancy and childbirth, she was brewing beer the week before she gave birth. Still, her father was concerned about her, and hoping to see Thomas in Williamsburg once John Wayles cleared up the matter of a business deal that was not working out.

Wayles and his partner, Richard Randolph, were acting as selling agents for a consignment of 490 people, captured in Africa and brought over on a slave ship called the *Prince of Wales*. As fate would have it, the ship might more aptly have been named the *Price of Wayles*. The two partners financed the deal with a loan from the British merchant house Farell and Jones, intending to hold a slave auction at Bermuda Hundred, pay off the loan, and keep the profit. But trading in captive people, potentially enormously lucrative, was also incredibly risky. By the time the ship arrived, ninety of the miserable passengers had died, a horrifying but by no means unusual incidence of mortality for a slave ship. Those who lived were in terrible condition. The purchasers at the auction bought these people on—what else?—credit, pledging to pay in tobacco. Wayles would die with those debts uncollected, leaving Richard Randolph and Wayles's own heirs holding the bag.

John Wayles was worried about his daughter, his slave ship, and the rising fervor of opposition to Britain. He expressed his concern to Thomas Jefferson, who was then in Williamsburg aligning himself with the resistance: "I have heard nothing about our dear Patty since you left this place. . . . Our sale of Slaves go[es] on Slowly so 'tis uncertain when we shall be down but I suppose before the Rebel party leaves town."

WE DO NOT know how Martha felt about her father's ventures in human beings. She may have been ignorant of the financial and legal aspects, and though she was certainly steeped in the daily regimes of slavery, she may never have attended a slave auction herself. But even if Martha did not personally witness the buying and selling of people, she took for granted her right to exploit that terrible commerce to solve her intimate problems. In January 1773, at Martha's behest, Thomas attended a slave sale. He went to a plantation called Maiden's Adventure, where he spent £210 (on twelve months' credit) to purchase three people: Ursula Granger, her fourteen-year-old son,

George, and her five-year-old son, Bagwell. Martha wanted him to buy Ursula, a large and formidable person who could do everything from laundry and ironing to caring for children, from smoking hams and making pastry to "switching" miscreants. To get Ursula, who would become a "favorite housewoman," Martha was willing to also take the children. Martha and Thomas agreed that enslaved families should be kept together, the owners' finances permitting. Jefferson would shortly buy Ursula's husband, George Granger, from another planter, and the Grangers were soon central members of the Jefferson household. Isaac Jefferson, Ursula's youngest son, recalled the way that "Mrs. Jefferson would come out there with a cookery book in her hand and read out of it to Isaac's mother how to make cakes, tarts, and so on." But the relationship between the mistress and her slave woman was more intimate than cakes and tarts. Martha did have trouble nursing, as she had anticipated, and Patsy continued to be small and sickly. The Jeffersons asked Ursula to wet-nurse Patsy, providing what Thomas Jefferson called "a good breast of milk." Patsy rapidly began to thrive, although Ursula's own baby, Archy, died in 1774.

AS BABY PATSY began to bloom, the Jeffersons left the mountain. Thomas attended the legislature, while Martha had family business. Her sister Elizabeth Eppes, like Martha, had already lost a son, but was pregnant again. She gave birth to her second child, John Wayles Eppes (to be known as Jack) at Eppington, on April 7, 1773. Martha had worries as well as joy: her father was seriously ill. She stayed at or near the Forest at least through the spring, perhaps through the early summer.

Consequently, the Jeffersons were absent when another new cousin arrived at Shadwell, when Thomas's sister, Martha Carr, gave birth to her sixth child. As we have seen, Dabney Carr could not linger with his namesake baby boy. He headed off to Williamsburg for that fateful session of the legislature, when the Burgesses voted to establish the first colonial Committee of Correspondence, and the royal governor, Lord Dunmore, in retaliation dissolved the assembly.

This time of political upheaval was another season of tragedy for Martha and Thomas, as each lost the most important man in her and his life. Dabney Carr went to Shadwell after the history-making legislative session, intending to return to politics in the capital. Carr was feeling poorly while at Shadwell, and felt so ill on his attempt to ride back to Williamsburg that he returned to his mother-in-law's house and took to his bed. Whatever was wrong with him, the Jeffersons' doctor, George Gilmer, diagnosed the ailment as "a bilious fever." Following the practices common to the so-called heroic medicine of the day, Gilmer treated Carr with ipecacahuana (to induce sweating and vomiting) and a cathartic that caused severe diarrhea. Doctors believed that if such dosing did not kill the patient, it would provoke a cathartic cure. On May 16, 1773, Dabney Carr died.

As we have seen, Dabney Carr's body was buried not once, but yet again when the grief-stricken Jefferson returned and insisted on having the corpse moved to Monticello. Carr's widow, Jefferson's sister, had already returned with her children to her house at Spring Forest in Goochland County. Thomas Jefferson's terrible grief at his friend's death was compounded by his own wife's absence. Jefferson had left his father-in-law "in so low a situation that his life could not be depended on, which makes me extremely anxious to return." Carr's second grave had scarcely been dug and filled when John Wayles died, on May 28, at the age of fifty-eight. Martha had spent most of that spring at the Forest, taking care of her dying father.

Historian Rhys Isaac pointed out that when Thomas Jefferson

brought Martha to his mountaintop, "he marked Monticello strongly as an example of the novel setting that was becoming increasingly prevalent in the North Atlantic world at this time—a household sentimentalized by the married couple at its center as the secluded domestic sphere of 'home.'" The death and reburial of Dabney Carr, the first person interred in Thomas Jefferson's Monticello cemetery, was similarly a sacred origin tale for Monticello. "With Carr," wrote Isaac, "the mythologizing of the mountaintop as a place of destiny, the place of their shared last rest, had begun."

But these were Thomas's visions and dreams, reiterated and embroidered and treasured by daughters and grandchildren as mementos of the founding mother most of them had never known. Those visions foundered on the rocks of reality and mortality. Martha's experiences of Monticello were starkly different from those of her husband. In the case of the tragic demise of Dabney Carr, that mythic moment in the Monticello graveyard, she wasn't even there.

JOHN WAYLES DIED when Martha was not yet twenty-five years old. Her world would never be the same. Her father had been her source of security her entire life, as a motherless child, a bereaved widow, the heartbroken mother of a dead son. He was still looking out for her when he amended his will in February 1773. His health failing, he worried about the debt he owed Farell and Jones, growing larger on account of his last, immense foray into the slave trade. Wayles stipulated that all the tobacco he was growing on his various lands be shipped to pay that debt, "unless my children should find it to their interest to pay and satisfie the same in a manner that may be agreeable to the said Farrel and Jones."

John Wayles had always taken care of Martha. He had written a first will long before, in April 1760, soon after his third marriage. Martha was then twelve years old, a tough age for a girl faced with yet another stepmother. Many fathers, either through neglect or to please the new wife, disinherited children from their previous marriages. Wayles, however, made it clear that Martha must inherit the legacy spelled out in her mother's marriage settlement, and he went even further. He worried that Martha would feel that she had been treated unfairly when he left the rest of his estate—"all & singular my Lands Tenements & Hereditaments, and also all my slaves and all my other Estate both real and personal"—to his other daughters, Elizabeth, Tabitha, and Anne. Thus he declared, "It is my desire that, if my Daughter Martha thinks her portion not Equal to her Sisters, that her Portion may be thrown into Hotchpotch with her three sisters above and the same Equally Divided among them."

Martha chose not to intermingle her inheritance in "hotchpotch" with her sisters' legacies. Her share already encompassed some eleven thousand acres of land and 135 human beings. With Martha's inheritance, Thomas Jefferson became, for the first time, a truly rich man, more than doubling his own fortune. But he also inherited the debt that so worried John Wayles, an obligation that did not seem onerous at the time but would bedevil Jefferson for all the years to come.

8

Martha's Property

IN THE SUMMER of 1773, Thomas Jefferson began the journey to his ringing embrace of life, liberty, and the pursuit of happiness. Martha Jefferson contemplated death, duty, and the fate of her slaves. The three surviving Wayles sisters—Martha, Elizabeth Eppes, and Anne Skipwith—now had to come to grips with the consequences of their father's death. They had land to partition, people to divide up and move around. Martha had already begun to assemble her household, beginning with her maid, Betty Brown, and the redoubtable Ursula and her family. Thomas too was attending to his human property, claiming his mother's slaves in return for assuming Jane Jefferson's debts. Digging and hammering and brick burning at Monticello continued.

Now Martha had to make some decisions about the Hemings family, from thirty-eight-year-old Betty Hemings on down to Martha's youngest half-sister, the infant Sally Hemings. Since Martha had inherited Betty and her descendants, the Hemingses were now Thomas Jefferson's property. As long as John Wayles lived, they had been part of the household at the Forest. But what would happen to them now?

Martha's sister Elizabeth and the latter's husband, Francis, had temporarily given up their new house at Eppington and moved to the Forest, to manage John Wayles's estate. The oldest Hemings sons, Martin and Robert, would stay there to serve the Eppeses, but Betty and her younger children would leave. Anne and Henry Skipwith, recently married, were moving to the Appomattox River plantation John Wayles had named Guinea but that the Skipwiths gave a more high-toned name, Hors du Monde. Betty Hemings and her children went there with the Skipwiths, far from Williamsburg.

Packing their late father's concubine and their youngest half-sisters and half-brothers off to Hors du Monde was a good way for the Wayles sisters to keep the Hemingses out of sight. Anne Skipwith, like Martha Jefferson, had inherited thousands of acres of land and scores of slaves of her own. Presumably Henry Skipwith also came to the marriage with human property. Surely there were others who could help with the housekeeping for a newlywed couple.

If Betty Hemings had stayed at the Forest, there would have been two babies around the house, Jack Eppes and Sally Hemings, nephew and aunt, respectively. There might be family resemblances that everyone would have to ignore or deny. John Wayles may have taken his mixed-race household for granted, but as the attacks on his character following the Chiswell case suggest, some of his neighbors may have taken a dimmer view. Given the murder of Francis Eppes's brother by Sukey, the slave girl, seven years before, how did Eppes feel about the light-skinned Hemings children, who provided such indisputable evidence of master-slave intimacy?

Whatever the emotions of their white relatives and owners, Betty Hemings and her children had no claim to a home, or, really, to anything at all after the death of their master and father. The person who had the power to determine their fate was Thomas Jefferson. This newly wealthy man had immense plans for his domestic establishment. He was in love, and eager to please his wife. And he was certainly aware of the risks that slaves faced on plantations remote from the home quarters. It was only three years since the murder of Hannah at Snowdon, an incident likely known to the Hemingses and to Martha as well. The Jeffersons preferred to act as if such things did not happen, but that kind of news traveled far and fast in colonial Virginia, and left deep scars in its path.

Thomas Jefferson had the legal right to decide what happened to the Hemingses, right up to putting them on the auction block. Such a course may have occurred to him. His brothers-in-law, Francis Eppes and Henry Skipwith, were preparing to sell 150 of the slaves their wives had inherited from John Wayles. Jefferson already owned whole families of people who had staffed the household at Shadwell.

But it seems Jefferson never thought about selling the Hemingses. Instead he began to bring them to Monticello, installing them in the foremost positions of responsibility, supplanting some of the people who had served his mother and father before him. He was clearly doing what Martha wished. Still, the Hemingses had to earn his trust. Martin Hemings left the Eppeses at the Forest and came to Monticello, and so did nearly five dozen bottles of Jamaican rum. Jefferson noted his intent to "keep a tally of these as we use them by making a mark in the margin in order to try the fidelity of Martin."

Elizabeth Hemings had known Martha all her life, and Martha had grown up with the Hemings children. She knew what had transpired between her father and his concubine, and Martha had just spent months with the pregnant Betty Hemings, nursing John Wayles through his last illness. She saw to it that the Hemings family came to live with her. But we should not romanticize the relationship between Martha the mistress and her enslaved kin. Whatever affection existed between them was shot through with the stubborn fiction of white supremacy and the inescapable fact of human bondage. Love, as we have seen in the case of the Jeffersons, did not imply equal power or responsibility between people—far from it. Instead, a man's love for a woman, or a master's affection toward a slave, expressed a belief that the superior person must protect the loved (and in some measure, despised or pitied) inferior. Thomas Jefferson loved his wife but would never have imagined her to be his peer. Martha may have loved Elizabeth Hemings and her children but she would not have seen them as her equals. If their skin color and family ties made them, in her eyes, a caste apart from other enslaved people, they were also a caste apart from her.

Trying to wrap our twenty-first-century minds around the entanglements of the Wayles-Eppes-Hemings-Jefferson family is a little like trying to eat spaghetti with a knife. Annette Gordon-Reed has rightly called such a confusion of cross-caste, cross-race kinship "bizarre." The white members of this extended family practiced a denial so deep that it became second nature. The black members had to pretend that they saw and knew only what whites wanted them to see and know, while among themselves they kept alive the larger story. The strangeness and silencing of southern interracial kinship was so pervasive, and so weighty a legacy, that six children and their mother could disappear inside it, not just for days or years, but for decades and centuries. In 1948, Dumas Malone would write blithely that John Wayles's death was "less tragic" than that of Dabney Carr, "for he was a widower of fifty-eight and his children were all grown or nearly so." That cavalier pronouncement would have come as bitter but not surprising news to Elizabeth Hemings, nursing little Sally and wondering about her future.

Love never occurs in a vacuum, and love is never, ever simple. Love can be exploitative and terribly cruel. Even in today's small nuclear families there is plenty of room for warmth and rage, for gratitude and resentment, for soothing and laughing and fighting, for lies, secrets, and silences. How much more volatile and confusing was the world of

Martha Jefferson's family! For one thing, Betty Hemings's older children—Mary, Martin, Nancy, and Betty Brown—had reason to feel differently about their new owners than the younger ones would. The older Hemingses had grown up under the control of John Wayles, a man who bought and sold human beings by the hundreds, right up to his last days, and who had taken their mother as his concubine. The younger ones would come of age as possessions of Thomas Jefferson. As a young lawyer, Jefferson had represented a slave suing for his freedom. He lived well off the labor of the enslaved but he hated the institution. He resented the debt John Wayles had left as a result of the voyage of the slave ship *Prince of Wales* and did what he could to keep from paying his part of that debt. And, of course, Thomas Jefferson would become the most celebrated lover of liberty in American history.

For her part, Martha Wayles Skelton Jefferson depended upon and took for granted the right to own slaves. She may have cared for them, may have loved some of them. She might even have considered the possibility of freedom for some of those closest to her. But she would not have imagined that it was within her power to do anything at all about the larger institution. More, even, than most women of her time, place, and class, she was willing to leave public matters entirely to men, trusting them to do the right thing. Unlike her mother and her daughters, she never signed a marriage contract, asserting her legal rights over her own property. Her father had always taken care of such matters, and her husband believed women were happiest when they confined themselves strictly to matters of hearth and home. She could not, and perhaps did not want to change the law, or even men's minds. Her way, instead, was to focus on what she *could* do personally, and that was no simple matter. Every day she faced dozens of choices about how to treat people she was related to but could not openly recognize, people she needed and owned, people who were skilled and knowledgeable and emotionally invested and conflicted in their own right.

Martha's family—the nucleus of what Jefferson would come to refer to, in the slaveholder's patriarchal language, by the same word—was tailor-made for ambivalence and pettiness, generosity and anger. If she harbored any jealousy of Elizabeth Hemings, if she resented the Hemings children, she had the right to express any or all of those feelings toward the Hemingses, while they could not respond in kind. If she felt like hitting any one of them, at any time, law and custom gave her complete license to do so. Few of her contemporaries questioned the necessity of using the rod to keep order and to teach moral lessons. Even Thomas Jefferson, no advocate of violent punishment, on occasion resorted to the whip. We have no way of knowing what kind of discipline John Wayles, the poor boy turned slave trader, used on the people he owned, or for that matter, on his legitimate daughters. We do know that on at least one occasion Thomas Jefferson admonished Martha for being too hard on little Patsy, who would recall to her own daughter, Ellen Randolph Coolidge, Martha's "vivacity of temper," a "little asperity [that] sometimes shewed itself to her children, and of course more to my mother, her oldest child, than the others who were much younger."

Martha Jefferson was a charming woman. She had a gentle, amiable, cheerful way about her. But she expected to give orders and to see her commands obeyed. Her father had held hundreds of slaves, and through her inheritance, her husband would do likewise. While she may have known the names of some who sweated out their lives in the tobacco fields, she had little personal contact with most of those people. From her point of view, it was enough that they kept the crops growing and selling, kept her father's or husband's line of credit flowing. She took her own job, as manager of the household, seriously, and kept her accounts not out of some childlike desire to emulate her document-loving husband, but at least in part as a hedge against theft by those she supervised. She watched closely over the slaughtering of hogs to make sure that nobody made off with a hunk of her meat.

The enslaved people Martha saw and lived with every day had to please her. If they did not, she could use the whip to compel obedience, or order an overseer to administer punishment . She may have disagreed with her husband about matters of discipline. Jefferson hated violence; as Marie and Edmund Morgan write, "It was as natural as breathing for Jefferson to prefer wheedling to whipping." If he stayed her hand with Patsy, perhaps he did likewise with those bound to obey Martha's will. But it seems just as likely that Martha used familiar feminine tools—gentle persuasion, indirection, manipulation—to get her way with those who served, as well as those who ruled.

THE HEMINGSES DID not go all at once to Monticello. There was at least one good reason not to move more people to the mountain in the summer of 1773: the well was dry. But the Jeffersons began to bring them closer. In 1774, Martin, Robert, James, and Mary Hemings joined their sister, Betty Brown (and their half-sister, Martha Jefferson), on the mountain, raising the number of enslaved people there to forty-five. Betty Hemings went with her older daughter Nancy and the younger children, Thenia, Critta, Peter, and Sally, to Elk Hill, bringing the slave population at that establishment to seventy-four.

Martha sent the Hemingses to Elk Hill as a way of claiming the place. Even though she had not insisted on a prenuptial agreement, she was determined to shape the future of her property, in real estate as well as people. Thomas needed to find some way to pay his third of John Wayles's debts, and in July 1773 he began to think about which of his newly inherited lands to put up for sale. He planned to keep Poplar Forest, the Wayles plantation in Bedford County that would eventually become his home away from home. But he thought he might sell Martha's lands at Elk Island. Though Martha had lived at Elk Hill, John Wayles had left the place not to her, but instead to Anne and Henry Skipwith. In the months after Wayles's death, Jefferson thought it might be a good idea to get rid of all his Goochland County properties.

Instead, in January 1774, as he sold more than half the land Martha had inherited, he decided to buy Elk Hill from the Skipwiths. The deed for the property reflected Martha's reticence about public matters; both her sister and brother-in-law signed as sellers, but only Thomas Jefferson was listed as purchaser. The same held true later, when Jefferson bought two more tracts of land adjoining the original Elk Hill property, more than doubling the size of that estate to a total of 669 acres.

Why would Jefferson keep Elk Island and seek not simply to own but also to expand the plantation where his wife had lived with her first husband? Judging from their visit so soon after their wedding, and the fact that she returned there again and again, the place meant something to her. She had an established, peaceful house at Elk Hill; at the unfinished and half-habitable Monticello, a shifting cast of white workmen and enslaved laborers was still blasting roadbeds and firing bricks. Elk Hill had particular charms—a great view of the river, an abundance of game. Thomas Jefferson had learned to shoot from his father, and was known to hunt small game from time to time, in part as a means of getting off in the countryside by himself. Isaac Jefferson, Ursula's son, recalled that "Mr. Jefferson used to hunt squirrels and partridges; kept five or six guns. Oftentimes carred Isaac wid him. Old Master wouldn't shoot partridges settin'. Said 'he wouldn't take advantage of 'em'—would give 'em a chance for thar life. Wouldn't shoot a hare settin' nuther; skeer him up fust." But Thomas Jefferson never showed any particular interest in the kind of hunting so adored by the Virginia gentry, with foxes and hounds and grand, bibulous breakfasts. The opportunity to host hunting parties was one of Elk Hill's attractions, more Martha's idea of fun than her husband's.

Thomas had reasons of his own for deciding to make Elk Hill a second residence. It was near his widowed sister's place at Spring Forest, and on the way to Tuckahoe as well as Williamsburg. Elk Hill was also closer than Monticello to Martha's sisters at the Forest and Hors du Monde. It was convenient and comfortable, and being there pleased Martha. They could afford two houses. If Monticello was then and would always be his creation and his passion, it was not necessarily the center, and certainly not the compass, of Martha's world. For her, Elk Hill was a beloved place.

IN THE WAKE of John Wayles's death, the Jeffersons spent most of their time with Martha's family, at Williamsburg, the Forest, Bermuda Hundred, and Elk Hill. But they were, after all, building a home of their own. They returned to Monticello in January 1774. With another baby expected in the spring, Martha pursued her housekeeping. She saw to the hog slaughtering, borrowed ten pounds of sugar from her mother-in-law, and used the sugar to brew fifteen gallons of beer. She churned butter and paid back those ten pounds of Jane Jefferson's sugar. She played cards (and lost a shilling and threepence), a pursuit of which her husband was said to disapprove, though he played a little backgammon himself. The closer she came to giving birth, the more beer she brewed. If this musical woman ever conceived of keeping house as being a little like playing a song, her steady work at brewing was a refrain in merry measure. But the tune would falter. As far as we know, this was the last beer she ever brewed.

February brought the frightening earthquake and the drowning of Thomas's sister Elizabeth. As he recovered from that tragedy, Thomas turned to gardening at Monticello with a passion, laying out a vast new garden bed, seeing to the planting of radicchio, salsify, cippolinis, lentils, all sorts of plain and exotic vegetables; hills of nasturtiums and cresses; apples, cherries, and almonds from seed and seedlings. Their second daughter was born on April 3, 1774. In homage to a mother-in-law coping with her own daughter's death, they named the baby Jane Randolph Jefferson.

9

His World and Hers

AS THE PEACH trees bloomed and the shoots of early peas poked up through the soil, events conspired to pull Thomas Jefferson more and more away from home. He returned to Williamsburg shortly after his daughter Jane was born, in May 1774. The assembly met again, in the wake of the Boston Tea Party and closure of the port of Boston. Martha stayed behind at Monticello and tried to notice things Thomas would want to know when he returned. She duly recorded eating the first ripe cherries from the trees he had planted, and noted those first peas of the season. When Thomas got back, he would look over her journal and record her observations in his Garden Book.

Much as he treasured the small pleasures of home, the torrent of public life was sweeping Thomas away. Down in Williamsburg, when Jefferson and his allies proposed a day of fasting and prayer in solidarity with their "sister colony" of Massachusetts, the governor, Lord Dunmore, responded by dissolving the assembly. Jefferson, by now a leader of the radicals in the legislature, joined the unofficial meetings at the Raleigh Tavern. As he looked back later, he would describe his younger self as "bold in the pursuit of knowledge, never fearing to follow truth and reason to whatever results they led, and bearding every authority which stood in the way."

The stalking of truth and reason was about to become a very dangerous hunt, and we may wonder how a mother of two little girls felt about her young husband's willingness to take such risks. Thomas was embroiled in controversy and formulating his first great statement of political philosophy, an incendiary pamphlet that would be printed, without his knowledge or consent, though not without pride in his authorship, as *A Summary View of the Rights of British America*. Martha, back at Monticello, was suffering from a painful and worrisome breast abscess. Dr. Gilmer came to treat her, though she could not take time away from her growing household. At the end of June, she distributed clothing to the household slaves, counted up her china and pewter ware, made soap and candles, and bought and butchered beef and mutton and shoats.

This was the season in which Thomas Jefferson, planter, lawyer, and provincial aristocrat, became a revolutionary. In *A Summary View*, he rejected the authority of Parliament in America, arguing that though the colonies owed allegiance to the king, they elected their own representatives to local legislatures. The Continental Congress, then meeting in Philadelphia, would not tread that far, not yet. As historian Fawn Brodie pointed out, "Jefferson must have known that his *Summary View* invited hanging."

He was on perilous political ground, but Jefferson situated his argument deeply and firmly in the terrain of his real life, as an Albemarle County planter and lawyer, clearing his lands, traversing the breadth of Virginia, leaving his family at home for days and weeks on end. Should such a man's fate be tied to a distant, negligent, sometimes abusive government? As he saw it, the original British colonists, like their Saxon ancestors, had left "the country in which

chance, not choice, had placed them." They had conquered and settled their new lands as individuals: "For themselves they fought, for
themselves they conquered, and for themselves alone they have the
right to hold." Railing against the colonists' lack of representation in
Parliament, Jefferson pointed out the immensity and remoteness of
Virginia, a colony that had "as yet affixed no boundary to the westward. Their western counties"—such as Bedford, where Martha had
so recently inherited the Poplar Forest lands from her father—"are,
therefore, of indefinite extent. Some of them are actually seated many
hundreds of miles from their eastern limits." The inhabitants of such
far-flung places, he insisted, had a right to govern themselves in a way
that suited their lives and livelihoods.

The free man depicted in the *Summary View* sounded very much
like the master of Monticello, king in his own vast domain, though a
man who ruled uneasily. Jefferson insisted that "the abolition of slavery is the great object of desire in those colonies where it was, unhap-
pily, introduced in their infant state," just as he was coming to grips
with his life as holder of hundreds of enslaved people, some of them
his wife's kin. But if nature abhorred slavery, nothing in nature prevented certain forms of dominance, certain habits of deference. On
any given day, he could sit and write thrilling words about liberty
and democracy while his wife and enslaved workers slaughtered a
sheep and rendered the fat. Martha might stir the vat of lye and ashes,
making soap to wash the ink off Thomas's stained fingers, taking a
moment to offer him a refreshing drink. Ursula might wipe her dripping knife, take off a blood-soaked apron, rinse off her hands and
face, and take a Jefferson baby to her breast.

MAKING REVOLUTION DID, of course, entail sacrifices. Most of those
were ahead of him in the summer of 1774, but even then Thomas Jefferson had his hands full, with his legal work, his enlarged estate, and

his house project. He gave up practicing law (the British had closed the Virginia courts, in any case), but he was having problems making progress on the house, by any measure an ambitious project. Jefferson had ordered fourteen—fourteen!—pairs of sash windows from Britain for Monticello; he expected that they would be seized when they reached Virginia (he would eventually buy them back at auction). The want of those windows added one more incentive to the Jeffersons' decision to move the family to Elk Hill for the winter. Work on the house continued, with the arrival of carpenters Joseph Neilson and William Fossett, and the family would return to the mountain from time to time, of necessity. Thomas had been elected to the Albemarle County committee charged with enforcing the Continental Congress's trade ban with England. Martha had to supervise the winter slaughtering in January, when twenty-five hogs and a goose met their maker at Monticello.

While Thomas attended the Virginia Convention in Richmond, Martha and the girls stayed nearby, at Elk Hill. Patrick Henry called for liberty or death and the Virginia delegates voted to organize and arm militias. Amid the rising preparation for violence, Thomas was chosen to go to the Continental Congress. By now her husband had been a member of what her father called "the rebel party" for years, and Martha must have known what an important part he played in that bold faction. As much as they had been apart before, they had managed to not be far from one another. Now he would go to Philadelphia, more than three hundred miles and seven days' travel away.

As Thomas sallied forth into the bright light of history, Martha retreated into invisibility. He left from Williamsburg on June 11, 1775, arriving in Philadelphia on June 20. For the next five weeks, an abundance of public and private records tells us in vivid detail where Thomas Jefferson was, and what he was doing—paying for punch at City Tavern, buying books and boots and buckles, getting a whip repaired and a key mended, purchasing pickled oysters, corn salve, violin strings, and a tomahawk.

During that same time, we have no idea where Martha was, or who was with her, or what she was doing. She had seldom stayed at Monticello when he was not there. We do not know whether they exchanged letters. He was a devoted husband and a great correspondent, but given the unreliable post and Thomas's plan to return as soon as possible, they may not have done so. In any case, no letters between them have been found. But the fact that he expected to return by way of Virginia's convention at Richmond suggests that Martha may have been at Elk Hill. They would soon head for Monticello. Going to the mountaintop, whatever its allures, had been something less than an exercise in domestic tranquility before. It would be anything but that this time.

During the first three years of their marriage, Thomas Jefferson had been a prominent man in his colony, a man whose wealth and influence were increasing. Martha had married him expecting as much, and knowing that her own inheritance would add to his stature. Now he had taken a perilous road to a distant place, leaving her behind with her fears for him, for her own safety, for her children. One of those terrors became a reality in September, when little Jane, only a year and a half old, died at Monticello. No stone was laid in the graveyard to mark the child's passing.

Thomas could not stay to mourn with Martha. He set out again for Philadelphia on September 25, and this time he would be gone for more than three months. Instead of going with him, Martha went to the Forest to be with her sister, Elizabeth Eppes. Both women had recently borne children who died. For a person as private as Martha, the intimacy of home and the sympathy of family appealed more than the noise, cold, and dirt of a city full of strangers.

But privacy did not ensure safety. That fall of 1775, being in Virginia, so near to Williamsburg, was riskier than going to Philadelphia. There was fighting along the coast and a rising threat of invasion. Lord Dunmore tried to burn the town of Hampton, and issued his proclamation offering to free any slave who took up arms against rebel masters. The Eppeses knew firsthand how even a weaponless girl could find a way to kill her erstwhile master, and the prospect of armed rebellion could not have been reassuring.

Back in Philadelphia, with matters in Congress increasingly critical, Jefferson wrote regularly to Martha, telling her the political news and worrying about events back home. Historians have presumed that he destroyed all their letters to one another, but we know that he wrote long letters to her and shared with her his views about politics, because he said so in letters to Francis Eppes. "I wrote to Patty on my arrival here," he said on October 10, "and there being then nothing new in the political way I include her letter under a blank cover to you. Since that we have received from England news of much importance," he added, offering a summary of military developments. But instead of repeating what he'd written to his wife, Jefferson advised Eppes that for a more detailed account of developments in the war, "I must refer you to Patty."

Even in Philadelphia, family tragedy seemed to follow Thomas Jefferson. On October 22, he went to dine with his relative and mentor, Peyton Randolph, speaker of the Virginia assembly, at the country house of a Philadelphia wine merchant. That night Randolph suffered a stroke and died. Jefferson wrote the sad news to Martha almost immediately, adding to Francis Eppes, "Our good old Speaker died the night before last. For the particulars of that melancholy event I must refer you to Patty."

While Jefferson could set aside only one day a week to write letters, he wrote to his wife at least every two weeks, and followed up with letters to his brother-in-law. He heard nothing in return. Maybe

Martha and Eppes did write back, and their letters fell victim to unreliable postal service. Or perhaps they were worried that anything they wrote to him could put them or him in greater danger. Or possibly they were too busy or distraught to write. By the beginning of November, as the Congress boiled with rumors of invasion and insurrection in Virginia, Jefferson was frantic. "I have never received the scrip of a pen from any mortal in Virginia since I left it, nor been able by any enquiries I could make to hear of my family," he wrote to Francis Eppes. "I had hoped that when Mrs. Byrd came I should have heard something of them, but she could tell me nothing about them. The suspense under which I am is too terrible to be endured. If any thing has happened, for god's sake let me know it."

Two weeks later, a terrified Jefferson urged Martha and the Eppeses to flee the Forest and head for a safer place, probably Monticello. "I have written to Patty a proposition to keep yourselves at a distance from the alarms of Ld. Dunmore. To her therefore for want of time I must refer you and shall hope to meet you as proposed." Within days, Robert Carter Nicholas would send his dire warning to the Virginia delegates, conjuring a vision of a country in flames, open to the depredations of Tory militias and the vengeance of rebellious slaves: "The Person of no Man in the Colony is safe, when marked out as an Object of their Vengeance."

Still, Jefferson could not go to Virginia until December 28. For her part, Martha was back at Monticello on December 14, butchering hogs for the smokehouse and killing cattle "for the workmen," making candles and breaking a loaf of sugar. She must have been a very brave woman to journey across Virginia, from the Forest to Monticello, in that fearful time, traveling with a three-year-old. In all likelihood, Martha's trip also required the assistance of enslaved people she felt she could trust, despite Dunmore's proclamation of freedom. All of them would have been safer in Philadelphia.

*   *   *

AS THOMAS JEFFERSON made his way home, Lord Dunmore rang in 1776 by bombarding Norfolk. Martha was stocking up. Someone at Monticello was making clothes—Martha had paid a weaver to make twenty-five yards of cloth and purchased stays and scissors—and she slaughtered hogs on a larger scale than ever. Ursula presided over most of the work of killing animals and cutting them up, salting and applying saltpeter and hanging the meat in the smokehouse. But Martha was deeply involved as well, if only to stand nearby and make sure that no one stole away with any of her hams. Amid such bloody abundance, the Jeffersons counted themselves well provisioned and safely removed from the war, far enough from the coast to escape the British navy. Work went on at the house, still not fully habitable but rising faster now with the efforts of the white carpenter Joseph Neilson and his apprentice, William Fossett. Life seemed to go on normally enough.

So did death. Thomas Jefferson's mother died on March 31 at Monticello. Whether Martha was at her side, we do not know. There was, of course, contact and commerce between Monticello and Shadwell, visits back and forth. Martha sometimes referred to Jane as "my mother," just as Robert Skipwith had referred to Martha as "my sister" rather than sister-in-law. But in the four years Martha had been married to Thomas Jefferson, she had spent relatively little time in Albemarle County. When her husband was away, Martha generally left, too. Having never had a mother of her own, she relied on her sisters, especially Elizabeth Eppes, for support. Jane Jefferson died at the age of fifty-seven, one year younger than John Wayles, and older at the time of her death than many of the women Martha had known. We do not know how Martha felt about her mother-in-law, whether they were close, how she felt the loss. She may have had her hands full caring for the living, in any case, including her husband, who was home at this point suffering with a six-week-long migraine headache.

Jefferson was due back in Philadelphia, and his friend Thomas Nelson, Jr., wrote from there in February, saying that he'd brought his own wife, and Jefferson should bring Martha along when he returned. Martha would have to be inoculated against smallpox if she came, but Nelson insisted, "You must certainly bring Mrs. Jefferson with you. Mrs. Nelson shall nurse her in the small pox and take all possible care of her."

Whether or not Martha wanted to go with her husband to Philadelphia, circumstances conspired to prevent her from taking the trip. Sometime during their months together at Monticello, Martha once more became pregnant. This pregnancy, Martha's fourth as far as we know (she may also have miscarried in 1775), nearly killed her. Historians have wondered about Martha's health problems, which accelerated in the years of the Revolution. Fawn Brodie speculated that Martha may have suffered from "debilitating monthly hemorrhaging, or from a tendency to miscarry when pregnant, or from dangerous anemia after childbirth, or from all three." Whether those hypotheses were correct or not, Brodie was surely on target in asserting that "one would understand why Jefferson could not bring himself to explain even in a private letter the nature of any of these problems. Such was the commonplace taboo."

THOMAS JEFFERSON WAS finally ready to depart for the Congress on May 7, and was clearly worried about Martha. Before he left, he gave her ten pounds (presumably in Virginia currency), more money than he'd ever given her before. Though he would try to get back as soon as he could, he expected to be gone for a while. She would spend the months of April and May at Monticello, but in June she decided to risk going to the Forest. However much she wanted the company of her sister during her pregnancy, both she and Jefferson knew that by moving close to Williamsburg, Martha and three-year-old Patsy would be in greater danger from the British than they were at Monticello. Jefferson's friend John Page, then president of the Virginia Council of State (the provisional government), had sent an alarming letter from Williamsburg to Philadelphia obliterating any imagined distinction between the battlefront and the home front in Virginia, where wartime shortages and instability were eroding morale and stirring up anger at the rebels. "I have snatched a few Moments to scribble you a few loose Thoughts on our present critical Situation," Page wrote.

I think our Countrymen have exhibited an uncommon Degree of Virtue, not only in submiting to all the hard Restrictions and exposing themselves to all the Dangers which are the Consequence of the Disputes they are involved in with Great Britain, but in behaving so peaceably and honestly as they have when they were free from the Restraint of Laws. But how long this may be the Case who can tell? When to their Want of Salt there shall be added a Want of Clothes and Blankets and when to this there may be added the Terrors of a desolating War raging unchecked for Want of Arms and Ammunition, who can say what the People might not do in such a Situation, and tempted with the Prospect of Peace Security and a Trade equal to their wishes? Might they not be induced to give up the Authors of their Misfortunes, their Leaders, who had lead them into such a Scrape, and be willing to sacrifice them to a Reconciliation?

With the fear of social upheaval added to his concern about Martha's health, Jefferson attended the Congress, where there was more bad news about the Continental Army's attempts in Canada. The time for independence was at hand; Virginia itself was already functioning as an independent entity, if not a fully governed state. As spring gave way to summer, and Thomas Jefferson took up the perilous, sometimes terrifying, sometimes tedious, eventually exhilarating work of separating from England, he was a man torn in two, dedicated to the liberty of his country but frightened half to death about the state of his family, especially the woman he loved above all other human beings. He had begged Martha and the Eppeses to write to him weekly, and waited anxiously for the arrival of their letters even as the business of the Congress became more and more urgent and absorbing.

10

Domestic Tranquility

WHILE THOMAS JEFFERSON assisted at the birth of his country in Philadelphia, Martha Jefferson fought for her life in Virginia. This pregnancy had gone horribly wrong. She was never far from his mind, even as he drafted his immortal Declaration of Independence, squirmed through the Congress's revisions, and readied himself for the step that put his head irrevocably on the imperial block and inscribed his name in the history books. His original draft of the Declaration reflected his state of mind. As is well known, in one passage deleted by the Congress he passionately condemned King George III for "waging cruel war against human nature itself," by capturing "a distant people who never offended him" and selling them into slavery in America. But in a far less celebrated passage, he also excoriated the king for "exciting those very people to rise in arms among us, and to purchase that liberty of which he has deprived them, by murdering the people on whom he also obtruded them." Philadelphia might be a dangerous place, but he was desperately worried about his ailing wife back home, surrounded by enslaved people, any of whom might take Dunmore's proclamation as a signal to rise against their masters.

*   *   *

ON JUNE 30, he wrote to Edmund Pendleton, President of the Virginia Committee of Safety, to ask that he be replaced in the Congress, for reasons he expressed euphemistically but with force:

> I am sorry the situation of my domestic affairs renders it indispensably necessary that I should sollicit the substitution of some other person here in my room. The delicacy of the house will not require me to enter minutely into the private causes which render this necessary.

Concerned as he was, Jefferson held on to hope with tenacity and tenderness. On July 4, 1776, he made time to go shopping, purchasing seven pairs of women's gloves for twenty-seven shillings, acting like a man who meant to spend a good long time hand in hand with his wife. But Martha's condition worsened. Jefferson was frantic. "I have received no letter this week, which lays me under great anxiety," he wrote to Francis Eppes on July 23. "I shall leave this place about the 11th of next month. Give my love to Mrs. Eppes, and tell her that when both you and Patty fail to write to me, I think it shall not be unreasonable in insisting she shall." Letters soon arrived that did nothing but feed his anxiety. He was desperate to leave Congress and get home. To Richard Henry Lee, the replacement delegate who had not yet arrived in Philadelphia, he wrote, "For god's sake, for your country's sake, and for my sake, come. I receive by every post such accounts of the state of Mrs. Jefferson's health, that it will be impossible for me to disappoint her expectation of seeing me at the time I have promised. . . . I am under a sacred obligation to go home." He told John Page, "Every letter brings me such an account of the state of her health that it is with great pain that I can stay here."

We do not know how far Martha's pregnancy had advanced when

she miscarried sometime in late June. That sad event saved Martha's life. On the day before independence was declared, Francis Eppes wrote to Jefferson to say that she was recuperating at Elk Hill. "We return'd last Sunday from Elk-Hill whare we had been for a week on a visit to your good Lady; she is perfectly recover'd from her late indisposition and except being a little weak, is as well as ever she was. She is in great expectation of seeing you in August, if your appointment to serve in Congress the insuing year don't prevent." By the end of that month, Edmund Pendleton was writing to wish Jefferson a pleasant journey home and to say that he hoped "you'll find Mrs. Jefferson recovered, as I had the pleasure of hearing in Goochland that she was better." Martha was eager to join her husband, who was heading to Williamsburg to attend the assembly, but Jefferson wrote to Elizabeth Eppes hoping "to stay Patty with her awhile longer."

It took Jefferson only six days to get from Philadelphia to Monticello, and we do not know whether Martha was there to greet him. He had been gone long enough that his wine cellar had run low; someone went down to Shadwell to fetch the bottle he credited to his mother's estate. Martha and Thomas were together by October 4, when he gave her money to tip two slave women at the Forest. Now they would make their way to Williamsburg, where Jefferson's friend George Wythe, then attending the Congress in Philadelphia, had offered the use of his house.

Despite the perils of war, the Jeffersons lived in the capital in comfort and style. Robert Hemings had replaced Jupiter as Jefferson's valet, and he and his older brother Martin attended them. Presumably Martha also had a maid of her own and someone to help with the children. While there were wartime shortages of some goods, the Jeffersons nonetheless managed to buy coffee and tea, bread and cake, oysters and mutton, and shoats and fowl. There was ribbon and gauze and lace to be had, and Patsy even got a new doll. That fall Martha became pregnant for the fifth time. Once again she was ill, or at least uneasy; a doctor visited her in early December.

For the moment, they believed, Virginia was secure from the British. Dunmore had sailed away in May, taking with him the "shattered remains" of the "Ethiopian Regiment" of fugitives from slavery, with smallpox on board the ship. In December, Martha and Thomas took a meandering course homeward, visiting their sisters along the way. Jefferson's friend John Page had worried that the shortage of salt was the first step to hardships that would turn the common people away from their revolutionary leaders, but Thomas Jefferson overcame that problem for himself. On the way home, he bought five bushels of salt, a good thing with all the hogs awaiting slaughter at Monticello.

WHEN MARTHA RETURNED to the mountaintop this time, after all the drama and difficulty and danger, Monticello seemed like home. In the best situations there is some tension between mothers-in-law and daughters-in-law, especially when they live as neighbors. We will never know how Martha and Jane Jefferson felt about one another, but one thing is certain: Martha was now indisputably in charge of her household, and at the center of her family's social life. She had another baby coming to replace the children she had lost. As the house at Monticello grew more complete and more majestic, her husband was near at hand, full of high ideals and great plans. In January, she and Ursula killed sixty-eight hogs. Life was good.

Thomas Jefferson treasured the distance between his Albemarle County sanctuary and the war theater. His friend Thomas Nelson, Jr., wrote from Baltimore, describing the horror of the scene of British invasion and the particular dangers to American women:

Could we but get a good Regular Army we should soon clear the Continent of these dan'd Invaders. They play the very Devil with the Girls and even old Women to satisfy their libidinous appetites. There is Scarcely a Virgin to be found in the part of the Country they have passed thro' and yet the Jersies will not turn out. Rapes, Rapine, and Murder are not sufficient to rouse the resentments of these People.

But at Monticello, peace reigned. Amid the usual routine of slaughtering and curing and storing, of candle- and soap-making, Martha inventoried her bedding and linens, made a list of the family's clothes, and generally acted like an expectant mother in the throes of a nesting frenzy. Martha's version of cleaning closets was to make eight dozen candles and sixty-eight pounds of soft soap when she was eight months pregnant. At the end of April, Thomas went off to the legislature in Williamsburg, and as her lying-in time approached in May, she recorded the planting of beans and peas and made still more candles. Finally, on May 28, her son was born, with the assistance of a midwife. Thomas made it back to the mountain just in time.

The baby lived little more than two weeks, not even long enough to acquire a name. Martha resumed her housekeeping, trading with enslaved people, buying their chickens with her bacon. But she lost track of time. She was usually meticulous about dating her household activities in her account book, but in the months of June and July, no dates appeared for her transactions. In August, she determined to get control over her affairs. That month, nearly day by day, she carefully listed every duck or goose or lamb killed, and made a point of mentioning which hams and sides of bacon and pork shoulders and legs they took out of the smokehouse to pack into bags "for our own eating," and which "for workmen." As August flowed into September, she dreamed over her accounts and drew a winsome sketch of two birds on a leafy branch.

In the wake of their son's death, Thomas stayed close, neglecting his public duties. His colleagues noticed, and some were critical. "It will not perhaps be disagreeable to you in your retirement, sometimes to hear the events of war, and how in other respects we proceed in the arduous business we are engaged in," wrote a sarcastic Richard Henry Lee, in a letter Jefferson did not answer.

Martha's health, and her state of mind, were sometimes too fragile for outdoor work. So she kept busy in the house, making inventories of every bed, blanket, and sheet at Monticello and Elk Hill and Poplar Forest, enumerating Patsy's frocks and pockets and kerchiefs, counting her own nightcaps and aprons and "suits of brussels lace" and Thomas's breeches and coats, his ruffled shirts and white silk stockings. In November, six months after losing her last child, she was pregnant yet again, and as another new year dawned, was back at her slaughtering—forty-two hogs from Bedford, twenty-two from Monticello, another twenty-eight from Elk Hill. On March 17, she echoed the first entry in her housekeeping journal: "opened a barrel of flower." But now she would be thrown into the maelstrom of politics and warfare. Her journal fell silent, not to resume for years.

IN THE SPRING of 1778, the war grew wider. The British had shifted their strategy after the American victory at the Battle of Saratoga and were now putting more redcoats in the South. Thomas Jefferson crisscrossed the state, between Charlottesville and Williamsburg. Sometimes he was at Elk Hill and whenever possible, he was at Monticello. He planted his vegetable garden and tended a tree nursery he hoped would one day yield quinces, apricots, almonds, plums, peaches, nectarines, and a profusion of apples. But Jefferson's memorandum books made no mention of his wife.

Their third daughter, Mary Jefferson, was born on August 1, 1778. Jefferson paid Mrs. Gaines, the midwife, twenty pounds for attending Martha, along with another twenty shillings for assisting Nell, an enslaved woman, who gave birth to a daughter named Scilla. Dr. Gilmer, who had made multiple visits during the preceding months, was there as well. After bearing five children and suffering at least one miscarriage, the repeated ordeal of pregnancy and childbirth had begun to take a serious toll on Martha's body. But she had reason for hope, and for joy. This time, the baby lived. Little Mary, to be called Polly by those who knew her, would be one of only two of Martha's children to live to adulthood. When Polly herself set out on the road to marriage and motherhood, Thomas Jefferson would present his daughter and her new husband with gifts including Scilla, the child born on the same day, at the same place, as the woman who would own her.

Jefferson had lingered at Monticello with Martha, but eventually he was compelled to go to Williamsburg to attend the legislature. He went reluctantly. The House of Delegates went into session on October 5, but when he finally made an appearance on November 30, he was in the custody of the sergeant at arms. As often as he expressed his desire to remove himself from public office and political life, this heavy-handed compulsion of duty did nothing to change his mind. He paid a fine for nonattendance, then hastened to join his family at the Forest before going home to Monticello to greet the new year.

THE WAR FOR Independence came to Albemarle County in a deceptively bloodless way. Following the defeat of British and Hessian troops at Saratoga, four thousand prisoners of war were marched from New York to Charlottesville, to be quartered until they could be exchanged or deported. Among those prisoners were the British general William Phillips and a number of German noblemen who shared Jefferson's love of music, gardening, and the finer things in life. Jefferson offered a nearby property to the German general, Baron Friedrich Adolf von Riedesel, along with his wife and three daughters. As the German prisoners planted gardens, and their aristocratic officers joined in musical evenings at Monticello, the Jeffersons and the Riedesels struck up a friendship that included their children.

Frederika Charlotte Louise von Massow, Baroness von Riedesel, was three years younger than Martha, but she had seen far more of the world. The baroness had lived through the hardship of crossing an ocean to join her husband, only to find herself swept up in the war at Saratoga, nursing the wounded in battle and suffering the devastation of defeat. She had journeyed to Albemarle amid deprivation and terror; she and her little girls had nearly starved on the passage through Virginia. "Often our lives were in danger when we passed over breakneck roads, and we suffered terribly from the cold and, what was even worse, from lack of food," she wrote in her vivid memoir of her time in America. To make matters worse, the locals were anything but friendly to the captured woman:

> When we arrived in Virginia and had only another day to go before reaching our destination, we had nothing left but tea and some bread and butter, nor could we get anything else. One of the natives gave me a handful of dried fruit. At noon we arrived at a house where I asked for some food, but it was refused harshly with the remark that the people had nothing to give to the royalist dogs. I saw some Turkish flour [Indian meal] and begged for a couple handfuls so that I could mix it with water and make some bread. The woman replied, "No, that is for our Negroes who work for us; you, however, wanted to kill us." Captain Edmonstone offered her a guinea or two for it because my children were so hungry, but she replied, "Not for a hundred would I give it to you; and if you die of hunger, so much the better."

The Riedesels must have been grateful indeed to be in the hands of the generous Jeffersons. Frederika von Massow von Riedesel was likely the first, and probably the only baroness whom Martha ever met, but the two women had much in common. The baroness prided herself on her good cheer and resilience, as did Martha. She too had a passionately devoted husband. And like Martha, she had lost children, a son and a daughter, and was caring for a baby girl. Her title notwithstanding, the baroness was in some regards amazingly down-to-earth. Her husband, like Jefferson, loved gardening, though the baron was foolish enough to refuse to wear a hat, and as a result suffered severe sunstroke. The baroness nursed him while she too traded with entrepreneurial slaves for poultry and vegetables, and took her turn in slaughtering oxen and pigs.

For all their earthy activities, however, Martha and the baroness were both accustomed to certain privileges and amenities. Martha had slaves to command; the baroness found soldiers to do her bidding. For her part, the baroness was appalled at the way most Virginians treated their enslaved workers:

Many of them let the slaves walk about stark naked until they are between fifteen and sixteen years old, and the clothes which they give them afterward are not worth wearing. The slaves are in the charge of an overseer who leads them out into the fields at daybreak, where they have to work like cattle or suffer a beating; and when they come home completely tired out and sunburnt they are given some Indian meal called hominy, which they make into baked stuff. Often, however, they are too exhausted to eat and prefer sleeping a couple of hours, because they must go back to work. They look upon it as a misfortune to have children, because these, in turn, will also be slaves and unhappy men. As they have no time to cultivate their own bit of land that is given to them, they have no money whatever, except what they can get from the sale of poultry, with which to buy their clothes.

She nonetheless admitted, "There are, of course, good masters too. One can recognize them immediately, because their slaves are well dressed and housed. These Negroes are very good servants, very faithful to their master, and very much attached to him."

Whether the baroness had Thomas Jefferson in mind when she pointed to the exceptional "good master," we cannot be sure. The families did spend time together, judging by letters the baron later wrote to Thomas Jefferson, presenting "my respects and Madame de Riedesels best Compliments to Mrs. Jefferson, whose very amiable Character and the many proofs which we have experienced of Her Friendship can never be effaced from out of our Memory, and she will ever possess a high rank among Madame de R's particular Friends." They shared a love of music and attended evenings at the now-completed and impressive Monticello, "an elegant building, projected according to [Jefferson's] own fancy." A Hessian officer whose painting Jefferson admired remarked, "As all Virginians are fond of Music, he is particularly so. You will find in his House an elegant Harpsichord, Pianoforte, & some Violins. The latter he performs very well upon himself, the former his Lady touches very skillfully & who is in all respects a very agreeable, sensible & accomplished lady." Even after the troops were sent off to New York, and war thundered across Virginia, the Baron and Jefferson sent one another affectionate letters, always appending their greetings and good wishes for each other's wives.

For all their friendliness, when the baroness wrote her memoirs she said nothing of the Jeffersons. By the time Frederika von Riedesel looked back, Martha Jefferson had died. Perhaps the baroness shared Thomas Jefferson's belief that silence was the best remedy for grief. Or perhaps their congenial moments had come only intermittently. The entire time the Jeffersons and Riedesels were together in Albemarle, and indeed, for the first nine months of 1779, Martha Jefferson appeared nowhere in Thomas's accounts. He gave money to Martin

Hemings on a regular basis, and Martha may have been too ill to manage her household, leaving daily duties to the Monticello major-domo. Whatever the state of her health, Martha had managed to rally for social occasions and to present a gracious and cultured welcome to the noble prisoners.

This interlude of comity between enemies did not last long. Thomas Jefferson sold the pianoforte he'd bought for Martha in 1772 to General Riedesel, who pledged to pay a hundred pounds. At the beginning of May, Jefferson set out for the legislature at Williamsburg, by way of Elk Hill and the Forest. Martha, Patsy, and Polly remained with the Eppeses at the Forest, where they learned that Jefferson had been elected governor of Virginia. He had rather narrowly defeated his friend John Page, who hastened to offer congratulations and assured Jefferson, "As soon as Mrs. Jefferson comes to town Mrs. Page will wait on her." But Jefferson replied that Martha did not intend to come to Williamsburg any time soon. He himself was to depart immediately for a weekend at the Forest. When Martha did decide to join her husband at the capital, Jefferson assured Page, "She has too much [value] for [Mrs.] Page not to consider her acquaintance as a principal among those circumstances which are to reconcile her to her situation." Martha was not eager to take her place as the governor's lady, and her own reservations surely weighed upon a husband always ambivalent about his duty to the public, always longing to return to the peaceful shelter of his home and family.

11

The War Comes Home

DURING HIS FIRST year and a half as governor, Thomas Jefferson presided over a state that had not yet felt the lash of invasion. But the British were coming. Jefferson struggled to secure money, supplies, and soldiers, and kept an uneasy eye on reports from the northern front, while coping with urgent requests for help from the Continental Army. At least Martha was with him in Williamsburg, sharing something of his public life. For the first time, instead of trading bacon for eggs and chickens and cabbages, she dealt extensively in cash. She started out asking for small sums for her household expenses, but soon found she needed much more of the fast-inflating Virginia currency. In February 1780, she paid almost £120 for an apron.

Martha was more at home in the country than the town, but keeping house anywhere required familiar skills and familiar faces. Ursula and George and their children were there, along with Jupiter, acting as driver and chief groom, Suck (Jupiter's wife and the cook), Martin, Robert, James and Mary Hemings, and Betty Brown. Ursula and George's son, Isaac (later known as Isaac Jefferson), was only five years old at the time, old enough to make fires and carry water. For him the move to town was a momentous event. He recalled much later the impressive procession of the Jefferson entourage, "coming down to Williamsburg . . . at the time Mr. Jefferson was Governor. He came down in the phaeton, his family with him in a coach and four. Bob Hemings drove the phaeton; Jim Hemings was a body servant; Martin Hemings the butler. . . . Mary Hemings rode in the wagon." The state capital was relocated to Richmond in April 1780, a move Jefferson promoted over the objections of Tidewater leaders, arguing that getting away from the coast would make the capital both more secure and more convenient to upcountry citizens. "It was cold weather when they moved up," remembered Isaac Jefferson. "Mr. Jefferson lived in a wooden house near where the palace stands now. Richmond was a small place then, no more than two brick houses in the town—all wooden houses what there was."

Being governor did not assure luxury, but at least the horror of war still seemed far away. Thomas and Martha Jefferson received a letter from their friend and putative enemy, General Riedesel, then in New York, announcing "the happy recovery of Madame de Riedesel after having presented me a fourth Daughter, near three weeks ago . . . we both beg leave to reiterate our assurances that it will ever give us much pleasure, not merely from gratitude but our real personal attachment, to hear of your and Mrs. Jeffersons uninterrupted Happiness." Jefferson wrote back quickly, offering facetious congratulations and his own assurances of friendship:

I sincerely condole with Madame de Riedesel on the birth of a *daughter*, but receive great pleasure from the information of her recovery, as every circumstance of felicity to her, yourself or family is interesting to us. The little attentions you are pleased to magnify so much never deserved a mention or thought. . . .

opposed as we happen to be in our sentiments of duty and honor, and anxious for contrary events, I shall nevertheless sincerely rejoice in every circumstance of happiness or safety which may attend you personally, and when a termination of the present contest shall put it in my power to declare to you more unreservedly how sincere are the sentiments of esteem & respect (wherein Mrs. Jefferson joins me) which I entertain for Madme. Riedesel & yourself.

Jefferson's teasing tone belied his own concerns. By this time, it was clear that Martha was enduring her seventh (or perhaps eighth) pregnancy. Only seven-year-old Patsy and two-year-old Polly had survived. Jefferson, like the baroness, clearly hoped for a son.

While Martha remained devoted to her family and household, she dipped a toe into the fast-moving stream of public affairs. At the behest of Martha Washington, she joined in a campaign to make clothes and raise money for the army. She wrote what until recently most historians have assumed was her only surviving letter, to Eleanor Madison, wife of the Reverend James Madison, endorsing the plan. Her letter echoed her pride in her husband's high ideals and his work in founding the new nation:

Richmond, August 8, 1780

MADAM

Mrs. Washington has done me the honor of communicating the inclosed proposition of our sisters of Pennsylvania and of informing me that the same grateful sentiments are displaying themselves in Maryland. Justified by the sanction of her letter in handing forward the scheme I undertake with chearfulness the duty of furnishing to my country women an opportunity of proving that they also participate of those virtuous feelings which gave birth to it. I

cannot do more for its promotion than by inclosing to you some of
the papers to be disposed of as you think proper.
I am with the greatest respect Madam Your most humble servant,
                              MARTHA JEFFERSON

Martha could not "do more for its promotion" than to send on per-
tinent papers, because she was once again in poor health. But there
is no reason to assume that Martha opposed the war or failed as a patriot. If the letter said nothing else, it plainly stated that she counted
herself among those women of her country who "participate in those
virtuous feelings which gave birth to it."

We should not be surprised to find Martha using the words *virtue*
and *birth* in the same sentence. Other women of her time may have
tried to control their fertility by using herbal concoctions, the rhythm
method, or abortion, the only birth control methods known at the
time. But though she struggled with her fragile body, Martha Jefferson staked her life on perpetual pregnancy. Her husband worried
about her, and wrote friends that he hoped to retire "at the close of
the present campaign." That autumn brought rumors of an imminent British invasion. General Alexander Leslie sailed up the James
and skirmished with militias at Portsmouth, but withdrew, much to
the relief of the denizens of the capital. On November 3, Martha gave
birth to Lucy Elizabeth, who came into the world weighing ten and
a half pounds. Such birth weights have become more common in the
twenty-first century, but in the eighteenth, babies this large were a serious hazard to the mother, and perhaps an indication of a more serious health problem, gestational diabetes. If Martha suffered from
diabetes, she would surely have had difficulties with the Monticello
diet, so heavily laden with ham and sugar, butter and flour. With a
wife who may have needed lighter fare, Thomas Jefferson's devotion
to his gardens, to those first peas of spring and the peaches of high

summer, appears less a matter of caprice than a carefully considered labor of devotion.

Within the month, Martha was well enough to resume her house-keeping, while Jefferson worried about the fighting both north and south of Virginia. He worked to raise and supply the state militia, unable to rely on Congress or the hard-pressed Continental Army for help. He struggled with declining civilian morale, untested and un-reliable recruits, prisoners of war now a menace rather than guests of his house. Things went from bad to worse: no food, no arms, no horses or boats, spectacularly inflated paper currency, general fear and instability. Now word came from General Washington that a Brit-ish fleet had left New York, sailing south. Scouts sighted twenty-seven sails off the Virginia coast. Jefferson hesitated before calling up the militia, and paid the price for his tardiness. The winds proved good for the British fleet heading up the James, and disastrous for the Vir-ginians. British troops under the command of Benedict Arnold, the turncoat American general whose name had already become synony-mous with treason, reached Richmond on January 5.

The day before Arnold's troops arrived to burn and pillage in Richmond, Martha, Patsy, Polly, and baby Lucy Elizabeth fled in the carriage, with Robert and James Hemings (and, presumably, Betty Brown), heading for Tuckahoe. Governor Jefferson stayed behind, fe-verishly mustering his forces and sounding the alarm. Isaac Jefferson was among the slaves left behind as every white person who could get away did so and the British marched into town, formed their lines, and fired their cannons. Isaac never forgot the experience: "In ten minutes not a white man was to be seen in Richmond; they ran hard as they could . . . Isaac was out in the yard; his mother ran out and cotch him up by the hand and carried him into the kitchen holler-ing. Mary Hemings, she jerked up her daughter the same way. Isaac run out again in a minute and his mother too; she was so skeered, she didn't know whether to stay indoors or out." When the British fired again, Jefferson had his horse fetched and rode away. The British troops told the slaves that they were disappointed not to find Jefferson, since they had a "nice pair of silver handcuffs" they wanted to put on him. He spent the next days on horseback, riding frantically in pursuit of General von Steuben, then in command of the Virginia militia. But to the small slave boy left behind, Thomas Jefferson had simply run away: "Isaac never see his Old Master arter dat for six months."

The British moved on to blow up the powder magazine at Westham, only to return to Richmond the next day to round up the abandoned slaves and march them to the encampment near Yorktown. Jupiter and Suck, Ursula and George, Mary Hemings, and four children (Mary's daughter and sons: Molly, Daniel, the infant Joe, and Isaac himself) were taken. "All of 'em had to walk," Isaac recalled, "except Daniel and Molly . . . and Isaac." There was smallpox in the British camp, and many died, though none of "Mr. Jefferson's folks." Amid such frightening misery, Isaac's memory bespoke the concerns of a slave child: "The British treated them mighty well; give 'em plenty of fresh meat and wheat bread."

What went through Martha's mind as she abandoned her beloved husband and the people she knew so well, driving off in a panic with her half-brothers, clutching her daughters about her? What were Robert and James Hemings and Betty Brown (pregnant herself, just then) thinking as they left behind their sister and her children? And what did those who were taken think about the Jeffersons' willingness to leave them in the hands of the enemy? During all the time that Isaac and his family and friends remained with the British, nobody who had escaped could know who among the captives starved or suffered, who lived and who died. They did know that wherever the British army went, smallpox followed.

The Jefferson slaves remained with the British into the siege of Yorktown, where little Isaac saw and heard "tremendous fire and smoke—seemed like heaven and earth was come together. . . . Heard the wounded men hollerin'. When the smoke blow off, you see the dead men laying on the ground." Washington gathered together the surviving slaves and took them back to Richmond, notifying their owners. "Old Master sent down two wagons right away, and all of 'em that was carred away went up back to Monticello. Old Master was mightily pleased to see his people come back safe and sound." George had even saved the family silver by hiding it in a mattress ticking, and told the British they'd already sent the silver up to the mountain.

BENEDICT ARNOLD'S FURIOUS forces wrought havoc along the James, then fell back to Portsmouth. Governor Jefferson did what he could to manage the situation, but he was no military leader. He had waited two critical days before calling upon the militia. His enemies deemed his behavior during the invasion erratic and cowardly. They launched an inquiry into his conduct, which wounded him to the bone and compounded his own feelings of failure. Though George Washington assured Jefferson that he had done all he could, the widespread criticism rankled. He was determined to clear his name and retire once more from public office.

Jefferson joined Martha and the children, then moved them to his father's plantation at Fine Creek before they returned to Richmond. Amid so much turmoil, Martha understood the dire situation her husband faced. The militia needed wagons and horses and guns and food and men, and so did the Continental Army. He was struggling to keep the populace from turning on his government and joining with the British. Jefferson hoped that reinforcements would come sailing in, but instead, in March, the British returned to Chesapeake Bay, to join Arnold and await General Charles Cornwallis, coming up from the south. The newly arrived British troops were commanded by General William Phillips, who had dined at Monticello only a few months earlier.

In this most turbulent time in the lives of Thomas and Martha Jefferson, there fell another devastating blow. On April 15, baby Lucy Elizabeth Jefferson, not yet six months old, died. The Governor's Council was to meet the next day, in miserable weather, but Jefferson wrote to say he could not bear to take part: "The day is so very bad that I hardly expect a council, and there being nothing that I know of very pressing, and Mrs. Jefferson in a situation in which I would not wish to leave her, I shall not attend to-day."

Martha had now lost four children. The way the war was going, she had reason to fear she might lose everything else. Little more than a week after the baby's death, the British massed for another push up the James. Martha, Patsy, and Polly fled Richmond again, with Jupiter driving the carriage, headed this time for Elk Hill. She and the children remained there through the terrifying weeks that followed. A guest at John and Mary Bolling's place in Goochland County gave Jefferson an account of the worry and confusion in the neighborhood:

We receive every day vague reports of the conduct of our cruel foe, but can't tell what degree of credit to give thereto. If you can spare so much time, I should be extremely obliged in receiving from Your Excellency by the return of the bearer an account of the present situation of both armies, the strength of each, the probable designs of the Enemy, our loss in the action on Appomattox, the particular depredations and injury done *at* and in the vicinity of Petersburg and at Osbornes, and in short every other interesting circumstance, for I had rather know the worst that can have happened than continue any Longer in a state of suspense and uncertainty.

The anxiety could not have been easier to bear at Elk Hill, though Martha could draw comfort from familiar surroundings in that awful spring. Patsy, at the age of eight, was old enough to have developed an attachment to this place her mother cherished. This particular interlude at Elk Hill made a powerful impression on that bright child, who had been hauled back and forth across Virginia in the terror and turbulence of war. It was, after all, springtime, with greening grass, flowers beginning to bloom, a time of rebirth. A young girl and her mother might walk out to see cows licking their newborn calves, and spindly-legged foals frolicking in the fields. But even at Elk Hill, the war pressed in. Cornwallis's troops were ready to move up the river. Jefferson was working to have the capital moved to Charlottesville, prior to his anticipated retirement on June 2. Martha would have to leave Elk Hill and travel to Albemarle County, a more difficult proposition than ever before. She had to cross the James to get home, and boats were in short supply. "Mrs. Jefferson and your little family were very well yesterday at Elk-hill," a friend assured the governor, "and were endeavouring to procure a vessel to cross over the river to Mr. C: Harrisons, but I doubt they would find it difficult, for the Q:Master had the day before collected all the canoes in the neighbourhood and sent them down the river loaded with grain for the use of the army."

Cornwallis arrived in mid-May, launching a campaign up the James and into the very heart of Virginia. He knew Jefferson was at Monticello, and sent Colonel Banastre Tarleton, the notoriously ruthless cavalry commander, in pursuit of the rebel governor and assembly. Once again the Jefferson family took flight, with Thomas sending Martha and the children as far away as he could, off to Poplar Forest, far to the west in Bedford County. He promised to join them as soon as he could.

Tarleton arrived on June 4, only hours after Jefferson himself fled the mountaintop, once again leaving enslaved people behind and at the mercy of the invading army. Where "Great George" Granger had been the man to save the family silver in Richmond, that fabled task now fell to twenty-six-year-old Martin Hemings. According to one of the most famous stories in Monticello lore, Tarleton's troops were pounding up the mountain while Martin and another slave hid the silver beneath the planks of the steps of one of the front porticos. The British arrived just as they finished, with Martin slamming the planks down on the other man, who was trapped below. That man would be stuck in the tight, dark hole until the next day; meanwhile Martin faced down soldiers armed with loaded guns and bayonets. They threatened to shoot him if he did not reveal the whereabouts of the master and his treasures. "Fire away, then," Martin reportedly told them, a cocked pistol pointed at his chest. This display of bravery was not simply a selfless gesture of loyalty to the master, but was also a defiant assertion of Martin's manhood. As Annette Gordon-Reed has written, "Martin Hemings was as much his own man at that moment as he could ever have been in his life to date."

TARLETON'S CAVALRY LEFT Monticello intact, for reasons passing understanding. But Cornwallis, in Jefferson's words "the most active, enterprising and vindictive Officer who has ever appeared in Arms against us," inflicted a cruel blow. He aimed at Jefferson but struck the lives of Martha and many enslaved people the hardest. Cornwallis took his army to Elk Hill and occupied the place for ten days. There he wrought his vengeance on the fugitive governor "in a spirit of total extermination." Seven years later, the memory of Cornwallis's depredations at Elk Hill still burned bitterly for Thomas Jefferson. He recalled that the British general

destroyed all my growing crops of corn and tobacco, he burned all my barns containing the same articles of the last year, having first taken what he wanted; he used, as was to be expected, all my stocks of cattle, sheep and hogs for the sustenance of his army, and carried off all the horses capable of service: of those too young for service he cut the throats, and he burned all the fences on the plantation, so as to leave it an absolute waste.

There was also a heavy human cost. Some thirty slaves left with Cornwallis, either as captives or, as Jefferson put it in his Farm Book in 1781, "fled to the enemy," "joined enemy," or simply "run away." In his later recollection, Jefferson blamed Cornwallis for "carrying off" those enslaved people, and commented, "Had this been to give them freedom he would have done right, but it was to consign them to inevitable death from the small pox and putrid fever then raging in his camp." Most died in enemy hands. Some made it back to Elk Hill and Monticello, bringing smallpox with them.

Jefferson scholars have, until recently, taken an oddly sanguine view of the losses the Jefferson household endured at the hands of the British. Dumas Malone acknowledged the devastation at Elk Hill, but commented blithely, "His supply of slaves was not seriously depleted, for he still had more than two hundred," including "his very special 'people,'" Jupiter and Suck, George and Ursula, "and the superior Heming [*sic*] family of 'bright' mulattoes.'" Life at Monticello, said Malone, "resumed its normal character and tempo."

One wonders what Martha Jefferson would have made of such an assessment by her husband's most distinguished biographer. True, the "normal character and tempo" of Martha Wayles Skelton Jefferson's life throbbed with death and loss, but nothing had ever come close to this: A husband in disgrace and despair. Ursula and her family, Mary Hemings and her children taken prisoners by the British, and dozens of people seized by, or running to, the enemy. Her most intimate domain had been invaded. If she had any letters there from her beloved husband, Cornwallis would have found them, and done with them what he pleased. Her lovely place had been laid waste, the new colts lying blood-soaked, their throats slashed, bellies bloated to bursting and swarming with flies, amid ruined fields and the smoke-blackened remnants of fences.

Her own thirty-three-year-old body was itself a war zone, torn by the ravages of eight pregnancies, perhaps more. She had flown from place to place in terror. She must have been exhausted. Still, some of her ramparts had held. Thomas was alive and well; so were Patsy and Polly. Monticello was unharmed. The Hemings family, along with Jupiter, had stood by the Jeffersons: from Robert and James, bravely transporting Martha and the girls across frightful terrain, to Elizabeth and the other children, looking after things at Monticello, to Martin, legendary savior of the family silver. With what she had been through, and what was yet to come, tea services and cruet sets were the least of her problems.

12

The Butcher's Bill

WHILE CORNWALLIS RAGED at Elk Hill, the Jeffersons took refuge at Poplar Forest, some ninety miles to the south and west of Monticello. There, Thomas, an expert, hard-riding horseman, was thrown from Caractacus, his favorite mount, and "disabled from riding on horseback for some months." Such accidents could be fatal, as Martha well knew. But Jefferson was a resilient man, and Martha, who had suffered so much, had that in common with her husband. He seized his enforced immobility as an opportunity to write his *Notes on the State of Virginia*. This remarkable document, the product of those months together at Poplar Forest and then, finally, back at Monticello, bespoke his continuing love for Virginia, for places they had shared, people they knew, illuminated by a mind as searching and scintillating as any in the history of their country. Jefferson's *Notes* also revealed some of the less admirable dimensions of his mind, including the depth and breadth and scientific oddities of his faith in white supremacy.

When they got back to Monticello, they settled in with purpose, ramping up their household, keeping the careful accounts that proved their worth as industrious and well-schooled plantation owners. While Thomas inventoried his homeland, Martha counted out her sheets and blankets, bolsters and pillows, napkins and table-cloths, duly noting her tallies in her long-neglected housekeeping journal. Martha ran a patriotic household, eschewing imported cloth for the homespun and homemade. They hired a man to weave the cotton, hemp, and woolen and flaxen threads spun by slave women at Shadwell, Monticello, and Elk Hill. Martha kept track of all aspects of their textile production, from the raw fibers to the cloth that the family and slaves used and wore: fine cotton for her children and her counterpanes, fine linen for Mr. Jefferson's shirts, coarse linen and "yarne cloth" for "our negroes," good linen for "house servants." In November she sent bolsters, blankets, and sheets for two beds from Monticello to Elk Hill. Thomas was surveying his world while Martha rebuilt hers, and it seems she looked forward to making the place that Cornwallis had savaged into a home once again.

Every battlefield is something else, the site of a farm or a church, a pasture, a pond. Some places recover. Others never do. Martha's body was scarred and weakened by pregnancy and fear and war. On August 15, 1781, Thomas Jefferson "Left with Mrs. Jefferson £165." On September 25, she returned £120. This was the last time money ever changed hands between them. Fawn Brodie observed that Martha's disappearance from her husband's accounts was a signal that she was sick. That September, she was certainly pregnant again. She kept up her record of the spinning and weaving, but during the months Martha carried her last child, she did not record any spending or slaughtering, no soap, no candles. On April 30, she wrote down "5 lb. picked cotton from Elk-hill," and on May 1 she made the final entry in her housekeeping journal, noting the weaving of "5 yds. Of fine mixt cloth for a coat, mr. Jefferson." As far as we know, with one famous exception, these were the last words she ever wrote.

A week later, on May 8, she gave birth to her fifth daughter. Thomas recorded the birth of "Lucy Elizabeth (second of that name)."

*   *   *

HISTORIANS HAVE PORTRAYED Martha Jefferson as slight and delicate, gentle and submissive, cheerful despite her frail body and withdrawing temperament. But these are retrospective judgments, rendered alongside the regret that we can never know Thomas Jefferson's wife, since he, or someone else, destroyed every letter between the two of them. "Because of this impenetrable silence on his part, probably we shall never know much about Martha Wayles Jefferson and her life with him," wrote Dumas Malone.

But Jefferson's act of possessive vandalism did not obliterate all traces of this ordinary and remarkable woman. Those who say we have too little left of Martha to know her, speak only in relative terms. Compared to what we know about her husband, we do not know much about Martha. Compared to what we are able to learn about most of the people historians have written about, let alone most of the people who have lived on this earth, Martha left an immensity of information about her life, enough, indeed, to say a very great deal about how she lived, who she was, what and whom she loved.

Martha Wayles Skelton Jefferson survived a life of perpetual loss with amazing vivacity and resilience. She liked beer and cards and hunting parties. If she cultivated sensibility and delicate feeling, she was also a landed, slaveholding plantation woman, a woman who could ride a horse through a mountain blizzard, give orders to scores of people, run several households at once, preside over the slaughter of a herd of hogs. She loved her family and nurtured them faithfully, though it appears she was capable of sharp speech and of using manipulation to get what she wanted. She persuaded her smitten husband to buy the place where she had lived with another man, a place where she had borne her only son who lived beyond his first days. She took herself to that place again and again. But Thomas Jefferson had no reason to doubt Martha's devotion to him. Their passion for each other would prove fatal to her, and devastating to him.

Martha was a strong woman to endure what she did. By the summer of 1782, only three of the eight children she had carried still lived. She had sustained recurrent physical traumas amid the horror and destruction of a war that tore right through her household, a campaign of kidnapping and burning, of panic-stricken flight, of destruction of her livestock, barns, and fences, of the disgrace and depression of her idealistic husband. From the first, she had suffered in pregnancy and childbirth. She had survived potentially lethal breast infections, and borne at least one baby weighing over ten pounds. Any one of her pregnancies carried risks that could have killed her. Repeated childbearing and the ravages of revolution sucked away her strength and ripped her body to pieces.

On May 20, with a very sick wife and a tiny infant in a room nearby, Thomas Jefferson wrote from Monticello to his friend James Monroe, refusing absolutely Monroe's entreaties that Jefferson return to public life. He had been elected to the Virginia House but had refused to attend. He risked being arrested and compelled to go to Richmond.

Jefferson's letter to Monroe drew on his personal anguish and anxiety about Martha to make a strong political argument about citizens' right to privacy. The state, he insisted, had no "*perpetual* right to the service of all it's members." Such a claim "would be to annihilate the blessing of existence; to contradict the giver of life who gave it for happiness and not for wretchedness, and certainly to such it was better that they had never been born. . . . I may think public service and private misery inseparably linked together." While Jefferson invoked divine authority to justify his determination to stay home with his desperately ailing wife, when he referred to "the giver of life who gave it for happiness and not for wretchedness" he had Martha in mind.

When he spoke of wishing that someone had never been born, the infant Lucy Elizabeth lay close at hand. "Mrs. Jefferson has added another daughter to our family," he wrote Monroe, in closing. "She has been ever since and still continues very dangerously ill."

Some of Jefferson's other friends and acquaintances questioned his motives and his judgment in not answering the call of service. Fawn Brodie observed, "The callousness of Jefferson's admirers and friends in refusing to heed the impending tragedy seems now almost incomprehensible." But Monroe was deeply sympathetic. "I have been much distress'd upon the subject of Mrs. Jefferson and have fear'd, as well from what you suggested yourself as what I have heard from others, that the report of each succeeding day would inform me she was no more. . . . It may please heaven to restore our amiable friend to health and thereby to you a friend whose loss you would always lament, and to your children a parent which no change of circumstance would ever compensate for. . . . Nothing will give me so much pleasure as to hear of Mrs. Jefferson's recovery, and to be informed of it from yourself."

There would be no letter from Thomas Jefferson to James Monroe, or for that matter, to anyone else. While Martha lived, Thomas stayed close. According to their daughter Patsy, "For four months that she lingered he was never out of calling. When not at her bed side he was writing in a small room which opened immediately at the head of her bed" and took his turn "administering her medicines and drink to the last." Sometime near the end, Martha began to copy out poignant lines from Laurence Sterne's *Tristram Shandy*:

> *Time wastes too fast: every letter*
> *I trace tells me with what rapidity life*
> *follows my pen. The days and hours*
> *Of it are flying over our heads like*

Clouds of windy day never to return—
More every thing presses on—

But she was too weak to continue. And so Thomas, in anguish, took up a pen and went on:

and every
time I kiss thy hand to bid adieu, every absence which
follows it, are preludes to that eternal separation
which we are shortly to make!

He would wrap this scrap of verse around a lock of her hair, and keep it with him, all his days.

AT THE END Martha had gathered those closest to her around her deathbed. Elizabeth Eppes and Anne Skipwith and her daughters, Patsy and Polly, were there. But they were not alone. Edmund Bacon, a later Jefferson overseer, told a story preserved by the enslaved people at Monticello, a story in which certain details were wrong or muddled, but which featured the shadow family Martha Jefferson had kept with her throughout her life. "The House servants," said Bacon, "were Betty Brown, Sally, Critta, and Betty Hemings, Nance and Ursula. They were old family servants and great favorites. They were in the room when Mrs. Jefferson died."

They have often told my wife that when Mrs. Jefferson died they stood around the bed. Mr. Jefferson sat by her, and she gave him directions about a good many things that she wanted done. When she came to the children, she wept and could not speak for some time. Finally she held up her hand, and spreading out her four fingers, she told him she could not die happy if she thought her four children were ever to have a stepmother brought in over them. Holding her other hand in his, Mr. Jefferson promised her solemnly that he would never marry again. And he never did. He was then quite a young man and very handsome, and I suppose he could have married well; but he always kept that promise.

Martha Jefferson had only three remaining children when she died, not four. But no one stepped forward to challenge the other details of Bacon's secondhand account.

On September 6, 1782, Thomas Jefferson wrote down a sadness he could scarcely speak: "My dear wife died this day at 11:45 a.m." Many years later, Patsy Jefferson, by this time an aging wife and mother with many sorrows of her own, recalled her father's reaction to her mother's death. "A moment before the closing scene he was led from the room almost in a state of insensibility by his sister mrs. Carr who with great difficulty got him into his library where he fainted and re-mained so long insensible that they feared he would never revive. The scene that followed I did not witness but the violence of his emotion, of his grief when almost by stealth I entered his room at night to this day I dare not trust myself to describe."

For weeks after Martha's death, Thomas Jefferson was prisoner to his unquenchable grief. "He kept his room for three weeks and I was never for a moment from his side," Patsy recalled. "He walked almost incessantly night and day only lying down occasionally when nature was completely exhausted on a pallet that had been brought in during his long fainting fit. My Aunts remained constantly with him for some weeks, I do not remember how many."

JEFFERSON'S FRIENDS WORRIED about his sanity. Edmund Ran-dolph, then serving in the Continental Congress, wrote to James

Madison that "Mrs. Jefferson has at last shaken off her tormenting pains, by yielding to them, and has left our friend inconsolable. I ever thought him to rank domestic happiness in the first class of the chief good; but scarcely supposed that his grief would be so violent as to justify the circulating report of his swooning away whenever he sees his children."

And what of those children? Like her own mother, Martha Jefferson had left a motherless baby, little Lucy Elizabeth, too young to have any memory of the woman who had borne her. Daughter Polly, at four, would be left with a terror of abandonment, and would struggle to come to terms with her father for the rest of her own life. Patsy, at age ten, reacted differently, appointing herself her father's life companion in their mother's stead. "When at last he left his room," she remembered, "he rode out and from that time he was incessantly on horseback rambling about the mountain in the least frequented roads and just as often through the woods; in those melancholy rambles I was his constant companion, a solitary witness to many a violent burst of grief, the remembrance of which has consecrated particular scenes of that lost home beyond the power of time to obliterate."

Martha Wayles Skelton Jefferson was buried at Monticello, her grave marked with a tombstone inscribed in Greek: "Nay, if even in the House of Hades the dead forget their dead / yet will I even there be mindful of my dear comrade." Below that message is the inscription: "To the memory of Martha Jefferson, Daughter of John Wayles; Born October 19th, 1748, O.S. Intermarried with Thomas Jefferson January 1st, 1772; Torn from him by death September 6th, 1782: This monument of his love is inscribed."

IT TOOK JEFFERSON a month or more to pull himself together enough to write a letter. When he sat down to write to his sister-in-law, Elizabeth Eppes, he said he did so on behalf of his daughters. He was still shattered, obsessed with mortality, including his own. He showed Elizabeth Eppes his feelings without restraint. "This miserable kind of existence is really too burthensome to be borne," he wrote, "and were it not for the infidelity of deserting the sacred charge left me, I could not wish it's continuance a moment. For what could it be wished? All my plans of comfort and happiness reversed by a single event and nothing answering in prospect before me but a gloom un-brightened with one cheerful expectation." He was longing to flee his sorrows, to the grave or elsewhere. But he had to hang on, for the children's sake, and because Martha would want him to look after their girls. "The care and instruction of our children indeed affords some temporary abstractions from wretchedness," he said, "and nourishes a soothing reflection that if there be beyond the grave any concern for the things of this world there is one angel at least who views these attentions with pleasure and wishes continuance of them while she must pity the miseries to which they confine me."

Even in this private letter to Martha's sister, he could not bring himself to utter Martha's name. He assured Elizabeth Eppes that the children "are in perfect health," but he seemed both dazed and of-fended at the fact that the girls were "as happy as if they had no part in the unmeasurable loss we have sustained." But he hinted at one reason for their seeming happiness, an injunction on the part of their aunt, and possibly a plea from their own mother, not to lose them-selves in sadness. Elizabeth Eppes had told Jefferson not to mourn forever, to seek happiness at the first opportunity. He was finding that task impossible:

> I forget that I began this correspondence on behalf of the chil-dren and am afflicting you at the distance of 70 or 80 miles with sorrows which you had a right to think yourself out of the reach of. I will endeavor to correct myself and keep what I feel

to myself that I may not dispirit you from a communication with us. . . . I say nothing of coming to Eppington because I promised you this should not be till I could support such a countenance as might not cast a damp on the chearfulness of others.

Jefferson's letter to Elizabeth Eppes was the cry of a man in the grip of an emotional riptide, in the anguish of simultaneously remembering and trying to forget the woman he loved so well. It was the literary version of his tortured rides across the countryside, his young, worried, faithful daughter by his side, and he invoked those rambles in the letter: "Patsy rides with me 5 or 6. Miles a day," he wrote, "and presses for permission to accompany me on horseback to Elkhill whenever I shall go there. When that may be however I cannot tell; finding myself absolutely unable to attend to any thing like business."

Some historians have seen Jefferson's wild grief as a sign of his guilt about his own part in Martha's death, about his relentless claim to her body, a passion and a possession that led to the pregnancies that wore her down and finally killed her. Martha had surely suffered from the physical ordeal of carrying and bearing children. But her husband believed that her death had been hastened not just by childbirth, but also by the repeated traumas of invasion and war, by the Revolution that he himself had helped to birth. If Thomas Jefferson held any truth to be self-evident, it was the notion that happiness lay in preserving a high, impregnable wall between the turbulent public world of politics and strife, a realm assigned to men, and the peaceful sphere of domestic tranquility, a place associated with women. The Revolution had breached that wall, and violence had flowed into his home, his wife's sheltering domain, with the force of a spring freshet tearing away a mill dam, with the smell of smoke and the taste of blood and a sound as horrible as the shriek of a dying horse. War, he thought, had killed Martha Jefferson as surely as the babies she relentlessly bore, and this war, like those babies, was his fault.

Thomas Jefferson loved his wife with all his heart. The only way he knew to grieve was to draw a shroud of silence over her, to obliterate all trace of her, to ruthlessly suppress memory of her presence. In the shadow of her death, at a moment when he was hardly able to function rationally, he determined to sell Elk Hill, the place Martha cherished and had tried to reclaim despite Cornwallis's horrible violation. But Patsy's feelings about that place, like her thoughts about her mother, differed from those of her father. She begged to go with him to Elk Hill whenever he could bring himself to ride there. The daughter's plea bespoke her longing for the place where she could best sense the presence of the mother she had lost, a place she identified with happier times, and not a desire to erase grief.

Isaac Jefferson, Ursula's son, remembered Elk Hill well. "Old Master had a small brick house there where he used to stay, about a mile from Elk Island on the north side of the James River. The river forks there: one half runs one side of the island, tother the other side. When Mr. Jefferson was Governor, he used to stay thar a month or sich a matter; and when he was at the mountain, he would come and stay a month or so and then go back again." Jefferson scholar James A. Bear, Jr., editor of Isaac's memoir, pointed out that Jefferson's memorandum books, "which chronicled his whereabouts, do not support Isaac's report of the visits to Elk Hill," though Bear acknowledges that some Farm Book entries do suggest that the Jeffersons visited there. But Isaac Jefferson, who must have been taken to Elk Hill by his mother, was not wrong about family visits to Martha's beloved private retreat. Martha and the children went there often, and Thomas Jefferson visited them at Elk Hill whenever he could get away from the work of creating a new nation.

Like so many transactions in Thomas Jefferson's life, the plan to sell Elk Hill dragged on for years. The deeds for the second and third parcels he purchased there were not recorded until 1782 and 1783—after the sacking by Cornwallis, even after Martha's death. Much as he labored to reduce that beloved, tragic place to a business proposition, he could never fully wipe away the memory of his life there with Martha. When he advertised Elk Hill for sale in 1790, he had not been there for some time. Yet he could describe the place with precision: the rich red loam of the highlands and dark, rich loam of the low grounds, the "good dwelling house, of 4. Rooms below, and two above; with convenient out houses, on a very high and beautiful position, commanding a fine view of the Blue mountains, of James river for several miles, and of Elk Island." He could draw a fine map, too, boundaries not quite as precise as in the maps he drew from survey notations, but by his own lights reflecting "a General idea of the lands, drawn from memory, yet not far from the truth."

Thomas Jefferson could not forget Elk Hill. How much harder it was for him to suppress his yearning for the woman who had given him so much happiness despite the difficulties of their days together. He would come to terms with her death by rebuilding and defending the wall between the private world he shared with the women he loved, and the contentious realm of his public life. He—or someone close to him—burned his private letters, systematically destroying those documents, just as meticulously as he cataloged and copied his public correspondence. Dumas Malone wrote that Jefferson "carefully preserved and deeply cherished small souvenirs of his dead wife, but eventually he also saw to it that none of their letters should ever be open to prying eyes. . . . He was determined that the sacred intimacies of a lover and husband should remain inviolate. His wife did not belong to posterity; she belonged to him."

But Martha did not belong entirely to him. She also belonged to others who knew her, who loved her, who had raised her and been raised with her and raised by her, commanded by her, even owned by her, worked and played and laughed and cried alongside her. Thomas Jefferson could not wipe out their memories, however he might try. They too would have to come to grips with Martha's influence on their lives.

Thomas Jefferson himself assuredly belonged to her. His promise never to wed again bound him to her, far beyond the grave. Somewhere over the course of her own life, Martha Wayles Skelton Jefferson had acquired a horror of stepmothers, but not, it seems, of half-siblings, or Hemingses. The tension between remembering and forgetting the tangled, sometimes warmly joyous, too often tragic life of Martha Wayles Skelton Jefferson would shape the relationships between Thomas Jefferson and the women he would love for the rest of his life.

Part III

SALLY

13

Stories and Shadow Families

JOHN WAYLES'S YOUNGEST daughter, like all children, had four bio-logical grandparents. Three of those grandparents were English. Her mother's mother was African. In other places or times—a hundred years earlier in Virginia, or sixteen hundred miles distant in Nuevo Mexico, or four thousand miles across an ocean, in Spain or France—Sally Hemings's maternal heritage would not have sealed her destiny. But because of where and when Sally was born—in Virginia, in 1773—the accident of birth determined her race—black, or negro—and her legal status—slave.

Sally Hemings's foremothers also gave her another legacy. They bequeathed to her a set of stories to be used as weapons against en-slavement, and against the lacerations of race. Sally, in turn, passed those stories on to her children, and we know them because her son, James Madison Hemings, preserved them through slavery and free-dom, through secession, war, and reunion, and told them to a news-paperman named S. F. Wetmore, the editor of the *Pike County* (Ohio) *Republican*, in 1873. "I never knew of but one white man who bore the name of Hemings," Madison affirmed. "He was an Englishman and my great grandfather. He was captain of an English whaling vessel which sailed between England and Williamsburg, Va., then quite a port." His great-grandmother, he explained, "was a fullblooded African, and possibly a native of that country. She was the property of John Wales [Wayles], a Welchman."

Madison Hemings's family story began with a tale of attempted rescue, in which his great-grandfather, discovering that the woman he had sold had borne his child, played the role of hero, and his grandfather, John Wayles, took the part of villain. "Capt. Hemings happened to be in the port of Williamsburg at the time my grandmother was born," he told the journalist, "and acknowledging her fatherhood he tried to purchase her of Mr. Wales who would not part with the child, though he was offered an extraordinarily large price for her. She was named Elizabeth Hemings." The captain, said Madison, was "determined to own his own flesh and blood." But he would be thwarted, not just by John Wayles, but more treacherously, by informers in Wayles's household. Captain Hemings "resolved to take the child by force or stealth, but the knowledge of his intention coming to John Wales' ears, through leaky fellow servants of the mother, she and the child were taken into the 'great house' under the master's immediate care."

According to Madison Hemings, his grandfather Wayles was not acting out of simple greed. He was also curious about how this new creature, half-English and half-African and neither black nor white, but something else, might turn out. "I have been informed that it was not the extra value of that child over other slave children that induced Mr. Wales to refuse to sell it, for slave masters then, as in later days, had no compunctions of conscience which restrained them from parting mother and child of however tender age," Hemings told S. F. Wetmore, "but he was restrained by the fact that just about that time amalgamation began, and the child was so great a curiosity that its owner desired to raise it himself that he might see its outcome." His heroic attempt at redemption thwarted, "Capt. Hemings soon afterwards sailed from Williamsburg, never to return. Such is the story that comes down to me."

In Madison Hemings's telling, John Wayles's first motive in claiming Betty Hemings as his slave had been curiosity. Wayles's later actions bespoke more carnal impulses. "Elizabeth Hemings grew to womanhood in the family of John Wales," Madison Hemings continued, "whose wife dying she (Elizabeth) was taken by the widower Wales as his concubine, by whom she had six children—three sons and three daughters, viz: Robert, James, Peter, Critty, Sally and Thena. These children went by the name of Hemings."

GENEALOGIES ARE FAMILY stories with a purpose. They are intended as much to exclude as to include, and as they emphasize some details, they omit or mistake others. There is another way to tell the story of Sally Hemings's family, not simply as an unfriendly transaction between men, but as a tale of wedding gifts and women's legacies. At the time of Betty Hemings's birth, about 1735, when Captain Hemings was supposed to have made his offer, Betty's mother did not belong to John Wayles. She was the property of Francis and Sarah Eppes, Martha Jefferson's grandparents. In 1746, they gave Betty and her mother to their daughter Martha, who was marrying John Wayles. The bride's property passed instantly to her new husband, and in turn, to Martha and her own husband, Thomas Jefferson.

Such details would not have mattered to Madison Hemings, but other things did. He was careful to note that his great-grandfather commanded a whaling boat, not a slave ship. Madison Hemings distanced his heroic progenitor from that unholy traffic. He likewise never referred to his great-grandmother, grandmother, and mother as "slaves," though he took pains to explain that Elizabeth Hemings was different from "other slave children" and had been betrayed by "leaky fellow servants," in other words, by tattling slaves. The Hemingses embraced a genealogy that linked them by blood to white men and slave masters—the whaling captain, the planter-lawyer, the author of the Declaration—and set them apart from other enslaved people. Generations of Hemingses stubbornly preserved the story of their British progenitor and their kinship with Wayleses and Eppeses, Jeffersons and Randolphs. Most importantly, they linked themselves to Thomas Jefferson. The linchpin of this celestial connection was Sally Hemings, one of the most famous, least known women in American history. She was not the first, or the last, Hemings woman to have a long relationship and children with a white man. She was the middle woman in a multigenerational dual lineage, granddaughter, daughter, mother, aunt, sister, and niece to women who lived as partners of white men.

SALLY HEMINGS WOULD not have remembered her father, since she was born in 1773, possibly after his death. Surely she heard stories about him from her mother and siblings, from other enslaved people, from the white half-sisters who inherited their father's property, and perhaps from their husbands. Monticello would be the first home she remembered. In that not-yet-famous place, Sally Hemings came to consciousness in the heat of the American Revolution.

Sally's world was full of Hemingses, her mother and five brothers and six sisters all close at hand. The eldest, Mary, was twenty years older than Sally. She worked as a seamstress and took care of her own children. The youngest, a little brother and sister, were John, whose father was the carpenter Joseph Neilson, and baby Lucy. As war came up the river and into the neighborhood, the Hemings family would be pulled apart. Sally was five years old when British and German prisoners came to Albemarle County, a time, it seems, of relative tranquility and plenty, but a harbinger of things to come. If she did not hear firsthand, from the voluble Baroness Riedesel or the baroness's little daughters, the story of their ordeals in battle and as prisoners of war, surely such a colorful, horrible tale spread through the Monticello grapevine.

When Sally was six, Thomas Jefferson became governor of Virginia. Her sisters, Mary and Betty, and her brothers, Martin, Robert, and James, moved away, first to Williamsburg, and then to Richmond. Sally remained with her mother, her older sister, Nance, and the other youngest Hemingses—Thenia, Critta, Peter, John, and Lucy—at Monticello. Though she was too young to understand the maneuverings of politicians or the movements of armies, she was old enough to recognize that many of the people she knew best were gone. Now came the rumors of British invasion, and the redcoat army itself, under the traitor Arnold, making its way toward the state capital, toward so many in her family.

Sally would have been at Monticello when the Jefferson carriage rolled up, driven by her brothers, Robert and James, carrying the frightened mistress and her three small girls, bearing tales of the terror in Richmond. Sally's mother would learn that her daughter Mary and grandchildren had been left behind to be seized by the British. And what did the Hemingses know of those who were not taken captive, but who had voluntarily gone with the British, in the hope of claiming their freedom? Some died. Some returned, carrying smallpox. Sally, fortunately, did not contract that hideous and deadly disease. Not all scars are physical.

When Sally was eight, the Revolution swept through the door. The master fled the majestic house he had spent so many years building. Once more Thomas Jefferson left his slaves to fend for themselves, assuming they would defend his home and property. Sally was at Monticello when Banastre Tarleton's cavalry arrived. If she did not personally witness her brother Martin's fierce resistance to the British, the story of his heroism would be told again and again. In the months of transience and uncertainty that followed, the Hemingses were dispersed over the landscape of Virginia, from the British encampment at Yorktown to the western outpost of Poplar Forest. Some of them went with Martha Jefferson as she made her last visits to the Forest and Elk Hill. Elizabeth and the youngest children, it seems, remained at Monticello through this time of instability and anxiety.

WHEN MARTHA JEFFERSON came home to Monticello for the last time, Sally Hemings was among those who cared for her. As Annette Gordon-Reed explained, "Just as Elizabeth Hemings and her daughters had seen Martha in her weakest and most vulnerable moments, they had seen her husband at his lowest point as well, and they shared memories of this defining time at Monticello." They would learn too that Thomas Jefferson "was not the master of everything." Martha's death set off shock waves that scattered the Hemingses like shrapnel from a hand grenade.

In October 1782, Thomas Jefferson left his home, convinced he could never be happy at Monticello again. He took along his three daughters and Martin, Robert, and James Hemings. He planned to stop at Eppington, the long-neglected plantation on the Appomattox to which Martha's sister, Elizabeth Eppes, and her husband, Francis, had lately returned. Jefferson had only rarely visited Eppington. In fact, he had to hire a guide to show him the way, so that he might leave his tiny baby daughter, Lucy Elizabeth, in the care of her aunt. He was making plans to leave the country.

Jefferson had spent the final years of his wife's life fending off the claims of public service, even turning down an enticing appointment as a peace commissioner in Paris. He had not yet emerged from the torture of fresh grief when the Congress, at James Madison's urging, renewed the appointment. The news came to Jefferson in December, at a friend's plantation, where he had taken his older daughters, Patsy and Polly, to be inoculated against smallpox. He saw in the opportunity a chance to flee his sorrow, to travel to a country he ardently longed to see. He hurried to arrange his departure, sending four-year-old Polly to join her baby sister at Eppington, while he planned to take Patsy with him to France.

And now came months of uncertainty and wandering. Jefferson traveled from Virginia to Boston in search of a boat that might take him safely to Europe, in the dead of winter and with the risk of capture by British warships. Amid many delays, the peace treaty was signed without him. He returned to Monticello for the summer, gathering his family about him again, when Virginia reelected him to the Continental Congress. Over the course of the next year, he followed the Congress from Philadelphia to Princeton and then to Annapolis. He traveled with Robert or sometimes James Hemings. He installed Patsy in Philadelphia, while the two younger girls stayed at Eppington. He would never see his youngest daughter again.

JEFFERSON WAS APPOINTED minister plenipotentiary to European nations in May 1784. He was to join John Adams and Benjamin Franklin in negotiating treaties of amity and commerce. Before leaving he shuttered and shut down his remarkable house at Monticello. Jefferson left the management of his business affairs in the hands of his friend and neighbor, Nicholas Lewis, and gave his power of attorney to his brother-in-law, Francis Eppes. Enslaved people would still tend the master's tobacco fields, under the eyes of hired overseers, rather than under the governance of a man who hated the brutalities of slavery. Elizabeth Hemings and her daughters, now with no household duties to perform, would retreat to their cabins. Jefferson left instructions that the Hemings women not be forced to do field work, or as he phrased it, be "put into the ground."

Jefferson also made provision for Betty's older sons. James Hemings accompanied him to France, first in the role of body servant, but ultimately, to be trained in the art of French cuisine. Martin and Robert Hemings found employment away from Monticello, with their master's explicit approval. Mary Hemings was hired out to Charlottesville merchant Thomas Bell. And Sally Hemings, at nine or ten years old, about the age Thomas Jefferson had been when his mother and father sent him off to be tutored by a stern and narrow minister, would be separated from her mother and sent to Eppington to serve as maid to Polly Jefferson, her half-niece, now six years old.

THE EPPESES AND Wayleses and Jeffersons and Hemingses were united by generations of blood. Francis Eppes was Martha's first cousin as well as her brother-in-law. Their grandfather had owned Sally Hemings's grandmother and had refused to sell Elizabeth Hemings back to her English father. Martha and her half-sister, Elizabeth Eppes, were so close that Elizabeth took in Martha's two youngest daughters after Martha's death. Thomas Jefferson and Francis Eppes were also intimate friends, and Jefferson would in time make his nephew, Jack Eppes, one of his protégés.

Martha Jefferson had made a point of keeping the Hemingses close, dancing a minuet of intimacy and denial with her father's shadow family. Elizabeth Eppes was also half-sister to six of the Hemings siblings, but her relation to them differed from Martha's in one important regard: she did not own them. Still, she was familiar to the enslaved members of the Monticello household; Isaac Jefferson, Ursula's son, recalled that "Mrs. Eppes was a sister of Mrs. Jefferson—mightily like her sister." Elizabeth Eppes remained close to Martha, nursing her through her last illness. But if either Mrs. Eppes or her husband felt any obligation to the Hemingses, any impulse to see to their welfare after Martha's death, they did not make use of their labor or their talents, with one exception: they permitted Sally Hemings to come into their household, to give comfort to little Polly Jefferson.

Elizabeth Eppes's life had followed a course similar to Martha's. She married a man devoted to science with a passion for gardening, a landowner and slaveholder who hoped to build a big house on property he had inherited from his father. She bore eight children, two of whom died young. She inherited her share of her father's wealth and his debt, and her husband struggled with that legacy his whole life.

Francis Eppes, like Thomas Jefferson, had grand plans for his home, a two-story house, white stucco with a red-shingled hipped roof, with a commanding view of the Appomattox River from the rear, where he planned and planted extensive gardens. Guests who arrived by road traveled down a long drive through the woods, the view opening up to a sweep of lawn and the vista of the imposing house. Eppington was impressive, though nothing on the extravagant scale of the Monticello house where Thomas and Martha Jefferson lived together. Eppes had begun to build in about 1770, but his project was stalled by the death of his father-in-law, John Wayles. The management of the Wayles estate, wartime disruption, and perhaps even the needs of Martha Jefferson kept the Eppeses at the Forest through the Revolution. When they returned to Eppington in 1783, Francis Eppes undertook to expand the house, adding two wings and a porch. They had to tear down chimneys and cut doors, no easy process for the people living there. Like Monticello, Eppington would be a dwelling designed by the master to suit his wants and needs, a place long under construction. The west wing, not accessible from the main house, served as Francis Eppes's office and study, his sanctuary.

Hemingses had lived at various Wayles, Eppes, and Jefferson holdings, from Bermuda Hundred and the Forest to Hors du Monde and Elk Hill. But Sally Hemings had spent most if not all of her life at

Monticello. When she left her mother and brothers and sisters for the first time, she was heading nearly eighty long miles away, into unknown territory. Polly Jefferson, taken to Eppington to join Lucy Elizabeth, was too young to understand what such a journey meant, and in any case, she had traveled a great deal in the first turbulent years of her life. Over the next few years, Polly developed a fierce attachment to her loving aunt and uncle, and to the place that seemed to her more home than anywhere else she had known. But for Sally Hemings, Eppington was a place of exile from and abandonment by nearly everyone she had loved. She bid good-bye to her mother at Monticello, and went to a strange place, probably taken there by her brother, Robert, in July 1784. When Robert left, Sally was pretty much on her own.

VIRGINIA WAS A dangerous place to be a child in the waning years of the eighteenth century. Surviving the ordeal of birth was the first challenge. And then there were the recurring epidemics of childhood diseases, from measles and mumps to scarlet fever and pertussis, or whooping cough. Sickness came to Eppington in the autumn of 1784, less than two months after Thomas Jefferson left for Paris and deposited his daughters and their slave maid at the plantation on the Appomattox. People began to suffer the symptoms of pertussis—the runny nose, sneezing and fever, the cough that becomes increasingly sharp and wracking. Sufferers struggle for air through an excruciating cough that has a distinctive barking or whooping sound. Some victims cough so terribly that they vomit. Some cough so incessantly that they cannot retain food or water, and die of malnutrition or dehydration. Some develop pneumonia and other acute infections that can prove deadly. The disease is spread through contact with airborne discharges from the mucous membranes—in other words, by spending time in proximity to coughing or sneezing people. The old and the very young are at greatest risk of dying from whooping cough, though anyone can catch it.

People at Eppington got very ill, and some died. Francis Eppes was plainly worried when he wrote to Thomas Jefferson in September, in a letter that warned of financial as well as physical dangers to Jefferson's family. Crops were bad at Monticello, Poplar Forest, and Elk Hill. Creditors clamored to be paid, and Eppes was expecting lawsuits. John Wayles's heirs—Francis Eppes, Thomas Jefferson, and Henry Skipwith—would have to sell property to pay the debts from Wayles's estate. And the children were terribly sick. "I wish it was in my power to inform you that your children were well," Eppes wrote. "They as well as our own are laid up with the hooping cough. Your little Lucy and our youngest and Bolling are I think very ill. Polly has it badly but she sleeps well and eats hartily."

Enslaved people at Eppington, living in crowded, drafty quarters and in far from sanitary conditions, would have been extremely vulnerable to infection and to complications. Sally Hemings, as maid to Polly Jefferson, may have slept in her young mistress's room, or perhaps in a dwelling with other slaves, but she undoubtedly shared her sleeping place with other people. Sally was repeatedly exposed to the whooping cough virus, since Polly and Lucy Elizabeth, and their cousins, Martha (called "Bolling") and Lucy Eppes, all came down with the disease. Polly and Bolling Eppes suffered, but survived. The two Lucys did not. The grief-stricken Elizabeth Eppes wrote the news in a heartbreaking letter to Thomas Jefferson:

It is impossible to paint the anguish of my heart on this melancholy occasion. A most unfortunate Hooping cough has deprived you, and us of two sweet Lucys, within a week. Ours was the first that fell a sacrifice. She was thrown into violent convulsions linger'd out a week and then expired. Your dear angel was confined a week to her bed, her sufferings were great though nothing like a fit. She retain'd her senses perfectly, calld me a few moments before she died, and asked distinctly for water. Dear Polly has had it most violently, though always kept about, and is now quite recovered. My heart shudders for my poor Bolling, who is reduced to a skeleton, and the cough still very obstinate. Life is scarcely supportable under such severe afflictions.

It took nearly seven months for this letter, and a similar one from Francis Eppes, to reach Thomas Jefferson. Their letters arrived at precisely the moment Jefferson learned that he would be staying in Paris, to succeed Benjamin Franklin as minister to the French court. He had, however, found out about his daughter's death earlier, in a letter sent by James Currie, the doctor who had treated the children at Eppington. Currie wrote that Lucy Jefferson "fell a Martyr to the Complicated evils of teething, Worms, and Hopping Cough which last was carried there by the Virus of their friends without their knowing it was in their train."

If Lucy Jefferson had intestinal parasites as well as whooping cough, chances were good that others at Eppington suffered from the same malady, which would have made people there miserable long after the whooping cough had passed. Sally Hemings may have suffered from any of these afflictions, but she was far from people who loved her, who might have offered particular care and comfort.

Thomas Jefferson, grieving anew, made the decision that would change Sally's life forever. From the moment Jefferson received the Eppes's letters informing him about one daughter's death, he was absolutely determined that the other must leave Eppington and come to France. He wrote to Francis Eppes to say that his new appointment would keep him in Europe longer, so "I must have Polly." He knew that his letter would take months to reach Virginia, so he could not expect her to come for another year at the least. He hoped that would allow time to make proper arrangements, to find a woman in Virginia who might be hired to accompany his daughter on a long and daunting ocean voyage.

14

Summoned and Sent

NEARLY THREE YEARS passed between the death of Lucy Jefferson and the moment when Polly Jefferson and Sally Hemings were put on a ship bound not for Paris, but for London. The delay in their departure was not simply a matter of slow mail service. Three other things kept Polly in Virginia: the fact that she was dead set against leaving, the problem of finding the right ship to transport her, and the challenge of finding the right person to take a terrified little girl across the Atlantic.

Since her father's and sister's departures, Polly had learned to think of Eppington as her home. For Polly, family now meant aunts and uncles and cousins. The Eppeses doted on her, and she was deeply attached to them. Her father, on the other hand, had left her, newly motherless, when she was only four years old. However much he wanted her with him, and however many letters he wrote to other people about his concern for her and his plans to bring her to him, Jefferson never wrote a single letter *to her* during all the years that an ocean lay between them. While he told Francis Eppes that "dear Poll . . . hangs on my mind night and day," those words were not addressed to Polly herself. Polly, for her part, was learning to read and write. By the time she was seven, she wrote well enough to send her father a letter of her own, notable for its firmness and its brevity: "Dear Papa, I want to see you and sister Patsy, but you must come to Uncle Eppes's house. Polly Jefferson."

Thomas Jefferson felt sure that Polly would grow accustomed to the idea of leaving Eppington. She never did. She clung to her resistance with a steadfastness that grew into desperation and flashed into frenzy, as her father relentlessly demanded that she come to him. In the end he had to force her to leave the home she had come to love, to embark on a hazardous voyage across the sea to join a father she barely remembered. The dangers were very real, from deadly weather to the precarious seaworthiness of vessels too new to be tested, or too old and battered to be watertight. Jefferson acknowledged the problems when he wrote to Francis Eppes in August 1785, affirming that "I must now repeat my wish to have Polly sent to me next summer":

This, however, must depend on the circumstance of a good vessel sailing from Virginia in the months of April, May, June, or July. I would not have her set out sooner or later on account of the equinoxes. The vessel should have performed one voyage at least, but not be more than four or five years old. We do not attend to this circumstance till we have been to sea, but there the consequence of it is felt. I think it would be found that all the vessels which are lost are either on their first voyage or after they are five years old; at least there are few exceptions to this. . . . I will only add that I would rather live a year longer without her than have her trusted to any but a good ship and a summer passage.

No one knew better than Thomas Jefferson, United States minister to France, that these were not the only perils. Algerian pirates had been a problem in the Mediterranean and the Atlantic for centuries. Even as he wrote to Francis Eppes, pirate corsairs were attacking American ships. "The Algerines this fall took two vessels from us, and now have 22. of our citizens in slavery," Jefferson told Francis Eppes. "Their dispositions are . . . hostile, and they very possibly will demand a higher tribute than America will pay. In this event they will commit depredations on our trade next summer. . . . My mind revolts at the possibility of a capture; so that unless you hear from myself (not trusting the information of any other person on earth) that peace is made with the *Algerines*, do not send her but in a vessel of French or English property: for these vessels alone are safe from prize by the barbarians."

Jefferson was so worried about pirates that he repeated his warning to Eppes in January, adding one detail: "I write the present chiefly to repeat a prayer I urged . . . that you would confide my daughter only to a French or English vessel having a Mediterranean pass. This attention, tho' of little consequence in matters of merchandize, is weight in the mind of a parent which sees even possibilities of capture beyond the reach of any estimate. If a peace be concluded with the Algerines . . . I pray you to believe it from nobody else."

Such warnings did nothing to reassure the Eppeses that they ought to bow to Jefferson's wishes and send a stubbornly resistant little girl across the ocean to join her equally obdurate father. Finding the right ship, sailing at the right time and with the right captain and credentials, was enough of a problem. How much more complicated was the task of recruiting someone to take care of Polly on the trip. Jefferson had begun by proposing the idea of hiring a woman to serve as a nanny on the voyage, and asked the Eppeses for their advice about such a person. By August 1785, he had given the matter further thought. "With respect to the person to whose care she should be trusted," he wrote to Francis Eppes, "I must leave it to yourself and Mrs. Eppes altogether." But he had some suggestions.

Some good lady passing from America to France, or even England, would be most eligible; but a careful gentleman who would be so kind as to superintend her would do. In this case some woman who has had the small-pox must attend her. A careful negro woman, as Isabel, for instance, if she has had the small-pox, would suffice under the patronage of a gentleman. The woman need not come farther than Havre, l'Orient, Nantes, or whatever port she should land at, because I could go there for the child myself, and the person could return to Virginia directly.

As months went by, Jefferson and Francis Eppes worked to recruit a chaperone for Polly. At first Jefferson hoped Polly might accompany Thomas Barclay, the American consul in Paris, who was expecting to travel to Philadelphia and then return to France. "She would be in the best hands possible; and should the time of his return become well ascertained, I will write you on the subject." But he did not want the Eppeses to wait for Barclay if they had already located the right ship and the right escort. "In the mean time it need not prevent your embracing any opportunity which occurs of a sound French or English ship, neither new nor old, sailing in the months of April, May, June or July under the care of a trusty person." And he added, in a teasing tone, "You see how much trouble I give you till you get this little charge out of your hands."

Elizabeth Eppes hated Jefferson's scheme from the beginning. Jefferson tried to overcome his sister-in-law's resistance with a combination of flattery and patriarchal firmness, working through his brother-in-law. "I know that Mrs. Eppes's goodness will make her feel her separation from an infant who has experienced so much of her tenderness," he wrote to Francis Eppes. "My unlimited confidence in her has been the greatest solace possible under my own separation

from Polly. Mrs. Eppes's goodness will suggest to her many consid-
erations which render it of importance to the future happiness of the
child that she should neither forget, nor be forgotten by her sister and
myself."

In the end, Francis Eppes decided that a father's insistent claim
outweighed a child's frantic resistance, and looked for a ship and an
escort. Overruling his worried wife and his terrified niece, Eppes
told Jefferson in April 1787, only two weeks before the vessel was
to set sail, that he had found an appropriate ship. The *Robert* was
scheduled to depart for England on May 1, commanded by Captain
Andrew Ramsay, "a man of very good temper." "She is a fine ship
and has every accommodation to make [Polly] cumfortable except a
Female attendant," Eppes wrote. He had hoped to be able to send
Polly with the French consul and his wife, but that eventuality had
fallen through. Thus Polly's chaperone was to be "a Mr. John Amonit
a young man of caracter who promises to do every thing in his power
to make her happy . . . recommended to you by our Governor and
some others of your particular Friends." As to the question of the
female attendant, Eppes reported that "Isabel or Sally will come with
her either of whome will answer under the direction of Mr. Am[onit]."
Some of the letters between Eppes and Jefferson have not been found.
Perhaps they were destroyed, by Thomas Jefferson or his protective
descendants, because they discussed the possibility that Sally Hemings would be going to Europe with Polly Jefferson.

THE LAUDED MR. AMONIT did not sail on the *Robert* as chaperone to
Polly Jefferson. Instead, the nine-year-old girl crossed the ocean under
the direct protection of the captain of the ship, Andrew Ramsay. Her
sole traveling companion was fourteen-year-old Sally Hemings, who
had come instead of Isabel Hern, a twenty-seven-year-old enslaved
woman from Monticello whom Jefferson had mentioned. The Eppe-

ses had fully intended to send Isabel, who was taken from Monticello to Eppington, leaving behind her husband and four children, in the spring of 1786. Francis Eppes set about pursuing "the necessary ceremony of enoculating" Isabel, as Jefferson had directed. All that took time, delaying Polly's departure another year. In the meantime, Isabel returned to Monticello and became pregnant again. She had a difficult birth with her fifth child, and was too sick to make the trip. Two weeks before the ship sailed, Francis Eppes was still holding out hope that Isabel would recover. But by that time he had settled on Sally as a suitable replacement.

Why? Sally Hemings hardly answered Jefferson's description of the person he required to accompany his daughter. She might have been a careful girl, but Sally was no mature woman. She had not been inoculated against smallpox. She was to be supervised by John Amonit, but he did not make the trip. And yet the Eppeses saw fit to go through with the plan, with Captain Ramsay's assurances that he would look after Polly. That would be no minor responsibility. The child was so distraught at the thought of leaving that the Eppeses had to trick her into boarding the ship. They brought their own children on board at Bermuda Hundred to play with Polly for a day or two, hoping to "reconcile her to" the voyage. The children played until Polly fell asleep, and then the Eppes family slipped away, leaving Polly and Sally on board. When Polly awoke, the ship had sailed.

If the Eppeses were concerned about Polly's safety under Sally's care, they could have simply canceled the plan and written to Jefferson that the situation had become impossible. They decided to push ahead. Surely they could have found some other slave woman to make the trip, including Elizabeth Hemings, who was then doing light duty at the shuttered Monticello. So why send a fourteen-year-old slave girl across the ocean, on a dangerous voyage with a child who burst into wild hysterics at even the thought of leaving her Virginia home?

The Eppeses clearly considered Sally Hemings to be healthy, trustworthy, intelligent, and diligent enough to see the journey through, and to deliver Polly safely to her father. Nobody had a closer acquaintance with Polly Jefferson's desires and tantrums than Sally Hemings. Sally had known Polly since she was born. At Eppington, Sally had been charged with Polly's personal care, which included far more than washing out her linen, mending her stockings, and emptying her chamber pot. The Eppeses knew that Polly would not make it easy on whoever was with her when she woke up aboard the *Robert*, anchors aweigh. Sally, as Polly's slave, had no choice but to deal with Polly's fury, and she surely knew what would or would not work when the storm broke. When nothing could be done to calm Polly down, Sally perforce must wait for the fit to play itself out, tolerating tears or even blows, ready to fetch a drink of water or to tuck an exhausted little girl into bed.

For Francis Eppes, that may have been enough. But for Elizabeth Eppes, there may have been something more, something complicated. As Abigail Adams would later observe, Sally was fond of Polly, and it appears that Polly liked to have Sally nearby. Whatever affection lay between these two girls was both a product of, and in defiance of, biological heritage. Family resemblances are quirky things, even in shadow families. Especially in growing children, we see fleeting glimpses of the father one day, the mother another, and sometimes even of ourselves. As much as Elizabeth Eppes ignored or rejected their kinship, and as much as Sally played her part in the approved family drama, surely there were times when, unwittingly and unwillingly, Elizabeth Eppes noticed an expression or a gesture, a look about the eyes or angle of the head, the shape of hands or feet or a way of laughing, that reminded her of her father, or one of her Wayles sisters (two of them now dead), or of her own children, or of herself. Sally Hemings was Polly Jefferson's flesh and blood, her aunt, to no less a degree than Elizabeth Eppes. Disconcerting as those resemblances were, they also offered some whisper of consolation.

And if Sally remained at Eppington once Polly was gone, what would they do with her? No matter how much they needed hands to do the backbreaking job of growing tobacco, Sally could not be sent into the fields, since Jefferson preferred that Hemings women not do heavy farmwork. If they kept her on as a maid in the Eppes household, Sally posed a particular kind of risk. She was, according to the few descriptions we have of her, very light-skinned and beautiful, "mighty near white . . . very handsome, long straight hair down her back" according to Isaac Jefferson, and "light colored and decidedly good-looking" in the words of Thomas Jefferson's grandson, Jefferson Randolph.

Jack Eppes, Elizabeth and Francis's son, was then fourteen, just the age when young masters began to assert their authority. Some boys also began to trumpet their budding sexuality by exploiting slave girls. Francis Eppes's brother, Richard Henry Eppes, had been around Jack's age when Richard Henry was murdered by a desperate slave girl. Did the master of Eppington worry about his own son? All this would be pure speculation, if we did not know more about Jack Eppes. He had a tendency, as his father would later say, to "fall in love." He would eventually marry his first cousin, Polly Jefferson, and years later, after Polly's death, Jack would follow in his grandfather's and father-in-law's footsteps, keeping his own shadow family with Betsy Hemings—Sally Hemings's niece.

For her part, Elizabeth Eppes had grown up in a household where her father had a sexual relationship with his slave, Betty Hemings, and maintained a slave family right alongside his free family. Sally Hemings, Elizabeth Eppes's half-sister, was biologically Jack's half-aunt. Did it occur to Elizabeth Eppes that if Jack determined to set his sights on Sally, he would be pressing a sexual relationship on her own sister?

The Eppeses thus may have had ample reasons to see Sally on her way—back to Monticello, preferably, but in the jumble of events, to England with Polly. Sally, of course, had no choice in the matter. If life at Eppington had been hard in many ways, there must also have been good moments, times when Polly was in a good mood, charming and wanting to play; warm spring days when Sally could steal a few minutes to walk through Francis Eppes's blooming gardens, maybe even visits back to Monticello. Sally may well have wanted to return to Monticello, which was, after all, her home, a lovely place where she was a member of a special family. But at Monticello, the kind master had been replaced by an overseer. Her brothers, Martin, Robert, and James, and sister Mary, were away, working on their own.

It is also possible that Sally wanted to go to France with Polly. Her brother James was in Paris, as was the master she doubtless remembered better than Polly did. Having seen Thomas Jefferson in the depths of his grief, knowing Polly's resistance to him, and separated from her own family, Sally might have felt sympathy for his longing for his children. Surely she sympathized with little Polly, who was to be cruelly forced away from the people she had come to love, at the very age when Sally herself had been sent away from her own Hemings kin. Sally knew that making the trip would require some bravery. Her brother Martin had demonstrated his courage when the British came to Monticello. Simply to board the ship and head off into the utterly unknown, Sally Hemings had to be brave, too.

IF POLLY JEFFERSON had dreaded the voyage with a vengeance, how much more perilous it was for Sally to take that trip! For one thing, Polly had been inoculated against smallpox, and Sally had not. But just as important, the two girls were miles apart socially. Polly quickly became the pet of the captain and crew. She was the daughter of the American ambassador, traveling under Captain Ramsay's protection. She would cling to Andrew Ramsay like a human barnacle, and he became attached to her in turn. For all her terror, little Polly was in a considerably more secure position than the pretty, very vulnerable Sally Hemings. Even if Ramsay tried to offer Sally some measure of protection, he clearly could not watch over her every second of the five-week journey. She would have to venture off on her own to fetch water or food, to get help if Polly was sick or disgruntled, to dispose of slops. Seagoing men were not known for their fine manners, even where genteel women were concerned. What might the sailors have had to say to a comely slave girl? What unsolicited contact could occur in the close passages of the ship? And what did Sally Hemings know of Algerian pirates who captured people and sold them into slavery, what did she hear either from her rough and ready shipmates, or from Virginia slaves who had their own memories of Arab slave catchers and traders?

The depredations of the Algerian pirates were, after all, common knowledge on both sides of the Atlantic. They even worried Patsy Jefferson, in school at the fashionable Abbaye de Panthémont in Paris, awaiting word of her little sister's voyage. Patsy wrote to her father, who was on tour in the south of France, to remind him to hurry back, "as you must be here for the arrival of my sister." Being in a convent school assuredly did not prevent Patsy from hearing or discussing the latest news. She related vivid details of a skirmish between an American ship and an Algerian corsair. "A Virginia ship coming to spain met with a corser of the same strength," she wrote. "They fought and the battle lasted an hour and a quarter. The Americans gained and boarded the corser where they found chains that had been prepared for them. They took them and made use of them for the algerians themselves."

Some who heard the story doubtless believed turnabout was fair play, but Patsy saw the event as a story of the iniquity of slavery.

"They returned to virginia from whence they are to go back to algers to change the prisoners to which if the algerines will not consent the poor creatures will be sold as slaves. Good god have we not enough? I wish with all my soul that the poor negroes were freed."

The *Robert* had the proper credentials to keep pirates away, and as long as she was with Polly, Sally would be relatively safe. But Sally must have been told that she would likely have to return across the ocean alone. She would have to cope, on her own, with the sea and the sailors and maybe even with slave-trading pirates. Sometimes even the brave have excellent reason to be afraid.

SMALL WONDER, THEN, that when they arrived in London on June 26, 1787, to be delivered to Abigail Adams by Captain Ramsay, Sally Hemings was not a very impressive figure. Jefferson had developed close relationships with both John Adams, now American minister to England, and his wife, Abigail, when the couple were still in Paris. He had written in December to let Abigail Adams know that Polly would be sailing to London, and that he hoped that she would "take her under your wing till I can have notice to send for her, which I shall do express in the moment of my knowing she is arrived. She is about 8. years old, and will be in the care of her nurse, a black woman, to whom she is confided with safety."

Adams had a terrible time prying Polly loose from the captain, and she was appalled, from the first, at Polly's resistance to her father. She was also aghast that "the old Nurse whom you expected to have attended her, was sick and unable to come. She has a Girl about 15 or 16 with her, the Sister of the Servant you have with you." Sally was only fourteen. Perhaps Abigail Adams overestimated her age because she looked older than she was. Or perhaps Adams simply could not believe that Jefferson's relatives would send his daughter across the ocean with someone that young.

By the next day, Adams had managed to calm Polly down; Polly rapidly transferred her attachment from the captain to her new protector. Adams, who had found Polly in such ragged condition that she had taken her shopping for "a few articles which she could not well do without," remained shocked at the idea of such a child being sent across the ocean with a young slave: "The Girl who is with her is quite a child, and Captain Ramsey is of the opinion will be of so little Service that he had better carry her back with him." Adams was understandably reluctant to give her approval to that plan without explicit instructions from Jefferson. "But of this you will be the judge. She seems fond of the child and appears good naturd."

Abigail Adams had considerable knowledge of the culture and character of men who made their living on the sea. Her husband had famously defended the British soldiers charged in the Boston Massacre by arguing that the mob that had taunted the redcoats into firing was nothing more than a rabble of "saucy boys, negroes and mullatoes, and outlandish jack tars." Abigail expressed no personal attachment to Sally Hemings, but she did see fit to purchase clothing for her, as she had for Polly, "as I should have done had they been my own," since both girls arrived with "cloaths only proper for the sea." If she had any thought of simply sending Sally back with Andrew Ramsay, she would likely not have put herself to that expense and trouble.

INSTEAD OF COMING to get Polly himself, Thomas Jefferson sent his French mâitre d'hotel, Adrien Petit. Polly, disappointed and betrayed once again by her father, fell into a fresh round of fits, which Abigail Adams sought in vain to relieve. Still, she believed that Polly would come around. When the child had first arrived, after five weeks at sea "with men only . . . she was rough as a little sailor, and then she had been decoyed from the ship, which made her very angry, and no one having any Authority over her; I was apprehensive I should meet with some trouble." But Abigail Adams was captivated by Jefferson's younger daughter, "a child of the quickest sensibility, and the maturest understanding . . . the favourite of every creature in the House." What a shame, Adams offered, that Jefferson must lose the pleasure of Polly's company by "committing her to a convent. Yet situated as you are," she agreed, "you cannot keep her with you. The Girl she has with her, wants more care than the child, and is wholly incapable of looking properly after her, without some superiour to direct her."

Dumas Malone took from Adams's remark a general lesson about Sally Hemings's role as Polly Jefferson's escort across the sea: "This girl proved to be of little help." Malone, one of the people who most vehemently denied Thomas Jefferson's later relationship with Sally Hemings, had reasons of his own for dismissing Sally Hemings as a nameless, useless nobody. But rather than following Malone's lead, we must put Abigail Adams's words in context. Polly Jefferson might be enchanting, but she was quite a handful, liable to pitch a shrieking fit at the thought of separation from whatever person served as her protector of the moment. She had been repeatedly deceived and manipulated, in ways that strike a modern parent as singularly cruel. Polly had learned to get her way by alternately charming and raging. One minute an "amiable lovely Child" who "reads to me by the hour with great distinctness, and comments on what she reads with much propriety," she was at the next moment "almost in a Frenzy."

Sally Hemings had no standing to take Polly in hand and make her behave. Her job was to do as Polly commanded. No one should have expected Sally to take on the job of correcting Polly, and Abigail Adams was not suggesting that she do so. In Adams's mind, Sally simply did not merit that much thought. Instead, Adams rather acidly pointed out that apart from arranging for Polly to go to a Catholic boarding school, something of which Adams clearly disapproved, Thomas Jefferson had not taken any steps to see that she was properly supervised, including during her five weeks at sea "with only men." Under the circumstances, he could hardly expect Sally to provide all the care and direction Polly needed.

And what did Abigail Adams mean when she wrote that Sally Hemings "wants more care than the child"? Adams obviously found Sally immature and seems to have regarded the enslaved girl with a mixture of pity and contempt. Sally had come to her poorly clothed and, to her eyes, too young, ignorant, and soft to govern the tempestuous and scintillating Polly Jefferson. The two girls were, to Adams's eyes, a study in contrasts. Polly Jefferson was educated: at nine, already a great reader and a writer of letters. Francis Eppes, like Thomas Jefferson, believed in schooling for girls and had written to Jefferson to ask him to find a tutor, "a man or Woman not younger than forty capable of teaching our girls French English erethmatick and musick." Polly was also a hearty eater, who had once said she was unable to write to her father because she had a rash on her arms, a malady her aunt Elizabeth chalked up to "eating too freely of butter'd muffins."

No one would have taken pains to procure an education for Sally Hemings, or have expected Sally to court the approval of a strange white woman by reading to her. If Sally could read at all, she would have had to persuade someone to teach her. She would have spent her years at Eppington dining not on butter'd muffins, but on slave rations, typically corn and fatty pork, and whatever vegetables, eggs, or meat she might get from an enslaved person who kept a garden or chickens. Sally probably had to work for those treats. On board the ship, Polly Jefferson would have been fed the choicest tidbits from the captain's table, while Sally Hemings ate whatever the cook saw fit to give her.

If the two girls arrived in London in torn and dirty dresses, desperately needing decent clothing, the quality of even their shabby garments marked the difference in their ranks. Abigail Adams would soon outfit Polly with fine Irish Holland frocks and muslin trimmed with lace, stockings and nightcaps and a brown beaver hat with a feather, leather gloves, and a blue satin sash and a comb and brush and a toothbrush. Adams bought for Sally Hemings enough calico to make two short gowns and coats, and Irish linen for aprons, stockings, and a handkerchief shawl. She paid six shillings and eight pence "for washing," presumably for the clothes in which Sally had arrived. Adams had also paid to have Polly's trunks delivered; we may assume that Sally's baggage was modest at best.

Though Abigail Adams was silent on the matter, Sally Hemings was very light-skinned, and may have borne some obvious physical resemblance to her niece. Such things are sometimes more apparent to strangers than to those who have schooled themselves not to see. That would have made the contrasts between the two girls all the more painfully plain.

While Polly Jefferson was emotionally unhinged when Abigail Adams knew her, she was evidently in good health. We cannot be sure of the same for Sally Hemings, although if she had been very sick, Adams would have mentioned the fact. But if Polly was distraught at the thought of being taken to her distant but loving father, with what emotions must Sally have faced the wild uncertainty of her own fate?

Sally too had been separated from all she knew and thrust on board a ship, subjected to five weeks with a volatile little mistress and a boatload of strange men. She was facing the prospect of staying in London, a dirty, noisy, scary place, the likes of which she had never seen, awaiting a long and frightening voyage back, alone, in worsening weather. Andrew Ramsay may have offered to "carry her back with him" but he said nothing at all about Sally Hemings in the letter he wrote to Thomas Jefferson on July 6, 1787, offering to take Polly all the way to Paris if necessary. Ramsay might have been, as Annette Gordon-Reed has written, "just a bit too eager" to take Sally Hemings away; Gordon-Reed reminds us that "sexual exploitation—either the potential for it or the actual experience of it—was a constant threat" in the lives of enslaved girls. But even if Ramsay had only noble motives for wanting to take Sally back to Virginia, members of the Hemings family knew that the best intentions of white sea captains were easily thwarted. Sally's brother James was in Paris. She may have wanted badly to accompany Polly, when the little girl was at last persuaded or compelled to go.

In the end, Sally Hemings found her way to Paris not because of her own wishes, but because Polly Jefferson wanted her to go. More importantly, she boarded a boat bound for France and not America because Thomas Jefferson was willing to have her come.

15

Paris

THE FOURTEEN-YEAR-OLD GIRL who traveled to France in the summer of 1787 was unsophisticated, but not innocent. Sally Hemings had grown up with revolution and invasion. Members of her family had been taken captive, and a place she knew had been pillaged. She had seen the British cavalry come riding up to the great house at Monticello. People close to her had died: her mistress and half-sister, two Lucys at Eppington (both her half-nieces), and her own nine-year-old sister, another Lucy. She knew people who had been bought and sold. Her master at Eppington had seen a slave girl hanged for the murder of his brother.

Sally had lived on Virginia farms her whole life, but the remoteness of such places did not keep out violence or sin or sorrow in the lives of the free or the enslaved. She had felt cold and heat and sickness and sadness. But she had known peaceful times, too, when Monticello and Eppington were quiet, green places ruled by the seasons and the habits of slavery, which were orderly and familiar.

Thomas Jefferson, awaiting the arrival of his daughter and her maid, surely believed he was waiting for two young girls, though he must have wondered how the years had changed his daughter and this slave who was also a blood relation, his beloved Martha's half-sister. Then again, he may not have given the matter a lot of thought. He had plenty to occupy his mind. He had only just returned from a mostly idyllic tour of southern France and Italy, and like many people who have been on vacation, he had a lot of catching up to do. In addition to his mundane duties—processing passports, negotiating for Americans who had business in France, seeking economic and political ties—he was contending with an international crisis. War between Turkey and Russia threatened to inflame all of Europe, with unclear but troubling consequences for the newborn United States.

Adrien Petit, Polly Jefferson, and Sally Hemings arrived in Paris on July 15, 1787. Polly "had totally forgotten her sister," Jefferson reported to Abigail Adams, "but thought, on seeing me, that she recollected something of me." Her reaction was understandable, as was Jefferson's similar response: "She neither knew us nor should we have known her had we met with her unexpectedly." Of all the Virginians present at the reunion in Paris, Thomas Jefferson had surely changed the least, in physical terms. True, he was dressing far more fashionably than he had three years earlier, but the three girls would have been absolutely transformed, the two eldest now heading into womanhood.

Madison Hemings, Sally's second son, would tell an interviewer that his mother had come to Paris as nearly a "young woman grown." Sally may have chosen to portray herself as more or less mature, for reasons we will soon explore, when she told her children about her time in Paris. Abigail Adams, on the other hand, had deemed Sally "quite a child" but "fond" and "good naturd" when she hosted the two girls in London. One way or another, Sally Hemings's time in Paris would change her forever.

PARIS MUST HAVE struck Sally and Polly as another planet. The dark and teeming streets, the fabulous boulevards, cacophonous with oxcarts and wagons groaning with stones or meat, driven by cursing teamsters; gilded carriages ferrying women with coiffeurs a foot high, gowned in silk and dripping with jewels, and men in satin and lace and silvery wigs; the harsh cries of street vendors hawking everything from cherries and chestnuts to live birds, old hats, snuffboxes, and soap; the plaintive wails of the unemployed, selling the rags they had picked from garbage heaps; the emaciated young girls, selling themselves. How marvelous, the magnificent colonnaded buildings, immense lush gardens, imposing statues of men on horseback. And how intimidating, the hulking women carrying heavy loads and brawling with one another at the top of their lungs. Strange men leered and hurled incomprehensible, threatening suggestions. And then there were the pitiful tattered figures of begging children and starving mothers, crying for bread. What did not assault the girls' eyes or ears would have attacked their noses, the outdoor privies of plantation life having nothing on the infamous open sewers of the French capital. Especially in July. If they were not feeling faint by the time they reached the Hôtel de Langeac, they must have had strong stomachs indeed.

As the hired coach turned off the Champs-Elysées and onto the Rue de Berri, into the courtyard, they beheld the two-story neoclassical façade of Thomas Jefferson's rented home, the Hôtel de Langeac. Sally Hemings and Polly Jefferson had known some grand houses, on the Virginia scale. Eppington, while no architectural novelty, was stately and imposing, with its white façade and red roof, its high ceilings and sweeping views. Monticello, though not yet the domed landmark it would become, was a fine brick building in command of a mountaintop, equipped with the columned porticos and grand salon that bespoke the importance and vision of the owner. But neither Sally nor Polly had ever seen anything like the great houses of Paris.

The Hôtel de Langeac was located at what was then the western edge of Paris. It was built in the shape of a trapezoid, squeezed into the place where the streets met at a sharp angle. The front doors opened into a great elliptical entrance hall, illuminated from above and leading to a circular salon with a skylight that inspired Jefferson in his later design of the dome room at Monticello. His private suite, upstairs, included an oval study overlooking the garden. The place was a refuge from the clamor of the city, with its bright, airy rooms, its extensive gardens, its gilded mirrors and gleaming floors, pianoforte and paintings and clocks, the kitchen hung with its immense battery of shiny copper pots and pans. Jefferson's house was also equipped with an indoor privy, a convenience that must have seemed a wonder to girls from the Virginia countryside.

THOMAS JEFFERSON WAS a creature of order and routine, in matters ranging from the laying of fires and winding of clocks, to the settling of girls who depended upon him. Within a week of her arrival, Polly had been dispatched to the Abbaye de Panthémont, the elite Catholic girls' boarding school that Patsy had attended since coming to France. Polly would live and study with her sister, with the promise of seeing her father once or twice a week.

Sally had a reunion of her own, with her brother James. He was just finishing up his apprenticeship in cooking and was about to be promoted to chef de cuisine in Jefferson's household. James was eight years older than Sally, and even before the journey to Paris, he had traveled more broadly than Sally ever had or would again, once she returned to America. How formidable he must have seemed, in his chef's toque and work uniform, speaking French and, very soon, earning regular wages.

Sally too would develop new skills during her time in France, but first there was some unfinished business. Jefferson would have to make a place for this young female slave in his decidedly masculine, French-speaking household. In addition to Petit, Jefferson employed a valet de chambre, a coachman, a *frotteur* (who polished the parquet floors by skating around on brushes), and a gardener, all Frenchmen. He had previously hired a woman to cook, but now James Hemings was making the transition from personal servant to chef de cuisine. However trustworthy Sally had proven herself by getting Polly safely across the ocean, she could not be sent out on errands, since she spoke no French and did not know the city. As soon as he could, Jefferson sent her off to the outskirts of town. She was to be inoculated against smallpox, a weeks-long ordeal of risk and recovery brilliantly reconstructed by historian Annette Gordon-Reed. Both Jefferson and Francis Eppes had made so much of the need for immunization that Sally must have been relieved that she would finally be protected from the dreaded disease. Jefferson entrusted her to the care of Dr. Robert Sutton and his sons, the foremost "inoculationists" not only in Paris, but in the world at the time. Sally would be isolated and carefully nursed while she suffered whatever symptoms she endured, and she evidently survived the experience without lasting effects. But what a painful, bizarre, and confusing way to be introduced to life in a foreign country, among complete strangers, most of whom spoke no English.

For more than two years, Sally Hemings lived in Paris. According to her son, Madison Hemings, she learned to speak French with some facility. She had to communicate with the other servants in the Jefferson household, and James had hired a tutor to help him learn the language. Polly and Patsy were also studying and speaking French at school, and Patsy was already beginning to forget her first language, and to resort to French sentence constructions even when she wrote in English. "I begin to have really great difficulty to write in English," she told her father in one letter, asking about the wrist he had broken earlier by writing, "Pray, how does your arm go?" By the time Sally Hemings returned to America, she was thinking in French, too, at least sometimes. Like many people who have treasured their time abroad, Sally would sprinkle French words into her sentences for years after.

In that summer of 1787, Thomas Jefferson gave Sally Hemings the attention due one more person for whom he was responsible, and probably not much more than that. It was his duty to take care of the people who depended upon him, especially females, even when he was occupied with a thousand other things, from matters of war and peace to the pursuit of his own happiness. Just as he made certain that Sally was secure against smallpox, he also needed to see that she had a place to stay, food to eat, clothing to wear. She may have lived in his house, or in the nearby servants' quarters. She ate what the other servants did, although her brother the chef likely introduced her to special treats, like his delicate "Snow Eggs," a custard and poached meringue confection known to later gourmet cooks as "Floating Island."

Sally had new words to wrap her mouth around, and new food to tempt her palate, and new clothes to make her presentable in the eyes of those who would identify her with her distinguished master. Patsy began to go out more in society, requiring her own elaborate dresses and accessories, including a maid to accompany her on social visits and to evening events. So Jefferson spent money on clothing for Sally. Just as he began to pay James Hemings for serving as his chef, Jefferson also began, on New Year's Day of 1788, to pay wages to Sally. It is not clear what kind of work she did to earn her pay. Now that Polly was at school, Sally was no longer serving as her maid on a daily basis, though she would likely have assisted both Patsy and Polly when they came home on weekends and for more extended visits, carrying their water and their waste, sewing up their ripped hems, tending their hair, scrubbing stains out of their gloves. She learned to care for the fine fabrics the Jefferson girls began to wear, and to do fancy sewing, a skill at which her eldest sister, Mary, excelled, and which Thomas Jefferson believed all women should master. With so little to do much of the time, Sally likely began her lifelong job as Thomas Jefferson's chambermaid, or *femme de chambre*.

A Virginia slave girl with money in her pocket may have found Paris a magical place full of wonderful things to see and do, to hear and taste, to inspect and buy. But if the city offered delights, it was also a place of unspeakable poverty, seething with the resentment of the many who labored for little, in the shadow of the glittering excesses of the few. The working women of Paris might roam the streets to ply their trades, to flirt and bargain and brawl, but the pretty young servant of a luminary like Thomas Jefferson, raised in relative isolation in Virginia and with an imperfect knowledge of French, must have found the clamor and bustle of the streets daunting, and sometimes dangerous.

There were other reasons that Sally might not have embraced all that Paris offered. Her brother James needed to be out in the city, elbowing his way through the markets and haggling for the things he required to prepare meals for an exacting master and numerous guests. But Sally's work would not often have taken her away from the house. The men who watched over her would not have given her a lot of room to roam on her own. James, a Virginian, after all, might well have felt that it was his duty to keep an eye on his beautiful little sister, amid so many perils and temptations. And the master, for all his own fascination with "the vaunted scene of Europe," was a man who believed, to the depth of his soul, that women needed to be protected, and men's duty was to provide that protection. Jefferson was absolutely appalled at the way European women of all ranks flaunted themselves in public.

*   *   *

THOMAS JEFFERSON HAD long believed in a natural law of gender, a separation of the roles and responsibilities of women and men that, ideally, confined women to the protected sphere of domesticity while giving men both the freedoms and the burdens of public life. The American Revolution had breached that divide, with mortal consequences for his beloved wife, and perhaps even some of his children. In Paris, experiencing wondrous sights, sounds, and sensations, amid heady talk of liberty and progress and even perfectibility, in the company of scintillating friends, including some notably intelligent, assertive, and ambitious women, Jefferson had begun to recover from Martha's death, to enjoy life, and to reimagine his own future.

But much as Jefferson relished the companionship of women in Paris, much as he learned to practice the gallantries and flirtations that made French society so effervescent, his time in Europe deepened and solidified his belief that nations could not be virtuous and progressive unless they safeguarded the differences between men and women, the separation of politics from polite society, the segregation of public from private life. In the months just before Polly Jefferson and Sally Hemings arrived in Paris, Thomas Jefferson had been traveling in the south of France and in Italy. He had seen endless examples of women out in public, doing men's work. For him, such sexual disorder was both a cause and a symptom of social injustice. He observed that in the least prosperous parts of Europe, the natural order of things had been upended. He began his "Notes on a Tour through Southern France and Italy" with a description of the countryside, and a critique of social life:

I observe women and children carrying heavy burthens, and laboring with the hough [hoe]. This is an unequivocal indication of extreme poverty. Men, in a civilized country, never expose

their wives and children to labour above their force or sex, as
long as their own labour can protect them from it.

Jefferson glossed over his own hypocrisy in making such a pronouncement, he who sent women by the scores out to his Virginia
fields to plow and hoe and cut tobacco on the frozen ground of late
winter and in the blazing summer sun. Back at Monticello, Ursula
presided over the slaughter of dozens of pigs and hung hundreds of
pounds of ham in his smokehouse. He did not extend the privileges
or responsibilities of free women to enslaved women, any more than
he affirmed the liberties of enslaved men.

But he had, after all, been away from Virginia for three years. Far
across the ocean, he was nurturing and polishing a nostalgic vision of
his life at Monticello as an unbroken idyll of happiness, an arcadian
counterexample to the artifice and corruption of Europe's most lush,
decadent, and teeming capital. As he thought about how women lived,
and where they belonged, he became more and more persuaded that
the United States was more progressive, more civilized, more moral
than Old Europe. In Languedoc, he saw women working as barge
hands and lock keepers on the canals, jobs that he considered "much
too laborious for them," though he did not suggest that those women
were physically unable to do their work. Presumably they were laboring "above their sex" rather than "above their force." But doing
such inappropriate work, Jefferson argued, not only taxed women's
strength, but also imperiled their morals. "Can we wonder if such of
them as have a little beauty prefer easier courses to get their livelihood,
as long as that beauty lasts?" he asked. He blamed the elite women who
hired male hairdressers and domestics for the corruption of working
girls: "Ladies who employ men in the offices which should be reserved
for their sex, are they not bawds in effect? For every man they thus
employ, some girl, whose place he has taken, is driven to whoredom."

(Left)
Thomas Jefferson
(1791), by Charles
Willson Peale.

(Below)
Page from Martha
Wayles Skelton
Jefferson household
accounts (1777).

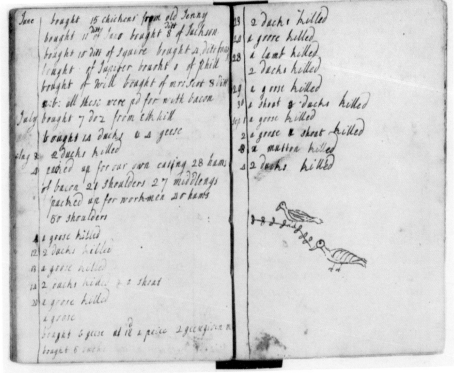

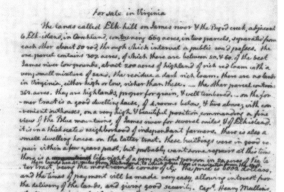

(Left)
Map of Elk
Hill property,
drawn from
memory by
Thomas
Jefferson
(1793).

(Below)
The house at
Eppington.

(Right)
Maria Cosway self-
portrait, mezzotint by
Valentine Green.

(Below)
The Monticello mansion.

(Above)
Thomas Jefferson's
bedroom and study.

(Right)
Martha Jefferson
Randolph, portrait by
Thomas Sully.

(Above)
Martha Jefferson Randolph's
sitting room (south square
room) at Monticello.

(Left)
The Monticello staircase.

(Above)
Cook's Room
in the south
dependency,
similar to the
room in which
Sally Hemings
may have lived
for a time.

(Right)
Ann Cary
Randolph
Bankhead,
portrait by
James Ford.

Ellen Wayles
Randolph
Coolidge,
portrait by
unknown artist.

Cornelia Jefferson
Randolph, bust by
William Coffee.

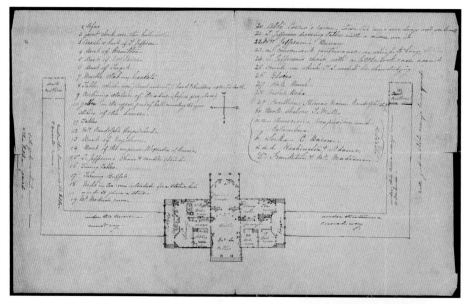

(Above) Floor plan of Monticello, with estate inventory, by Cornelia Jefferson Randolph.

(Below) Photograph of Virginia Randolph Trist and Ellen Randolph Coolidge, (ca. 1850s).

(Above)
Bell used by Martha Jefferson, given to Sally Hemings.

In March and April of 1788, nine months after Polly and Sally came to Paris, Jefferson set out on a seven-week tour of Holland and the Rhine valley. Once again he was alarmed that "the women here, as in Germany, do all sorts of work." In his journal, he proceeded to lay out his view of women's nature in greater detail than he ever had before:

While one considers them as useful and rational companions, one cannot forget that they are also objects of our pleasures. Nor can they ever forget it. While employed in dirt and drudgery, some tag of a ribbon, some ring or bit of bracelet, earbob or necklace, or something of that kind will show that the desire of pleasing is never suspended in them. How valuable is that state of society which allots to them internal employments only, and external to men. They are formed by nature for attentions and not for hard labour. A woman never forgets one of the numerous train of little offices which belong to her; a man forgets often.

Jefferson's attention to women's eagerness to please, their weakness and vulnerability to whoredom, verged on the obsessive. The arrival of his younger daughter and her maid strengthened his determination to see that the girls and women who lived under his protection were sequestered, not simply from hard labor, but from men's salacious gazes and thoughts. He prided himself on his ability to control his base impulses, but he knew that other men were not so virtuous. His daughters, and young Sally Hemings, the girl who, in fleeting moments, may have raised the ghost of his lost Martha, were members of his family, deserving of his care, his protection, his possession. Paris was a wicked and enticing place. He sent his daughters to a convent. He would certainly have done what he could to shield Sally Hemings from hungry eyes, even as he looked at her with eyes of his own.

16

Amazons versus Angels

OVER THE MONTHS that followed, Sally Hemings grew from a child into a woman, a coming of age that was, according to her son, bound inextricably with becoming the mistress—or, to use Madison Hemings's word, concubine—of Thomas Jefferson. Jefferson was a vigorous, charismatic, powerful man of forty-four living in a city renowned for its wickedness. He could have picked out sexual partners like a man at a morning market, inspecting a bin full of dewy ripe peaches. He knew any number of gorgeous, talented, well-born, and willing women. What in the world was going on in Thomas Jefferson's mind?

IN THE THREE years since he'd come to France, Thomas Jefferson had been amazed, amused, attracted, captivated, annoyed, and appalled by the women of Paris. While his gregarious predecessor, Benjamin Franklin, had reveled in his status as the ladies' favorite, Jefferson was more reserved and quite a bit more priggish than the celebrated Franklin, Paris's favorite bon vivant in a coonskin cap. But like Franklin, Jefferson presented himself as an American original, a sunny-tempered, democratic rustic. The Virginian was no stranger to politics, and Paris society was nothing if not political. He learned very quickly to sense the undertones, to watch out for intrigue in every gesture or glance.

Jefferson loved the concerts and theater and opera, so he found himself in places where women displayed themselves to the public. He was a popular figure at the salons and levees where women ruled. He learned to flirt and gossip, to clothe himself with elegance, to know fine food and wine. He spent time with flamboyant women and enjoyed socializing with them more than he ever had before, and a good deal more than he ever would again. The women of haute Paris were often pretty and sometimes witty, and a few were even learned. They dressed with elaborate care, cultivated the art of conversation, and in some cases excelled in the arts of music and painting. While he sought out a more conventional crowd than Franklin's circle of "atheists, deists and libertines," in John Adams's waspish phrase, Jefferson liked artists and musicians and writers and radicals who questioned the rules. He was well acquainted with women who dared to probe the edges of propriety. In one case, as we will see, he was simply bedazzled by an accomplished, mildly daring lady.

But even as Jefferson took his place in the social whirl, even as he insisted that he did "love this people," he remained a little aloof and considerably critical. He recoiled at the sight of peasant women and their city-dwelling sisters doing work he considered above their abilities and against their nature. Elegant ladies were also doing all kinds of things they should not have been doing. Their idleness and extravagance disgusted him; their forwardness took him aback. Some of them were especially aggressive, like the Dutch baroness he met when he attended a *lundi gras* masquerade with William Stephens Smith, John Adams's secretary, in 1786. Jefferson managed to slip out of her clutches, but "when Mr. Jefferson had made his escape," Smith said, the baroness "fastened her talons on me." The more Jefferson saw of

Parisian women, the more his memory of Martha's many trials faded and sweetened, leaving behind a vision of familial peace and bliss. He began to imagine America as the land of manly men who lived up to their responsibilities, and modest, genuine females who created domestic tranquility.

Paris changed Thomas Jefferson in many ways, from the quality of the lace at his cuffs, to the vintage of the wine on his table, and not least, to the scope of his architectural and philosophical imagination. But while he enjoyed watching and escorting, flattering and flirting with lovely ladies, he hated hearing them challenge and disagree. The more they insisted and disputed, the more he convinced himself that for the good of society, women must be protected from politics, and public business in turn must be protected from the disruptive presence of meddlesome and seductive females.

It was not just that women were not made for such things (though they weren't, in his view). They had an innate desire to please men, and that made them dangerous indeed, potential, if not actual, agents of corruption. Jefferson chose his friends and allies carefully, with an eye to their discretion and their judgment. Years earlier, he had decided not to hire a man who "appears to have a good enough heart, an understanding somewhat better than common but too little guard on his lips. I have marked him particularly in the company of women where he loses all power over himself and becomes almost frenzied. His temperature would not be proof against their allurements were such to be employed as engines against him." In Paris, he grew ever warier of men who lacked control, of men who used women to get ahead, of designing females with agendas of their own.

One such alluring woman was the immensely wealthy and beautiful Philadelphian Anne Willing Bingham. She was the daughter of Thomas Willing, the richest banker in America, and the wife of the second richest, William Bingham. Anne Bingham enchanted Jefferson when he met her in Paris, in the winter before Polly Jefferson and Sally Hemings arrived. But he despised William Bingham, whom he regarded as an ambitious and unscrupulous arriviste. As the Binghams made their way back to America, he wrote to warn James Madison that William Bingham "will make you believe he was on the most intimate footing with the first characters in Europe and versed in the secrets of every cabinet. Not a word of this is true. He had a rage for being presented to great men and had no modesty in the methods by which he could effect it." Not only was Bingham obnoxious, but he was using his wife to gain influence. "If he obtained access," Jefferson commented, " . . . it was with such as who were susceptible of impression from the beauty of his wife."

Anne Bingham was not just beautiful. She was intelligent and broad-minded. She relished the freedom with which French women moved and talked and acted, and had told Jefferson as much. On the heels of his warning to Madison about her husband, Jefferson wrote Mrs. Bingham a long letter, asking her, "Tell me truly and honestly, whether you do not find the tranquil pleasures of America preferable to the empty bustle of Paris." Then he painted a picture of the Parisian grande dame, a passage that ranks as one of the funniest and most savage in Jefferson's entire correspondence:

At eleven o'clock it is day chez Madame. The curtains are drawn. Propped on bolsters and pillows, and her head scratched into a little order, the bulletins of the sick are read, and the billets of the well. She writes to some of her acquaintance and receives the visits of others. If the morning is not very thronged, she is able to get out and hobble round the cage of the Palais royal: but she must hobble quickly, for the Coeffeur's turn is to come, and a tremendous turn it is! Happy if he does not make her arrive when dinner is half over! The torpitude of digestion a little passed, she flutters half an hours thro' the streets by way of paying visits, and then to the Spectacles. These finished, another half hour is devoted to dodging in and out of the doors of her very sincere friends, and then away to supper. After supper cards; and after cards bed, to rise at noon the next day, and to tread, like a mill-horse, the same trodden circle over again.

Jefferson figured that Anne Bingham would get a laugh out of his biting portrait, but he also attached a serious moral: "Thus the days of life are consumed, one by one, without an object beyond the present moment: ever flying from the ennui of that, yet crying it with us; eternally in pursuit of happiness which keeps eternally before us."

At that moment, he was, of course, insisting that his youngest daughter be taken from her home in Virginia and sent across the ocean to France. Still, he embraced a romantic image of home life in America, a vision of peace and harmony that he himself had known only fleetingly over the course of his own time-tossed, tragic marriage:

In America, on the other hand, the society of your husband, the fond cares for the children, the arrangements of the house, the improvements of the grounds fill every moment with a healthy and useful activity. Every exertion is encouraging, because to present amusement it joins the promise of some future good. The intervals of leisure are filled by the society of real friends, whose affections are not thinned to cob-web by being spread over a thousand objects.

Jefferson closed his letter by offering to send Mrs. Bingham news of the latest fashions, and perhaps even some items of couture, although he declined to pick them out himself. He ended with a poke at the political pretensions of some ladies. Mrs. Bingham should designate someone to choose any clothes he sent her, or perhaps "we will call an assembleé des Notables to help you out of the difficulty, as is now the fashion."

That winter, as he awaited word of Polly's voyage, it seemed to him that Paris women really were doing outrageous things, right out in public. The brawny market hawkers who hollered and quarreled could be forgiven their unladylike behavior, having to make a living, after all. But even fine ladies were forgetting themselves, intruding into business in which they had no place. Jefferson was willing enough to talk a little politics with women who did not push things too far. In letters to his learned female friends, he routinely mixed observations on events of the day with gossip, fashion news, and light flirtation. He told his friend the Comtesse de Noailles de Tessé that he had some ideas for a reorganization of the French government along more democratic, American lines, ending his proposal with a morsel of flattery: "This is my plan Madam; but I wish to know yours, which I am sure is better." He corresponded with Abigail Adams on matters great and small. Her outraged response to the "mobbish insurgents" who fomented the backcountry revolt in Massachusetts known as Shays' Rebellion had prompted Jefferson to observe, "I like a little rebellion now and then." But we should see these exchanges as news swapping, not policy making. Neither of these learned women advocated a real role for women in government, and neither proposed to the famous apostle of liberty that he ought to think about extending the Rights of Man to woman.

POLLY AND SALLY arrived in the summer of 1787, in the midst of international turmoil and rising civil unrest. That fall, with his daughters installed in the convent and Sally Hemings recovering from her inoculation at a house on the edge of the city, Thomas Jefferson wrote a staggering number of letters about everything from commerce to science. He handled myriad matters for American citizens with affairs in France, and French persons with business in America. He paid for wine and art and furnishings, dishes and phosphorescent matches, a bust of Lafayette for the state of Virginia and a consignment of American flora and fauna (including a moose skeleton!) for the Comte de Buffon.

But Jefferson also had women on his mind. The previous year, he had shaken off the worst of his grief over Martha. In July 1786, he learned that William Stephens Smith, the man with whom he had attended the menacing masquerade in Paris, had married the Adams's daughter, Abigail. In an exuberant letter studded with exclamation points, Jefferson offered his congratulations to the groom, adding a mildly bawdy suggestion: "May your days and nights be many and full of joy! May their fruits be such as to make you feel the sweet union of parent and lover, but not so many as that you may feel their weight! . . . I will wish you a good night. I beg your pardon, I had forgot that you would have it without my wishes."

This warm testament to the husband's joys bespoke Jefferson's memory of the passion he and Martha had shared. The dangers of pregnancy, those "private miseries" that had caused Martha's death and his own unspeakable pain, seemed to have vanished from Jefferson's mind. He concluded another letter to Smith with jocular greetings to "Mrs. Adams and Mrs. Smith. I hope the former is very well and that the latter is, or has been, very sick, otherwise I would observe to you that it is high time." How could he have forgotten so much? People in love are susceptible to amnesia, and by this time, Thomas Jefferson was wildly in love.

THE OBJECT OF Jefferson's passion was a beautiful artist and musician, Maria Hadfield Cosway. She had been born near Florence, Italy, in 1759, the daughter of English parents, her father a wealthy Manchester merchant who operated a fashionable hotel for English tourists. Educated at convent schools, Maria had been a child prodigy in music, painting, and languages. She had studied with celebrated artists in Rome, including Joseph Wright of Derby and Henry Fuseli. She painted mostly religious subjects, and by the age of nineteen was elected to the Academy of Fine Arts in Florence.

From her earliest days, Maria was torn between her desire for a religious vocation and her love of art and music. In 1778, when her father died intestate, she wanted to enter the novitiate, but her many friends and promoters convinced her to go to London and concentrate on painting and composing. Her mother was desperate to see her married, settled, and secure. At nineteen, Maria was charming, blond, blue-eyed, and lovely as well as talented and ambitious. She became a protégé of Angelica Kauffmann, the great Swiss-born painter who was among the founders of the British Royal Academy of Painting and Sculpture. Soon Maria was the toast of London society. She fended off numerous suitors before finally settling on—and settling for—the brilliant, rich, and famously eccentric painter Richard Cosway, the most successful miniaturist of his day, who was evidently as grotesque as Maria was beautiful. One historian described him as "a preposterous little Dresden china manikin with a face like a monkey," a dandy in the extreme who was determined to turn Maria into the chief ornament of his overadorned salon. She was ambivalent about the marriage from the first, to say the least. For all her education, Maria had the naïveté of a convent-bred girl, and her new husband ran in fast company. Richard Cosway was said to have had affairs with people of both sexes, and he painted pornographic snuffboxes for clients including the libertine Prince of Wales. While Richard attempted to mold her into a submissive English wife, Maria resisted his attempts to confine and control her. She painted, even exhibiting at the Royal Academy, and continued with her music, giving "Great Concerts" in the enormous parlor of their ostentatious mansion. Maria Cosway also made friends by the dozens. She had plenty of artistic talent, but her gift for friendship was perhaps even greater.

THE AMERICAN PAINTER John Trumbull introduced Maria Cosway to Thomas Jefferson in the late summer of 1786, when the Cosways were visiting Paris. Jefferson and Maria likely met at the Halle au Bléds, the domed grain market that was as much an architectural wonder as it was a place of commerce. From that moment on through the autumn, Jefferson and Maria spent every possible moment together, sometimes all by themselves. Richard Cosway was busily drumming up commissions for himself, painting miniatures for the nobility of Europe, and pursuing his own amours. He had kept a close eye on his wife when they first married, but by this time, by mutual consent, the Cosways seem to have given one another considerable room to move. If Richard Cosway was jealous of the time Maria spent with the tall, charming American ambassador, no hint of his feelings has surfaced.

But we do know that Maria Cosway and Thomas Jefferson were smitten with each other. They took advantage of every moment together to nurture a romantic friendship that both found sweet and stimulating. Over the rest of Jefferson's life, he and Maria Cosway exchanged a series of warm, admiring letters unparalleled in his correspondence, letters that reflected the changes in their fates and fortunes as Jefferson rose to power, retired, and grew aged, and as Maria abandoned marriage and the madding crowd for a life less frivolous, as the founder of convent schools for girls. No one could imagine that the sweet and simpering coquette depicted in Richard Cosway's drawings of his wife would one day be the stooped, blocky, beatific old lady who was appointed a baroness of the Austrian empire for her work as an educator of women. Of course, Jefferson scholars have cared mostly about Maria's Paris interlude with Thomas Jefferson, and their speculations about the liaison between the two sometimes read like schoolgirl gossip. Arguing about whether they ever had sexual relations is a little like playing tennis with an invisible ball. Still, Maria Cosway was the first woman to capture Thomas Jefferson's attention after the death of his wife.

Maria and Richard Cosway left Paris for Antwerp, Belgium, in October 1786, leaving Jefferson suffering not only from the pain of her departure, but from the agony of a broken wrist, injured while "vaulting a stile" on some recent, unwise frolic. He rode part of the way out of town with the Cosways in their carriage, got out, and "walked, more dead than alive" to the other side of the street, where his own carriage waited to take him back to the Hôtel de Langeac. That night, he sat down to write to Maria Cosway, producing (painfully, with his left hand) the most celebrated letter in his voluminous correspondence, his extended "Dialogue between My Head and My Heart." In the form of a mock debate between restraining reason and unruly emotion, Jefferson rehearsed every memorable moment of their time together. For propriety's sake, he sang the praises of both Cosways, "these good people," but the letter was addressed to "My Dear Madam," and his thoughts clearly dwelled on the lady. He celebrated her "qualities and accomplishments belonging to her sex, which might form a chapter apart for her; such as music, modesty, beauty, and that softness of disposition, which is the ornament of her sex and charm of ours." He insisted on imagining that she might come to America—"I see things wonderfully contrived sometimes to make us happy"—tempting her with the chance to paint "the Cascade of Niagara, the passage of the Patwomac thro the Blue mountains, the Natural Bridge . . . And our own dear *Monticello*." Maria, he said, wanted "only subjects worthy of immortality to render her pencil immortal." That summer, he traveled in northern Italy, missing her mightily: "I am born to lose everything I love. Why were you not with me?" But he did not seriously expect that when he returned home, as inevitably he must, this woman both accustomed to the worldly pleasures of London and Paris, and devoted to the Church of Rome, would follow him back to faraway Virginia.

Maria Cosway returned to Paris without her husband in the fall of 1787. But by this time, Polly Jefferson had arrived. To Maria's annoyance, Jefferson was too busy to make time for her when she was available. Much to Jefferson's frustration, Maria was herself caught up in a social whirl that kept them from spending time alone. She may, moreover, have been nursing something of a grudge against him. The morning she left Paris, they were to have breakfast, but instead she fled at 5 A.M., without even telling Jefferson good-bye. "I leave you with very melancholy ideas," she wrote him. "You have given, my dear Sir, all your commissions to Mr. Trumbull, and I have the reflection that I cannot be useful to you." She may have been referring to the various errands Jefferson had asked Trumbull to do for him in London. But Jefferson was also devoting some of his precious time to posing for Trumbull, who was then working on his famous painting of the signing of the Declaration of Independence, as well as at least one miniature of Jefferson. A painter of portraits and miniatures herself, Cosway may have been jealous of Trumbull. When she returned to England in December, the romance had cooled considerably.

Such histrionic gestures did not impress Thomas Jefferson, who hated public displays of temper, particularly on the part of women. Maria Cosway had charmed and vexed him. But she never challenged his ideas of what a woman should be. Indeed, if anyone in Paris struck him as the embodiment of desirable femininity, of the yielding warmth and sweetness that he treasured and craved, it was Maria Cosway. In later years she would display the devotion to duty, seriousness of purpose, and regard for peace and harmony that made him rejoice when her letters arrived, remember their delightful time together, and value her friendship all the rest of his days.

*   *   *

OTHER LADIES, HE believed, were going a little crazy. As winter turned to spring, the people were hungry, the French government was in financial crisis, and the fever for politics swept through the most exalted circles of Parisian society. Jefferson was appalled. The salons that had once delighted him with conversation about art and music, architecture and science, humor and coquetry, were now arenas of raging argument. "Society is spoilt by it," he wrote to his friend the Marquise de Bréhan, then traveling in America with her brother-in-law (and lover), the Comte de Moustier. "Instead of the gaiety and insouciance which has distinguished it heretofore, all is filled with political debates into which both sexes enter with equal eagerness." That summer of 1788, as bread riots broke out and the danger of wider rebellion loomed, he complained to Maria Cosway that "the civil dissensions, tho' they have yet cost no blood and will I hope cost none, still render conversation serious, and society contentious. How gladly I would take refuge in your coterie. Your benevolence, embracing all parties, disarms the party-dispositions of your friends, and makes of yours an asylum for tranquility."

If only the soothing ministrations of ladies could calm, instead of inflame, the rising rage on the way to revolution. But to his alarm, the contagion threatened to cross the Atlantic and infect even his own countrywomen. Anne Willing Bingham had replied to his letter satirizing the women of Paris with a ringing defense of her French friends. "I agree with you that many of the fashionable pursuits of the Parisian Ladies are rather frivolous . . . but the Picture you have exhibited, is rather overcharged. You have thrown a strong light upon all that is ridiculous in their Characters, and you have buried their good Qualities in the Shade. It shall be my task to bring them forward, or at least to attempt it." She admitted that the ways of French women might not play so well in America, and owned that "the state of Society in different Countries requires corresponding Manners and Qualification." But Anne Bingham was not stepping back; quite the contrary. Imagine Thomas Jefferson's dismay as he read Bingham's letter making the case for female assertiveness in the boldest political language:

> The women of France interfere in the politics of the Country, and often give a decided Turn to the Fate of Empires. Either by the gentle Arts of persuasion, or by the commanding force of superior Attractions and Address, they have obtained that Rank and Consideration in society, which the sex are intitled to, and which they in vain contend for in other Countries. We are therefore bound in Gratitude to admire and revere them, for asserting our Privileges, as much as the Friends of the Liberties of mankind reverence the successful Struggles of the American Patriots.

It took Jefferson nearly nine months to reply. When he did, he seemed to be responding as much to the tumult around him as to Anne Bingham's letter. She had requested fashion magazines as well as some theater pieces, and he sent both. "We have now need of something to make us laugh," he said, "for the topics of the times are sad and eventful. The gay and thoughtless Paris is now become a furnace of Politics. All the world is run politically mad. Men, women, children talk nothing else; and you know that naturally they talk much, loud and warm. Society is spoilt by it." He appealed to her vanity, even as he reminded her of her place:

> You too have had your political fever. But our good ladies, I trust, have been too wise to wrinkle their foreheads with politics. They are contented to soothe and calm the minds of their

husbands returning ruffled from political debate. They have the good sense to value domestic happiness above all other, and the art to cultivate it beyond all others. There is no part of the earth where so much of this is enjoyed as in America. You agree with me in this: but you think that the pleasures of Paris more than supply its want: in other words that a Parisian is happier than an American. You will change your opinion, my dear Madam, and come over to mine in the end. Recollect the women of this capital, some on foot, some on horses, and some in carriages hunting pleasure in the streets, in routs and assemblies, and forgetting that they have left it behind them in their nurseries; compare them with our own countrywomen occupied in the tender and tranquil amusements of domestic life, and confess that it is a comparison of Amazons and Angels. . . . As for political news of battles and sieges, Turks and Russians, I will not detail them to you, because you would be less handsome after reading them.

To Thomas Jefferson, there was nothing strange about telling a thoughtful and accomplished woman that her life's mission lay in devoting her every effort to creating a peaceful household for a man he considered a pompous and unscrupulous self-promoter. If anything, Anne Bingham's insistence on women's right to stand up for their beliefs had lessened his esteem for her. In his mind, she had joined the party of the unruly Amazons of Paris, betraying her sister Angels of America.

Jefferson was not in the habit of talking about angels. But when he did, he thought of Martha. He had referred to her as an angel in that first wrenching letter to Elizabeth Eppes after Martha's death; in this letter to one of the most cosmopolitan women in America, he drew on a memory of life at Monticello gone gauzy with nostalgia. In his imagination, no wells went dry, no slaves were whipped (let alone murdered), no babies agonizingly pushed out, only to die, and certainly no tramp of soldiers' boots disturbed domestic peace. All that remained was the vision of a cheerful, submissive, saintly female, serving without question or complaint the needs of her weary man. Doubtless Thomas Jefferson had enjoyed precious moments of love, ease, and acceptance, had basked in the warmth he shared with Martha. Doubtless she had waited for him, on so many nights when he had been away in Philadelphia or Williamsburg, and welcomed him joyously back to the home he had missed so much. But what man could edit life so ruthlessly, produce a vision so appealing, and not want to find a way back to that protected, tranquil, imagined home? What kind of woman would be able to—would be compelled to—play the part assigned to her in this domestic fantasy?

Martha herself was no angel. Angels do not generally extract death-bed promises. With one foot in the grave, Martha had half dragged him in with her, with a request that conveys a possessiveness that may seem to us the height of cruelty. She was, after all, a widow herself, who had found a second husband she evidently loved dearly. Why deny Thomas his own chance at happiness? In truth, this was a very particular type of promise. She had asked that he forgo marriage, saying nothing of sex, not even anything of love.

Let's not forget that Martha Jefferson made her husband swear his oath never to remarry in front of Elizabeth Hemings, the enslaved woman who had replaced her own mother and stepmothers in her father's bed, and Critta and Sally Hemings, two of the children of that union. During that last illness, when she needed to call a servant, she rang a small bronze bell she kept by her bedside. After she died, that bell, according to Hemings family tradition, was given to Sally Hemings.

Martha's death was both a devastating loss and a liberation for Thomas Jefferson. He had ventured as far as Philadelphia that summer of 1776 when Martha almost died, and he had resolved that he would never be so far from her again. Had she survived, it is unlikely that he would have taken the offer to go to Paris, or been able to throw himself into politics as he did after her death.

Jefferson cloaked his burning ambition with a modesty his political enemies saw as the cunning of a born liar. But ambitious as he was, he sincerely believed that he had a duty to serve the people, his state, and his nation, and to further the cause of democracy. Much as he would have loved to have an angel in his house, he could not have had a wife who made claims on his time and distracted him from the affairs of state as he charted his rise to the top. Maria Cosway delighted him and awakened his sexual desire. But captivating as she was, she was too European, too sophisticated, too formidable, too public a woman for Thomas Jefferson, and in any case, she was married (a fact that actually suited his needs). The Jefferson who conducted American business in Paris was a man in his prime and on his way up. He had no intention of retiring from politics. He had made his promise to remain unmarried, and he did not, it seems, want a wife at all. But he did long for the comfort and joy of a woman who would welcome him home, make no demands, be content with an entirely domestic life, and accept his authority and his affections without cavil or complaint.

Who could more perfectly fulfill his vision than the young, impressionable, beautiful, enslaved half-sister of the departed angel, now growing into womanhood before his very eyes?

Sally's Choice

When Mr. Jefferson went to France Martha was a young woman grown, my mother was about her age, and Maria was just budding into womanhood. Their stay (my mother's and Maria's) was about eighteen months. But during that time my mother became Mr. Jefferson's concubine, and when he was called back home she was enceinte by him. He desired to bring my mother back to Virginia with him but she demurred. She was just beginning to understand the French language well, and in France she was free, while if she returned to Virginia she would be re-enslaved. So she refused to return with him. To induce her to do so he promised her extraordinary privileges, and made a solemn pledge that her children should be freed at the age of twenty-one years. In consequence of his promises, on which she implicitly relied, she returned with him to Virginia. Soon after their arrival, she gave birth to a child, of whom Thomas Jefferson was the father. It lived but a short time. She gave birth to four others, and Jefferson was the father of all of them. Their names were

Beverly, Harriet, Madison (myself) and Eston—three sons and one daughter. We all became free agreeably to the treaty entered into by our parents before we were born.

—Madison Hemings in an interview with a radical
Republican newspaper editor in 1873

SALLY HEMINGS SPENT her first months in Paris adjusting to an alien culture, recuperating from inoculation, learning her way. She must have struggled to make herself understood to anyone except her brother James and the three Jeffersons. Patsy and Polly were in school, and Thomas Jefferson was busy with his work, his friends, and his frustrating not-quite-romance with Maria Cosway. In the spring of 1788 he traveled in France, Holland, and Germany and was gone for seven weeks. By the time he returned to Paris, the political crisis in France was approaching a crescendo.

Then came a killing winter, more horrible than anything Jefferson had ever known. "We are here experiencing a Siberian degree of cold," he wrote to Francis Eppes. "In November the thermometer was down at 8°. and twice this month at 6°. with every prospect of long continuance. A snow and cold North-Easter carry off houseless and ill-fed men here, as a cold Northwester carry off houseless and ill-fed cattle in Virginia." By December 1788, the temperature had dropped further, down to nearly ten degrees below zero, and Jefferson told Francis Eppes, "the cold still continues and occasions very general sickness." Still, it was Paris, where misery and magic dwelled side by side. The grandest Parisians drove their carriages on the ice of the Seine, which was "covered with thousands of people from morning to night, skaiting and sliding."

Sally Hemings may or may not have been among those who were ill, but Patsy and Polly, in close quarters at Panthémont, contracted typhus.

They were stricken with fevers and chills and wracking coughs and thready pulses. "I have for two months past had a very sick family, and have not as yet a tranquil mind on that score," Jefferson wrote to Maria Cosway in January. Both girls were taken out of school and brought to the Hôtel de Langeac to recover. Jefferson had sent them to be educated and protected, but the convent had been the source of infection. Paris had become a more and more threatening place for his daughters.

Sally also knew some of the girls from Panthémont. Patsy's friend Marie Jacinthe de Botidoux wrote a letter to Patsy years later, asking her to "kiss Polly for me and give my best to Mlle. Sale [Sally]." Had Marie de Botidoux thought of Sally Hemings simply as her friend's slave, she might not have referred to her with the honorific title of "mademoiselle." But unless Patsy or Polly offered the information, the convent students may not have understood that the very light-skinned Sally was a slave or, for that matter, that she was of African as well as English descent. If the girls at Panthémont did know, they would not have had American ideas about race. Neither might they have been surprised at a family resemblance between Patsy or Polly and Sally. Convent schools often served as places of refuge for impoverished noblewomen and girls, some of whom played the role of servant/companion to their better-off relatives. Some, assuredly, were illegitimate daughters. Doubtless everyone gossiped about such mysterious relations.

Of course, this was an unprecedented time in French history, even at the Abbaye de Panthémont. The daughters of the French nobility were no more immune to political passions than their mothers and fathers. Some showed their radicalism by fraternizing with the lower orders. Patsy Jefferson had expressed the fervent wish that "the poor negroes were freed," and she may have treated Sally, who was only one year younger than Patsy, with affection. Friends like Marie de Botidoux also avowed a fervent devotion to democracy and the unfolding revolution; Marie boasted about gossiping with "the fish-wives" about the queen.

When the Jefferson girls brought typhus home to the Hôtel de Langeac from Panthémont, Sally Hemings would have served as their nurse, if she was not herself too sick to help. During the darkest days of that dire, frigid winter, cooped up in a chilled and afflicted house, all the shivering Virginians must have ached for the heat of home. "Surely it was never so cold before," Jefferson wrote to Maria Cosway. "To me who am an animal of a warm climate, a mere Oran-ootan, it has been a severe trial. . . . The weather has cut off communication between friends and acquaintances here."

Thomas Jefferson was a frozen, worried, lonely man. Who would not have been susceptible to the comforting warmth of another body, a fellow sufferer from the care and the cold, a beautiful, kindhearted girl? Sally Hemings, whatever fear, doubt, and even anger she may have felt toward him, was a long way from home, in a frigid city. Surely she longed for comfort of her own.

Sally was probably near or past her sixteenth birthday when Thomas Jefferson claimed her as his sexual partner, his mistress, his concubine. Whatever passed between them was tinged with secrecy and shame. Perhaps for that reason, Sally was sent away, to spend five weeks with Jefferson's launderer, Dupré. Jefferson paid Dupré for her board and "washing" (or laundry) at the end of April 1789, a week after he paid the final bill for Patsy and Polly at Panthémont. Sally may have been learning how to clean and repair the fine clothing Jefferson was now buying for himself and his daughters. Or there may have been other reasons why Jefferson determined to send her off for a time at the very moment that his daughters were coming home. Still, Sally was back at the Hôtel de Langeac by the first week in May. In that spring of 1789, Jefferson laid out money for clothing for Sally, uncharacteristic expenses for a servant to whom he was paying wages and providing room and board. Wherever she was, she was in his accounts and in his thoughts.

THOMAS JEFFERSON WAS thirty years older than Sally Hemings. His conduct toward her was predatory and exploitative. This young woman without her own means or home, living in a foreign country far away from nearly all her family, depended upon Jefferson for her life and livelihood. As a slave, she possessed neither the right to consent to nor to refuse his attention, no matter how she felt about him. She was unspeakably vulnerable. When Thomas Jefferson took Sally Hemings to his bed, he made her his victim.

But in doing so, he was, as they used to say, no worse than he should have been. In Jefferson's universe, men and women never met as equals. Of course, as a slave, Sally could not hope to aspire to the title her half-sister had held, that of Mrs. Jefferson. But by the time Sally Hemings and Thomas Jefferson had sexual relations, she had already learned that in France she was not enslaved at all. The minute she set foot on French soil, she had become a free woman. Her brother James had been in Paris for three years when Sally arrived. If he decided to claim his freedom and remain in France, Jefferson could not make him go back to America. Given the agreement he and Jefferson made in 1793, James Hemings may well have seized hungrily on that freedom, with an energy that reflected the cries for liberty ringing through the streets of Paris, roiling the markets and threatening the merchants and terrifying and exhilarating peasants and bourgeois and nobles all. James did go back to Virginia, but he would make a deal with Thomas Jefferson: he agreed to train his replacement in Jefferson's kitchen, and Jefferson promised in turn to grant James his emancipation. The young man who bargained with no less a personage than the cool and commanding Ambassador Jefferson would not have hesitated to let his little sister know that she too was free in France. Why would conversations in the scullery be any less ablaze with politics than they were in the salons? In the unlikely event that James had not told Sally she was free, surely someone else did.

According to Sally's son Madison, his mother used her knowledge of her freedom to cut her own deal with Thomas Jefferson. Sometime after that brutal winter of 1788–89, Sally Hemings had become pregnant with a child who was destined to live only a short time. Madison Hemings used the French word *enceinte*, perhaps his mother's way of both invoking her time in France and speaking in a genteel euphemism. Madison may have been in error about this pregnancy; there is no evidence of such a child in any written document, and the man who would later claim to have been that child, Thomas Woodson, was evidently not the son of Thomas Jefferson. Generations of Jefferson scholars have denied that the child existed. But Madison Hemings has proven a reliable source of information on his family's history in nearly all regards. We have two particularly strong reasons to assume that Sally was pregnant, and that Jefferson was the father of her child: the fact that Sally Hemings chose slavery in Virginia over freedom in France, and the fact that Thomas Jefferson freed her children.

Jefferson wanted to take Sally back to Virginia. He must have understood the overwhelming advantages he possessed in making his case. As a young, unwed pregnant woman "just beginning to understand the French language well," Sally's prospects for supporting herself in Paris were anything but bright. She had been dealt a very weak hand.

But she played her best card with skill. Whatever else she knew about Thomas Jefferson, she understood that they were doing something together that they should not have been doing. His conscience must have plagued him even as he worked to persuade her to come back to America with him. Jefferson would have been troubled by the idea of depriving a free person, even a free woman, of her liberty, even as her womanly weakness and dependence provoked in him a sense of obligation. As we have seen, Madison Hemings reported that his mother let Jefferson know that she meant to dispose of her freedom on her own terms.

As ambassador to France, Thomas Jefferson's job was to make treaties. Calling this agreement a treaty had the ring of Jefferson's joking with Anne Bingham about calling an Assembly of Notables to pick out her clothes. But the language, in this case, belonged to Sally Hemings. When she told her children that she had made a treaty with Thomas Jefferson, it carried the inflection of an inside joke between a woman who knew the position and the power of the man she was dealing with, and a man who was willing to be made fun of by a serving girl, a young female of mixed racial ancestry, a woman even then surrendering her freedom. There was something teasing and flirtatious and affectionate, and sardonic and ironic, in the tale Sally Hemings told, something that gives us a glimpse of a woman some called "Dashing Sally."

Treaties are also solemn, stately agreements with the force of international law. Treaty breaking is cause for war. Despite powerful incentives to violate his part of the agreement, Thomas Jefferson lived by the spirit and the letter of his treaty with Sally Hemings to the very end of his days.

THOMAS JEFFERSON HAD his pick of female companions in Paris, and surely could have selected one of any number of American angels in Virginia. He chose Sally Hemings. In the strange hall of mirrors that he inhabited, her insistence upon her freedom may have given him a rationale for wanting to possess her. She was already exceptional in his eyes, not simply a slave girl, but a Hemings, a Wayles, Martha's sister. She was, moreover, very light-skinned, and of mixed heritage. Jefferson had expressed his views on race mixing in his *Notes on the State of Virginia*, arguing that "blacks" were by nature inferior to "whites" in most regards. He argued, with confident circularity, that in order to prevent mixing, the races must keep separate. But like many southern slaveholders, Jefferson was fully capable of believing African Americans to be inferior to whites, of being, in short, a racist, while taking to his bed a woman who had African ancestors. Generation upon generation of white southern men did so, and no amount of social disapproval, of legal sanction, of shame or blame or personal peril ever stopped them.

Still, we are talking about Thomas Jefferson, a man to whom liberty was a cause worth pledging one's life, fortune, and sacred honor, who had fumed as the Continental Congress eviscerated the antislavery passages from his immortal Declaration. Why wouldn't Sally's insistence on her freedom make sense to him, help him see her as a woman and *not* simply a slave? Jefferson was, as Joseph Ellis has so eloquently explained, a brilliant rationalizer. Surely no one was in a better position to protect Sally Hemings than he was, and he owed her that much. Having brought her across the sea into a gathering revolution and then debauched her, he could not abandon her, even if he was leaving her a free woman. As he saw it, his honor lay not in letting her go, but rather in keeping her, in taking care of a woman to whom he had made a solemn vow. Recollecting the presence of Betty Hemings and her daughters alongside his own children at his wife's deathbed, he might even have told himself that Martha would have wanted it that way.

AND NOW WE come to the heart of the matter. Sally could not have known, as she stood her ground in Paris and made the fateful decision to return to America, whether Thomas Jefferson would keep his word. White men lied to slave women. Trusting Thomas Jefferson,

and agreeing to go home with him, was not an entirely rational decision on her part. Why would she do so?

Sally Hemings had all kinds of reasons to want to go back to Virginia. It was her home, and most of her family was there. As a Hemings, she had been shielded from the worst burdens of slavery. But
any slave could be sold, even—sometimes especially—those who
were blood kin to the master. They could be torn from their homes,
parted from loved ones, put into the hands of strangers against their
will. Thomas Jefferson had never been a man to buy and sell people as
if they were land or horses or harpsichords, but you never knew what
might happen.

Of course, no reasonable person could rule out the possibility that
money worries would force his hand. Jefferson was spending more
than he was making, as his brother-in-law kept reminding him. Once
he got back home, he would have to deal with his tangle of debts. But
Sally Hemings may not have known his real financial situation. From
all appearances, he was a very rich man. His house gleamed with elegant furniture and magnificent art, expensive books and paper, sump-
tuous food and fine wine. He attended the theater and the opera, rode
in a fine carriage, traveled whenever and wherever he pleased. How
could a sixteen-year-old girl not be impressed?

Sally was not the first woman of her family to enter into a liaison
with a white man. She had an African grandmother and an English
grandfather, Captain Hemings. When Sally Hemings put herself in
Thomas Jefferson's hands and returned to America, she walked in the
shadow of Elizabeth Hemings's long relationship with John Wayles,
the parallel family that Martha Jefferson had honored in her own way.
Sally's oldest sister, Mary, carried on the legacy. By the time Sally
went to France, Mary Hemings had children by at least one white
man, probably the Monticello carpenter William Fossett. During
Sally's time in Paris, Mary was hired out to the white Charlottesville

merchant Thomas Bell, with whom she had two more children. Bell would purchase Mary Hemings from his friend Thomas Jefferson and not only free their children, but bequeath his property to them.

Thomas Jefferson did not make Sally's sons and daughters his heirs, but he did promise to protect and provide for her, and to free their children. Sally also knew that he had promised Martha he would never remarry. If he kept that solemn vow, there would never be a new Mrs. Jefferson in charge at Monticello, bringing in a coterie of new servants to displace the Hemingses, or insisting that Sally herself be sent away or sold. Still, Thomas Jefferson might tire of her, or come to regret their affair. He must have been insistent and persuasive in making the case for going home with him, and against her remaining a free woman in Paris.

And yet there was as much to recommend against staying as there was to argue for going. Her prospects as an unwed mother in Paris were grim. Brother James might give her some support, and with his training and connections he may have been able to find them both places in another great household. But she had no secure employment options and only a tenuous command of the language. She was no muscular French fishwife, shouting her wares in the streets and gossiping with noblewomen about politics. Once the baby was born, if she stayed, she would have to find a way to both earn a living and care for her child.

And what of the world outside? Sally had to make her decision amid the surging upheavals of the French Revolution, with mobs of women breaking into bakeries and battling each other for bread, and crowds swelling to storm the Bastille and set the prisoners free. Thomas Jefferson might hope that the revolution would be achieved without bloodshed, but by the late summer of 1789 the people had taken to the streets. Even Jefferson admitted the possibility of violence to come.

Sally Hemings had seen what revolution could do, had been formed by war from her earliest days. The rebellion that had catapulted Thomas Jefferson to political power and everlasting fame had been, for her and her family, traumatic. Jefferson and his fellow patriots had committed their treason in the name of freedom, but the Hemingses remained slaves. Would she have been eager to subject herself to an uncertain, even terrifying future? Jefferson doubtless reminded her of the dangers. Recalling his letter to Anne Bingham, we can easily imagine him comparing the perils of Paris to the peace of Monticello.

Thomas Jefferson could not force Sally Hemings to go home to Virginia. But even had he been able to do so, Jefferson, by temperament, preferred to get his way with what he would have called persuasion, but which we may see equally as manipulation. He never hesitated to use his daughters' desire to please him, to merit his love, in order to get them to do what he wanted. Why would he not have used similar tactics on Sally Hemings?

AND FINALLY, OF course, at that momentous instant in her life, Sally Hemings faced a lover and antagonist who was not just any American man, not just any Virginia slaveholder, but Thomas Jefferson. Arguably the most revered, vexing, contradictory, complicated figure in American history, a man just ascending to the peak of his power. She was thirty years younger than he was, a girl just becoming a woman, raised in slavery, though in relatively protected circumstances. She told her son that his father had beseeched her and made big promises. Jefferson was a person of rare charm, warm and kind, devoted to his children, with seemingly infinite prospects in the world. Few women in America or in France, slave or free, had a chance at such an offer. Maybe she should have been more skeptical of his intentions, less vulnerable to his pleas and promises. We may, in the way of our

Puritan and Victorian forebears, disapprove of women who become mistresses without any hope of marriage, even as our society steeps itself in sex for sale, and even though most women of Sally's time had to treat marriage as a practical, rather than romantic, matter. But who could blame a woman like Sally Hemings, under the circumstances, for hoping to claim such a man's loyalty or protection, or perhaps his affection, or even his love?

18

Coming Home

IN THE SUMMER of 1788, Thomas Jefferson was thinking about going home. He wanted Patsy, then sixteen, to find a suitable husband, an American, preferably a Virginian. His debts had festered and swelled since his departure. Virtually from the moment Jefferson left for France in the fall of 1784, his brother-in-law, Francis Eppes, had been sounding alarms, sending letters warning that crops were bad, and that "your creditors are very pressing for their respective balances." The practical Eppes told the cavalier Jefferson that he could not expect to make enough money selling tobacco or wheat to meet his obligations: "Whenever the time arrives for their being paid a sale must take place." When Francis Eppes spoke of selling, he meant slaves. He and Henry Skipwith had together auctioned off more than a hundred people to cover some of their share of John Wayles's debt, but Jefferson thought he could manage by selling off land, including Martha's Elk Hill.

As the time to return neared, money was not his only worry. What was he to do with Sally Hemings? He had no intention of acknowledging their relationship, but people would talk. He was planning to return to France, and would not even be around to protect her from gossip or worse. And what did he mean by protection? At the moment that he was promising Sally Hemings that he would provide security for her and freedom for their unborn child, Jefferson was pressing her to make an ocean voyage in the middle of a pregnancy. He would never have put Martha through such an ordeal.

Jefferson asked Congress for a leave of absence of five or six months, expecting to spend part of that time at Monticello. He told himself that he was taking his family home for their own good. Whether or not Sally Hemings was still thinking about staying in France, Jefferson made his arrangements fully expecting her to return. "Mine is a journey of duty and affection," he wrote to Maria Cosway in September 1788. "I must deposit my daughters in the bosom of their friends and country. This done, I shall return to my station. My absence [from Paris] may be as short as five months, and certainly not longer than nine. How long my subsequent stay here may be I cannot tell. It would certainly be longer had I a single friend here like yourself."

Meanwhile, he let the folks back home know that he was headed their way. Jefferson told the Eppeses that he and his daughters "look forward with impatience to the moment when we may be all re-united tho' but for a little time." He wanted to get his debts settled once and for all, and though his brief time in Virginia would be "filled with business and disagreeable things," he was still looking forward to renewing "my antient friendships."

Sally Hemings may have had doubts about going back to Virginia, and she and James both might have expected to return to France after visiting family. But in the end she had reason to conclude that she had as good a chance of a satisfying life in America as she did in Paris. Thomas Jefferson always tried to put the best face on things, and they may have shared that predisposition. She too had lived through a Paris winter so grim and gray and frozen and frightful that the sunny skies and green slopes of Virginia must have beckoned like a loving embrace. Lonesome and vulnerable and pregnant, she could remind herself that at Monticello, her mother, and her sisters and brothers, and her old friends would be there to help her, even if the master proved false.

And then there was all that baggage. Sally surely helped with the packing, and for a man who planned to return to France as soon as possible, he was not exactly traveling light. By the time he purchased and packed everything he wanted to take back with him—busts of his heroes and paintings of classical scenes, cases of wine and leather trunks and clocks and plants and a macaroni machine and a "chariot" (minus its driver's seat, unfortunately)—there were thirty-eight boxes, trunks, and crates to be shipped. True, he was leaving behind all the furnishings of the Hôtel de Langeac, the gilded mirrors and framed pictures and furniture and even his new cabriolet. But perhaps he would not go to the immense expense of sending a mountain of goods across an ocean, if he was only going for a short visit?

JEFFERSON HOPED TO embark in April 1789 so that he might be at Monticello in summertime. He expected that things would be pretty much as he'd left them, with George and Ursula and Betty Hemings "of course" to greet him there. Martin and Robert Hemings had hired themselves out for the years of his absence, but he wanted them back, too, at least for his visit.

To his frustration, he did not receive permission for his leave of absence, and so the winter wore on with no real prospect of leaving. The Jeffersons and Hemingses were still in Paris for the fateful summer of 1789, the dawn of a revolution that would truly turn the world upside down. Ambassador Jefferson kept close tabs on political developments, visiting Versailles daily and closeting himself with the high-minded aristocrats and ambitious politicians who pushed for enlightened reform. Jefferson was excited about the prospect of a new government dedicated to liberty and equality, and hopeful that the transition to a constitutional monarchy would be orderly and peaceful. He put his faith in leaders he found "cool, temperate and sagacious," and at the end of June he believed that the great crisis was over.

He was dead wrong, of course, and narrowly missed being embroiled in violence himself, as the revolution began. He rode in his carriage past the king's foreign mercenaries just before an angry crowd attacked the troops with rocks and forced them to retreat. He heard about the storming of the Bastille and watched as the king was brought to Paris by the deputies of the Assembly, surrounded by thousands of shouting citizens brandishing pikes and pruning hooks and pistols, swords, and scythes. In the days that followed, he would ride out to observe "the mobs with my own eyes" and visit the great scenes of Revolution in the days after the Bastille fell, "for nothing can be believed but what one sees, or has from an eye witness."

If Sally Hemings overheard the philosophical speculation and political maneuvering in Jefferson's parlor, in the kitchen the talk of revolution would have been hungrier and angrier, forged in muscle and blood and the faces of malnourished children. If she was permitted to venture out at all to see what was happening, she did not view the chaos of the streets from a high perch on the back of a fine horse.

THEY FINALLY LEFT Paris on September 26, bound for Le Havre, where they waited out the blustery weather for ten days before crossing the English Channel. John Trumbull had helped Jefferson book passage, staterooms for himself and his two daughters, convenient to unspecified quarters for his servant and theirs. But the party of five, three Jeffersons and two Hemings servants, James and Sally, were something more: a dual family, the kinship among them thrust into the shadows. Martha Jefferson's blood ran in the veins of four of them. Two of her half-siblings were saying good-bye to freedom. One of them carried the child of her widower back into slavery.

Jefferson bought a shepherd dog, "big with pup." Dumas Malone imagined the moment when "shortly after midnight the Jeffersons—with slaves, bitch and baggage—left Havres on the packet *Anna*," bound for Cowes, on the Isle of Wight. Back in Paris, a political tempest blew up. On October 5, a crowd of some six thousand women, desperate for bread, gathered a horde of male allies as they marched to Versailles to confront the king and queen and force the royal family to return to the city. Though Thomas Jefferson had hoped that the revolution might be decorous, he understood the potential for shattering violence. The spectacle of women armed with pikes and guns, at the head of a mob that killed two palace guards, beheaded them, and paraded their heads on pikes, would have revolted him to the core.

John Trumbull had booked passage for the Jefferson party as the only passengers on the American ship *Clermont*, under the command of Captain Nathaniel Colley. They weighed anchor from England with a convoy of more than thirty ships, on October 23. Malone envisioned the voyage as a placid one for Jefferson, marked by little seasickness, fair winds, and good weather. The great biographer pictured his subject as a little wistful and a little bored. Thomas Jefferson had conducted his country's business at the highest levels for five years, had moved in glittering circles, had squired beautiful and accomplished women and reveled in the greatest art and most stirring music. He had seen and studied magnificent architecture and plunged into the headiest discussions of science and knowledge and progress. "More even than Maria Cosway," wrote Malone, "the music which had delighted him must have seemed like a lovely dream as he listened to the lapping of the waves." As he sailed homeward on this temporary errand, in Malone's view, he "could have had little adult conversation except with Captain Colley. . . . Patsy and Polly occupied much of his time no doubt, and after a while he could observe his new shepherd pups but he probably spent a good many hours merely reminiscing."

Or perhaps he spent many hours burdened with weighty thoughts. Or he may have simply decided he would not see Sally Hemings as a problem; he would not have been the first or last man to decide that a mistress, even a pregnant one, was more or less on her own. It would have been like him to refuse to discuss the matter with any of his traveling companions, including Sally herself. Thomas Jefferson believed that families should not talk about some things, in the interest of domestic tranquility. Those unspeakable things were, of course, the very worries and dilemmas, the insecurities and injuries, that mattered most.

Patsy Jefferson knew that her father hoped to see her married soon. Only recently out of the convent, having even considered taking vows herself, she was feeling the pressure to find a husband quickly. Jefferson was headed back across the ocean, and if she was going to take such a momentous step, she wanted him there giving his blessing. She may have been aware of Sally's pregnancy and may even have suspected her father's part in the predicament. Could she help wondering, as they sailed home to Virginia, what had happened, what would happen, what people would think, what her mother would have thought? She had comforted and cajoled him since her mother's death. Did her father even care about what Patsy herself thought?

Polly doubtless looked forward to getting home. She assumed that she would be sent to Eppington, to be reunited with her beloved aunt and uncle. Once again her father would abandon her. The last time, Sally had gone to Eppington to be her servant. Now, as Polly approached womanhood, she would need a lady's maid. Sally was better qualified than anyone in Virginia to take that job, but this time Sally

Hemings would remain at Monticello. Did Polly have any inkling what her father, her slave, and her sister might be thinking on that subject?

James Hemings was sailing back into slavery, though he, like Thomas Jefferson, anticipated that the voyage would be temporary. Much as he might have looked forward to seeing his home and family, he may have intended to leave Monticello as soon as he could. And what of Sally? She had Jefferson's word that he would take care of her, but he was planning to leave her at Monticello. She was pregnant for the first time. If she had seen some women grow big and give birth and raise babies without terrible trouble, she also remembered Martha Jefferson's agonies, and the dead children of Monticello and Eppington.

In the last days of the voyage of the *Clermont*, the coastline of Virginia was shrouded in fog so thick that they could not even see any pilot boats sent out from port. "After beating about three days," Patsy Jefferson recalled, "the captain, a bold as well as an experienced seaman, determined to run in at a venture." Even years later, Patsy would recall the moment in vivid detail, the mortal danger so close to the native land she had not seen in five years:

> The ship came near running upon what was conjectured to be the Middle Ground, when anchor was cast at ten o'clock P.M. The wind rose, and the vessel drifted down, dragging her anchor, one or more miles. . . . We had to beat up against a strong head-wind, which carried away our topsails; and we were very near being run down by a brig coming out of port, which, having the wind in her favor, was almost upon us before we could get out of the way.

They managed to escape and landed at Norfolk, but before their baggage was unloaded, the *Clermont* caught fire. As nearly every sailor in the harbor jumped in to fight the blaze, it seemed that all might be lost. But the fire was successfully contained, and everything they had brought with them was saved.

IF THOMAS JEFFERSON had illusions about returning home for a brief domestic idyll, picking up his marching orders, and getting on the next boat across the Atlantic, his hopes were dashed when he arrived in Norfolk. The newspapers proclaimed that George Washington, newly elected president of the United States, had nominated Jefferson to be secretary of state. He longed to return to Paris, Sally Hemings or not, but he would not refuse the president. Sally could now be confident that he would not be abroad when her baby came. But neither would he be available to her. Jefferson was ascending another rung on the ladder of public service and personal ambition. For the next twenty years, despite busy and productive interludes at Monticello, Jefferson devoted himself to the politics he claimed to detest, in the name of principles he felt bound to defend.

The Jefferson party made its meandering way back to Monticello, along the way going to see Martha's (and Sally's) half-sisters, Elizabeth Eppes at Eppington and Anne Skipwith at Hors du Monde. While Patsy and Polly visited with their aunts, Thomas Jefferson met with his brothers-in-law to work out payment of their shared debt. They stopped at Spring Forest to see his sister Martha Carr, and at Tuckahoe, where Patsy found herself suddenly swept into courtship with Thomas Mann Randolph, Jr., son of her father's companion of his early days.

They arrived at Monticello on December 23, 1789, after a journey through bad winter weather along sodden, treacherous roads. The mud-caked horses were utterly exhausted. Slogging painfully up the deeply rutted, nearly impassable Three-Notched Road, they found a jubilant welcome. Word had spread that they were on the way, and the enslaved people on Jefferson's plantation asked to have the day off. They gathered near Shadwell, surrounded the carriage, and escorted the returning master with shouting and cheering all the way up the mountain.

Wormley Hughes, Sally Hemings's nephew, was just a little boy at the time, but he had a vivid memory of the return of the three Jeffersons and the two Hemingses. As an old man who had spent a lifetime running Jefferson's stable, Hughes told biographer Henry Randall in 1858 that the slaves had unhitched the horses, and pulled and pushed the carriage up the hill. Patsy Jefferson recalled that when they arrived at the house, the overjoyed slaves took her father out of the carriage and carried him, refusing to let his feet touch the muddy ground. The crowd parted for the Jefferson girls, who must have been impressive in their Paris couture.

Jefferson had been in France for five years. But for all intents and purposes he had not called Monticello home since Martha's death, more than seven years before. Many of those who cheered remembered him as a kind man, and those who had not known him had likely heard stories of his mildness and decency. They had reason to be happy that he was back. As Jefferson biographer James Parton noted, "A Virginia estate was a poor thing indeed in the absence of the master." The house was dilapidated, the crops had been poor, and the people eking out a living at Monticello had been subjected to the rule of overseers with no personal stake in their welfare. They were doubtless glad to see this man who was ultimately responsible for and to them.

Sally Hemings returned to the joy of reunion with her mother and brothers and sisters, and the pain of resuming her chains. Both she and James must have impressed their relatives with their French words and garments. But however she had changed, it was just a matter of time before the free woman of Paris took her place as just another slave at shabby Monticello.

JEFFERSON WAS QUICKLY consumed with the family business he had to do before leaving to join the new government in New York. He was knee-deep in matters involving his parents' affairs, a lawsuit against his brother Randolph, the estates of his long-dead sisters Jane and Elizabeth, and his late friend Dabney Carr. He wrote endless letters full of intricate calculations to resolve nagging problems. He attended to his neglected lands and ramshackle house, made plans for the spring planting, and worked over the design of his famous moldboard plow, as lingering diplomatic business and the press of his next set of duties closed in.

Before he knew it, he was also dealing with the betrothal of seventeen-year-old Patsy to Thomas Mann Randolph, Jr. Only a month after they returned to Monticello, Patsy was rushing into marriage with a young man her father found suitable and promising, but a man neither of them knew very well. Patsy and Tom Randolph were married on February 23.

If Sally Hemings was recently pregnant when they left Paris at the end of September, the fact must have been obvious by the time of Patsy's wedding. Jefferson had suffered through Martha's eight pregnancies, her hideous births, the miscarriages and the dead children. In April, he wrote to his friend Madame de Corny to thank her for her many kindnesses during his time in Paris. He was concerned about the volatile situation in France but ventured the "hope that a revolution so pregnant with the general happiness of the nation, will not in the end injure the interests of persons who are so friendly to the general good of mankind" as herself and her husband. Sally's pregnancy surely caused some dissension, if not full-fledged revolution, at Monticello, but everyone must have hoped that mother and child would not be injured by the experience. Such events often harmed people Jefferson loved. And if word got out that he was the father of Sally's child, his own interests would assuredly be injured, to say the least.

Still, he was glad to be home. He wrote from New York to a discontented friend in Virginia, saying that the path of his own life had "not been strowed with flowers. The happiest moments of my life have been the few which I have past at home in the bosom of my family. Emploiment any where else is a mere mouser of time; it is burning the candle of life in perfect waste for the individual himself. . . . Public employment contributes neither to advantage nor happiness."

Sally Hemings's mother had given birth to twelve children, and Betty Hemings lived to be more than seventy years old. Some of Sally's sisters did well with childbirth, and some, like Martha, did not survive the repeated traumas. Sally was surrounded by female kin who had vast experience in the matter. Madison Hemings never said whether his mother's first child was a boy or a girl; he probably did not know. The baby, he said, "lived but a short time." As far as we know, the child was never named.

Part IV

PATSY AND POLLY

19

Patsy and Polly

THOMAS JEFFERSON WAS a little nervous about running the Department of State. The United States of America was a frail, fledgling nation, facing a Europe in turmoil and rebellion in the American backcountry. He had only one previous experience with an executive position, as governor of Virginia during the Revolution. That time his public and private lives had crashed together with bloody fatality, bringing him disgrace and misery. He told George Washington that "when I contemplate the extent of that office, embracing as it does the principal mass of domestic administration, together with the foreign, I cannot be insensible of my inequality to it: and I should enter on it with gloomy forebodings from the criticism and censures of a public just indeed in their intentions, but sometimes misinformed and misled." In an ideal world, he would be free to enjoy the fruits of his farm, the labors of his field hands, and the attentions of his family in uninterrupted harmony. But Washington had nominated him. He could not refuse.

Before he went off to do his duty, he meant to settle his family according to his desires. He counted on Patsy and Polly to give him love and comfort, just as surely as he relied on the Hemingses to lay out his clothes, build his fires, clean his house, carry his messages, shell his peas, and fricassee his chickens. He wanted his daughters and their families close by.

He expected his domain to be a peaceful place, but by no means a democracy. At Monticello he ruled as a benevolent patriarch over people whose loyalty should be beyond question. He would be guided by his loving concern for their best interests, and they would understand that to obey him was to return that loving care. Much as he lamented the distance between his home and his political life, he believed that keeping the private separate from the public was the only way to ensure the safety and happiness of his women, his children, his family, his people.

The reality no more resembled Jefferson's ideal than an unripe persimmon resembles a perfect pear. He left behind a house at Monticello fallen into disrepair, a farm in general neglect, and a scattering of underproducing plantations in Albemarle, Bedford, Goochland, and Cumberland counties. Hundreds of people depended on him, from his daughters and his mistress to his house servants and his field workers. He in turn depended on them to look after his property, to pay his bills with their labor, or to support themselves by finding work elsewhere, until he summoned them back. One of those people was pregnant with his child, or perhaps had already given birth. His two daughters and new son-in-law, meanwhile, were trying to find their place in a world all three had left years before.

THOMAS MANN RANDOLPH, Jr., was an intellectual and an aspiring scientist who had seen something of the world. He had spent the years between 1784 and 1788 at the University of Edinburgh, a hothouse of the Enlightenment, studying languages and philosophy, mathematics and anatomy. Young Randolph had corresponded with Jefferson, who perceived "by his letters he has good genius, and every body bears witness to his application, which is almost too great." In short, Randolph seemed a little intense to his future father-in-law, but he had plenty of curiosity and talent, the right bloodlines, and excellent prospects in Virginia.

As wedding presents, the two fathers gave the couple land, livestock, and slaves. Jefferson tendered a thousand acres in Bedford County and twenty-seven slaves, inventoried in family groups, as was his careful habit. Thomas Mann Randolph, Sr., offered 950 acres of land at "Varina" in the lowlands of Henrico County, southeast of Richmond, along with forty unnamed slaves. The Varina land was a disappointment to the couple and to Thomas Jefferson, since Jefferson was urging his friend to offer a tract he owned at Edgehill, only three miles from Monticello. Randolph Sr.'s own father had done as much for Peter Jefferson, after all, trading the land at Shadwell for the famous bowl of arrack punch. But for the moment, Patsy and Tom Randolph resigned themselves to making the best of a situation they could not change.

After the wedding Polly left Monticello with the newlyweds, expecting to be taken to her aunt and uncle at Eppington. Jefferson, on his way to take his place in the government in New York, missed the girls terribly. "I am anxious to hear from you, your health, your occupations, where you are &c.," he wrote Patsy. "Having had yourself and dear Poll to live with me so long, to exercise my affections and chear me in the intervals of business, I feel heavily the separation from you." But he fell back, as usual, on optimism. "It is a circumstance of consolation to know that you are happier; and to see a prospect of it's continuance in the prudence and even temper both of Mr. Randolph and yourself." Patsy Jefferson Randolph was indeed a young woman who turned a mild face to the world. But the same could not be said of Tom Randolph, a man who later stood on the floor of the Congress of the United States and announced, "Lead and even steel make very proper ingredients in serious quarrels." His own sympathetic biographer would call Randolph "thin skinned and sensitive to the point of violent contentiousness."

Adjusting to married life was no easy thing, Jefferson counseled his elder daughter. "Your new condition will call for abundance of little sacrifices, but they will be greatly overpaid by the measure of affection they will secure to you." And then he gave Patsy a piece of advice that sent a fierce double message, seeming to cast off the bond between the loving father and his fervently devoted daughter, while tightening the cinch: "The happiness of your life depends now on the continuing to please a single person. To this all other objects must be secondary; even your love to me, were it possible that that could ever be an obstacle."

Patsy Jefferson was a mature seventeen years old. She knew a lot about devotion to one person. From the moment of her mother's death, her father had relied on her to be his chief comfort and companion. She had embraced that role, riding with him through the woods and meadows of Monticello as he fled his wild grief, accompanying him on the restless rounds from Baltimore to Philadelphia and ultimately to Paris. By making herself indispensable, she earned the chance to go with him across the ocean, to dedicate herself to her studies at Panthémont, to be the girl who deserved his love. "The more you learn the more I love you," he had written to her, "and I rest the happiness of my life on seeing you beloved by all the world, which you will be sure to be if to a good heart you join those accomplishments so peculiarly pleasing in your sex."

Pleasing as those accomplishments might be, acquiring them was no stroll down the Champs-Elysées. Jefferson expected a lot from Patsy, more, he said, than he recommended for most girls, because "the chance that in marriage she will draw a blockhead I calculate at fifteen to one." Over the years he wrote dozens of letters reminding her that if she wanted him to love her, she must work hard and do her duty. In 1783, he'd left her behind in Philadelphia, while he followed the Congress to Annapolis. He'd written to remind her to obey the woman with whom she was boarding, and to lay out the schedule of work he expected her to follow:

from 8. to 10 o'clock practice music.
from 10. to 1. dance one day and draw another.
from 1. to 2. draw on the day you dance, and write a letter
   the next day.
from 3. to 4. read French.
from 4. to 5. exercise yourself in music.
from 5. till bedtime read English, write & c.

Jefferson was particularly exacting when it came to the matter of letter writing. "I expect you will write to me by every post. Inform me what books you read, what tunes you learn, and inclose me your best copy of every lesson in drawing. Write one letter every week either to your aunt Eppes, your aunt Skipwith, your aunt Carr . . . and always put the letter you so write under cover to me." Lest Patsy scribble off some careless lines, between dancing and drawing and music and reading in two languages, Jefferson let her know he expected polished productions. "Take care that you never spell a word wrong. Always before you write a word consider how it is spelt, and if you do not remember it, turn to a dictionary. It produces great praise to a lady to spell well." As if Patsy needed reminding of the devastating loss they had suffered, Jefferson took care to let her know how much he depended on her:

I have placed my happiness on seeing you good and accomplished, and no distress which this world can now bring on me can equal that of your disappointing my hopes. If you love me then, strive to be good under every situation and to all living creatures, and to acquire those accomplishments which I have put in your power, and which will go far towards ensuring you the warmest love of your affectionate father, Thomas Jefferson.

P.S. Keep my letters and read them at times that you may always have present in your mind those things which will endear you to me.

Patsy could not hope to escape his scrutiny on any matter, from the way she spent each minute of her day, to every stitch of her clothing. "Be you from the moment you rise till you go to bed as cleanly and properly dressed as at the hours of dinner or tea," he instructed her. "A lady who has been seen as a sloven or slut in the morning, will never efface the impression. . . . Nothing is so disgusting to our sex as a want of cleanliness and delicacy in yours. . . . The moment you rise from bed, your first work will be to dress yourself in such a stile that you may be seen by any gentleman without his being able to discover a pin amiss."

As much as he tried to control Patsy's outward behavior, Jefferson even hoped to be able to dictate the commands of her conscience. When, in 1783, religious zealots predicted that the world was about to end, Jefferson wrote to reassure his daughter that the prophecies were false. He could not help taking the opportunity to insist that she really ought to behave herself as if Judgment Day could come any time, and balanced his cheery prognostication with a ladleful of gloom: "never do or say a bad thing . . . you will always be prepared for the end of the world: or for a much more certain event which is death."

Patsy was smart and spunky, and she learned to fire back. She chided him when he failed to write to her, and she knew that guilt was the gift that kept on giving: "Being disappointed in my expectation of receiving a letter from my dear papa," she wrote him from Paris, when he was traveling in the south of France, "I have resolved to break so painful a silence by giving you an example that I hope you will follow, particularly as you know how much pleasure your letters give me."

Still, for the most part, she strove to live up to his expectations. At Panthémont, she practiced the pianoforte and harpsichord, struggled to read the classics in Latin, and grew so proficient in French that her English began to desert her. When he admonished her to be busy and avoid boredom as a poison to both body and spirit, she responded, "I am not so industrious as you or I would wish, but I hope that in taking pains I very soon shall be. I have already begun to study more." Jefferson let her know that a lot was riding on her diligence. "My expectations for you are high; yet not higher than you may attain. Industry and resolution are all that are wanting. No body in this world can make me so happy, or so miserable as you. . . . To your sister and yourself I look to render the evening of my life serene and contented. It's morning has been clouded by loss after loss till I have nothing left but you."

PATSY LOVED PANTHÉMONT. She made friends easily, but just as important, at Panthémont she had the attention of educated nuns who encouraged the efforts and soothed the longings of a talented, motherless girl. The papal nuncio in Paris, a close friend of Jefferson, had hopes that the nuns might even make a convert out of the daughter of the well-known Deist. He reported to a correspondent that sixteen-year-old Patsy "seems to have great tendencies toward the Catholic religion." According to Jefferson family tradition, Patsy so fully embraced the all-female religious community that she at one point even considered taking the veil. Her father quickly quashed the idea, and in some versions of the story, after receiving a letter from her declaring her intentions, got into his carriage, rode to the school, had his daughters brought to the door, and drove them away. Such a scene may never have happened, but if Patsy did raise the idea, she made her proposal to her father in the midst of his liaison with the devoutly Catholic Maria Cosway. Patsy knew how to get her father's attention.

She returned to America a polished and educated young woman of seventeen, tall and serene, bilingual, cultured, dressed in the latest Paris fashion. But she did not know the first thing about running a plantation household. Her father had hoped to settle her for a time at Eppington, to be trained by Elizabeth Eppes. He had written to his sister-in-law to say that Patsy would need "your finishing to render her useful in her own country. Of domestic economy she can learn nothing here; yet she must learn it somewhere, as being of more solid value than everything else."

There was no time. Patsy married Tom Randolph only two months after she arrived at Monticello. Biographer Fawn Brodie saw in this hasty marriage a flight from Jefferson's relationship with Sally Hemings. It may have been that, but Patsy had other reasons for the marriage. Her father was planning to leave her for the first time since she had been ten years old. If she remained single, she would have been sent to Eppington, a place that was a beloved home to her sister but that Patsy had only visited in the very stressful months after her mother's death. Tom Randolph was tall and dark and fit, a dashing horseman and deep thinker, who avowed his intention to make her happy and provide for her. Plus her father approved of the match.

Jefferson continued to hope that the young Randolphs would find a way to settle at Edgehill, though the elder Randolph seemed determined to fix them at Varina, the heavily mortgaged plantation far to the south and east of Monticello. They hated the place. Varina was fundamentally a "cropping" plantation, a place where gangs of enslaved people sweated to grow tobacco under the lash of a hired overseer. The place had no stately home for the owners, and only two small houses with two rooms each for overseers. It was, moreover, so hot there, even in May, that the athletic Tom was "prevented altogether from taking exercise by the excessive heat," and he developed a nasty rash that "kept me for several days in excessive torture." Patsy, who had reveled in the female world of Panthémont, had no companions, not even her sister Polly (who had gone to Eppington) or her maid. Sally Hemings, the obvious candidate for that job, had not accompanied either of the sisters, but instead had stayed behind at Monticello.

Until such time as Randolph Sr. could be persuaded to turn over Edgehill to Patsy and Tom, the obvious solution was to have them return to Monticello and run the place in Jefferson's absence. While they would not have the satisfaction of setting up an independent household, they needed a home. Jefferson's neighbor, Nicholas Lewis, had acted as his steward for the property while the Jeffersons were in Paris, but Lewis was getting old. Patsy and Tom wanted to go back to Albemarle County. Tom hoped to buy a small farm near Monticello, no more than one hundred acres, an operation he felt he could handle himself without hiring an overseer. The property at Varina had been run into the ground, he thought, because "ignorance of Agriculture is so evident in our common Virginia Overseers that it must decrease in value every day under the management of one of them."

Glad as the Randolphs were at the thought of leaving Varina for Monticello, Polly preferred to be at Eppington, being mothered by Elizabeth Eppes in familiar surroundings. Mrs. Eppes was delighted to have her there and was hoping that Patsy would remain at Varina, near enough to Eppington for regular visits. Convenient as it was for Jefferson to leave Polly with her doting aunt and uncle, it was also hard for him to realize that Polly had come to see the Eppeses as surrogate parents. "I am sensible of your goodness and attention to my dear Poll," he wrote Elizabeth Eppes from New York, "and really jealous of you; for I have always found that you disputed with me the first place in her affections. It would give me infinite pleasure to have her with me, but there is no good position here."

Just as he had with Patsy, Jefferson tried to control Polly from afar. He reignited the battle over letter writing that Polly had fought with him since she had first learned to read and write. At some point, in Paris, the family had begun to address her as Maria, and Jefferson used the name in an instructive voice. "I have written you, my dear Maria, four letters since I have been here, and I have received from you only two. . . . This is a kind of debt I will not give up." We can hear him rehearsing previous arguments with Polly as he went on. "You may ask how I will help myself?" he inquired, and provided a stern retort. "By petitioning your aunt, as soon as you receive a letter to make you go without your dinner till you have answered it." He could not help adding, "How goes on the Spanish? How many chickens have you raised this summer?"

Thomas Jefferson was a formidable opponent, but Polly Jefferson had some moves of her own. She was beguiling when she chose to be: "She is a Sweet Girl, reads and Sews prettily and dances gracefully," Martha Jefferson Carr had told her brother four years earlier. But she could also be as stubborn as a stump. She had used every weapon at a small child's command, from sweet pleading to quivering tears, from charm and clinging to all-out shrieking tantrums, to fight his plan to force her to go to Paris. Elizabeth Eppes had been Polly's rock and refuge and had enlisted Jefferson's own sisters in her attempts to keep him from hauling Polly across the ocean, "draged [sic] like a calf to the Slaughter."

Polly's aunt Eppes had, in the end, been unable to defy Thomas Jefferson, which taught the child a lesson in the limits of women's power. So she learned to resist passively. "Laziness" was her weapon of choice. Her letters to Jefferson and to Patsy were often affectionate, but they were never as frequent as they admonished. Both her father and her elder sister could be sarcastic in addressing Polly, as they never were with each other. "No letter from you yet, my dear Maria," Jefferson wrote, reminding her of her literary debt to him and adding that "I think you have quite as little to do as I have, so that I may expect letter for letter."

Polly returned the favor with a measure of sullenness. "You tell me in your last letter that you will see me in September," she chided her father, "but I have received a letter . . . that says you will not be here before February. . . . I am afraid you have changed your mind." She acknowledged herself as his "Affectionate daughter," but she signed the letter not "Polly" or "Maria," but with the name that Elizabeth Eppes would have used when she introduced her niece: "Mary Jefferson."

The sisters returned to Monticello, from Varina and Eppington, in the fall of 1790. Jefferson had work to do putting his household and his family in order. He continued to promote the Randolphs' plan to get a place in Albemarle County. "I have always believed it better to be settled on a small farm, just sufficient to furnish the table, and to leave one's principal plantations free to pursue the single object of cropping without interruption," he wrote to Thomas Mann Randolph, Sr., endorsing the idea of absentee slave owning while he outlined a potential deal for some of Randolph Sr.'s land at Edgehill. Patsy and Tom could use the land, slaves, and crops at Varina to pay Tom's father for Edgehill. Meanwhile, Jefferson would be delighted to have them live at Monticello until they could build a house of their own.

Young Tom Randolph wanted Edgehill rather than Varina partly because he had some hope that by living on a smaller place, he might find a way to farm without using slave labor. As they negotiated over the purchase of Edgehill, Randolph Sr. was determined that his son buy a larger tract of land than he wanted and take slaves along with land. The son insisted that he wanted a smaller parcel of land alone. Patsy had expressed her hatred of slavery in Paris. Both she and her husband hoped to find some way to avoid a lifetime of owning human beings. "My father continues to press the purchase of Edgehill on me," Tom Randolph wrote to Jefferson. But Tom felt he had to refuse his father, despite the fact that taking what was offered would be the easiest thing to do. "My aversion to increase the number of my negroes would be an insurmountable objection," he insisted. "My desire to gratify my Father would induce me to attempt it if there was a prospect of my making myself whole, without employing slaves in the cultivation of the lands. It will be better I believe to confine my views to a small tract, just sufficient to supply me with provisions. Patsy agrees with me," he told her father, "but we both wish to be guided by you."

Tom Randolph took a reasonable tone with Jefferson, but not with his own father. He threw the kind of temper tantrum that would cause him trouble all his life, and the two quarreled bitterly. Jefferson tried to forge a compromise, urging that his son-in-law take slaves in family groups rather than simply as undifferentiated chattel. But the Randolph father and son were so at odds that negotiations broke down. Jefferson was frustrated with Patsy's husband. He wanted his family in Albemarle County, and Tom Randolph seemed to him to be stubbornly standing in the way. Jefferson was sympathetic to Randolph Sr.'s annoyance with his son, and surprisingly indifferent to Tom and Patsy's attempt to renounce slavery. "Nature," he told the elder man, "knows no laws between parent and child, but the will of the parent."

In the end, indeed, he would have his way. Meanwhile, it suited him, and them, to have them at Monticello, "perhaps for some years," he told his sister, Mary Bolling.

Patsy proved to be as fertile a bride as her mother had been, and was pregnant with her first child. She could hardly have forgotten Martha's travails, and even if she maintained outward calm, she was surely apprehensive. So Jefferson decided that twelve-year-old Polly would have to leave Eppington to be with her sister at Monticello. Patsy would hardly be all by herself on the mountain, but Jefferson insisted that "the solitude she will be in induces me to leave Polly with her this winter," he wrote to a disappointed Elizabeth Eppes. "In the spring I shall have her at Philadelphia if I can find a good situation for her there. I would not chuse to have her there after fourteen years of age." Perhaps he thought he had kept Patsy in Paris too long. But Jefferson was also making plans to bring Elizabeth's son, Jack Eppes, to live and study with him in Philadelphia, though he considered the city a dangerous place for young people. He cautioned Jack's mother that she had better warn him about city girls. "I know no such useless bauble in a house as a girl of mere city education," Jefferson sniffed. "She would finish by fixing him there and ruining him."

Eighteen-year-old Jack Eppes was, it seems, already a young man with an eye for the ladies. After he joined his uncle in Philadelphia, in the spring of 1791, Jefferson reported to his sister-in-law that her son was doing well with his studies. "If we can keep him out of love," said Jefferson, "he will be able to go strait forward."

THOMAS JEFFERSON WAS an exacting householder, and he expected his elder daughter to run his Monticello according to his standards. Preparing for his return to the capital, he left behind with his retiring steward, Nicholas Lewis, careful instructions regarding his household and family. He wanted two meat-houses (smokehouses) built, one for himself and one for the Randolphs, along with a dairy and a stable, and he asked that the fences around the house, garden, and orchard be repaired. As for the inhabitants, Jefferson meant to establish the Randolphs' control in his absence while also protecting the

Hemingses. "Mr. Randolph and my daughters . . . are to be furnished with whatever the plantations will furnish, to wit, corn, fodder, wheat, what beeves there may be, shoats, milch cows, fire-wood to be cut by the plantation negroes. . . . They are to have also the use of the house servants, to wit, Ursula, Critta, Sally, Bet, Wormley and Joe. So also of Betty Hemings, should her services be necessary. To be always cloathed and fed by me." Thus he prepared to leave his household in a state of domestic tranquility. But powerful as he was, there were some things he could not control.

20

Trouble in the Neighborhood

THOMAS JEFFERSON ENJOYED playing intellectual guide to his male kin. Soon after he returned to America, a young cousin named John Garland Jefferson asked for his help in studying the law. Jefferson offered to let the young man share the law books he had loaned to his favorite nephew, Peter Carr. The two came to Charlottesville in the fall of 1790, while Jefferson was still at home. He expected them to buckle down and get to work, and did not imagine that they would be much trouble. But they disappointed their fastidiously discreet mentor. Garland Jefferson and Peter Carr made the mistake of getting involved with a hotheaded lawyer named James Rind.

The trouble began with gossip, but the matter was serious enough that Thomas Jefferson decided he had to get Garland Jefferson out of town. He described the uproar in a carefully oblique letter to his sister Martha, Peter Carr's mother:

That you may have no uneasiness from what you will hear from Peter, I will mention to you that a worthless fellow, named Rind, wrote a libel on the inhabitants of Charlottesville and neighborhood, which P. Carr and G. Jefferson were imprudent enough to suffer him to communicate to them. Rind then pasted it up in Charlottesville, and from expressions of his, the suspicions were directed on all three. Peter has I believe satisfied every body that he was innocent, and has taken proper notice of the much more scurrilous peice [*sic*] written against the three. The matter is over as to him. But not as to G. Jefferson. He leaves the neighborhood therefore, and I wish him to be boarded in yours, that he may be convenient to the books he is to read.

Jefferson asked his sister to find Garland Jefferson a place to stay, somewhere in Goochland County, "at a reasonable rate, distant from public places, and rather distant from you . . . the less he is with your family the safer their reputations will be. . . . Do not let it be delayed. . . ."

Thomas Jefferson hated having people gossip about his family. But however vicious the talk, he would not have bothered to involve himself unless he had some personal stake in settling things down. In this instance, he not only got rid of his young relative, but also sent him into seclusion and paid his bills. Jefferson further wanted both Carr and the younger Jefferson to sever all relations with their new friend Rind. The two, accordingly, wrote a letter to Rind, cutting off this "acquaintance formed in one week." Garland Jefferson insisted to his mentor that he had taken no part in Rind's original libels. "I was not the author of a sentence," he told Jefferson, "yet by my intercourse with Rind, I laid myself open to the suspicions of the people, and incurred the imputation of having done that which in my though[t]ful moments I look upon with a degree of horror."

Jefferson hoped that the matter would be put to rest by hustling his cousin off to the country. But he had underestimated James Rind's sense of personal betrayal, and overestimated his own capacity to manipulate people and events. Rind was angry, relentless, and determined to have satisfaction. When John Garland Jefferson got to Goochland County, Rind was already there, waiting for him. He was furious that young Jefferson had tried to break off their friendship. Rind had a reputation as a duelist, and when he told Garland Jefferson "ironically" that "a man who wou'd not from selfish principles give up a friend, ought to be damned," he knew he was tossing out fighting words. Garland Jefferson responded that "that was a language he had no right to hold," courting the very challenge Thomas Jefferson had hoped to prevent. Fortunately, the matter did not come to blows, or worse, a dawn meeting with pistols.

But what was in the letter James Rind "pasted up" in the middle of town? What kind of gossip about "inhabitants of Charlottesville and neighborhood" could have bothered Thomas Jefferson personally, and caused so much trouble for the Jefferson family? What accusation could be so damaging when it was posted in a public place and then turned back on three young men, that it could provide grounds for a duel? Such altercations typically involved any or all of three things: honor, money, and sex.

The Rind and Jefferson families had a history, going back to Jefferson's father-in-law, John Wayles, and forward to the moment when Jefferson's presidency would be rocked by revelations about his private life. James Rind's father, William, was the publisher of the *Virginia Gazette*. He had printed the satirical doggerel and angry letters attacking John Wayles's breeding, reputation, and character in the 1766 Chiswell affair. People in the neighborhood knew that John Wayles had fathered six children with his slave, Elizabeth Hemings, surely a subject that raised the question of "breeding," and his reputation and character were undoubtedly open to gossip on that score.

Whatever particular charges were hurled back and forth in Charlottesville nearly a quarter of a century later, Thomas Jefferson too was among those men who were vulnerable to shaming accusations of sex across the color line. And he was not the only one. At the time of James Rind's altercation with Garland Jefferson and Peter Carr, Jefferson's friend Thomas Bell, the prominent Charlottesville merchant, was living openly in a sexual relationship with Sally Hemings's sister, Mary Hemings. Years later, Jefferson's grandson, Jeff Randolph, insisted that Peter Carr, one of the accused, was the father of Sally Hemings's children, while Jefferson's granddaughter Ellen Randolph Coolidge fingered Carr's younger brother, Samuel, for that deed.

As historian Joshua Rothman has pointed out, white Virginians of this era, and Albemarle County residents in particular, did not exactly approve of interracial liaisons, but they tended to look the other way unless they had reasons other than offended morals to cause trouble for mixed couples. But this 1790 episode was also only one moment in a long-running family feud. Ten years later, in 1800, James Rind's brother William, who had carried on the family newspaper business, was publishing the Jefferson-hating *Virginia Federalist* and claiming to have "damning proofs" of Jefferson's "depravity."

Jefferson's response to the Rind imbroglio of 1790 foreshadowed his actions ten years later, when tales of his domestic doings threatened to destroy his presidency. He would dispose of the matter as quietly as possible and do everything he could to preserve the wall between his private and public lives. "I hope that this affair will never more be thought of by any body, not even by yourself except so far as it may serve as an admonition never to speak or write amiss of any body, not even where it may be true, nor to countenance those who do so," Thomas Jefferson told Garland Jefferson. "The man who undertakes the Quixotism of reforming all his neighbors and acquaintances will do them no good and much harm to himself."

He continued to pay Garland Jefferson's bills at least until the summer of 1793, when Jefferson received a letter from the Charlottesville merchant with whom he had set up a credit account for his relative. Garland Jefferson evidently decided he preferred to deal with somebody more "convenient" who would loan him cash as well as give him goods. The young man had not bothered to let his benefactor in on his change of plans. Worse yet, he had left behind a larger debt in Charlottesville than Thomas Jefferson had expected, "which has Swelled you're a/c. Some thing more than you had a right to expect." The merchant promised they would work it out. No doubt they did; the creditor in question was Jefferson's good friend Thomas Bell, a member of the family.

THE GARLAND JEFFERSON–JAMES Rind quarrel, and the ensuing scandal, could not have helped Patsy Jefferson Randolph establish peace and harmony at Monticello. She was, in the winter of 1790–91, eighteen years old, very pregnant, and struggling to get control of a house full of enslaved kin who had been operating pretty much on their own while the Jeffersons were in Paris. When last she had lived at Monticello, Patsy had been a motherless ten-year-old child, sticking to the side of the widowed father who was by turns numb and inconsolable. She had lived those first ten years in the midst of revolution and had rarely known the ease and comfort of a healthy mother in a peaceful home—perhaps mostly at Elk Hill. Now she must be the lady of the house.

As she moved to take command of the servants whom her mother had brought to Monticello, Patsy Jefferson Randolph may have claimed some of their sympathy, but she had not yet earned their obedience. Her father and mother had always relied on Martin Hemings to run the household at Monticello, keeping everyone in line with fierce discipline. But "Martin has left us," Patsy reported, without elaboration. She was having trouble with nine-year-old Wormley Hughes, Betty Brown's son, and ten-year-old Joseph Fossett, Mary Hemings's son, who had a tendency to break things. "Not relying much in the carefullness of the boys particularly when left to them selves I took an account of the plate china and locked up all that was not in imediate use." She even counted and locked up the "spoons &c." that were in daily use, every night and after breakfast. "It was very troublesome in the begining," she wrote to her father, "tho now I have the boys in tolerable order every thing goes on pretty well."

The two boys were not the only targets of Patsy's domestic crackdown. "I have wrought an entire reformation on the rest of my household. Nothing comes in or goes out without my knowledge and I believe there is as little waste as possible. I visit the kitchen smoke house and fowls when the weather permits and according to your desire saw the meat cut out." Thus young Patsy Jefferson, lately out of the convent school in Paris, joined her mother and a long train of plantation women, locking up the cupboards and carrying around the big ring of keys. In the dead of a Virginia winter, she hauled her cumbersome body out to the smokehouse to monitor the seasonal hog slaughter. Like Martha Wayles Skelton Jefferson before her, Patsy stood close as the strong-armed Ursula wielded her bloody knife, watchful lest any hungry or greedy or unruly person pilfer her pork.

Polly too came under Patsy's eagle eye. Though Patsy complained that she herself could not find a moment to read, she did make Polly keep up with her studies. "She is remarkably docile where she can surmount her Laziness of which she has an astonishing degree and which makes her neglect what ever she thinks will not be imediately discovered," Patsy complained to her father. She ferreted out every task Polly failed to complete, from studying Spanish verb tenses to practicing the harpsichord. Being a surrogate mother was a chore, but one she seized with a vengeance; Patsy reported to her father with a touch of humor that Polly found her older sister "inexorable." The sheltered young woman, with no training at all, grew up fast. She had no time for romance before the wedding, and few months after to enjoy marriage without impending motherhood. Now she shouldered the heavy responsibility of presiding over her father's cherished, demanding refuge. There is something wistful in the way Patsy closed that first letter to her father, detailing her myriad housewifely efforts: "Believe me ever your affectionate child."

Patsy came through the birth of her first child, a daughter, in fine shape, attended by her neighbor Mary Walker Lewis. Polly was kept away from the proceedings, or maybe chose to absent herself; she complained to her father that Patsy "had been very sick all day without my knowing any thing of it as I stayed upstairs the whole day." The new parents asked Thomas Jefferson to choose a name for the infant, a process that took over a month due to the slow mails. The first-time grandfather was thrilled, congratulating his daughter on becoming both a "notable housewife" and a mother: "This last is undoubtedly the key-stone of the arch of matrimonial happiness, as the first is it's daily aliment." He named the baby Anne, after his own sister, his wife's sister, and Tom Randolph's mother. From this moment forward, Martha Jefferson Randolph, devoted daughter and housekeeper, would have a long, demanding second career in motherhood. She would bear twelve children, eleven of whom lived into adulthood.

WHILE THOMAS JEFFERSON felt keenly his distance from Monticello every moment he was away, slavery wove the warp and weft of his family and finances, his emotional life and his business obligations, even as it divided his house. The Hemings family had come to the mountain with his bride, and they had taken over his household. Betty Hemings and her daughter Betty Brown had lived at Monticello with various of their children during his absence in Paris. Patsy Randolph would keep his house, relying on the steadfast Ursula, and Betty Hemings and her descendants.

But four of Sally's sisters and brothers—Mary, Thenia, Martin, and Robert—had been hired out in the years that Jefferson had been away, and they were all making plans to depart Monticello for good. In 1792, Jefferson sold Mary Hemings, "according to her wishes," to Thomas Bell, along with their two young children, Robert Washington Bell and Sally Jefferson Bell. Jefferson had given Mary's oldest son, Daniel, to his sister Anna Marks while he was in Paris, and in 1790 gave her oldest daughter to Patsy and Tom Randolph. Mary's son, Joseph Fossett, and daughter, Betsy Hemings, remained Jefferson's property, though there would be much visiting between the Bell and Jefferson households. Thenia Hemings was sold to James Monroe, along with her five daughters, in 1794, presumably according to her own preference.

Martin Hemings, who had served as majordomo at Monticello for nearly twenty years, had been on his own in Jefferson's absence. He was evidently not prepared to resume his position in a household dominated by Thomas Jefferson and run by Tom and Patsy Randolph, and there may have been other reasons for his discontent. Martin Hemings quarreled bitterly with Jefferson in 1791 and insisted that Jefferson sell him. Jefferson, who seldom permitted himself displays of temper, was as angry as Martin was, and by 1795 they had parted company by mutual agreement. No record of sale exists, and of course Jefferson would have been within his rights to do anything he pleased. But Jefferson may well have simply let Martin leave to make his own way in the world, freeing him by passive consent if not legal action, demonstrating some implicit respect for the man who had stared down Tarleton's raiders and now openly defied his own master.

Robert Hemings had been working in Fredericksburg when Jefferson returned. But while Jefferson was gone, Robert had found a wife, and he was arranging to purchase his freedom by paying off his debt to his employer in Fredericksburg, who would then pay Jefferson. On Christmas Eve, 1794, Robert Hemings became the first enslaved person Thomas Jefferson ever formally freed. But Jefferson complained that Robert's employer had "debauched" him of the slave who had been at his side at the height of the American Revolution. The man had paid only sixty pounds for this skilled, well-traveled, and trusted individual, and Jefferson felt he'd been cheated of a fair price. Perhaps there was also a hint of hurt feelings in Jefferson's reaction, a suggestion that he felt personally betrayed by Robert's desire to be his own master.

The wrenching separation between Thomas Jefferson and Robert Hemings, so entangled by kinship and shared experience, almost amounted to a divorce. On a visit to Richmond in the winter of 1795, Patsy Randolph "saw Bob frequently" and reported to her father that Robert "repeatedly declared that he would never have left *you* to live with any person but his wife." Patsy was genuinely sympathetic, knowing how deeply any hint of displeasure on Thomas Jefferson's part could wound those who wanted so badly to please him. "He appeared to be so much affected at having deserved your anger that I could not refuse my intercession when so warmly solicited towards obtaining your forgiveness." But much as she felt Robert Hemings's pain, she stood on the ground of racial superiority as she pled his case with her father. "The poor creature," she wrote, "seems so deeply impressed with a sense of his ingratitude as to be rendered quite unhappy by it but he could not prevail upon himself to give up his wife and child." Whether or not she intended her words to hurt her father, they may have had that effect. In pursuit of his own duty, after all, that was precisely what Thomas Jefferson had done.

IN 1793, JEFFERSON wrote up an agreement with James Hemings, stipulating that once James had taught someone at Monticello to master the art of French cooking, he would be granted his freedom. James took his brother Peter as his apprentice and by 1796 had fulfilled his part of the bargain, and left Monticello to find his own way.

But Sally Hemings made no plans for independence. She remained in Virginia, to bear and lose the first child she had conceived with Thomas Jefferson, to take her place as one of three housemaids, alongside her sisters Critta Hemings and Betty Brown, under the domain of the young, inexperienced, and determined Patsy Randolph. Jefferson had made it clear that Sally and her mother and sisters and brothers, and now her nephews Wormley and Joe, were "always to be fed and cloathed by me." He meant to avoid imposing on Tom Randolph's slim resources, but he also let his daughter know that the Hemingses were under his protection.

There was reason they needed protecting. Jefferson owed money to people who were growing tired of not getting paid. Ironically, his father-in-law, the debt collector, had left him an inheritance that brought men of the same loathed profession to Jefferson's door. Much as he might hope to clear his accounts by selling tobacco or land (he was still trying to unload the Elk Hill plantation), he could not raise enough quick money to satisfy his creditors.

Jefferson resigned himself to selling human beings. His brothers-in-law, Francis Eppes and Henry Skipwith, were frantic about their shared debt, and both sold large numbers of slaves to pay it off. Jefferson approached the matter obliquely, obscuring even from himself what he was doing. "I do not (while in public life) like to have my name annexed in the public paper to the sale of property," he once wrote to the Poplar Forest overseer who was selling eleven people on Jefferson's behalf.

Even in private correspondence, he found roundabout ways to discuss the business of trafficking in people. "I heartily congratulate you on the success of your sale," he wrote Francis Eppes, in a typical letter. "It will determine me to make a decisive stroke in the same way next winter." He could only bring himself to speak bluntly about what he was doing when he was signaling desperation, and begging others to pay their IOUs to him. In a letter trying to collect a debt from John Bolling, his sister Mary's husband, he said, "I hope you will not think it unkind in me . . . I find myself obliged this winter to make a very considerable sale of negroes in addition to the sales of land I have already made and shall further make." When the sales finally occurred, Thomas Jefferson was far away in Philadelphia, and in the end he was badly disappointed with the proceeds, "miserable enough, the negroes having averaged only £45 a peice [sic]." His beloved Martha's eldest half-brother, Robert Hemings, had sold for quite a bit more than that.

WITH WHAT MIX of familiarity and strangeness did life go on at Monticello in those days, in that household cleft by the fierce fiction of race, where a daughter ruled over her aunt, who was also mistress to her father? Patsy Randolph could not have been ignorant of the fact that six of Betty Hemings's children were her aunts and uncles, or that another of Betty's daughters was living in Charlottesville, in a common-law relationship with a well-respected white man who came to dine at Monticello and assured his friend Jefferson that "the family are all well." Patsy may have convinced herself that her father was above sleeping with Sally Hemings, but she could not fail to notice that Sally never took a husband, though Thomas Jefferson strongly encouraged his slaves to form nuclear families, and did everything he could, when buying and selling people, to keep husbands and wives and children together. Sally's singleness spoke for itself.

Surely it occurred to Patsy over the years that the beautiful, traveled, and "mighty near white" young woman who served as her father's chambermaid never conceived a child except when the master was at home. Between the time Jefferson took the office of secretary of state and the time he retired from the presidency, Sally Hemings gave birth to at least six children, at least some of whom bore a stunning resemblance to Thomas Jefferson. Four of those children lived to adulthood. All of them were, one way or another, set free. For their entire adult lives, often thrust together at Monticello, Patsy Randolph and Sally Hemings lived with a lie that split them into dual, unequal families, doubled the rhythms of daily life, etched in words and gestures and rote routines, over and over and over again. In the course of her sixty-four years of life, Patsy Jefferson Randolph kept silent about the matter. Only late in life, at the urging of her son, did she break that silence and offer her children a denial of the connection between her father and her enslaved half-aunt.

Families are where lies, secrets, and silences go to live. All of us find ways to live with falsehood, to pretend that we can't see what we don't want to tolerate. Thomas Jefferson loved his daughter. He knew how much pain it must cost her to pretend not to notice what was plainly in front of her face. In his selfish, slaveholding, possessive, and patriarchal way, he also loved Sally Hemings. He understood, on some level, that he owed her a great deal for her willingness to endure the denigration and invisibility of the concubine, the silent submission of the servant/lover, and most of all, the unconscionable vulnerability of the enslaved.

Both his daughter Patsy and his slave Sally were, in turn, deeply devoted to him, although their feelings toward him must have been so convoluted that they stymie the modern imagination. So even as Jefferson remained solicitous of Patsy's desire to deny his relationship with Sally, and just as he worked to respect and reinforce his daughter's domestic authority, he continued in his efforts to take care of Sally and her family. He made the point, in a letter to Patsy, of inventorying "the following articles for your three house-maids":

36 yds. callimanco

13 ½ yds. calico of different patterns

25 yds. linen

9 yds. muslin

9. pr. cotton stockings

thread.

By the time he wrote this letter, Polly was with him in Philadelphia, boarding with a local woman who kept a school for girls. She may have helped him figure out precisely what the Hemings sisters needed, and how much of each item to buy. But more likely, Sally Hemings, by this time an accomplished seamstress, had given him a shopping list, and he was fulfilling her commission down to the last thread.

WHILE JEFFERSON TRIED to keep everyone happy, in his absence there had been some trouble at Monticello. He imagined his home as a place of enduring sweetness, sequestered from the nastiness and strife that beset public life. But the people in his household did not always play their parts dutifully, and sometimes they were furious with one another. When there was some kind of unspecified friction in his household in the winter of 1791–92, he did what he could to support Patsy long-distance by reminding her of "the love I bear you, and the delight with which I recall the various scenes thro which we have passed together, in our wanderings over the world." Patsy and Tom Randolph were by then looking to move into a home of their own, but Jefferson wanted to keep them in his house as long as possible. So he told Patsy that he hoped "I shall be able to make you both happier than you have been at Monticello, and relieve you from the *desagremens* to which I have been sensible you were exposed, without the power in myself to prevent it, but by my own presence." His use of the French word for "annoyances" may not have been casual. Sally Hemings used her knowledge of the language to emphasize her exceptional place in Thomas Jefferson's life, to put herself, in at least this regard, on equal footing with Patsy Jefferson Randolph.

Still, Patsy was the master's daughter, the free white mistress of the household. She had endless ways to maintain her superiority. Jefferson was her steadfast ally in that effort, reminding her often that he wanted every slave at Monticello to look first to the needs and desires of the Randolphs, and only then to the tasks he wanted them to do. "I wish every other object to be considered as secondary in my mind to your accomodation [sic]," he insisted.

Jefferson understood that he was asking Patsy and Sally, and everyone around them, to perform an emotional trapeze act, sometimes in the midst of family upheaval. In the fall of 1792, two of Tom Randolph's sisters, Judith and Nancy Randolph, were embroiled in a spectacular scandal. Judith was married to yet another cousin, Richard Randolph, master of the aptly named Bizarre plantation, on the Appomattox River. Her younger sister Nancy was living with the couple at the time. The three were on a visit to a neighboring plantation when the unmarried Nancy either gave birth or suffered a miscarriage. What happened next was never completely clear. Slaves reported finding the discarded body of an infant somewhere on the plantation grounds. The rumor soon spread throughout Virginia that Nancy Randolph had borne her brother-in-law's baby, and that the two had killed the child. Richard Randolph was charged with the murder. His beleaguered wife, Judith, was forced to testify at his trial, and so was Patsy Jefferson Randolph, who was called as a character witness. Richard Randolph was acquitted but the scandal lingered for years afterward.

The rumors spread all the way to Philadelphia, where Secretary of State Jefferson wrote to console his distraught daughter. He offered advice that bespoke his sense of responsibility for all the women under his care, and revealed a hint of his own guilt at having debauched a slave girl. He hoped that neither Patsy nor Tom felt "any uneasiness but for the pitiable victim, whether it be of error or of slander. In either case I see guilt in but one person, and not in her." Nancy Randolph, he held, was not to blame for her predicament. The man who was supposed to be acting as her protector and provider had taken advantage of the young woman. Patsy's beleaguered sister-in-law needed her friends' support, "when their commiseration and comfort become balm to her wounds. I hope you will deal them out to her in full measure, regardless of what the trifling or malignant may think or say." Jefferson reminded Patsy of the importance of loyalty, and of long family connection, and the danger of casting stones: "Never throw off the best affections of nature in the moment when they become most precious to their object; nor fear to extend your hand to save another, lest you should sink yourself."

Patsy replied that she was standing by Nancy Randolph but having trouble being entirely sympathetic to the fallen woman. She was speaking of her sister-in-law, but her words could easily apply to her half-aunt, Sally Hemings. "I have continued to behave with affection to her which her errors have not been able to eradicate from my heart," she told her father, "and could I suppose her penitent, I would redouble my attentions." Patsy was also worried about the potential injury to her own reputation, and she implied that she knew a thing or two about loyalty to close relatives who courted scandal, and women who were not penitent. "It is painful to an excess to be obliged to blush for so near a connection," she explained to Jefferson. "I know it by fatal experience."

PATSY RANDOLPH WAS in charge at Monticello, but even her father had told her that her first duty was to her husband. From the early days of her marriage, she discovered that answering to Thomas Mann Randolph's needs and desires, his caprices and his injuries, could be a tough job. Randolph had first exhibited his volcanic temper in his quarrel with his father over the purchase of Edgehill. In that instance, he had good reasons for standing his ground, but over the years he proved so touchy and quick to anger that he made more enemies than friends. He was nearly involved in several duels, quarreled with many of his relatives and even his solicitous father-in-law, and at length wore out the patience of even his long-suffering wife.

But Tom Randolph was not simply hot-tempered. His tendency to "nervousness" and melancholy led to repeated mental breakdowns over the course of his life with Patsy. They had been married less than five years when he first decided that he needed to travel, as treatment for a mysterious illness. Randolph's prolonged bout of ill health coincided with Jefferson's resignation from Washington's cabinet at the end of 1793 and return home to "retirement" at Monticello. Randolph took a long trip north, to New York and Boston, by himself. But his torments continued. In the summer of 1795, he decided to visit hot springs resorts in western Virginia. This time Patsy went along. They had three children by now, so leaving the older two, Anne and young Thomas Jefferson Randolph, at Monticello, they set out for the springs with baby Ellen in tow.

Thomas Jefferson was very worried about his son-in-law. No one seemed to know what was really wrong with Tom Randolph, and Jefferson was as concerned about the treatment as the disease. Various members of his family, from his wife to both of his daughters, had been subjected to "the potent doses of Dr. Currie," the favorite physician of the Eppes family and himself a friend of Jefferson's. Jefferson always held that letting nature take its course was far healthier than the heroic prescriptions of doctors, who believed in pushing diseases to crisis with bloodletting, purging, and the administration of toxic doses of lead and mercury, before deadening the pain with opiates. He hoped that a little respite from everyday care, along with the mildest treatments, would make Thomas Randolph feel much better.

That summer of 1795 brought devastation to Virginia. Torrential rains drowned the corn in the fields and washed away more topsoil than Jefferson had ever seen flow into the swollen Rivanna. Floods carried off dams and mills along all the rivers, sweeping the Appomattox nearly clean and raging all the way north into Pennsylvania. Everyone Jefferson knew was ill, and he described Monticello as "a mere hospital of sick friends." But the worst news of all came from the Randolphs, on their way to the Sweet Springs. On or about July 23, 1795, little Ellen Wayles Randolph, less than a year old, had died at Staunton, of unknown causes. Jefferson hastened to assure his son-in-law that it was "impossible that the journey could have had any effect on the accident which happened," though he had often worried about the effects of hard travel on babies, and had himself lost young children who had been forced to endure arduous journeys across the Virginia countryside.

Jefferson sent James Hemings to bring "the body of our dear little Eleonor" back to Monticello to be buried. Mourners included Jefferson's three sisters, Mary Bolling, Martha Carr, and Anna Marks. Jefferson paid his sisters' old tutor, Benjamin Snead, two dollars to read a funeral service. But the parents did not return for the sad occasion. Though Tom Randolph soon reported that his health was recovered, his hopes proved false, and his continuing mental problems caused tension in the family. The Randolphs seemed to withdraw into themselves, spending most of the fall and winter at Varina, while their children remained at Monticello with Jefferson. It was months before Patsy wrote another letter to her father.

21

Domestic Tranquility, Revisited

THOMAS JEFFERSON HAD gone into his retirement from politics with depressed spirits of his own. But he was a resilient man. As the terrible summer of 1795 slipped into autumn, he told his friend Angelica Church that he was "now in that tranquil situation which is my delight, with all my family living with me, and forming a delicious society." He wrote Maria Cosway that he had "bidden an eternal Adieu to public life which I always hated." He was a happy farmer, living in the outdoors, "eating the peaches, grapes and figs of my own garden," and permitted "from the innocence of the scenes around me, to learn and to practice innocence towards all, hurt to none, help to as many as I am able." He told Eliza House Trist that he was so busy with his farm, he had given up philosophy and science. "I read but little. Take no newspapers . . . and I have it in contemplation next to banish pen, ink, and paper from my farm. . . . The society of my family and friends is becoming more and more the sole object of my delight." His family had lost one tiny member. But they had gained another. On October 5, 1795, Sally Hemings gave birth to her second child, a daughter named Harriet.

Jefferson presented himself to those faraway friends as a contented country patriarch. But the reality was more complicated, as he admitted to those closest to him. Now that he lived off the soil, the weather was no longer simply a subject of his questing curiosity; it was a life-and-death matter. If too much or too little rain fell, or temperatures were too low or too high, crops failed. When that happened, he had to buy food to feed his field hands and his household. In times of dearth, prices rose sky-high for what little grain could be had. "There is vast alarm here about corn," he wrote Tom Randolph in the winter of 1796. "My situation on that subject is threatening beyond any thing I have ever experienced. We shall starve literally if I cannot buy 200 barrels."

Jefferson's household was also changing. In 1796, James Hemings made an inventory of his kitchen utensils and set out to seek his fortune, replaced as chef at Monticello by his younger brother, Peter. John Hemings, Elizabeth Hemings's youngest son, began to train as a carpenter and furniture maker, while Wormley Hughes and Joseph Fossett worked first in the nailery, and then took up trades of their own. Jefferson meanwhile appointed "Great George" Granger to be his first and only enslaved overseer, holding that job alongside a white overseer named William Page. The two were a curious pair. While Great George was solicitous of his fellow slaves, Page was, according to Tom Randolph, "anxious but peevish and too ready to strike."

The public business of buying and selling, like the private endeavor of tearing down and putting up his house, continually disrupted the peace of Jefferson's domain. To deal with his mounting debts, Jefferson mortgaged many of his slaves to "friendly" creditors, a strategy intended to stave off more hostile demands. Meanwhile, enslaved and free workers were tearing down walls at Monticello, and everyone had to step lively to keep bricks from falling on their heads.

Despite the heartbreak of losing a child, Patsy Randolph was a sturdy and determined woman. She went on bearing and rearing her passel of children, shuttling between her own household and Monticello, keeping house for her husband, her father, and myriad guests, making her own rounds of visits to an endless array of relatives. Her sister Polly was far more delicate and retiring. By now, the family addressed her more and more often as "Maria," the name they had given her during her cosmopolitan experience in Paris. But as she grew to womanhood, she was still the girl who had been christened "Mary" and mostly known as "Polly," a homebody who fully embraced her father's notion that "we love best those we loved first."

On October 12, 1797, Polly married John Wayles Eppes, her first cousin. She had known and loved Jack Eppes since her early childhood at Eppington. Thomas Jefferson was absolutely elated at the match. Just as he wished his slaves to "marry in," to build and create family ties that would not require trips away from home, his vision of his family, happily encamped in his neighborhood, was a lifelong idée fixe. "I now see our fireside formed into a groupe," he told Patsy, in a letter crowing over Polly's engagement to Jack Eppes. Now he would preside over a family "no one member of which has a fibre in their composition which can ever produce any jarring or jealousies among us. No irregular passions, no dangerous bias, which may render problematical the future fortunes and happiness of our descendants. We are quieted as to their condition for at least one generation more."

Jefferson expressed himself even more emphatically to Polly, when he wrote to congratulate her on her decision to marry Jack.

This event in compleating the circle of our family has composed for us such a group of good sense, good humor, liberality and prudent care of our affairs, and that without a single member of a contrary character, as families are rarely blessed with. It promises us long years of domestic concord and love, the best ingredient in human happiness, and I deem the composition of my family the most precious of all the kindnesses of fortune. I propose, as in the case of your sister, that we shall all live together.

As a wedding present, he gave Polly and Jack Eppes his plantation at Pantops, adjoining Monticello. He included in the bargain thirty-one enslaved people. As he had with Patsy, Jefferson took care to enumerate the people he was giving to Polly as members of families. Among them was Mary Hemings's fourteen-year-old daughter, Betsy.

But Thomas Jefferson's vision of domestic life as an unbroken idyll was naïve. The proposal to move Polly and Jack to Jefferson's neighborhood never came to pass. At the moment when Polly Jefferson and John Wayles Eppes married at Monticello, most of the house was unroofed and exposed to the elements. Polly's beloved aunt Elizabeth Eppes could not even attend the wedding. Tom Randolph too seems to have missed the festivities, due to a black mood that had him contemplating suicide. He was so depressed, in fact, that he was afraid to face his family, and remembering "the horrors of 94 and 95," he told Jefferson that "I should shun them by embracing death if it could be done no other way." Jefferson himself was headed back to Philadelphia, and Elizabeth Eppes was pressing hard for the young couple to spend at least half their time at Eppington. This time, Aunt Eppes proved victorious. Polly and Jack Eppes gravitated to Eppington, the home they both knew best, the place where Polly would spend most of the rest of her life.

JEFFERSON INSISTED THAT he had no appetite for public life, that "ambition is long since dead in my mind," and that "I have no wish to meddle again in public affairs, being happier at home than I can be anywhere else." In the meantime, in 1796, he let his friends nominate him for president of the United States. He greeted the news that he had come in second to John Adams, and was accordingly elected vice president, with apparent satisfaction, pronouncing the office a "tranquil and unoffending station." He insisted that he would go to Philadelphia for only a month, slipping quietly into town to avoid formal fanfare, and would return to Virginia as quickly as possible. In this instance, he was as good as his word. Later in that spring of 1797, he was back at Monticello, savoring the first tender asparagus from his garden amid the blooming peach and cherry trees.

Much as he might have wished to spend his entire term as vice president at home, Jefferson cared passionately about politics. He meant to shape America's destiny, to ensure that men like him would always be free to enjoy the control of their property, the love of their families, the fruits of their labor and that of the people they commanded. He was confident that his cause was just, and though he hated conflict and confrontation, he knew a thing or two about how to play the game. His pose of equanimity barely masked his fierce ambition. He tried to appear above the fray, but he was the leader of the opposition to Adams's Federalists and needed to be in Philadelphia to tend his political fires. Thus he was away from home when word arrived that he had once again lost a child. In the cold, wet winter of 1798, disease came once again to his family, free and enslaved. Tom Randolph reported the sad news of the "death of Sallies child." Patsy, then living in comfortless quarters at a rented Albemarle County plantation, offered more details. Her own household was experiencing "more sickness than I ever saw in a family in my life. pleurisie, rhumatism, and every disorder proceeding from cold have been so frequent that we have scarcely had at any one time *well* enough to tend the sick." She or Tom had managed to visit Monticello almost daily, where things were a little better, with one notable exception. "Poor little Harriot," she said, "died a few days after you left us."

Patsy Randolph knew the pain of losing a child, and here we sense a glimmer of sympathy for Sally Hemings's grief, and Thomas Jefferson's own, at the death of two-year-old Harriet. But if they held a funeral for Harriet Hemings, no record testifies to the occasion. It was Sally Hemings's lot to suffer loss without the comfort of a husband to share her sorrow. She was six months pregnant with the son she would name Beverly. Whatever Thomas Jefferson felt about baby Harriet's death was twisted with shame and secrecy. He responded to Randolph's letter with nearly pathological obliqueness: "Yours of the 13th. came to hand yesterday, and relieves my anxiety as to the health of the family." Sally Hemings may not have known what her lost daughter's father had written, but even as he kept to his practice of grieving through silence, his words carried the inescapable cruelty at the heart of their master/slave relationship.

We may wonder, too, about the extent of Patsy Randolph's compassion for her father's concubine, her mother's half-sister. At the very moment that Patsy delivered Sally's tragic news, she revealed her own jealousy and possessiveness toward her father. Patsy reminded her father of their unique bond, rooted in their shared, sad history. "I feel every day more strongly the impossibility of becoming habituated to your absence—sepparated in my infancy from every other friend, and accustomed to look up to you alone, every sentiment of tenderness my nature was susceptible of was for many years centered in you," Patsy wrote. No "connexion formed since that could weaken a sentiment interwoven with my very existence." She closed with a jab at Polly, reminding her father of her sister's lazy and sullen refusal to write letters: "I have heard from Maria through Mr Eppes she deals much in promises but very little in deeds that are to be performed with a pen she was in good health and better spirits than usual."

Three young women, bound together by kinship and dependency, vied to bask in the warmth of Thomas Jefferson's affections. We may never know what Sally Hemings expected from the man who owned her and fathered her children, what she said to him or he to her, how many things were simply impossible to say. But Patsy and Polly repeatedly told Jefferson how much they loved him and how hard they worked to please him. Polly was plagued by a sense of her own inadequacy compared to Patsy. "What an economist, what a manager she is become," she wrote to Jefferson, while on a visit to Varina. "The more I see of her, the more I am sensible how much more deserving she is of you than I am, but my dear Papa suffer me to tell you that the love, the gratitude she has for you can never surpass mine; it would not be possible." Even after she had married Jack Eppes, Polly told her father that "I feel more & more every day how much the happiness of my life depends on deserving your approbation." He, in turn, frequently reminded his daughters that they were his only reasons for living. "On my part, my love to your sister and yourself knows no bounds," he told Polly, "and as I scarcely see any other object in life, so would I quit it with desire whenever my continuance in it shall become useless to you."

JEFFERSON WAS GENUINELY sympathetic to his daughters' trials and sorrows, and he begged them to write and tell him every trivial thing. But he also believed that women should endure domestic difficulty in silence. Polly wrote him about a painful visit to his sister Mary and her estranged husband, John Bolling, the notorious alcoholic. "My uncle Bolling is much as usual, in a state of constant intemperance almost, he is happy only with his glass in his hand," Polly confided. As her father's daughter, she placed some of the blame for her uncle's drunkenness on her aunt Mary. "He behaves tho' much better to my aunt than he did, and appears to desire a reconciliation with her, and I think could she hide her resentment of his past behaviour to her, she might render her situation much more comfortable than it is."

Jefferson hated to hear the bad news. "Mr B.'s habitual intoxication will destroy himself, his fortune & family. of all calamities this is the greatest," he wrote to Polly. But "I wish my sister could bear his misconduct with more patience. it might lessen his attachment to the bottle, & at any rate would make her own time more tolerable." There was a lesson for Polly in the Bollings' misery. "The errors and misfortunes of others should be a school for our own instruction," Jefferson explained, warming to his "sermon" on wifely submission as the source of marital happiness. "Harmony in the marriage state is the very first object to be aimed at. nothing can preserve affections uninterrupted but a firm resolution never to differ in will, and a determination in each to consider the love of the other as of more value than any object whatever on which a wish has been fixed. how light in fact is the sacrifice of any other wish, when weighed against the affections of one with whom we are to pass our whole life."

Jefferson knew, of course, that sometimes a husband and wife would disagree. He counseled forbearance for both parties, but where disputes arose, wives should always yield, lest a husband find "his affections wearied out by a constant stream of little checks & obstacles." Jefferson warned Polly against questioning or criticizing her husband, especially in front of company. "Nothing is so goading," he explained. "Much better, therefore, if our companion views a thing in a light different from what we do, to leave him in quiet possession of his view. what is the use of rectifying him if the thing be unimportant; & if important let it pass for the present, & wait a softer moment, and more conciliatory occasion of revising the subject together."

Polly Jefferson Eppes had been only four years old at the time of her mother's death. She might not have remembered Martha's "tart" tongue, and indeed, in the traumatic wartime years of Polly's early childhood, Martha may have been so sick, weak, and harried that she could not muster the fire for which she had been known in her youth. But the wife Thomas Jefferson had loved so well was no mealy-mouthed miss. If Martha Jefferson learned, as Jefferson suggested, to speak softly in public, and make her sharper points in private, she had thoughts and desires and worries and wishes of her own. She had insisted that her second husband buy and maintain the home she had shared with her first. She had brought to her marriage a house full of enslaved half-siblings and installed them in positions of responsibility. She had made Jefferson promise never to replace her, never to endanger her daughters' safety or security by putting them at the mercy of a stepmother.

Polly's surrogate mother, Elizabeth Eppes, showed similar force of character. She disputed Jefferson's plan to haul Polly across the ocean and repeatedly resisted his pleas to visit Monticello. She managed to keep Jefferson's younger daughter close to her, in defiance of his wishes. The Wayles sisters were, in short, agreeable women, but they were capable of speaking their minds. They had been raised to command and "correct" legions of slaves, to brew beer and slaughter hogs. They were not pushovers.

If Thomas Jefferson had a mental image of some model of feminine deportment as he wrote his sermon on wifely submission, Martha could have filled that role only as a figment of nostalgia, not as a flesh-and-blood person. She remained a force in his life through the vow he had made to her, a promise he implicitly invoked every time he assured his daughters that they had become his only attachments, his only reasons for living. But the traces of their life together were fading. In 1793 he had sold Elk Hill, the place where they had passed some of their happiest times before the terror of Cornwallis. The deed was finally executed in 1799; by that time the place had become to him just an extra piece of property. He received "fifteen hundred pounds current money of Virginia" for Elk Hill, and the bonds for the property had gone directly to Farell and Jones, toward the payment of his debt.

There was another woman, very much alive, who had very little choice except to please Thomas Jefferson, and no standing whatever to quarrel or criticize. That woman could not even complain if he beat or starved her, or forced her to wear rags and plow frozen fields in the dead of winter. Jefferson counted himself humane, in that he evidently did not do any of those things, in return for Sally's silence and her obedience to his will. And while he pursued the public's business in Philadelphia, Sally Hemings, the woman who came closest to Jefferson's avowed ideal, was back at Monticello, quietly mourning their lost daughter as she anticipated the birth of the first son of Thomas Jefferson lucky enough to live to be an adult.

22

Danger

AS VICE PRESIDENT of the United States in 1796, Thomas Jefferson threw himself into the heat of political battle, after his fashion. Always a man to avoid confrontation, he often acted through indirection and innuendo, employing others to do his dirty work. Unlike his more openly Machiavellian enemy, Alexander Hamilton, or his rigid and pompous onetime friend, John Adams, Jefferson took care to maintain the calm demeanor that gave him plausible deniability, while his allies and acolytes took care of the fulminating and eye gouging and throat punching.

Ever since he had been secretary of state, he had used journalists to advance his views. In those days, Philip Freneau's *National Gazette* had been Jefferson's mouthpiece, against John Fenno's Federalist *Gazette of the United States*. But by 1796, Jefferson had turned to a new partisan to spread the stories that undermined his enemies: a newspaperman and pamphleteer named James Thomson Callender.

Callender was a Scotsman who had fled his native land. Having libeled Samuel Johnson, attacked George III, and angered his own noble patron, he had moved to Philadelphia and joined a group of radical Republican journalists. He published pamphlets outlining a

political philosophy to the left of Thomas Jefferson but was more notorious for his vicious, sarcastic attacks on Washington, Hamilton,
and Adams. Callender first gained fame in the United States with
his *History of 1796*, a pamphlet that exposed Alexander Hamilton's
affair with a married woman, Maria Reynolds. He insisted that his
concern was to expose Hamilton's political corruption and the plots
and crimes of the Federalists, but he specialized in a combination of
gossip and invective that smeared his targets even as it exposed him
to prosecution. He had an unstable disposition, a hot temper, and a
perpetual urge to lose himself in the bottle.

In 1798, the volatile Callender was in desperate straits. Now he was
in trouble in Philadelphia, and hoping to escape his enemies and his
debts and the law, he set up shop in Richmond, Virginia. He certainly expected Virginia to be friendlier to his brand of political advocacy than anywhere else. Thomas Jefferson had become the chief
sponsor of his attacks on the Federalists in general and John Adams
in particular. Callender kept Jefferson posted on the progress of his
work, the popularity of his pamphlets, and the pressure of his obligations. Jefferson, for his part, kept up the pretense of despising the
bare-knuckle political combat in the presses. He wrote to Patsy from
the capital, lamenting that he could not be with her, quiet and happy
at home: "You should know the rancorous passions which tear every
breast here, even of the sex which should be a stranger to them. politics and party hatreds destroy the happiness of every being here. they
seem, like salamanders, to consider fire as their element." At that very
moment, he was paying the venomous Callender, stoking the flames.

By 1800, the Adams administration had thrown Callender in jail
under the Alien and Sedition Acts. The Federalists had pushed these
hated measures through Congress, claiming that the laws would
protect the country from disruptive foreigners and punish Americans who undermined the government with criticism. But to the

Democratic-Republicans, the Alien and Sedition Acts were a direct assault on the Bill of Rights and the liberties of all citizens. Callender was imprisoned for "publishing false, scandalous, and *malicious writings*," having called John Adams a "hideously hermaphroditical character which has neither the force and firmness of a man, nor the gentleness and sensibility of a woman," among other things. When Abigail Adams learned that Jefferson was giving Callender money, she never forgave him. Though Jefferson was alarmed at the increasingly vitriolic tone of Callender's attacks and told James Monroe, "As to myself, no man wished more to see his pen stopped," he still saw fit to defend Callender as a symbol of the suppression of the press, the violation of the First Amendment, the Adams administration's assault on Americans' liberty. One of his first actions as president was to issue a pardon for the scandalmonger who had served as his political instrument.

Twenty-first-century readers accustomed to a twenty-four-hour news cycle might well wonder: How could Jefferson have blithely used a man who had exposed his enemy's adultery, and imagine that he himself would remain free from scrutiny? The answer, of course, is that he did not expect his adversaries to let him off the hook. The Federalist press had attacked him with as much vigor and venom as Callender had unleashed on Jefferson's adversaries. Jefferson believed, however, that he had insulated his private life from public prying. "Take care that nothing from my letter gets into the newspapers," he admonished Thomas Bell, who replied reassuringly, "Any confidential line I may at any time have the pleasure of receiving from you Shall never by me or my means be made publick. I see the unwarrantable and Shamefull attacks at your Character from the moment you stepd into office. Such infernal Scoundrels ought to be consign.d to the Algerens."

Ever since the Revolution had come to his door, Thomas Jeffer-

son had worked long and hard to rebuild the wall of separation between the women and children who inhabited his domestic realm,
and the potentially lethal conflicts of his political world. He had hated
seeing Frenchwomen inject themselves into politics, and as he rose
through the highest ranks of the new American government, he was
just as determined to segregate public life from what he perceived as
the corrupting influence of ambitious women. As president he dined
mostly with men and only rarely entertained the ladies of the capital.
In some instances, in fact, he violated his habitually scrupulous manners and was downright rude to women he believed had forgotten
their proper place. His intentionally discourteous behavior toward
Elizabeth Leathes Merry, the haughty wife of British ambassador Anthony Merry, nearly provoked an international incident.

Jefferson reasoned that he maintained his virtue by keeping away
from women in public. What he did in the privacy of his faraway
home was, he believed, absolutely his own affair. He did not spend
thirty-seven years building and rebuilding a house on a remote mountaintop for nothing. If he could bring the people he loved under his
long-in-the-making roof, or at least settle them on nearby plantations,
he might keep them safe from harm, or at least from prying eyes. His
closest neighbors, so many of them his friends and relations, understood. They shared his foibles—addiction to fine things in the face
of crushing debt, propensity for sex across the color line. He had
quelled local scandal in the John Garland Jefferson–Peter Carr–James
Rind affair of 1790, and had every reason to believe that what happened in Charlottesville stayed in Charlottesville, at least where the
most powerful man in town was concerned. He could maintain his
privacy by buying off or ignoring any lesser being that had the poor
judgment to cross him.

In some regards, Jefferson's relationship with Sally Hemings may
have seemed to him the *least* problematic aspect of his personal life.

He had far more trouble with his debts, his crops, and the seemingly endless vexations of trying to get his house built. Every absence from home compounded his problems. The overseers in his fields and his nail shop could not control their workers, or beat them too much. Construction supervisors pulled down in sections the columns that supported his portico, and then forgot to number the pieces. Putting the columns back up was like a muscle-straining Rubik's cube.

Jefferson's daughters, meanwhile, had married according to his wishes, but just as he demanded perpetual proof of their affections, they returned the favor. Patsy announced that she looked forward to his return "with raptures and palpitations not to be described." Her own family was growing rapidly, and she was perpetually busy, but she found moments to write him letters that reminded him of their unique relationship. "Dearest and adored Father the heart swellings with which I address you when absent and look forward to your return convince me of the folly or want of feeling of those who dare to Think that any *new* ties can weaken the first and best of nature—the first sensations of my life were affection and respect for you and none others in the course of it have weakened or surpassed them."

Sally Hemings did not require that kind of attention. In fact, she was obliged to accept a social invisibility that penetrated the very heart of her family, an anonymity and illegitimacy that her nieces, Patsy and Polly, never faced, no matter how much they confined themselves to private life. Even in family correspondence, Jefferson and his daughters almost never referred to Sally, and never by name. If he wrote to her, he made no record of the correspondence, and he or his daughters and descendants did all they could to see that no such letters survived.

Nonetheless, when Sally gave birth to her third child, a daughter, Thomas Jefferson could not help mentioning the event in a letter, addressed not to Patsy or Polly, but to John Wayles Eppes, who was then at Eppington awaiting the imminent birth of his and Polly's first child. "Maria's maid produced a daughter about a fortnight ago," Jefferson wrote, "& is doing well." While he often noted the births of slave children in his account books (in the form of payments to midwives), it was a measure of Sally's importance to him that he mentioned the event in a letter; no other birth of an enslaved child merited such notice on his part. But we can also read, in Jefferson's oblique phrasing, the pains he took to balance his attachment to Sally with his deference to his daughters, and to the proprieties of racism and slavery. When that daughter died not long after, no member of Jefferson's white family commented in writing on this latest loss.

Sally Hemings had borne four children and lost three. Only her son, Beverly, born in 1798, remained. Surely her children's father, and their half-sisters, Patsy Randolph and Polly Eppes, shared in Sally's grief. Surely there were moments of remembering Martha Jefferson's similar trials. But many things could not be written, and some could not be spoken aloud, and some could barely even enter the realm of thought, including the freshest, most searing memories.

Whatever Sally was thinking or feeling, by this time Jefferson and his daughters had begun to pretend in public that she did not exist. Sally had little choice in the matter. As far as we know, once she had agreed to relinquish her freedom and return from Paris with him, she did not press the matter, as her brothers Robert and James did. Instead, she held Thomas Jefferson to his promise to free their children, and made sure they knew their own family history, a story that included an African woman and a half-African grandmother, an English sea captain, the lawyer, John Wayles, and the president of the United States. That history survived, despite generations of denial, denigration, and disappearance, a legacy only recently penetrated by historians seeking to know Jefferson not simply as he and his daughters would have him known, but as he was.

*   *   *

SALLY HEMINGS, PATSY Randolph, and Polly Eppes were all pregnant in 1799. Experience had taught Thomas Jefferson a great deal about the dangers of childbearing. As reticent as Jefferson was about Sally's situation, he was, by contrast, volubly interested in his daughters' pregnancies and births. Patsy Randolph followed in the footsteps of her Randolph grandmother and great-grandmother, and proved herself a sturdy breeder and bearer of children. By the time Jefferson was elected president, she had borne five children, only one of whom had died. She would birth seven more, all of whom lived to adulthood. Though we do not know how Sally Hemings experienced labor and childbirth, we do know that she survived at least six and probably seven such episodes, and lived into her sixties. She was reportedly "doing well" after the birth of her daughter, despite the fact that there was sickness throughout the region at the time.

It is not clear what sort of illness swept through Albemarle County in the winter of 1799, but the malady came to Monticello with force. Sally Hemings's baby might have been a victim of the epidemic that felled enslaved people who had formed the core of Jefferson's household for most of his life. Jupiter, who had served Jefferson since childhood, who tended his horses and served as watchman when Jefferson was gone; "Great George" Granger, the plantation's only enslaved overseer; and Ursula Granger, George's wife, who reigned in the washhouse and smokehouse; along with their son George, who had been ill since 1798, were all so desperate for a cure that they turned to a "Negro conjuror" from Buckingham County. Jupiter, and perhaps all four, died horribly—vomiting and convulsing for hours, gasping for breath and sometimes lingering in that state after taking a dose that the man had said would "kill or cure." Ursula, in fact, held on in suffering for months, long after the black doctor had fled following

Jupiter's death. According to Tom Randolph, the man's "poisons" had been responsible for "numerous [deaths] in this part of the country." Patsy thought the culprit should be brought back and tried for multiple murders.

Under the circumstances, it may have been better that Polly Eppes did not heed her father's urgings and go to Monticello to have her baby. Childbirth, rarely a picnic, remained a life-threatening ordeal for any Virginia mother at the turn of the nineteenth century. There was little in the way of sanitation, but much practice of "heroic" medicine, a system of treatment that relied on near-toxic doses of purgatives and "physicks" intended to cure in the same way that the "Negroe conjuror" had recommended, by almost killing the patient. Martha Jefferson Randolph managed to survive her many pregnancies and deliveries mostly by having the good luck not to need too much doctoring. But for her fragile sister, childbirth and its aftermath proved torturous. While Monticello reeled under the loss of Jupiter and George Granger, Ursula lay prostrate, and Sally buried her daughter in an unknown grave, Polly was in Chesterfield County awaiting the birth of her first child.

Jefferson still hoped that he could induce Polly and Jack to settle at his Pantops quarter. The irritable and whip-happy William Page, now overseer for Jack Eppes at Pantops, had a crew clearing land for tobacco fields there. Polly insisted to her father that she hoped they could find a way to move to Pantops, "& we shall then always be one of the first to welcome your arrival." But the Eppeses now had a house of their own, "Mont Blanco," on the Eppes family's ancestral Bermuda Hundred plantation. Jefferson continued to push them to visit. "Promises must not be forgotten," he insisted. When the time came for Polly's confinement, they did go home: not to Monticello, but to Eppington.

Maria Jefferson Eppes bore a daughter in January 1800. Her father was in Philadelphia, presiding over the Senate and getting ready to stand for the presidency. When Jack Eppes wrote to let Jefferson know that "Maria was become a mother & was well," her father received the letter with "purest joy, my anxiety on that subject having been as great as yours." But within days, the baby died. Patsy wrote the sad news in the same letter in which she informed him of the death of Jupiter and Ursula's terminal illness, both Georges having already succumbed. Polly, meanwhile, suffered a ghastly infection that caused such severe abscesses in her breasts that they "broke" in multiple places. "I have not heard from her since," Jefferson wrote to Patsy; "there is abundant cause of deep concern in this."

Thomas Jefferson, who was intimately familiar with the feeling of losing a child, and worrying about a seriously ill mother, wrote to express his sympathy and offer his advice on how to deal with the loss: "I know that time and silence are the only medecines." But far from remaining silent in the face of her affliction, he opened his heart in a frank, expressive, almost effusive effort to heal his frail younger daughter with words, to erase any past tension or conflict between them, and to deal with his own empathetic terror:

Mr. Eppes's last letter informed me how much you had suffered from your breasts: but that they had then suppurated, & the inflammation and consequent fever abated. I am anxious to hear again from you, and hope the next letter will announce your reestablishment. it is necessary for my tranquility that I should hear from you often: for I feel inexpressibly whatever affects either your health or your happiness. my attachments to the world and whatever it can offer are daily wearing off, but you are one of the links which hold to my existence, and can only break off with that. you have never by a word or deed given me one

moment's uneasiness; on the contrary I have felt perpetual gratitude to heaven for having given me, in you, a source of so much
pure and unmixed happiness.

At that moment, Thomas Jefferson was heading into the fight of his
political life, the campaign for the presidency and the protracted contest for the electoral vote in the election of 1800. He was also telling
Patsy that "politics are such a torment that I would advise every one I
love not to mix with them." He likewise insisted that the only place he
could find true peace and contentment was at home with his family,
ironically in the very season when his household had been ripped to
pieces by the deaths of Jupiter and the Grangers, Jupiter's passing in
particular "leaving a void in my domestic arrangements which cannot
be filled." He spoke of domestic tranquility in the wake of the death
of his and Sally's daughter, in the awful aftermath of Polly's labor,
when her baby lay dead and she herself was in excruciating pain and
mortal danger. For all his acute sensitivity to the contentiousness of
public life, he could hardly bring himself to face the perils and agonies of private life.

Patsy, however, knew that the only way to conquer private dangers
was to confront them directly. The moment they learned of Polly's
predicament, Tom and Patsy Randolph determined to go to her side.
Leaving little Jeff behind, they packed up nine-year-old Anne, the
two-year-old daughter they had named Ellen, after their lost child,
and baby Cornelia, and set out for Eppington. In the wake of a blizzard that had left fifteen inches of snow on the ground at Edgehill, it
took them three days of "fatigue & some danger & suffering" before
they reached Eppington. There, Tom said, "We found Maria much
worse than we expected; still confined to her bed, greatly reduced
in flesh and strength and suffering extremely from inflammation and
suppuration of her breasts." The Eppes family doctor, Jefferson's

cousin Philip Turpin, had been with her for days, dosing her heavily with castor oil and other "little medicines," hoping to reduce her infection by inducing vomiting and diarrhea. Jefferson was skeptical of "the system of physicking," believing that "for every good effect it can produce, I am sure two bad ones will result." The Randolphs shared his view; they were appalled at what Polly had endured. When they tried to convince the Eppeses to dismiss the doctor and cease the treatment, they met fierce resistance.

But they had more success convincing Polly that she had to stop taking Turpin's purgatives and focus on recovering her strength. Polly's infection proved stubborn enough to keep her in bed and in pain for another month, and Jack Eppes worried that "the sores on her breast have proved most obstinate & will not I fear be easily healed without the aid of the knife to which she feels as is natural a great repugnance." But Patsy remained at her sister's side, and the Randolphs' intervention likely saved Polly's life.

23

Scandal

WHILE POLLY JEFFERSON Eppes lost her child and fought for her life, her father launched his run for the presidency. In that fierce campaign of 1800, he had more and more trouble maintaining the cherished wall of separation between his home and his politics. Virginia was a hotbed of partisan animosity. Some of his own relatives embraced the Federalist cause and turned against him for reasons sometimes real and sometimes spitefully imagined. Old hatreds festered. As early as June 1800, William Rind wrote in his *Virginia Federalist* that he had "damning proofs" of Jefferson's "depravity," though he did not go into details. A tavern conversation in Richmond, among men with a grudge, carried the added weight of touching on the leaders of the nation.

James Callender, broke again and in and out of jail, wrote frantic letters pressuring Jefferson for money. Callender had the notion that the president would reward the service he had so enthusiastically rendered by giving him a job as Richmond postmaster. But Jefferson was growing uncomfortable with the viciousness of Callender's tirades, and he dragged his feet. Callender gulped down whiskey, listened to gossip, and read the papers, increasingly aggrieved against his former patron. "There seemed to be some special necessity in him," wrote Fawn Brodie, "to destroy not only men of eminence, but also his own benefactors." Callender would soon make it his business to collect as much information as he could about Thomas Jefferson's private life.

He did not have much trouble doing so. When Jefferson was at home, the whole world tramped to his door. Patsy complained about the "strangers which continually crowded the house when you were with us." On one visit to Monticello, "I never had the pleasure of passing one sociable moment with you. Allways in a crowd, taken from every useful and pleasing duty to be worried with a multiplicity of disagreeable ones which the entertaining of such crowds of company subjects one to in the country."

Jefferson offered sympathy. "Nobody can ever have felt so severely as myself the prostration of family society from the circumstances you mention," he wrote Patsy from Washington, where he was "surrounded by enemies & spies catching & perverting every word which falls from my lips or flows from my pen, and inventing where facts fail them." He longed for the peace and harmony of home, "where we love & are beloved by every object we see, and to have that intercourse of soft affections hushed & suppressed by the eternal presence of strangers goes very hard indeed." But he urged Patsy to be patient with the need to entertain all comers. "The present manners & usages of our country are laws we cannot repeal. . . . Consider that these visits are evidences of the general esteem which we have been all our lives trying to merit. the character of those we recieve is very different from the loungers who infest the houses of the wealthy in general." Whatever the character of his multitudinous guests, they were assuredly capable of carrying tales.

THE ELECTION OF 1800 proved a political trial by ordeal for Thomas Jefferson. Though Jefferson won the popular vote by an overwhelming margin, the electoral college vote resulted in a tie between him and his own vice presidential candidate, Aaron Burr. The matter went to the Federalist-controlled House of Representatives, where Jefferson's enemy, Alexander Hamilton, found himself lobbying on Jefferson's behalf, against Burr, whom he detested even more. Jefferson waited out the protracted battle, and finally took office in Washington, D.C., on March 4, 1801. His inauguration marked a sea change in American politics, heralding the decline of the Federalist party and the ascension of his own Democrat-Republicans.

In the midst of such a volatile and heady political moment, Jefferson was still thinking of home. He entreated his daughters to come to live with him there, but he knew that their family affairs would keep them in Virginia. They may, indeed, have resented his political ambitions; as Fawn Brodie pointed out, Patsy never wrote to congratulate him on his election.

But they had plenty to keep them busy. Sally, Patsy, and Polly were again pregnant that year, with Sally giving birth to a second Harriet in May, named after the daughter she had lost. By that time, James Callender had been snooping around Charlottesville long enough to amass ammunition to blackmail the president. Jefferson at first tried to pay him off, using James Monroe and Meriwether Lewis as go-betweens. But Callender soon confronted him directly, threatening to publish what he knew about Sally Hemings if Jefferson did not give him the postmaster's job. Jefferson was indignant that his onetime instrument made such presumptuous demands; he was confident he could meet the threat with haughty denial. "Such a misconstruction of my charities [toward Callender]," he wrote to James Madison, "put an end to them forever. . . . He knows nothing of me which I am not willing to declare to the world myself."

While Jefferson tried to deal with Callender, he gathered his family together. He managed to convince Polly and Jack Eppes that they should come to Monticello for the birth of her child, and she and her sister had their babies, Polly's son Francis and Patsy's daughter Virginia, a month apart, at their father's home that September. Thomas Jefferson had been present for the birth of at least one of his Hemings children, but now, for the first time, he was at home for the arrival of two of his grandchildren. He gladly paid the midwife, as well as settling his debt to the woman who had attended Sally the previous spring, before he left his burgeoning family to return to the capital. He arrived in Washington only days after William Rind's *Washington Federalist* printed a report that a prominent officeholder, "Mr. J," had "a number of yellow children and that he is addicted to golden affections."

James Hemings was also at Monticello that September, visiting his family and cooking for the household. Jefferson had hoped that James would come to Washington to serve as presidential chef, but he never actually asked Hemings himself, instead relying on intermediaries to carry messages. Sally may have acquiesced as Thomas Jefferson took greater and greater pains to conceal his connection to the Hemingses, but James may have been hurt by Jefferson's game playing. James wanted to go to Washington, but if he agreed to cook for Jefferson, he would be "among strange servants" and other people who might have heard the rumors about his sister. He wanted Jefferson to "send him a few lines," specifying the "conditions and wages you would please to give him in your own hand wreiting." But Jefferson never wrote.

James Hemings returned to Baltimore, where he had been living and cooking. Jefferson made a point of telling his go-between that "I would wish James to understand that it was in aquiescence to what I supposed his own wish that I did not repeat my application, after having so long rested on the expectation of having him." The trust between Thomas Jefferson and his wife's half-brother, the man who had served him from childhood, had been broken. A month later, word came to Jefferson that the talented and volatile Hemings had gone on an alcoholic binge and committed suicide.

Jefferson mourned James's death as a "tragical end." The news was a terrible blow to the family at Monticello, then in the throes of a whooping cough epidemic that threatened the lives of the Hemings, Randolph, and Eppes children. Tiny Francis Eppes coughed so violently that he was "perfectly black with it in the face" and in "a very precarious state of being . . . the most delicate creature" Patsy Randolph had ever seen. "Ellen and Cornelia were particularly ill both delirious one singing and laughing the other (Ellen) gloomy and terrified equally unconscious of the objects around them. My God what a moment for a Parent," Patsy wrote her father. As if that were not enough, Tom Randolph was once again losing his grip. "The agonies of Mr. Randolph's mind seemed to call forth every energy of mine," Patsy told him. "I had to act in the double capacity of nurse to my children and comforter to their Father."

Those trials alone were enough to strain everyone's tempers, but some further mysterious incident touched off the flames of domestic discord in that hard winter of 1801. When Polly left Jefferson's crowded, contentious, and febrile house for Eppington, she took along Critta Hemings, Sally's sister, as a nurse for her fragile son. Something had happened that fall to make Critta want to get away from Monticello. "I hope you had no objection to her spending this winter with me," Polly wrote to her father. "She was willing to leave home for a time after the fracas which happened there and is now anxious to return."

But now that Jefferson had ascended to the presidency, Monticello was no longer a protected, private place, no longer a family sanctuary. "With how much regret have I look'd back on the last two months that I was with you," Polly wrote her father; "more as I fear it will always be the case now in your summer visits to have a crowd." Much as he wanted her to come to Washington in the spring, Polly demurred. "I have been so little accustom'd to be in as much company as I should be in there to recieve the civilitys and attentions which as your daughter I should meet with and return, that I am sensible it is best for me to remain where I am."

By the summer of 1802, Virginia gossip about Thomas Jefferson and Sally Hemings metastasized into a national scandal. The Federalist *Port Folio* published a satirical ballad hinting that Jefferson had a black wife. Callender, now on the staff of the Federalist *Richmond Recorder*, was telling people that his former patron has subsidized his defamations of Hamilton, Washington, and Adams, and Callender geared up his direct attacks on Jefferson. The Republican press, in turn, went after Callender for his "apostacy, ingratitude, cowardice, lies, venality and constitutional malignancy," which only infuriated Callender further.

On September 1, 1802, he went public with his charges: "It is well known that the man, *whom it delighteth the people to honor*, keeps and for many years has kept, as his concubine, one of his slaves. Her name is SALLY." Callender charged that Sally had a son named Tom, who was "said to bear a striking though sable resemblance" to the president. He held that "by this wench Sally, our president has had several children. There is not an individual in the neighbourhood of Charlottesville who does not believe the story, and not a few who know it." He further reported that Sally Hemings had gone "to France in the same vessel with Mr. Jefferson and his two daughters. The delicacy of this arrangement must strike every portion of common sensibility. What a sublime pattern for an American ambassador to place before the eyes of two young ladies!"

The Republican *Richmond Examiner* quickly moved to denounce Callender as a liar. "That this servant woman has a child is true," wrote editor Meriwether Jones, a close friend of Jefferson, but Jefferson was not the father of that child. "Is it strange, therefore, that a servant of Mr. Jefferson's at a house where so many strangers resort, who is daily engaged in the ordinary vocations of the family, like thousands of others, should have a mulatto child? Certainly not."

Once the imaginary wall between the private and the public was demolished, it would prove as difficult to put back together as the jumbled columns of Jefferson's portico. Now the glare of political debate flooded the complicated triangulations of the Monticello household. Jefferson's daughters and their descendants would take up his defense, insisting that someone else had fathered Sally Hemings's children. But despite Republican threats of tar and feathers and horsewhipping, Callender persisted, rubbing raw the points of friction between Jefferson's daughters and their half-aunt. He grew ever more vitriolic and insulting in his portrayal of a woman who had never done a thing to court attention, who had devoted her own life to serving Thomas Jefferson and to the hope of her children's freedom. "Jefferson before the eyes of his two daughters sent to his kitchen, or perhaps to his pigstye, for this Mahogany coloured charmer." Anyone who dared question his story, Callender said, could meet him in court. He had a dozen witnesses "as to the black wench and her mulatto litter."

The Federalist press ran gleefully with the story, though no one could compete with Callender in the category of sheer invective. Some labored for a tone of objectivity, partisan as their purposes were. Their information was off the mark in some cases (at that point, as far as we know, Sally did not have a son named Tom), but much of what Jefferson's enemies published squared with what historians have now come to accept as the truth. The *Frederick-Town Herald* assured readers that "Mr. Jefferson's Sally and their children are real persons, and that the woman herself has a room to herself at Monticello in character of a semstress to the family, if not as house-keeper, that she is an industrious and orderly creature in her behaviour, but that her intimacy with her master is well known, and that on this account she is treated by the rest of his house as one much above the level of his other servants."

No one knows if Sally Hemings was "treated by the rest of his house as one much above the level of his other servants," though the Hemingses, who were blood kin to Jefferson's late wife and daughters, considered themselves as special, and were treated as such at Monticello. But the editor of the Lynchburg *Virginia Gazette* touched on Jefferson's sorest spot when he deigned to sympathize with Martha Jefferson Randolph and Maria Jefferson Eppes, and asked a pointed question. "These daughters, who should have been the principal object of his domestic concern," wrote the editor, "had the mortification to see illegitimate mulatto sisters, and brothers, enjoying the same privileges of parental affection with themselves. Alas! Mr. Jefferson . . . Why have you not married some worthy woman of your own complexion?"

Thomas Jefferson did not treat his Hemings children with "the same privileges of parental affection" accorded to Patsy and Polly. As we have seen, he followed the joys and sorrows of his daughters' lives with the closest possible attention, given his many commitments and interests. He did what he could to inspire, reassure, console, and control them. By contrast, by virtue of his own views on race, by tacit agreement with his free daughters, and according to the custom of the country, he kept his enslaved sons and daughter at an emotional distance. If he ever wrote to any of the Hemingses, those letters have not been found. His son, Madison Hemings, told an Ohio newspaper editor in 1873 that his father's "general temperament was smooth and even; he was very undemonstrative. He was uniformly kind to all about him. He was not in the habit of showing partiality or fatherly affection to us children. We were the only children of his by a slave woman. He was affectionate toward his white grandchildren, of whom he had fourteen, twelve of whom lived to manhood and womanhood."

Callender continued his attacks over the months that followed. Thomas Jefferson stayed silent. Meanwhile, the scandalmonger had enraged so many people in Virginia that it seems almost inevitable that someone would be moved to violence. On December 20, 1802, a Virginia Republican named George Hay, a onetime ally of Callender, attacked him with a walking stick, bashing in his head and smashing his fingers. Callender took Hay to court to try to recover damages and hired two lawyers to plead his case. One was William Marshall, brother of the Federalist chief justice of the United States, an enemy of Jefferson. The other was a Republican, but likewise no friend to Thomas Jefferson: James Rind, featured player in the 1790 altercation with John Garland Jefferson and Peter Carr.

Callender was once more doomed to disappointment. The Republican-dominated jury would not convict Hay in even such a brazen assault. Jefferson's onetime mouthpiece continued to attack his former benefactor, this time publishing the story of the president's long-ago overture to the wife of a friend, a lapse Jefferson would ultimately admit. But though Callender had severely damaged Jefferson's reputation, he gained nothing by his efforts. Eight months later James Callender got drunk for the final time, fell into the James River, and drowned in three feet of water.

WHILE THE PRESS fulminated and Jefferson's allies scrambled to defend him from Callender's charges, Jefferson himself never uttered a word in public in his own defense. He did, however, attempt at once to protect his daughters, and to use them as human shields. With Callender privately pressuring him for money and the Federalist press hounding him for exposing such delicate ladies to their father's iniquities, Jefferson wanted Patsy and Polly at his side, providing proof of his virtue. He pushed them to make a visit to Washington in the spring of 1802. Failing that, he hoped they would both be with him at Monticello that summer, and then return with him to Washington in the fall. When Polly explained that she could not come to Washington, or even visit Monticello in the summer because her husband needed all his horses for plowing, Jefferson offered to send a coach from Washington to pick up both of his daughters.

Now that the wall was well and truly tumbling, he urged Patsy and Polly to take a greater public role. The man who had so long insisted that women could find happiness only by confining themselves to the pleasures of their households now needed his daughters' political support. Monticello itself was no longer the refuge he had desired and designed, but was instead besieged with visitors, including perfect strangers, whenever he was at home. And much as they wanted to be with their father, his daughters hated the constant and expensive company that diverted his attention and demanded to be greeted and seated and fed and flattered.

Jefferson tried to convince Polly that her annoyance at the Monticello crowds was a sign that she had grown too accustomed to shutting herself up at Eppington and Bermuda Hundred. "I think I discover in you a willingness to withdraw from society more than is prudent," he told her. "I am convinced our own happiness requires that we should mix with the world." He spoke, he said, from his own experience in the years between 1793 and 1797, when he had "remained closely at home, saw none but those who came there, and at length became very sensible of the ill effect it had upon my own mind . . . and irresistible tendency to render me unfit for society."

Of course, during those years at Monticello, Jefferson had hardly been all by himself. He had commanded a house full of enslaved servants, directed a consuming construction project, opened his nailmaking shop. Betty Hemings and her daughters, Sally, Critta, and

Betty Brown, had been on the scene, and for most of that time, until she married Jack Eppes, Polly had been there with him. Polly could not have failed to remember that in those years, Sally Hemings had conceived two children.

Polly resisted his pleas. She reported that both she and little Francis had been so sick that she'd asked "my dear mother," Elizabeth Eppes, to come to Bermuda Hundred to take care of her, and had kept Critta Hemings from returning to Monticello for the same reason. Meanwhile, there had been an outbreak of measles in Albemarle County. Jefferson still hoped Polly could be persuaded to come to Monticello when he was home, so he told her to stay away from Edgehill, where he feared Patsy's children would have the disease. So determined was he to have Polly at his house that he wrote to Patsy, then presumed to be nursing her own children through the epidemic, to ask her to go to Monticello herself, to make sure that any children on the mountain who had the measles would be isolated. "Should any one on the mountain have it they must remove," he told Patsy, and suggested that Sally Hemings and Betty Brown must take their children to stay at Elizabeth Hemings's house, a small dwelling on the Third Roundabout, several hundred yards south of the mansion. He assured Polly repeatedly that he was taking measures to remove any Hemings children who might be infected (not to mention Sally herself), and expressed his happiness that she had kept Critta with her: "At Monticello there could be nothing for her to do; so that her being with you is exactly as desireable to me as she can be useful to you." His message was clear: Polly should use the Hemingses as she wished, and he would make it easy for her to avoid them as she chose.

BOTH DAUGHTERS EVENTUALLY made their way to Monticello in the late summer, to join their father on the mountaintop where the Hemings children had, at least for a time, been tucked out of sight at Betty

Hemings's cabin. Jefferson still wanted Patsy and Polly to come to Washington as soon as possible, and tried to overcome every objection they raised. He would pay for the journey, send horses and coaches, even see that they had proper wigs, which Patsy asked him to order from a Philadelphia milliner. Dolley Madison had assured them that in Washington, fashionable wigs were "universally worn and will relieve us of the necessity of dressing our own hair, a business in which neither of us are adepts." Sally Hemings may have learned something of elegant hairdressing when she had served as their maid in Paris, but she was certainly not invited to accompany them to Washington for this show of family solidarity.

Still, as much as Jefferson hoped to erase any sign of Hemingses from his life in Washington, he counted on them for his private comforts. He made a point of asking Patsy to bring Peter Hemings's recipe for muffins. "My cook here cannot succeed at all in them," he told her, "and they are a great luxury to me."

TRAVELING THE RUGGED roads of Virginia was a trial even for men alone, and Thomas Jefferson complained often about the inconvenience and danger. How much more difficult it was for two young mothers to make the journey to Washington, especially under such emotionally charged circumstances. Delay piled upon delay, and as bad winter weather approached, the hazards of the journey mounted. Both husbands had business of their own to attend to in Virginia, so the women would have to go by themselves. Polly pronounced the visit "scarcely worth making for so short a time" and said she would rather wait until spring and travel with her father, but "my sister will not agree to put it off any longer."

The steely Patsy was, as Polly suggested, utterly determined to stand by her father at this moment of crisis in his public life. She made sure that Polly did not back out, though at twenty-four, Polly seemed again the fretful child who had resisted her father's order to leave Virginia and travel to France so long ago. It did not matter how short the visit would be, Patsy said, "as this is a flying visit only to shew that we are in earnest with regard to Washington." She left all four of her daughters at home and took along only her son Jefferson, reasoning that "it is better to part with them for a time than risk such a journey with a carriage full of small children." She planned to return to the capital with her father in the spring, taking all the children along. Patsy Randolph was only twenty-nine, but she had been her father's fiercest and steadiest support for nearly two decades, from the time that he had been left a widower and she a motherless child. However much he insisted that nature had fitted men to protect and provide for women, the weaker sex, in his own life, Thomas Jefferson had learned to depend on this rock-solid female.

Jefferson's daughters made their way to Washington in November, returning to Edgehill in January "after a most disastrous journey sufficiently distressing in itself," Polly wrote to Jefferson, "but more so at the time from the depression of spirits felt on leaving you." They had spent happy hours mostly in his private sitting room but had appeared enough in public to demonstrate their unfailing devotion to their father. Both sisters had, at Jefferson's insistence, shopped for nice things in Washington, and Polly worried about the "immense" cost to her father. Neither Polly nor Patsy had experience of such indulgent spending; life on isolated plantations did not require fancy gowns or fussy accessories. Indeed, Patsy's little daughter, Virginia, left behind for a few weeks, "would not recognize her [mother] till she changed her dress for one that she remember'd from its being a calico."

Both Martha Jefferson Randolph and Maria Jefferson Eppes knew what it was to live with debt. Both their husbands had financial problems, and both women worried perpetually about money. But Thomas

Jefferson turned a blind eye to his own distresses when he felt like spending. He insisted to Polly, "You did not here indulge yourselves as much as I wished, and nothing prevented my supplying your backwardness but my total ignorance in articles which might suit you." He hoped that she would return to Washington with Patsy in the spring. In any event, "Mr. Eppes's election will I am in hopes secure me your company next winter."

Thomas Jefferson, who had only two years earlier declared politics "such a torment that I would advise every one I love not to mix with them," had now drawn the husband of his shy and delicate daughter into that pit of public misery. While he blithely urged Polly to join them in the whirlpool of intrigue and malice, she had fought his entreaties before and she had no desire to submit in this case. Neither did Patsy return in the spring of 1803. She was pregnant once again, and Polly would shortly follow suit.

Tom Randolph also went to Congress, in the fall of 1803, and both sons-in-law lived with Jefferson at the White House. Polly moved to Edgehill to spend the winter with her sister. Whatever sibling rivalry had existed between them, they shared the loss of their mother, the common experience of bearing and rearing children of their own, the odd predicament of growing up with blood relations who were also their slaves, and the unique experience of being Thomas Jefferson's daughters. Together they defended the reputation of their beloved father against charges of racial mixing, charges they both knew to be true, and moreover, to be a family tradition. They had grown closer over the years. On November 2, 1803, Patsy bore her seventh child, a daughter she named Mary Jefferson Randolph, after Polly.

Just as their relationship with each other changed over the years, their feelings about Sally Hemings doubtless altered; no doubt Sally's feelings changed, too. As the three grew from girls into women, the tangled private bonds of race and enslavement, affection and possession, turned into national scandal, bringing denial and deception. The public controversy surely strained whatever affections they bore for Sally, and she for them, after a lifetime together. All the fuss must have made life more difficult for all their kin, Eppeses and Randolphs and Carrs and Bollings and, of course, Hemingses.

Jefferson's closest friends, James Madison and James Monroe, were both intimately familiar with life at Monticello, and both had been involved in the efforts to hush up James Callender. Surely those pragmatic gentlemen must have considered the idea that it would be best for everyone if Sally Hemings were sent away. She could go to another of Jefferson's plantations, or be packed off to live with some relative, perhaps his brother Randolph or one of his Carr nephews, particularly if any of those men were, as some of Jefferson's descendants would claim, the father of Sally's children. Jefferson might even have sold Sally to some sympathetic friend. Monroe, after all, had bought her sister Thenia years earlier.

But Thomas Jefferson stood by the woman who had given up her freedom to follow him home. Sally was not sold. She was not even sent off the mountain. Even at the height of the controversy, Jefferson was unwilling to concede anything more to public opinion, or to his white daughters' embarrassment, than to ask Sally and her children to move temporarily into her mother's house, a short distance from his own, on the pretext that they might have the measles. Sally had lived at Monticello most of her life. He revealed his devotion to her when he refused to make her leave then. And he never did.

24

Motherhood and Mortality

MARY JEFFERSON EPPES had endured a long train of illnesses in her twenty-five years of life. Her third pregnancy was as troubled as her first, and she dreaded the birth. Jefferson hoped that Polly would take heart from seeing her sister come through delivery in fine shape. "Take care of yourself my dearest Maria," he wrote to her at Edgehill. "Have good spirits and know that courage is as essential to triumph in your case as in that of the souldier." But he had frightening memories of his own. He tried to make light of their fears, assuring Polly, "Some friend of your Mama's (I forget whom) used to say it was no more than a knock of the elbow." If she had a good doctor near at hand, "nothing is ever to be feared." Polly's mother had had doctors aplenty, and her widower and daughters knew from heartbreaking experience that almost anything having to do with childbirth was worth fearing.

The Randolph household at Edgehill was chaotic at the calmest of times, with six boisterous children and a husband whose intermittent presence was a mixed blessing. The addition of the anxious and grouchy Polly and her sickly son tested Patsy's temper. "I write amid the noises and confusion of six children interrupted every moment by their questions," she wrote her father in January. She was coping as best she could without help from either Tom Randolph or Jack Eppes, who remained in Washington for the congressional session. "We are *all* of us 'as well as can be expected,'" she told Jefferson. "Maria's spirits are bad, partly occasioned by her situation which precludes every thing like comfort or chearfulness, and partly from the prospect of congress not rising till April. . . . I hope we shall do as well as if Mr. Eppes was here but certainly her mind would be more at ease could he be with her." Little Francis Eppes was having "dreadful fits; I cannot help fearing them to be epileptic," Patsy wrote, although she hoped he would outgrow them. She had, however, kept her suspicions to herself, knowing that Polly would be upset if the idea that Francis was epileptic became a subject of hurtful rumor.

Thomas Jefferson was determined to cheer up his daughters, despite his own worries. He hoped Congress would adjourn in time for Jack Eppes to "be with Maria at the knock of an elbow," and hoped that she too would "keep up her spirits." As for Francis's fits, "there is little doubt but he will out-grow them; as I have scarcely ever known an instance to the contrary, at his age." In Washington, Jefferson was enjoying the celebration of the Louisiana Purchase and happy not to have to deal socially with the haughty English ambassador, Anthony Merry, and his snobbish wife. "As much as I wished to have yourself and your sister with me," he told Patsy, "I rejoice you were not here." He was afraid; they all were. Polly must find a way to be brave: "Pour into the bosom of my dear Maria all the comfort and courage which the affections of my heart can give her, and tell her to rise superior to all fear for all our sakes."

Polly desperately wanted her husband home for the birth, and wished that her father might even manage to come to Virginia in time. Jefferson, who had, after all, a country to run, was sympathetic but realistic. "Let us all see that you have within yourself the resources of a courage, not requiring the presence of any body," he urged his younger daughter. But Polly continued depressed and weak. In a letter to her father on February 10, 1804, she avowed that the only thing that could cheer her up was the hope "of soon seeing you and Mr. Eppes." Five days later, Polly went into labor. Her daughter, Maria Jefferson Eppes, was born at Edgehill. The birth left the mother weak and feverish, and infection set in.

Patsy's daughter Ellen remembered the days that followed. Ellen was at the time only eight years old, but brilliantly precocious for her age, and childhood memories are often more sharply engraved than recollections softened and shaded by age and experience. She recalled her "poor aunt's pale faded, and feeble look," and the way that her own mother had slept in her aunt Maria's room and tended to her every need. Jack Eppes hastened to Edgehill as soon as he could, and Thomas Jefferson finally arrived at the beginning of April to find his younger daughter in mortal decline. He insisted on taking her to Monticello, borne in a litter by enslaved men who carried her the four miles from Edgehill, up the mountain. Little Ellen Randolph joined a poignant, almost macabre procession, as her aunt was "carried around the lawn in a carriage, I think drawn by men, and I remember following the carriage over the smooth green turf."

Mary Jefferson Eppes drew her last hard breath on April 17, 1804. She was twenty-seven years old. "This morning between 8. & 9. aclock my dear daughter Maria Eppes died," wrote Jefferson in his memorandum book. The deathbed scene recalled Martha Jefferson's last moments. Thomas Jefferson was likely by Polly's side, along with her husband, John Wayles Eppes, her sister, Martha Jefferson Randolph, and the Hemings women. Elizabeth Wayles Eppes, Polly's beloved "mother," would be there soon, if not in time. The other children were close at hand.

Thomas Jefferson had now outlived his wife and all of their children, save one. He asked to be left alone for several hours. His sole surviving daughter by Martha said that when she went to look for him, she found him with his Bible in his hands. Meanwhile, some-one—presumably Patsy Randolph, with likely assistance from one or more of the Hemings women—had prepared the body. By the time little Ellen was taken to the death chamber, Polly Eppes had been covered with a white cloth, strewn with "a profusion of flowers."

Ordinarily, by that time of the year, the jonquils and hyacinths would have already bloomed, and the tulips and irises might be open-ing. But the weather had been wet and bleak. "This has been a re-markeably backward spring," Thomas Jefferson wrote in his Garden Book. Monticello lay swamped, under a pall that chilled the bones and drenched the soul.

MARY JEFFERSON EPPES was buried at Monticello. Once again Eliz-abeth Wayles Eppes carried a motherless baby home to Eppington. She was accompanied this time by Francis Eppes and Patsy's oldest daughter, thirteen-year-old Anne Cary Randolph. Letters of condo-lence poured in. Even Abigail Adams, who admitted to Jefferson, "It has been some time since I conceived that any event in this life could call forth feelings of mutual sympathy," had found that "the powerful feelings of my heart burst through the restraint, and called upon me to shed the tear of sorrow over the departed remains of your beloved and deserving daughter—an event which I most sincerely mourn." Adams had waxed furious as Callender, Jefferson's hatchet man, had savaged her husband. Then she had watched as Callender lashed out at his patron with the story of Sally Hemings. She could not help reminding Jefferson of the "attachment which I formed for [Polly] when you committed her to my care upon her arrival in a foreign land, under circumstances peculiarly interesting." But she was not writing to taunt him about the peculiar circumstance of Sally Hem-ings. She had read an account of Polly's death in the newspaper and found herself remembering "the tender scene of her separation from me, when, with the strongest sensibility, she clung around my neck, and wet my bosom with her tears, saying, 'Oh now I have learned to love you, why will they take me from you?'"

Thomas Jefferson once more reeled with grief. It took him two months to reply to a letter from his old friend, John Page. When he did, he echoed the tortured words he had written to Elizabeth Eppes twenty-two years earlier. "Others may lose of their abundance," he wrote, "but I, of my want, have lost even the half of all I had. My evening prospects now hang on the slender thread of a single life. Perhaps I may be destined to see even this last cord of parental affection broken! The hope with which I had looked forward to the moment when, resigning public cares to younger hands, I was to retire to that domestic comfort from which the last great step is to be taken, is fearfully blighted."

Now his mind traveled back to the moment when he'd lost Martha, the casualty not only of his private desire, but of the revolution he had wanted and made, the war that had invaded her house and uprooted her family. A time when Martha Jefferson fled with her children, from Williamsburg to Richmond, from Monticello to Poplar Forest, when Cornwallis's men stomped through her house at Elk Hill, when they slashed the throats of the colts in the fields. "When you and I look back on the country over which we have passed," he wrote to Page, "what a field of slaughter does it exhibit! Where are all the friends who entered it with us, under all the inspiring energies of health and hope? As if pursued by the havoc of war, they are strewn by the way, some earlier, some later, and scarce a few stragglers remain to count the numbers fallen, and to mark yet, by their own fall, the last footsteps of their party." As he had after Martha's death, he contemplated, even longed for, his own. "We have, however, the traveller's consolation. Every step shortens the distance we have to go; the end of our journey is in sight—the bed wherein we are to rest, and to rise in the midst of the friends we have lost!"

For all his pain, Thomas Jefferson was the president of the United States. Eventually he had to go back to work. He had spent the best years of his life in politics, and now, at sixty-one and feeling the ravages of age, the weight of his office seemed nearly insupportable. Jefferson was an ambitious politician, sometimes a ruthless partisan, capable of ferocious focus and Machiavellian manipulation in the service of his ideological and institutional goals. He did not profit from office—quite the contrary—and the time he spent in office kept him from the home life he idealized, the women and children he loved.

But he insisted throughout his life that he had not entered politics because of a desire for fame, but precisely in order to preserve the sanctity and liberty of his private world, the place where he really lived, where he found the source of all true happiness. In 1801, as he had sat in frustration, waiting for the electoral college to decide his election to the presidency, he had written to Polly to reassure her that she was as important to him as Patsy was, and to explain his motives for spending so much of his life away from them:

The scene passing here makes me pant to be away from it: to fly from the circle of cabal, intrigue and hatred, to one where all is love and peace. tho' I never doubted of your affections, my dear, yet the expressions of them in your letter give me ineffable pleasure. no, never imagine that there can be a difference with me between yourself & your sister. you have both such dispositions as engross my whole love, and each so entirely that there can be no greater degree of it than each possesses. whatever absences I may be led into for a while, I look for happiness to the moment when we can all be settled together, no more to separate. I feel no impulse from personal ambition to the office now proposed to me, but on account of yourself & your sister, and those dear to you. I feel a sincere wish indeed to see our government brought back to it's republican principles, to see that kind of government firmly fixed; to which my whole life has been devoted. I hope we shall now see it so established, as that when I retire, it may be under full security that we are to continue free and happy.

For Thomas Jefferson, private happiness was the source of all that was good, and good government was the instrument that could ensure private happiness. But the peaceful, harmonious, private sphere he envisioned was a chimera. Life at Monticello was not peaceful and not harmonious. It was not even private.

Part V

A HOUSE DIVIDED

25

Domestic Diversification

IN THAT COLD, wet, disastrous spring of 1804, Martha Jefferson Randolph returned home to Edgehill to cope with her sorrows as best she could. Patsy Randolph was a strong woman. She would do her duty, tend her husband and children. But her sister's death left her desperately clinging to her bond with her father, who was making his muddy and miserable way to Washington. "I do not hesitate to declare if my other duties could possibly interfere with my devotion to you I should not feel a scruple in sacrificing them," she wrote to Jefferson, "to a sentiment which has literally 'grown with my growth and strengthened with my strength. and which no subsequent attachment has in the smallest degree weakened. It is truly the happiness of my life to think that I can dedicate the remainder of it to promote yours.['] "

At the age of thirty-one, Patsy had spent her life trying to make Thomas Jefferson happy, striving to live up to his image of the ideal American girl, woman, wife, and mother. She had studied the classics and practiced the harpsichord, written endless letters and married a man her father approved. She had come of age in a convent school in a foreign country, had worked to master the disciplines and arts of plantation housekeeping, a job she never learned to love. Patsy earned her father's esteem by seeming to have no trouble with childbirth, raising and educating a burgeoning passel of children, and most of all, by being devoted to him.

She had also labored to master herself. From the age of ten, when her mother died, Patsy had put aside her own grief and supported her father when he faltered. In the wake of another grisly death, of the loss of her only sister and beloved rival for their father's affection, she steeled herself to hold him up once again. Whatever it cost her, she would be as cheerful and stalwart and competent as he had raised her to be.

But losing Polly shook Patsy to the core. "We are as usual well here," she assured her father, and then proceeded to demonstrate that she was anything but well. "I have myself had an attack of something like the cramp in the stomach," she admitted, offering appalling details. "The spasms were violent and came on with a desire to puke which however produced nothing more than an insuperable distension of the breast at the moment and a difficulty of breathing amounting allmost to suffocation." Her speech had been affected, and for hours she had been unable to sit or lie down. She insisted that she had merely made the mistake of "eating radishes and milk at the same meal," though Tom Randolph "affirmed it to have been hysterics."

Patsy had a history of digestive disorders, some episodes so disabling that she could not attend "even to my common domestic affairs." She met them by putting herself on a diet, giving up "meat milk coffee and a large proportion of the vegetable tribe." But this time she was sure that the severity of her symptoms "proves it to have been some thing more serious than mere hysterics," and she worried that another such attack "may not be as easily checked the second time." She acknowledged that "I was much alarmed my self."

Patsy might have been poisoned by bad radishes or spoiled milk, but she was also suffering from what we would now call post-traumatic stress disorder. These days we would treat her condition with the respect it deserves. But in Patsy's time, "mere hysterics" were a sign of feminine weakness, a luxury for delicate females like her sister, not formidable women like herself. She tried to keep her father from worrying, but having lost Polly, he was terrified that something would happen to Patsy. The more she tried to hide things from him, the more anxious he grew. "In endeavoring to spare my feelings on your real situation it gives me the pain of fearing every thing imaginable," he told her, "even that the statement of your recovery may not be exact." He implored, "Let me pray you always to give me the rigorous state of things that I may be sure I know the worst."

As he had before, Thomas Jefferson felt the agonizing tension between the claims of public duty and beloved family: "Had not Congress been sitting, I would have seen you as soon as my horses could have carried me." But even as he lavished her with tender concern and sympathy, he reminded her of her responsibilities. "Consider my dear Martha to what degree, and how many persons have the happiness of their lives depending on you, and consider it as a duty to take every care of yourself that you would think of for the dearest of those about you." He knew, of course, that she counted him first among that number.

As the months went by, Patsy suffered recurring bouts of disabling illness. She finally admitted that "having what I never in my life had before (an hysteric fit) thought my self dying whilst in it." She insisted, once again, that she was on the mend, and avowed that what she needed was exercise. Her father and her doctor heartily agreed, and she took to "riding out" on horseback in good weather, as often as she could find the time. Thomas Jefferson's daughter wanted to be like her father. She would learn to deal with emotional trauma by getting on a horse and riding away.

*   *   *

SALLY HEMINGS, FOR her part, had spent much of her life with Polly Jefferson Eppes, the woman she had served and adventured with in girlhood: her niece, her mistress, her master's and lover's daughter. Whatever Sally felt or thought, Thomas Jefferson depended on her willingness to see to his needs. She had stood at Martha's deathbed, and now at Polly's. She had witnessed the ferocity and the helplessness of Jefferson's grief. Patsy had to go back to Edgehill soon after the tragedy, but Sally remained at Monticello to mourn with him. In his "Head and Heart" letter to Maria Cosway, Jefferson had described such a moment of affliction and had written, "When Heaven has taken from us some object of our love, how sweet is it to have a bosom whereon to recline our heads, and into which we may pour the torrent of our tears." Within a month of Polly's death, Sally conceived a child, her sixth, a son born in January 1805. She named him James Madison Hemings. He joined his older brother, Beverly, and sister, Harriet.

IN THE FALL of 1805, pregnant with her eighth child, Patsy took the unprecedented and never to be repeated step of going to Washington for her confinement. She insisted on going with her children to spend the winter with her father, even though she was leaving "at a time when it is so little convenient to Mr. Randolph." Having visited the capital once before, she knew that she would need expensive things to make herself presentable—a fashionable wig and combs, a "bonnet shawl and white lace veil, for paying morning visits"—not to mention paying the cost of travel and of boarding herself and her children. Tom Randolph, then serving in Congress and living at the White House himself, was having serious money troubles, and Patsy hated to saddle her father with her expenses.

Despite his mounting worries about his own financial difficulties, Jefferson pronounced himself glad to pay whatever was needed. Polly's ordeal had traumatized them both, and for the first time Patsy admitted that she was truly terrified of having her baby in Virginia. "My courage shrinks from the horrors of a trial so severe under the most favorable circumstances but rendered infinitely more so in this instance from the uncertainty of my accustomed medical aid and the want of a female friend," she told her father. Delivering a baby, she knew all too well, was no knock on the elbow. It was a matter of life and death.

Patsy gave birth to her child, a boy, in the White House. She gave her second son the same name Sally Hemings had given her child—Patsy's half-brother—a year before: James Madison. Her choice of name hinted at unspoken jealousy of Sally Hemings, but it also reflected Patsy's claim to her place as Thomas Jefferson's sole legitimate heir. She meant to bequeath her children a sense of their individual importance through their names.

The Randolph children's names testified to their parents' ambivalence about the burdens of their tangled family ties. Virginia families relentlessly named children after relatives, so much so that the only way to keep utter confusion at bay was to identify people either by nickname, or by place of residence. Patsy herself had been named after her mother and grandmother and Thomas Jefferson's sister, Martha Carr. Thomas Mann Randolph, Jr., not only bore the weight of sharing his father's name, but would also suffer the crushing indignity of seeing his father marry a second wife and bestow upon his much younger half-brother both his own name and most of his inheritance.

Patsy and Tom had asked Jefferson to name his first grandchild, and he had suggested "Anne" as a name often used on both sides of the family. They called their first son after Thomas Jefferson, and one daughter Mary, after Polly. All their other sons would be named in honor of Jefferson's distinguished friends: James Madison (born in 1805), Benjamin Franklin (1808), Meriwether Lewis (1810), and George Wythe (1818). But for their daughters, the Randolphs chose none of the family's usual names, Jane and Elizabeth and, of course, Martha. Instead, they made romantic choices: Ellen (born in 1796), Cornelia (1799), Virginia (1801). It seems they were so determined to avoid using a family name that when their seventh daughter was born, in 1814, they called her Septimia. Then again, Septimia, known as Tim, was the sixth of their living daughters, seventh only if one counted the first Ellen, the child who had died while Thomas Randolph shuttled restlessly from one water resort to another in search of a cure for his crippling depression. By the time Septimia was born, Martha Jefferson Randolph and Thomas Mann Randolph were living apart. The name Septimia was a reproachful reminder to the husband who blamed himself for the loss of the infant daughter whose tiny coffin had gone home to Monticello, borne in the arms of James Hemings.

MADISON HEMINGS WAS the first of Sally's children born after the Callender scandal. Jefferson had weathered that episode to be reelected handily. He had learned that whatever he did or said, in politics he could not avoid malice, slander, or the public's endless appetite for spicy secrets. His enemies had penetrated his personal life, but by gathering his family around him and refusing to acknowledge the rumors, he believed he had preserved his privacy. As Madison Hemings recalled, his father, Thomas Jefferson, "hardly ever allowed himself to be made unhappy any great length of time." He would do as he pleased, and meet attacks with silence, and when necessary, tolerant smiles.

Sally Hemings would bear Thomas Jefferson yet one more child. In May 1808, at the age of thirty-five, she gave birth to Thomas Eston Hemings, the son whose paternity has been genetically linked to a Jefferson male. Jefferson was sixty-five years old when Eston was born, but Sally was only thirty-five, assuredly still young enough to bear more children. She did not. In 1809, Patsy Randolph and her chil-

dren moved to Monticello, a fact that would not have made any difference in Sally's childbearing had anyone but Thomas Jefferson been
the father of her children. The permanent presence of his disapprov-
ing and possessive daughter may have put a damper on relations between Jefferson and his concubine. Or perhaps she had medical or
emotional issues of her own.

Sally's life too was changing. In 1807, Elizabeth Hemings died.
This founding mother had come to Jefferson's mountaintop with
Martha Jefferson and six of John Wayles's other sons and daughters
more than thirty years before. Betty Hemings raised her children
and grandchildren to educate themselves as best they could, to learn
skills, and to dream of freedom. That dream came true for at least
four of her five sons, perhaps all of them, and many of her grandchildren. She also bequeathed her daughters the example of a woman
making the best of her situation by seeking an alliance with a powerful man. Her oldest daughter, Mary, and her youngest, Sally, followed
in her footsteps.

When she was gone, the Hemings family, and indeed, all of Monticello, had lost a matriarch. Even though Sally Hemings emulated
her mother in her most important life choices, she was now nobody's
daughter and left to set her own course. It was she who must set the
example for the children; she who must teach them to dream free.
If age had dulled Thomas Jefferson's sexual desire, Sally Hemings
still enjoyed the protection of this possessive man. Once he had laid
claim to Sally Hemings as his concubine, once she bore his children,
he would expect and exact fidelity. We have no reason to believe that
Sally Hemings disappointed him.

AMERICANS—FOR THAT matter, people around the world—have been
fascinated by the strange relationship between Thomas Jefferson and
Sally Hemings, by the allure of sex across the color and caste line. But

if we are interested in complicated connections between women and men, we need look no further than Jefferson's daughter and son-in-law. When Patsy and Tom Randolph married, they had every reason to expect happiness. They had been born to privilege, and they inhabited the same social world. There had been warmth and respect between the Randolphs in the early years of their marriage. But in every marriage, expectation collides with experience, like a runaway wheelbarrow full of fragile flower pots, jolting over a rock-strewn path. The Randolphs endured the death of a child, the demands of their immense and intense families, Tom's myriad financial and emotional problems, and the continual claims of Monticello. While Patsy took pains to pretend that motherhood was no trouble to her, the repeated assaults of pregnancy and childbirth took a toll on her body and mind. And by the time of Polly's death, Thomas Mann Randolph knew that he could never best his father-in-law in the contest for his wife's affections.

Randolph alternately raged and despaired at the burden of living in Thomas Jefferson's shadow. He was a touchy man in any case, but competing with Jefferson inflamed an already volatile temperament. When he quarreled with his brother-in-law, Jack Eppes, while the two lived at the White House during their time in Congress, Randolph moved into a boardinghouse without telling his father-in-law, who was appalled to learn that Patsy's husband believed Jefferson favored Eppes. The tension, heaped on top of the already heavy load of public business and political intrigue, gave Jefferson one of his prolonged migraine headaches. It had a worse effect on Randolph. He developed a fever in the boardinghouse, and despite his earlier reservations about bloodletting, allowed himself to be bled repeatedly. By the time Jefferson persuaded him to move back in, Tom Randolph was so weak and feverish that Jefferson feared his son-in-law would die.

After tender nursing by Jefferson and an attentive doctor, Randolph slowly mended. Jefferson wrote to Patsy by every post, detailing the progress of Randolph's recovery. She was much relieved as Tom Randolph passed the point of danger, but more worried about her father's health than her husband's. "I make no exception when I say the first and most important object with me will be the dear and sacred duty of nursing and chearing your old age, by every endearment of filial tenderness," she assured Jefferson. "My fancy dwells with rapture upon your image seated by your own fire side surrounded by your grand children contending for the pleasure of waiting upon you."

Thomas Mann Randolph was conspicuously absent from his wife's rapturous fantasy. Even before Jefferson's retirement, before Patsy and the children moved to Monticello, Randolph often lived apart from his wife. When they were together, they had periods of amity, but he was prone to outbursts of temper and bouts of drinking. He was sensitive to a fault, manically impulsive, quick to take offense and to leap to unwise action. During his time in Congress, he quarreled with his vicious cousin, John Randolph of Roanoke, and was near to fighting a duel when Thomas Jefferson and others talked him down. He enlisted in the War of 1812, became an officer, and marched to Canada, but resigned in 1815 after disagreeing with his commanding general. After he returned, bitter and alienated, he spent much of his time away from his family.

No one can guess at the chemistry of passion and power, duty and despair, force, silence, acquiescence, affection, and anger that simmered between Jefferson's daughter and her tormented husband. Patsy bore Thomas Mann Randolph twelve children, nearly one every other year, despite their periods of friction and separation, exasperation and deep disappointment. In 1818, at the age of forty-six, she delivered her youngest son, George Wythe Randolph, named for her father's legal mentor. The Randolphs' marriage was many things. But it was not a haven of domestic tranquility.

* * *

NO ONE WHO reads Jefferson's correspondence with his grandchildren could doubt that Thomas Jefferson was a doting grandfather. They adored him in return. Patsy raised her children to compete for Jefferson's attention and affection. She devoted "every moment that I could command" to their education, and fretted when they did not make the progress she thought they should. Patsy Jefferson Randolph was a woman of prodigious intellectual gifts, in her time one of the best-educated women in the United States. She was a disciplined and demanding teacher, and her children too often frustrated her expectations. "My 2 eldest are uncommonly backward in every thing much more so than many others, who have not had half the pains taken with them," she complained to her father in 1801. Anne and young Thomas Jefferson Randolph gave her "serious anxiety with regard to their intellect," and Anne in particular "appears to me to learn absolutely without profit." Patsy was relieved, however, that "Ellen is wonderfully apt. I shall have no trouble with her." Ellen, at that time only five years old, was already emerging as Jefferson's pet, his little "Elleanoroon," and already competing with Cornelia, age two, for her grandfather's favor. "Ellen counts the weeks and continues storing up complaints against Cornelia whom she is perpetually threatening with *your* displeasure," Patsy noted, wryly. "Long is the list of misdemeanors which is to be communicated to you, amongst which the stealing of 2 potatoes carefully preserved 2 whole days for you but at last stolen by Cornelia forms a weighty article."

Instead of measuring all the children by one standard, Thomas Jefferson valued each grandchild for her or his particular gifts. He eagerly encouraged them as they revealed their individual aptitudes and fascinations. He tried to reassure Patsy that her eldest children, if not as bright as precocious Ellen, had their virtues. He thought Anne "apt, intelligent, good humored and of soft and affectionate dispositions and that she will make a pleasant, amiable, and respectable woman." He believed his namesake grandson had a good disposition, but declined to fret about whether the boy had much intellect: "It is not every heavy-seeming boy which makes a man of judgment, but I never yet saw a man of judgment who had not been a heavy seeming boy, nor knew a boy of what are called sprightly parts become a man of judgment." He insisted that "I set much less store by talents than good dispositions; and shall be perfectly happy to see Jefferson a good man, industrious farmer, and kind and beloved among all his neighbors."

Heavy-seeming or otherwise, Jefferson Randolph and his brothers went off from their mother's parlor classroom to study with tutors, and if they desired, to go to college. The girls learned their lessons at home and continued to study as it suited them. Patsy instructed her daughters in reading and writing, classics and languages, and music and the arts.

Educated as they were, both their mother and grandfather expected the Randolph girls to take up housekeeping as their vocation. Thomas Jefferson sent his granddaughters chickens to raise and plants to nurture. By 1805, fourteen-year-old Anne began to take on some of the household management at Monticello, documenting her work in a particularly poignant way. On the family's annual summer visit to the mountain, Anne came across Martha Wayles Skelton Jefferson's household account book. Taking up this memento of the grandmother she had never known, Anne began to keep track of her own housekeeping, beginning with the entry "paid John Hemmings in full discharge of every thing due." Like Martha Jefferson, Anne traded with Monticello slaves for chickens and eggs, fruits and vegetables. The Hemings family appeared frequently in her transactions. Betty Hemings, Sally's sisters Nance and Critta, and her brothers Peter and John, sold Anne chickens and eggs. Eight-year-old Beverly Hemings picked and sold Anne Randolph three quarts of strawberries one June day in 1806. But

Sally Hemings's name was absent from these accounts, which covered the years between the births of Madison and Eston Hemings, who were, like their brother Beverly, Anne Randolph's half-uncles.

Patsy was correct in thinking that her oldest daughter would never be a scholar. But Thomas Jefferson was equally right in believing that there was more to Anne than her mother credited. Anne Randolph was a gentle girl who shared her grandfather's passion for gardening. When she was only eleven, he wrote to her requesting a report on frost damage to his gardens and orchards, and asked her to ride over to Monticello from Edgehill to check on his peas and figs. By the summer of 1807, Jefferson was treating Anne as his Monticello gardening apprentice, asking her to report on "the state of our joint concerns there." He sent her seeds, plants, and roots. She in turn sent detailed accounts of which of his flowers and fruits and vegetables thrived and which died, and saved seeds. Anne developed a wide knowledge especially of flowers, enumerating the varied fates of his tuberoses and amaryllis, lilies and lobelia, anemonies and ranunculi, a flowering pea from the Arkansas River sent by Meriwether Lewis, and a plant commonly called twinleaf but known to Anne as Jeffersonia.

Of course, when Anne (or for that matter, her grandfather) spoke of gardening, they had no intention of wielding shovels themselves. "The tulips and Hyacinths," she told Jefferson, "I had planted before I left Monticello." The person who did the planting was almost surely Wormley Hughes, the Hemings cousin who served as Jefferson's master gardener, and also succeeded Jupiter in caring for and driving the master's horses. Wormley Hughes would one day dig Thomas Jefferson's grave.

JUST AS JEFFERSON imparted his love of gardening to his eldest grandchild, he shared his ardor for reading and writing with his second granddaughter, Ellen Wayles Randolph. By the time she had reached the age of five, Ellen had taught herself to read "by continually spelling out lines and putting them together and then reading them to who ever would listen to her." She clamored to learn to write as well, and Jefferson rewarded her enthusiasm by sending her a letter as soon as he knew she could read. He began by teasing her about her aversion to getting up early, telling her "I will catch you in bed on Sunday or Monday morning," a theme that soon became a comic refrain in their correspondence. Ellen would prove that anyone who wanted to get the better of her had best get up early in the morning, indeed. When Jefferson sent Ellen's ten-year-old brother, Jefferson Randolph, a French grammar, six-year-old Ellen demanded to learn French.

By that time, Patsy had reached the conclusion that even if others of her children were "blockheads," Ellen had inherited no small part of her grandfather's genius. Surviving childhood in the Randolph household was not easy. Ellen seemed to suffer even more than the others, catching everything from "eruptions" to whooping cough. But she endeared herself ever more to her mother with her zeal for reading. In the grip of a potentially lethal attack of dysentery, Patsy reported, Ellen "became thro the day delirious but employing every lucid interval in reading. Judge of my feelings My Dearest Father," wrote Patsy, "when hanging over her in agonies indescribable to have some question of natural history which she was reading at the time addressed to me by the little sufferer the activity of whose mind even the most acute bodily pain was never capable of subduing."

While he was president, Jefferson corresponded with his grandchildren, sending them books and bits of "newspaper poetry" for the literary scrapbooks he encouraged them to keep. Both Anne and Jefferson Randolph learned to read and translate Latin, and young Jefferson liked to read history and geography. They wrote to their grandfather with pride in their accomplishments. Ellen, though, soon outpaced her older siblings by writing to him frequently and at length.

By the age of nine, Ellen was engaging Jefferson in intellectual discussions. When she asked him to name the "seventh fine art," since she and her mother could only recall six ("Painting, Sculpture, architecture, Music, Poetry, Oratory"), he responded with a disquisition on the history of the concept of the fine arts, and, citing Lord Kames, made the case for including gardening ("Not horticulture, but the art of embellishing grounds by fancy"). He sent her a pair of bantam chickens, proposing "a question of natural history for your enquiry: that is whether this is the Gallina Adrianica, or Adria, the Adsatick cock of Aristotle? For this you must examine Buffon, etc." Ten-year-old Ellen replied that she had begun reading Greek history, doing multiplication, reading in French, and copying "the historical part of Lord Chesterfield's letters for a lesson in writing." At night, she said, she sewed while her sister Anne read aloud to the family. But she had not forgotten the matter of the chickens. Relishing an intellectual joust with her famous grandfather, the little girl added a postscript: "Mama says Buffon cannot answer the question you propose to me."

Jefferson could not answer Ellen's letters as fast as she wrote them, and pleaded for her patience, since "the tide of business, like that of the ocean, will wait for nobody." She conceded that he surely had more to do than she did, and amused him with the kind of "small stuff" from home that he craved in Washington. Ellen Randolph surprised, impressed, and delighted Thomas Jefferson. But if she was Jefferson's intellectual heir, she must play the role not of the man of genius, but of the accomplished woman. Her grandfather reminded her that however learned she hoped to be, she was destined for housekeeping. Jefferson urged Ellen to turn from the contemplation of higher things to "descend to the more useful region and occupations of the good housewife, one of whom is worth more than the whole family of the muses."

At one point Jefferson suggested to Ellen that she use her natural history books not to master a world of taxonomies and possibilities, but instead to learn about the four varieties of sheep he had recently acquired. For three of the varieties, he had only individuals of one sex, but thought he might interbreed them selectively and maintain pure strains, because "4. crossings are understood by naturalists to produce the true breed."

WITH THIS OFFHAND bit of interpretive animal husbandry, Jefferson raised with his small granddaughter the touchy subject of interbreeding. That likely did not resonate with Ellen Randolph at the time, but as it turned out, she would be preoccupied for the rest of her life with the problem of crossing and interbreeding. Ellen may only gradually have become aware of the tangled connections between her own family and Thomas Jefferson's shadow family, the Hemingses. But the fact that the young Randolphs and the four Hemings children, their uncles and aunt by blood, were all about the same age would suggest that they were very aware of each other. According to Virginia law, which Thomas Jefferson accepted as "our canon," the Hemingses, being less than one-quarter African, were already white people, just like Ellen Randolph herself.

Three of his four Hemings children claimed that white identity, two of them, evidently, with Thomas Jefferson's blessing. Ellen Randolph and her brother Jefferson, however, would vigorously deny the Jefferson connection to the Hemingses. They would carry on an elaborate family tradition of pretending that this shadow family virtually did not exist.

Thomas Jefferson showed them that this habit of denial was their duty, in the largest and smallest particulars. As he reminded Ellen of her responsibility to her chickens, he explained that "I rely on you for their care, as I do on Anne for the Algerine fowls, and on our arrangements at Monticello for the East Indians. These varieties are pleasant for the table and furnish an agreeable diversification in our domestic occupations." "Our arrangements at Monticello" was an oblique way to refer to enslaved people like the Hemingses, who raised chickens by the dozen, as we know from Anne Randolph's household accounts. Thomas Jefferson possessed two families who lived side by side, one enslaved and nominally black, the other entitled and putatively white. At a future date he would permit his slave children to go free, and to seek, if they chose, to cross over the racial divide, having already been "bred true." In the meantime, each in turn furnished "an agreeable diversification" in his domestic occupations.

26

The Pursuit of Happiness

FOR THOMAS JEFFERSON, the end to government service could not come soon enough. His second term as president was, in Dumas Malone's charitable estimation, "certainly not the most glorious of his public life." Others might call it something of a disaster, from Vice President Aaron Burr's alleged conspiracy to seize the lion's share of Louisiana Territory as a kingdom for himself, followed by Burr's trial for treason (he was acquitted), to the ill-conceived, ruinous embargo against Britain and France.

Nearly every letter Jefferson wrote to Patsy between 1805 and 1809 announced his weariness with public wrangling and his longing to get back home. Patsy had served as interim mistress of Monticello. Now both of them looked forward to her permanent move back to the place she had always considered her home. She would run her father's household and see to his comfort while her children diverted and revered him. He in turn would shower them all with love, inspire and instruct them, enjoy the luxury to read and think, refresh himself with wholesome country life, and generally pursue happiness. His grandchildren could hardly wait for his return. "How I long for the time that you are to come home to live and then we shall all go to

Monticello to live with you," wrote Ellen, a sentiment Anne enthusiastically seconded. "It wont be long now thank God before you come home to live with us."

Even as they spoke of surrounding the returning patriarch with peace and love, they all knew that Monticello would not provide a tranquil refuge. They would have to guard jealously their moments of privacy and pleasure. The crowds had come before, but now, as they welcomed a president home, there would be hordes eager to see the Sage of Monticello, to get their morsel of the famous Jefferson hospitality, to gawk and talk and eat and drink, to trample his grounds and peer in his windows and demand his attention. No doubt some intruders hoped to get a glimpse of Sally Hemings and her children. His presidency had survived the scandal, and Thomas Jefferson might pretend that he had laid the Hemings scandal to rest, but the rumors continued to percolate. The Federalist-sympathizing Irish poet Thomas Moore had visited the White House in 1803, receiving a cool reception from the president. He took his anger and Federalist gossip about Jefferson's private life back to England, where he composed the verse that kept the story alive for decades:

> *The weary statesman for repose hath fled*
> *From halls of council to his negro's shed,*
> *Where blest he woos some black Aspasia's grace,*
> *And dreams of freedom in his slave's embrace!*

Monticello was no longer at the edge of civilization and far above the babble and the rabble. Every day, especially on Sunday, friends and relations, acquaintances and utter strangers would pour down the roads from every direction to pound up his roundabouts, on foot and horseback, in carts and carriages, by the dozens, by the scores.

Anticipating the problem, Jefferson once again sought agreeable domestic diversification. Monticello had been a work in progress from the moment he had fled the smoking ruins of Shadwell to the time of his retirement from the presidency. In Europe, he had avidly studied every detail of great houses. When he returned, he had embarked on the great demolition and renovation that produced the white-columned brick Palladian masterpiece familiar to historians and tourists today. Monticello was a huge project, eventually encompassing eleven thousand square feet and forty-three rooms, including the workspaces under the house. Construction was not fully completed until 1809, when he finally returned home for good.

Toward the end of the renovation, Jefferson realized too late that in adding terraces on both sides of the house, he had made it possible for any curious person passing by to see right into his bedroom. Casting aside Palladio's insistence on symmetrical façades, Jefferson decided to add one more detail to protect his privacy. He ordered the construction of small louvered verandas, or "porticles," on either side of the greenhouse abutting his bedroom-cabinet-library suite. In these sheltered spaces he could sit outside without being seen. They also insulated his private apartments from prying eyes. If the porticles were intended to shield Sally Hemings's comings and goings from his bedroom, her family surely was not deceived; her brother John Hemings, the powerfully talented carpenter and furniture maker, built them. But at least the porticles hid Jefferson from the visiting multitudes.

Thomas Jefferson had taken a page from the noble apartments in the palaces of England and France and Italy in designing his spacious private quarters. He also followed the European pattern in turning the second floor of his house into a mezzanine, hidden from outside view, and in lighting the third floor with skylights. The majestic dome room, which gives the house its iconic profile, proved a bit of a puzzle to furnish and use. The porthole windows, designed for their pleasing aspect to outside viewers, were placed too high to see out of, and the space was too large to serve as a regular bedroom. Visitors sometimes lodged there, but most of the time it was used as a storeroom, full of extra furniture and bedding. Meanwhile, the Randolphs (and often other relatives) piled into the five second-floor and three third-floor bedrooms, along with surplus guests. Since there were often small children in residence (Patsy's children and, eventually, her grandchildren), enslaved nannies and nurses and child attendants would have been within calling, at least some of the time.

For all the grace and grandeur of the downstairs quarters, including the two elegant bedrooms that housed distinguished visitors, the upstairs bedrooms were dim, cramped, and stifling in hot weather. They were accessible only by two equally dark and narrow staircases, built to save both money and space. Anyone going up or down those stairs in skirts and petticoats would have had to squeeze through. Someone carrying a chamber pot or a child would have to step carefully, to say the least.

For Patsy's growing daughters, Monticello was a beloved place, but short on comfort and privacy. Few people of the time expected to have living space to themselves, but Thomas Jefferson insisted on his own grand and secluded quarters for reading, writing, and reflection. His learned daughter and her educated children envied his example. Ellen and Cornelia and their younger sisters Virginia and Mary all complained that between the demands of company and the lack of personal space, they could not study as they needed to do. They wrote letters in stolen moments, wherever they could find a place to perch, apologizing to the recipients for the hasty and disjointed "scrawls" and imploring the reader to "throw this scrap in the fire." Cornelia, who showed an early gift for drawing that blossomed into a talent for rendering architectural plans as well as domestic subjects, could never seem to find the time or place for her work.

Once the columns over the portico were completed, Jefferson had a floor laid in a space above to serve as a storage area, a not-quite-accessible drop down from the dome room. Virginia enlisted Cornelia's help in claiming the space. They piled up boxes to construct makeshift steps, hauled in an old cushionless sofa, and installed a couple of chairs and small tables to serve as writing desks. "I have taken possession with the dirt daubers, wasps and bumble beas," wrote Virginia, "and do not intend to give it up to any thing but the formidable *rats* which have not yet found out this *fairy palace*."

The Randolph children, of course, enjoyed luxurious accommodations at Monticello, compared to Jefferson's enslaved family. When Sally Hemings returned from France, she likely lived in a stone building on Mulberry Row, the slave "street" behind the main house, just above and at the edge of Jefferson's great vegetable garden. Later, Sally and her children may have moved into one of the twelve-by-fourteen-foot log cabins between the stone house and Jefferson's stable. If they lived with an earthen floor and a wooden chimney, Sally had to work at keeping things clean and managing her fires.

But just as likely, Sally may have had a room in the house. Jefferson's renovations called for stone "dependency wings" to be built under the terraces of the main house, as storerooms, kitchen, and housing for a few servants. Sally Hemings may have lived in one of the stone, brick, and wood rooms under the south terrace, close to the kitchen where her brother Peter served for a time as head cook. Those rooms may have been, as Jefferson's overseer Edmund Bacon described them, "very comfortable, warm in winter and cool in the summer," compared to the cabins on Mulberry Row. But any or all four of her children may have shared the space. Privacy was a luxury Sally Hemings had no right to demand, at least on her own behalf.

Though the Hemings children could not claim the privileges of Jefferson's free offspring, they saw themselves as a breed apart from most enslaved people. "We were free from the dread of having to be slaves all our lives long, and were measurably happy. We were always permitted to be with our mother, who was well used," Madison Hemings recalled. Up to the age of fourteen, the four Hemingses ran errands around the "great house," and after that they were taught a trade. Beverly, Eston, and Madison learned carpentry. Harriet worked in the "cotton factory," spinning and weaving. She had, of course, been expected to serve Jefferson and the Randolphs at their pleasure, though overseer Edmund Bacon insisted that Harriet "never did any hard work." But while Jefferson and Patsy relentlessly pressed the Randolph children to study their history and their Latin, to read great literature and write vivid, careful letters, no one looked to the education of the Hemingses. At the age of sixty-eight, Madison Hemings said he "learned to read by inducing the white children to teach me the letters and something more; what else I know of books I have picked up here and there till now I can read and write."

Monticello remained a musical place. Martha Wayles Skelton Jefferson had played guitar and harpsichord and pianoforte, and her daughters in turn played and owned beautiful instruments. The Randolph granddaughters were taught their music, and Virginia in particular developed a passion for the piano. Thomas Jefferson, of course, loved music, though the broken wrist he had suffered in Paris ended his violin playing for life. The Hemings children also inherited the love of music. Keyboard instruments were expensive and bulky, so Harriet may never have had her chance at a "feminine" mastery of music, but her brothers were well-known experts on the violin, who may have fiddled as they called the figures for country dances at Monticello and in the neighborhood. When Eston Hemings moved to Ohio, after his parents' deaths, his signature tune was a Scottish dance air, "Moneymusk," a song his father had copied out in manuscript years before.

*   *   *

THOMAS JEFFERSON IDEALIZED the domestic tranquility of Monti-cello, which he had spared no expense to transform into a beautiful and unique place. There were exuberant spring days when the hya-cinths bloomed in abundance, the peas fattened in their pods, the sounds of industry rang forth from weaving shop and kitchen and nailery, Mrs. Randolph hummed at her housework, and grandpapa set the young ones racing toward the house with a drop of his hand-kerchief.

There were other days when everyone was sick, when Cornelia or Virginia or whichever daughter had her month of housekeeping, that hated period of "carrying the keys" to the locked cellars and storage rooms. All the girls had to cope with quarreling children or angry servants, not to mention ten or twenty guests coming to dinner and staying overnight. Patsy worried at the toll so much company took on her aging father's health, not to mention the strain on his resources.

But Jefferson had his way of coping with the crush. He would, as he so often had, ride away. From the moment he ascended to the pres-idency, Thomas Jefferson had been planning his getaway. He began to make sketches for a noble villa, three days' travel southwest of his Albemarle residence, at Poplar Forest, the Bedford County property that Martha had inherited from John Wayles. The Jefferson family had stayed at an overseer's house there during their flight from Corn-wallis in 1781; Jefferson had written his *Notes on the State of Virginia* there while recovering from a fall from his horse. In 1805 he traveled to Poplar Forest to meet with his master bricklayer, to discuss his plans for the octagonal brick house that would be his second archi-tectural masterwork. The foundation would be laid in 1806.

By 1811, Jefferson began to make regular trips to Poplar Forest. He traveled to his sanctuary with his valet, Sally Hemings's nephew

Burwell Colbert, or with John Hemings, Beverly, Madison, or Eston Hemings, and usually with one or more members of his white family. Patsy only rarely got to enjoy the indulgence of a vacation from Monticello, but on occasion she got to go to Poplar Forest. In September 1816 she left most of her children, including two-year-old Septimia, back in Albemarle, putting her husband and her daughter Ellen in charge of the household. "You may consider your journey to Bedford at this season as very fortunate," Ellen wrote her mother, "for it has saved you from many disagreable intrusions; we have had several large parties from the springs, and a coach & four is by no means an uncommon sight at the door." The uninvited guests included "impudent and ungenteel people who behaved as if they had been in a tavern" and "dashing but not genteel Carolinians, [who] made a great noise asked a great many silly questions and at last went away leaving papa and myself weary & disgusted." Ellen consoled herself with the fact that at least her mother and grandfather had been spared the annoyance of such company. "These intruders," she said, "have pretty generally expressed their regret at Grand Papa's absence and I have rejoiced at it—on his account—not on my own God knows."

Ellen, like her sisters, had to take her part in inventorying the hams and counting the silver and bossing the servants, jobs her grandfather regarded as labors of love. But she would often enjoy the privilege of escaping. By the time they reached their teens, Ellen and Cornelia were Jefferson's most frequent companions on his journeys to his Bedford County refuge. All three reveled in the chance to read and think without interruption, and the girls competed with one another for the title of most serious scholar. At Poplar Forest, she and her sister had the rare luxury of a room of their own. "Ellen and Cornelia are the severest students I have ever met with. They never leave their room but to come to meals," Jefferson noted. Of course, at that very moment, the inveterate puller-down-and-putter-up was supervising "an alteration in that part of the house" which "deprived them of their room longer than I expected."

Whatever inconvenience they encountered, the girls seized the opportunity for quiet study at Poplar Forest. As with all vacation houses, the place sometimes showed the effects of absence and neglect. On a visit in July 1819, they found the weeds growing up to the kitchen door, the planks of the terrace torn up by the wind, and every window on the front of the house shattered by a recent hailstorm. Rain had poured in, staining the floors and leaving behind mold and must. The central skylight was shattered, but the windows in their own room had been spared. Both girls quickly unpacked their books and Cornelia set out her drawings and tools. Ellen wandered from room to room, cheered at the thought of how much she got done at a place that seemed "more dismal than usual," wild and desolate. "Here, every day for six weeks at a time I have devoted from seven to eight hours to my latin . . . there hour after hour, I have poured [*sic*] over volumes of history, which I should in vain have attempted to read at Monticello."

What to do with such passionate students? Thomas Jefferson willingly added to his burden of debt the cost of educating his eldest grandsons, Jeff Randolph and Francis Eppes. He was determined that Jeff go to Philadelphia to attend lectures in science, anatomy, and surgery, though the boy had neither appetite nor aptitude for the work. Jefferson likewise patiently endured Francis's endless complaints about his schoolmasters and studies.

But even as Ellen roamed the wreckage at Poplar Forest in an intellectual reverie, she had no illusions about her future. "I have often thought that the life of a student must be the most innocent and happy in the world . . . the pursuit of knowledge unlike other pursuits is subject to no disappointments." She would have loved to learn for learning's sake, as her grandfather seemed to do. But as a woman she could not afford to do so. "If I had been a man with the advantages of early education, I would have been just such a one, I think, but being a woman and not a rich woman, I must be content with peeping every now and then into a region too blissfull for my inhabitance, and after having felt myself for a short interval as 'passionless and pure' as Byron's Spirit, return to the vanities, follies cares and pleasures of ordinary life."

OF COURSE, EVEN the most brilliantly idealistic men had to come to grips with the follies and cares of ordinary life. Thomas Jefferson himself was still in the White House when he began to acknowledge the reality that would eventually overwhelm all others: his burgeoning debt. Jefferson was hardly alone in owing far more than he could pay. By the beginning of the nineteenth century, the Virginia gentry was sinking fast, and none faster than the Randolph clan. Patsy wrote to her father in January 1808, detailing the fading fortunes of her husband, who had already been forced to sell land and slaves to pay his most obdurate creditors, but who was perpetually fighting off bankruptcy. Tom Randolph's siblings had similar difficulties. Two of his sisters had been abandoned by their bankrupt husbands, and one brother was homeless. Another carried a pistol to keep the sheriff from arresting him, and when the gun went off in his pocket, he was crippled for life. "The ruin of the family is still extending itself daily," Patsy wrote, and though she had persuaded her husband not to co-sign his brothers' IOUs, they remained "both in a state of great anxiety."

Jefferson replied that he wished he could help his son-in-law, but he had his own problems. "I have now the gloomy prospect of retiring from office loaded with serious debts, which will materially affect the tranquility of my retirement," he admitted. Still, he insisted on taking an optimistic view of his difficulties. "Not being apt to deject myself with evils before they happen," he told Patsy, "I nourish the hope of getting along."

Far from being reassured, Patsy was appalled at her father's impracticality. "Your last letter has cast a gloom over my spirits that I can not shake off," she told him. "The impossibility of paying serious debts by crops, and living at the same time, has been so often proved, that I am afraid you should trust to it." She urged Jefferson to think only of his own comfort, and "not to consider the children but secure your own tranquility and ours will follow of course." Solicitous as always of her father's happiness, Patsy Randolph was a realist. Even at his best moments, her unstable husband could not pay what he owed, could not avoid the entanglements of his demanding family, and he definitely could not make a living growing tobacco with slave labor. How Thomas Jefferson would manage his even greater obligations, she could not tell.

Despite her mounting dread, Patsy Randolph urged her father to pursue his pleasures as he saw fit. Jefferson, in turn, begged her not to deny herself or her children anything that his credit could purchase for them. Patsy fretted and scrimped and saved, while he continued to play the lofty Virginia planter, spending lavishly, gratifying his architectural passions and his epicurean tastes, pressing his plans for educating his grandsons, for launching his granddaughters into society and onto the marriage market. Poplar Forest satisfied his need for privacy and peace, but that refuge from the hectic din at Monticello was yet another drain on his dwindling pool of resources. In his mind he was still the provider and protector of his family, and in theirs he was the revered patriarch. But more and more, Thomas Jefferson had come to rely on his purported dependents, enslaved and free, for his physical, psychological, and financial comfort and security.

27

The Perils of Matrimony

AS HE SETTLED into retirement at home, Thomas Jefferson devoted his still formidable talents to one of his proudest achievements, the building of the University of Virginia. He was determined to create a first-rate institution of higher learning, amply supported, felicitously designed, fully equipped, and preferably in Charlottesville. He had been thinking about a state university for years, and by 1817 he had managed to convince the state to fund the enterprise and to locate the university in his hometown. The process of getting the university adequately financed, built, and into operation lasted nearly the rest of his days.

Jefferson hoped to live to see his grandsons at the university. But in 1825, when the first students began to attend classes, the eldest among them, Jefferson Randolph, had already finished his education and was busy managing his grandfather's farm while trying to establish his own growing family. Patsy's younger sons, James and Ben, would eventually join the student body. None of his grandsons were serious scholars, but then, in general, the young men fortunate enough to go to the university were more notable for their family connections than their intellectual curiosity. One of Thomas Mann Randolph's nephews was among those expelled after a drunken student riot the first year of operation.

Even though Patsy Randolph's daughters were as well educated as any women in the United States, and better schooled than most American men of their time, there was no question of college attendance for them. Anne, Ellen, Cornelia, Virginia, and Mary Randolph were formally instructed by Jefferson's closest disciple, his curious, disciplined, patient, brilliant daughter. Martha Jefferson Randolph complained that child care, health problems, her husband's misfortunes, and the endless company at Monticello made it impossible for her to attend to her own reading and writing, but she was utterly determined to educate all her children, female as well as male. Ellen and Cornelia were her most dedicated students, but even the least intellectual among them had the benefit of a teacher who knew far more about most things than most people, let alone most women, because her father had worried that she might marry a blockhead. In 1962, President John F. Kennedy would famously tell a White House dinner gathering of Nobel Prize winners that "I think this is the most extraordinary collection of talent, of human knowledge, that has ever been gathered together at the White House, with the possible exception of when Thomas Jefferson dined alone." At Monticello, the earlier gathering of genius was multiplied. There, unlike the White House, Thomas Jefferson had the good fortune to dine with Patsy Randolph.

But the Randolph girls were not at liberty to use their education, their talents, or their ambitions to make their way in the world as they would. Anne could not take to the road on botanical expeditions as the Quaker William Bartram did. Ellen could not study Latin and Greek and law and run for the legislature. Cornelia could not turn her architectural drawings into houses for the wealthy. Instead they had to find a man who might provide them with prosperity and security. They brought to the marriage market some distinct assets: distinguished family, fine manners, sensible and even scintillating conversation, the skills of plantation mistresses, and not least, their close connection to their revered grandfather. But as time passed, their fortunes declined along with those of Thomas Mann Randolph and Thomas Jefferson. Without dowries, they had trouble attracting suitable men.

Jefferson's eldest granddaughter was the first to find a husband. On September 19, 1808, seventeen-year-old Anne Cary Randolph, the gentle soul who delighted in flowers, married the handsome Charles Lewis Bankhead, at Monticello. Anne's mother had her hands full, as usual, having given birth only two months before to her ninth child. But Patsy had reason to hope that Anne had made a good match. The groom's father was a distinguished Virginia doctor and Charles Bankhead himself was planning to study the law. Jefferson anticipated that Anne and her husband would live for at least a time at Monticello, where Bankhead would avail himself of Jefferson's law books. Anne obviously hoped for the same. Two months after the wedding, when they finally left the mountain to visit his family, Patsy reported that the bride was "in a state of such extreme dejection at the separation from her family that it rendered the scene a very distressing one."

By 1812, the Bankheads were living at Carlton, an eight-hundred-acre farm on the west slope of Monticello Mountain. It may have seemed to Thomas Jefferson that his long-standing dream of keeping his family close was coming true. But Anne's bridal anguish turned out to be prescient. Four years into his marriage, Charles Bankhead had proven himself a violent drunkard, already deep in debt and utterly unable to manage his affairs. Anne had taken refuge with her mother-in-law, with Bankhead evidently out of the picture for the time being. Jefferson and Bankhead's father assumed his debts and took control of his house and land, for the support of Anne and her children. Her husband was to have absolutely no part in that management.

Jefferson took the additional step of adding 130 acres to the property, exclusively for the benefit of his beleaguered granddaughter. He had to set aside his deep belief that women were fitted by nature to depend entirely on men, in order to provide for Anne. More than anything, Anne Bankhead needed protection *from* her husband, and only financial independence could give her any hope of security. "Hers," Patsy lamented, "has been a hard fate."

Patsy understated the matter. Anne Randolph Bankhead's marriage was a living hell. Charles Bankhead was locally famous for getting roaring drunk and beating up his wife and children. Virginia society tended to tolerate bad behavior in husbands (witness Jefferson's advice to his newly married daughter Polly, preaching the wife's duty to bow to her husband's wishes, and her obligation to conciliate even an alcoholic husband). But Bankhead was not gentleman enough to confine his brutality to his own household. Edmund Bacon, Jefferson's Monticello overseer, recalled that "I have seen his wife run from him when he was drunk and hide in a potato hole to get out of danger."

Thomas Jefferson prided himself on his peaceful household. Bankhead brought violence right into Jefferson's home. According to Edmund Bacon, one night Bankhead had attacked Burwell Colbert, the Monticello majordomo, in Jefferson's dining room, because Colbert refused to give him any more liquor. "Mrs. Randolph could not manage him," said Bacon, so she sent for the overseer rather than for her husband, who was too "excitable" to settle such matters reliably. But Thomas Mann Randolph heard the noise, rushed in, grabbed a fireplace poker, and knocked his son-in-law down "as quick as I ever saw a bullock fall," said Bacon. "The blow pealed the skin off one side of his forehead and face, and he bled terribly."

Anne's husband became so uncontrollable that he was at first consigned to his own father's medical care, and for a time, to an asylum.

In 1816 he returned to visit Monticello, but Patsy reported to her father that Bankhead had "recommenced his habits of drunkenness." Patsy and Tom Randolph were ready to send him to jail, if necessary, declaring, "If his family are much disturbed or endangered will take at once the steps necessary for their protection, as circumstances may require." Patsy did not see any use in "sending him to the mad house," since Bankhead would only return "with renewed health to torment his family longer." Instead she thought they should hire "a keeper" to prevent him from harming others, "and let him finish him self at once."

Charles Bankhead did not drink himself to death, as his mother-in-law wished he would. Anne, much to everyone's dismay, would not leave her husband and come permanently to live at Monticello. Thomas Jefferson admitted that he had "for some time taken for granted that she would fall by his hands." But he believed Anne was "too attached" to Bankhead to listen to her worried family and abandon her monster of a husband. Jefferson thought wives should love their husbands, but it seemed that love could turn to poison.

No one at the time understood the psychology of battered women, the demeaning and the isolation and the terror that decimate self-esteem and lead women who have been abused to imagine that they are the ones at fault. In Anne's time, neither the law nor the custom of the country gave a runaway wife much hope or support. Anne Bankhead, too ashamed to imagine herself worthy of her family's care, did what millions of women in her hideous situation did before and have done since. She stayed with her abuser.

Charles Bankhead, for his part, continued to embarrass and infuriate the Jefferson-Randolph clan. February 1, 1819, was court day in Charlottesville, a time when men came together from their scattered plantations to settle their legal disputes, to drink and socialize and politick, and to fight. Some incident—others later claimed that Bankhead had sent an abusive letter to Jeff Randolph's wife, but it may have been that Anne's brother had simply had enough of his brother-in-law's outrages against his sister—provoked the confrontation. Jeff Randolph was waiting for Bankhead at a Charlottesville store, armed with a horsewhip. Bankhead arrived carrying several knives. In the melee that followed, Bankhead stabbed Randolph in the hip and left arm, and Randolph, bleeding profusely, was carried into the store for treatment. Bankhead was taken to court and made to post bail. Thomas Jefferson had already come to rely heavily on his stalwart eldest grandson and heir apparent. Now news of the fight came to Monticello, with reports that Jeff had been seriously wounded. The old man had his horse saddled. He rode to town in the darkness, walked into the store where his cherished namesake lay suffering, and wept.

EVEN AFTER CHARLES Bankhead had stabbed her brother, Anne Randolph Bankhead remained with her husband, though a man was hired to live with them because, in Patsy's words, "They will always require a protector." Anne's younger sisters looked at her hideous life and dreaded the prospect of matrimony. "I am glad to hear sister Ann is going to be settled in a home of her own, particularly as she will have protection from that brute, for I am sure she must always be miserable," wrote twenty-year-old Cornelia to eighteen-year-old Virginia, wishing that Charles Bankhead would be sent away somewhere they would never see or hear of him again. But even had Anne's marriage not been a nightmare, their parents' long and difficult relationship provided them with plenty of reason to question whether getting married really provided any security. Husbands, it seemed, might not be worth the trouble they caused.

Patsy knew how they felt, and she shared their misgivings. "Ellen fulfills the promises of her childhood," she wrote to Elizabeth House

Trist in 1815. "She is a nurse to me in sickness a friend and companion in health and to her grand Father 'the immediate jewel of his soul'
I think sometimes she will never marry and indeed after her sister's
fate I almost wish she never may." Patsy was not simply worried about
her daughters' potential husbands. She was also perpetually on the
lookout for any exhibition of touchiness, instability, or anger in her
own children, any trace of what she and they referred to as "the Randolph" in their blood. Patsy thought Ellen had inherited a tendency
to hypersensitivity from her father, which might get in the way of a
happy marriage. Her daughter's feelings were "too acute for her own
happiness she is very much like her Father but with out his temper,
and such are not calculated for this selfish world."

Even when a seemingly perfect man presented himself, Patsy hesitated to part with her daughters. With every passing year, they in turn
were more aware of how much their mother and grandfather needed
them. When eighteen-year-old Nicholas Trist, grandson of Jefferson's
old friend Eliza House Trist and already virtually a member of the
Jefferson-Randolph family, wrote to Patsy in 1817 to ask for the hand
of seventeen-year-old Virginia, Patsy put him off on the grounds that
both he and Virginia were too young. Many warm letters passed between members of the Trist and Randolph families over the next
years, while Virginia remained at Monticello and Nicholas went first
to West Point, and then began to seek his fortune, eventually to use
his nimble intelligence and family connections to pursue a career in
diplomacy. By the time they finally married, in 1824, the Randolph
sisters had long since learned to think of Nicholas as a brother, one
who could sometimes be as annoyingly arrogant as any of their bio-
logical brothers.

Trist was particularly close to Ellen, who wrote to him far more
frequently than he returned the favor, and who demonstrated that
she had inherited the family gift for sarcasm. "Really, my dear Nicho-

las, you are quite too modest and humble; you will never make your way in the world with so poor an opinion of your own merits . . . how could you so far underrate your own communications, & overvalue my poor returns as to think *one* of your letters worth only *ten* of mine—what disinterestedness & humility. the days of chivalry are reviving," Ellen told him. She pronounced herself, "tempted to quote from Sir Anthony Absolute 'Why Jack, you d—d impudent dog!' only I am afraid you might be shocked at so flagrant an usurpation of the rights of your sex, which reserves as a peculiar privilege, the use of such energetic expressions."

But Ellen loved Nicholas Trist, and the chance to converse with a learned and lively male companion overcame her irritation. She wanted to talk about John Locke's *Essay on Human Understanding*, which she had just been reading, wishing that she had read it ten years earlier, so that she might have pursued her education in a more systematic way. Still, even when she was discoursing on philosophy, Ellen could not help ribbing her almost-brother one more time for his presumption of manly privilege—"Was I a man, could my studies have any object of sufficient importance to stimulate my exertions, I would now, even now, commence my education . . . as it is, I am nothing but a woman, and could promise myself no competent reward for so much trouble—and perhaps you will say if I had not been a woman I should not have thought myself & my concerns so entertaining a subject as I appear to have done, talking to you of nothing else."

It took Nicholas Trist more than six years to marry Virginia Randolph. His bride remained at Monticello long after they had married, even after they had children. If this most beloved and promising young man had to serve such a long probationary period to be accepted by a Jefferson granddaughter (and her protective mother), how much more difficult was the task for lesser mortals. Thomas

Jefferson's grandchildren had grown up seeing their connection to him as proof of their special standing in the world. They were by no means all scholars, but they certainly were accustomed to high-powered conversation, and to being listened to in their own right. Ellen and Cornelia, launched into society at Monticello and Poplar Forest and Richmond, routinely contrasted the sophisticated talk at Monticello with the vapid babble they endured elsewhere, and they were savage critics of the young people they met. Cornelia mocked a pretty girl who had caught the eye of her cousin Francis Eppes, by quoting a piece of doggerel: "All the brains / That little squashy head contains, Wouldent fill a musqueto's eye sir."

Ellen and Cornelia amused each other by heaping scorn on the people they met. Ellen wrote to her mother from Richmond, mentioning "Mr Wilson, the member of legislature, whom [Cornelia] may remember always neatly dressed and powdered, and talking of Philadelphia 'till even I got weary of the subject—if she does not know him by these tokens, bid her remember him as one of the alligators, whose open mouths and furious gestures, gave me such reasonable alarm at the governer's party." The Randolph girls made an inside joke of referring to their beaux as "alligators," much to their mother's amusement. But smart girls who imagined potential friends and suitors in terms of mosquitos' eyes and alligators' mouths tend not to be very approachable. Thomas Jefferson's granddaughters must have scared the life out of potential aspirants.

Cornelia and her younger sister Mary never married. Mary may have been too shy, and in any case, by the time she had reached the age of marriage, her father was already ruined and her grandfather was facing disaster. Cornelia was another story. Though Ellen was clearly Thomas Jefferson's favorite granddaughter, Cornelia competed with her older sister for her grandfather's approval. She was serious about her studies, disciplined about her art, and stalwart about bearing her share of the housekeeping duties. But Cornelia could not bring herself to engage in the dead-serious frivolity of finding a husband. When she and Ellen were sent to Richmond to stay with their aunt Mary Randolph, Cornelia was "bashful" to a fault, telling Virginia that "as to being able to enter into conversation wi[th] any one, it is a thing I find more difficult than ever." She chafed at social rituals and hated having to make conversation with "stupid" young men who impressed her as "puppies."

On a visit to Richmond, Cornelia could barely endure the ordeals of grooming and socializing. She wrote home to complain to Virginia that "I have either been sick or in an ill humour, or stupefied or more truly all three together ever since I have been here." She had borrowed some architectural books from a male acquaintance, but had "scarcely look'd into them," since she had "no time to do any thing useful or agreeable." Instead convention dictated that she fritter away her days doing pretty much nothing. Cornelia's bitter description of her life in Richmond recalled her grandfather's satiric rendering of the preening and boredom of Parisiennes:

> we get up evry morning just in time to dress for breakfast, & after that is over we come up & dress again to recieve company, we set in the drawin room from this time untill . . . it is time to adjust our dress for dinner, we cannot . . . work in the drawing room because . . . there is almost constantly some visitor there; after dinner it is too dark to do any thing & from that time untill ten oclock . . . we all set round the fire except the gentlemen who choose to play cards, & some talk nonsense, & some yawn & stretch, & pull out their watches & wonder at its being so early & would all fairly go to sleep at last if they did not seem to be afraid of this & do every thing in their power to keep themselves awake each exerts himself by turns to make a noise.

Cornelia retired early and gratefully from the field, but Ellen remained in the hunt. From the time she was eighteen, Ellen made frequent visits to Richmond, staying in her aunt Mary Randolph's thriving boardinghouse for weeks at a time. She wrote long letters home, describing the interesting and indolent gentlemen she met, the elegant dresses other young women wore. She was at first appalled by the cost of fashion. She sent her mother a piece of fine fabric "to have made for me," guilty at the thought of the other women of Monticello clad in rude cotton while she wore expensive linen, but her aunt had insisted that she could not go about town in "coarse and slazy" clothing.

As time passed, Ellen grew accustomed to spending money on herself, to paying for clothes and shoes and shawls and bonnets, and sometimes even for dressmaking. Ellen had traveled some distance, if not in miles, in habit, from the home where enslaved women wove the homespun garments that Patsy insisted the family wear during Thomas Jefferson's embargo. But even as she began to visit in town and receive callers at Monticello, Ellen could not think of dressing appropriately without calling on the skills of slaves back home. Anticipating her return from Poplar Forest in the spring of 1818, Ellen issued minute and imperious instructions for dressmaking by her own servant, Sally Cottrell:

I left cambric for one pair of sleeves, which Sally can cut out by the paper pattern, taking care to make them longer & larger, and besides this to allow for eight narrow tucks, which she must put in them as they are for my tucked frock which I brought have with me—she knows how to frill them . . . I wish my cambric frock with the pointed flounce, to have a new plain flounce, and new sleeves with three puffings like Cornelia's stuff—the cambric dress with the striped flounce to have new plain sleeves with straps to them, and the flounce ripped off—when she has done this and it is not a week's work; she may begin the tail of my striped muslin—which she is to trim with three puffings, in the manner of Cornelia's sleeves, set on above the hem the width of which she will know by a pin stuck in it—I hope she will work steadily for otherwise when I get home I shall meet a great deal of company & have no [. . .] clothes to wear—

She could not help adding a postscript: "Sally must make the tucked sleeves of the coarsest piece of [c]ambric," she insisted, and closed, "*Do* throw this letter in the fire."

Years passed, and Ellen remained single. Some combination of hesitation and haughtiness no doubt contributed to her unmarried state, but the well-known wreckage of her father's finances made things even worse. As she approached her twenty-third birthday, she lamented to her mother that "I have already been held to the world as a fortune-hunter in petticoats." Still single three years later, the trash talk had followed her to Washington, where she was still a belle but had been "galled more than once by the malicious gossiping of people who have nothing to do but exercise their spite against their neighbours." She could not help shopping in order to appear fashionable, and she needed money to pay her bills, but feared to approach her father. "Perhaps I had better write to him myself," she told her mother, but "I am so much afraid of his strange temper that . . . I know not what to do."

As she passed her twenty-seventh birthday, Ellen Randolph was the real-life embodiment of that combination of female arrogance and desperation later immortalized in the figure of Lily Bart, the tragic heroine of Edith Wharton's *The House of Mirth*. She was still single and nearly ready to give up trying when Thomas Jefferson received a visit from a learned young Bostonian. Joseph Coolidge was a Harvard graduate who had traveled in Europe and read widely. He was instantly enthralled by Ellen, and she, for a wonder, welcomed his attentions. Thomas Jefferson approved of Coolidge and encouraged his suit, though he told Coolidge that neither he nor Ellen's father could provide a dowry. Fortunately, Coolidge's fortune was enough to provide for his own family (though not enough, sadly, to rescue the Jefferson-Randolph clan from ruin). They were married on May 27, 1825, in the drawing room at Monticello, and soon after left on their journey north, to start a new life in Boston, farther from home than Ellen Wayles Randolph Coolidge had ever been in her life.

The family missed Ellen terribly, especially the aged and ailing grandfather who had doted on her and who must have sensed that he would never see her again. But they were delighted at the match she had made. Joseph Coolidge was a sort of anti–Charles Bankhead, as kind and solicitous of his new bride as he was prudent in his financial affairs. Her mother and sisters rejoiced at her rescue from their ruin. "I am not selfish enough to mingle with the sorrow I cannot help feeling at the loss of your society, any regrets for the cause that has deprived us of it," her sister Mary wrote, the following autumn, "since it has called you to a situation of more comfort and happiness than we could ever have hoped to see you enjoy among our fallen fortunes." As the clouds of ruin darkened "round us so thick as sometimes to shut out even the hope of better days," said Mary, they were happy to think that "you at least are exempt (except through the medium of sympathy with those you love) from a participation in whatever may befal our interests."

Even Thomas Jefferson, the congenital optimist, was succumbing to despair. His daughter and grandchildren watched disaster approaching, and each met the family's dire prospects in his or her own way. Patsy was nearly paralyzed with depression while her son, Jefferson, labored mightily to salvage what he could. While most of her daughters stood helplessly by, plucky Cornelia chafed at her feminine inability to change the family's fortunes. "I know I wish I could do something to support myself instead of this unprofitable drudgery of keeping house here," Cornelia wrote to Ellen, later that fall. "But I suppose not untill we sink entirely will it do for the grand daughters of Thomas Jefferson to take in work or keep a school, & we shall hold out for some time yet; ours is not a galloping consumption but one of those lingering deseases which drags on for years & years."

Cornelia was only partly right. In the months that followed, tragedy came to Monticello again and again, not as a lingering disease, but as a swift and vicious infection, not malingering at a frustrating shuffle, but bearing down upon them at a headlong gallop.

28

The Capriciousness of Fortune

THOMAS JEFFERSON'S FINE brick houses were built on mountains of shifty paper. He owed the merchants of Bristol and London and the book dealers of Paris, the Virginia storekeepers who sold him candles and coffee, the joiners and bricklayers and well diggers who waited to be paid, hat in hand, sometimes for years. Virginia gentlemen passed around IOUs like buckets at a house fire. At any moment, someone, or everyone, could get badly burned.

In 1819, the first great financial panic in United States history swept the nation, setting off a wave of bank failures and foreclosures that swamped the farms and plantations of Virginia. Jefferson, like other planters, was already in trouble. Over his long years of government service, his salary had never covered his living expenses. His crops had never paid his bills. He had inherited debt and borrowed heavily in his own right. From time to time, he sold land and people in the attempt to settle the larger claims against him, but his sales never brought what he expected or needed. He was generous to the point of pathology; while Patsy and her children fretted about expenses, he insisted that they buy whatever they need and treat themselves to extravagances, charging his accounts. As his debt mounted, he continued to spend freely on anything he wanted, from oil for his salads to art for his drawing room.

The Panic of 1819, that first great bust of a boomtime American economy, sealed his fate. He already owed nearly eighty thousand dollars, in today's terms a sum approaching $1.5 million. But the bonds of friendship and kinship dragged him down deeper. He had co-signed a note for Jeff Randolph's father-in-law, Wilson Cary Nicholas, in the amount of twenty thousand dollars. Thomas Jefferson was at Poplar Forest with Ellen and Cornelia, suffering from a crippling bout of rheumatism in his hands and knees, when word came that Nicholas had gone bankrupt and would have to sell everything to pay his debts. Thomas Jefferson would now be on the hook for the additional twenty thousand. "God grant, *we* may be enabled to weather the storm," Ellen wrote her mother. "After struggling all our lives with debt & difficulty, we may be reserved as another proof of the capriciousness of fortune."

Jefferson had staked his political life on a vision of an ideal society in which free men, living close to the soil, reigned as kings of their own domains. He had written his *Summary View of the Rights of British America* and the Declaration of Independence from the viewpoint of the liberty-loving Virginia planter, had conjured the masterful grid survey plan for the Northwest Ordinances, had consummated the deal for the Louisiana Territory, so that men across America might enjoy the freedom of living happily on the land with their wives and their offspring. Thus he imagined his own life. It was a magnificent vision, but fatally flawed. Like Thomas Jefferson, farmers throughout American history have enjoyed the freedom of space, of land of their own. Like him they have ruled and relied on their women and children and survived on mortgages and revolving credit. And like him, by the tens of thousands, so many have failed.

*   *   *

WHEN JOHN WAYLES Eppes married Polly Jefferson in 1797, Thomas Jefferson had been jubilant. He had predicted that his estimable sons-in-law would safeguard the family's fortunes for at least another generation. But by the beginning of the 1820s, both Jack Eppes and Tom Randolph were in serious financial trouble. Eppes had a health crisis that forced his resignation from the United States Senate in 1821. An "unskillful bleeder" tore a hole in his arm that left him "nearly a cripple." Between his infirmity, "bad crops and bad prices," and a warehouse fire that destroyed much of his tobacco, Eppes was not even able to pay his son Francis's school fees. Jack Eppes was only fifty when he died, in September 1823, at Millbrook, his Buckingham County plantation. He left behind his and Polly's son, Francis, a second wife, Martha Jones Eppes, and children ranging in age from three to thirteen.

But that was not all. Betsy Hemings, the niece of Sally Hemings who had been given to Polly Jefferson as a wedding present, also survived John Wayles Eppes. According to Betsy's descendants, Jack Eppes followed the family tradition established by the grandfather for whom he was named. After Polly's death, Jack Eppes had taken the enslaved Betsy Hemings as his concubine, and, like his father-in-law, Thomas Jefferson, started his own shadow family. Eppes's widow and her children moved to another plantation, but Betsy Hemings remained at Millbrook until her own death in 1857. Her descendants, like those of her aunt, kept alive the oral history of their interracial family. But while Sally Hemings's progeny relied on storytelling and memory to preserve their genealogy, Betsy Hemings's offspring possessed a powerful piece of material evidence to support their story. To this day, Betsy Hemings's impressive tombstone sits next to that of Jack Eppes in the remote Eppes family graveyard, and not, as might be expected, in the Millbrook slave cemetery.

Jefferson had long intended that Polly's son, Francis Eppes, should inherit the Pantops quarter of his Albemarle County lands, in keeping with his desire to hold his family close. But now his dream of populating his neighborhood with his descendants was as frail and tattered as his aging body. He salvaged what he could. Out of generosity to Polly's only surviving child as well as the hope of protecting his legacy from his creditors, he let Francis Eppes know that he intended to leave Poplar Forest to him. Meanwhile, he relied ever more heavily on the assistance and advice of his eldest grandson, the steady and conscientious Jeff Randolph, who would soon find himself in the position of having to rescue the family's fortunes.

Jeff had to begin by offering his own father what assistance he could. Thomas Mann Randolph was never able to escape either the financial or emotional burdens of slaveholding. Like Thomas Jefferson, Tom Randolph sold both land and slaves in the vain effort to pay what he owed. Randolph considered himself "a real practical farmer . . . devoted to my fields as a sea captain is to his ship." He paid close attention to his land and embraced efficient new ideas like contour plowing. But for the life of him, he could make no better headway against the undertow of debt, slavery, and hard luck than so many Virginia planters did. From the beginning of his marriage to Patsy Jefferson, Randolph had hated slavery even as he owned many slaves. He never lost his loathing of the institution that underlay his livelihood, never developed that hardness of heart that enabled slaveholders to see the people they owned as something less than human. We can read his anguish in a poignant letter to his agent in Richmond in 1815, when he made the heartrending decision to sell people he knew well and respected:

> The negroes, all of which I part from with very great regret, are as follows. One of the likeliest young mulatto women, about 19

years of age, which can be seen any where. Her name is Betsy, and it may very properly be mentioned that she is the daughter of that valuable mechanic and faithfull servant of Dr. Brockenbrough called Charles, now at the Sweet Springs. Her character is certainly good. A man called George of whom I can produce certificates that he is a healthy able hand, an excellent driver or teamster in every way raised in the low country. His wife Jenny, as faithfull a servant as ever lived. Two girls her daughters of the age to make waiting maids, both likely and healthy. And a man of about eight or nine and forty, (Mason by name) for whom I cannot expect much because he has a rupture although otherwise very healthy and an excellent hostler. I ask the favor of you to sell this man to someone who will treat him well at a sacrifice in price, even if I get only 200$ for him. I am attached to him and sell him from necessity.

Such necessities would become more urgent and more frequent, with every passing year. By the mid-1820s, Randolph had sold or mortgaged nearly everything he owned. Soon the auctioneer would come to cry the bidding at Edgehill.

WHILE THE BURDEN of debt pulled Jefferson and his kin ever deeper, the institution of slavery, the source of their livelihood and subject of their loathing, spread relentlessly westward. In 1820, Congress passed the Missouri Compromise, permitting slavery in the new state of Missouri, and in other parts of the Louisiana Territory south of 36°30' latitude. "This momentous question, like a fire bell in the night, awakened and filled me with terror," Jefferson famously told Maine congressman John Holmes. "I considered it at once as the knell of the Union. it is hushed indeed for the moment. but this is a reprieve only, not a final sentence." Perhaps, he thought, some scheme for gradual emancipation and expatriation might be concocted, but Jefferson had lost his optimism. "As it is," he said, "we have the wolf by the ear, and we can neither hold him, nor safely let him go. Justice is in one scale, and self-preservation in the other."

Jefferson's letter to Holmes was, as so many have noted, a comment on the evils of slavery and the generally desperate situation of Virginia slaveholders. But it was more than that. At this moment of peril to his own family, Jefferson vented a bitter and deeply personal rage against sons who squandered the freedom to which he had dedicated his life. "I regret that I am now to die in the belief that the useless sacrifice of themselves, by the generation of 76. to acquire self government and happiness to their country, is to be thrown away by the unwise and unworthy passions of their sons," he told Holmes, "and that my only consolation is to be that I live not to weep over it."

Looking to the insecurity of his descendants and dependents, the wreckage of his legacy, the desperate half-measures of his heirs, Thomas Jefferson knew that he had built a house divided, and that it could not stand. The deep and bloody fissure ran from the Tidewater, through Monticello and Poplar Forest, clear across his nation, wounding everything in its wake. He could not simply emancipate all his own slaves; they were too valuable, and his finances too dire, to do so without leaving Patsy utterly destitute. She hated slavery as much as he did, but he owed it to his beloved and increasingly desperate daughter and her children to hold others, including their own shadow family, in bondage.

He also owed something to Sally Hemings. She had given up her freedom in France to return to America with him. Jefferson had promised her that their children would be free. And so, as the vaunted Missouri Compromise spread the stain of slavery into Missouri and across the Southwest, he forged his own private compromise, his own personal moments of emancipation and expatriation. Beverly and Harriet

Hemings, Sally's oldest son and daughter, had both passed the age of twenty-one. He had not drawn up formal papers of manumission for anyone since their uncle, James Hemings, in 1796. He would not go through the legal process of granting Beverly and Harriet their freedom. He would find another way to solve the problem of his children's enslavement.

According to Jefferson's beliefs, his Hemings children, being the product of three generations of interracial intimacy and less than one-quarter African, were white. Though the enslavement of Sally Hemings made them slaves in the eyes of the law, Virginia statute also deemed them legally white. Beverly and Harriet Hemings wanted to be free, and to claim their father's racial privilege and pass into white society. Thomas Jefferson had learned that keeping people close did not mean keeping them safe. He had promised their mother that her children would be free. He would simply let them go.

BY THE TIME he was twelve years old, Beverly Hemings had achieved the status of "tradesman" on Thomas Jefferson's plantation, while his half-nephew, Jeff Randolph, went off to school. His sister Harriet learned the trade of weaving in the "cotton factory," at the same time that her Randolph half-nieces (Virginia was just Harriet's age) learned French and Latin, drawing and poetry, natural history and multiplication. The Hemings children were painfully aware of their clandestine genealogy, but as Madison Hemings insisted, they were also "markedly happy" in the knowledge of their eventual freedom. Their parents' Paris "treaty" gave the Hemings children hope and resilience.

By 1822, Thomas Jefferson's wealth had evaporated, and his lands, houses, treasures, and human property were in jeopardy. Whenever his creditors decided they had had enough, they would demand the auction of his property. It was time for Beverly and Harriet to fulfill their mother's plan and their father's promise. At the respective ages of twenty-four and twenty-one, they left Monticello. When Jefferson inventoried his slaves two years later, he simply noted that Beverly had "run away 22" and that "Harriet. Sally's run. 22." Their brother Madison reported that Beverly went to Washington to live as a white man, marrying a white Maryland woman whose family members were "people in good circumstances." They had only one child, a daughter who "was not known by the white folks to have any colored blood coursing in her veins." Harriet too went to Washington and passed into white society, marrying and having children who "were never suspected of being tainted with African blood."

Beverly, as a man, would have found it easier to leave Monticello than his sister. No neighbor who knew him would have questioned his setting out alone, as his uncles Robert, James, and John had often done, riding one of Thomas Jefferson's horses. No stranger, farther along the road, would think anything odd about an apparently white man traveling on his own. But a woman of any race, traveling by herself to an unannounced destination, would attract unwanted attention. Jefferson made sure that his daughter got the assistance she needed, from his overseer, Edmund Bacon. Harriet Hemings made a lifelong impression upon Bacon. "She was nearly as white as anybody," he recalled, "and very beautiful." Bacon later insisted that Thomas Jefferson was not Harriet Hemings's father, even though the master treated Sally Hemings's daughter with particular care. "When she was nearly grown, by Mr. Jefferson's direction I paid her stage fare to Philadelphia and gave her fifty dollars. I have never seen her since, and don't know what became of her."

Thomas Jefferson had freed Harriet Hemings's uncles, Robert and James, and had permitted her brother Beverly to leave Monticello. In his will, Jefferson would emancipate Harriet's uncle John Hemings, her cousin, Joseph Fossett, and her brothers, Madison and Eston. But

Harriet Hemings was the only woman Thomas Jefferson ever set free. He sent her away and likely never saw her again after Edmund Bacon put her on the stage. Jefferson may never have shown Harriet any sign of outward affection. He may well have told himself that he bore her no particular fondness. But he could not have given her a more precious testament of his love.

BY THE SUMMER of 1825, Patsy Randolph pronounced her family "irretrievably ruined." Tom Randolph had borrowed money at "usurious interest" and had gotten an injunction to put off the sale of his property. But Patsy knew that every day of delay simply added to their debts and postponed the inevitable. When the day of the auction came, four hours passed and nobody was bidding. People "got tired of waiting and were going off" when Jefferson Randolph, whose credit was still good enough that he could borrow money, stepped up and bought his father's Edgehill plantation and the people who were being auctioned with it. Patsy described the heartbreaking experience of seeing people she had known for so long put up for sale, "most of them old and . . . sold for little or nothing." Even Patsy's house servants went on the block: "Old Scylla Priscilla and Betsy with her children, Critty's 3 little orphan girls and an Orphan child of Molly Warren's making in all 3 women old and infirm and 8 little children all under Septimia's age, all girls but one." Despite her practical temperament and her long-standing anxieties, Patsy had never involved herself in the details of her husband's finances. She now found herself in the utterly new position of asserting her individual legal rights, at her son's insistence, to save the women and children who had worked in her household from being sold at a discount to strangers. Before the sale, Jeff Randolph had arranged for her to relinquish some of her dower rights—that is, her right to make a separate claim to as much as a third of her husband's property, for her own economic security.

He did so, paradoxically, as a means of protecting both Patsy and the people to whom she had a claim. "Under existing circumstances," Patsy insisted, "the word dower would never have been mentioned by Me, but My dear Jefferson who is the support of his family, had intended bidding for them for me to spare me the sorrow of seeing these my house servants and their children sold out of the family."

Thomas Mann Randolph was furious with his son. He thought Jeff had betrayed him and taken advantage of his impossible situation. He was also enraged at the wife who had stood by him so long, through so much. In the years since she had returned to Monticello, though they had been often apart, there was still affection and loyalty between them. But Tom Randolph could never get over the competition with his father-in-law for his wife's love, a contest Patsy simply refused to acknowledge. "My dear father wrote most kindly and pressingly to him to live with us altogether, for of late years he has spent most of his time at his plantations, but his independence of spirit will not permit him to stay where he could be doing nothing for himself or his family," she told Randolph's sister, Nancy. "His spirits are gone and he is completely overwhelmed."

BUT THERE WAS worse yet to come. Despite Charles Bankhead's periodic attempts to sober up, Anne Randolph Bankhead's marital miseries continued. The family was appalled, but helpless to do anything but disapprove. "Mama and myself were so peculiarly unfortunate the other day . . . as to have a encounter with Mr. Bankhead in one of his drunkest moods," Mary wrote to Ellen, in September 1825. "Fortunately for us, there was no one present but the family, and we were spared the shame and mortification of such a meeting (which I *know* was premeditated on his part) in the presence of entire strangers. Aunt Cary and Wilson succeeded at last in carrying him home but not until he had offered to shake hands with us. I *could not* have given him mine and acted from impulse in withdrawing it, though I still think I was right in doing so, whatever impression his cry of unrelenting malice and persecution on the part of our family towards him, may make on people who never can be fully acquainted with all the circumstances of the case."

At the time of that angry encounter, Anne Bankhead was pregnant with her fourth child. Then thirty-five years old, she had lived half her life in the loving embrace of her family, tending the flowers and trading for chickens at Edgehill and Monticello, and half as a terrified wife, surviving the assaults of her improvident, insane tormenter. Back when her marriage had only begun to go wrong, her grandfather had written her a letter offering a gloomy sort of comfort, in terms she understood. "Nothing new has happened in our neighborhood since you left us," he told her.

> The houses and trees stand where they did. The flowers come forth like the belles of the day, have their short reign of beauty and splendor, and retire like them to the more interesting office of reproducing their like. The hyacinths and tulips are off the stage, the Irises are giving place to the Belladonnas, as this will to the Tuberoses &c. As your Mama has done to you, my dear Anne, as you will do . . . and as I shall soon and cheerfully do to you all in wishing you a long, long, goodnight.

Now that long good night was at hand. Sometime after the new year of 1826, Anne Bankhead gave birth prematurely, at Carlton. She lingered for weeks, as had her aunt and her grandmother, before giving up the fight on February 11, 1826. Medicine was hardly a science, but the family felt certain that medical malpractice had contributed to her death. "Much cause have we to think that the mismanagement of

our ignorant Drs . . . has murdered the poor babys mother," Cornelia
wrote to Ellen.

Thomas Jefferson had been too ill to go to see Anne until the
morning that she died. By the time he arrived, she had lapsed into
unconsciousness. Crushed by the burden of his debts, his legendary
health failing, he could hardly bear the loss, weeping uncontrollably.
"Bad news, my dear Jefferson, as to your sister Anne," he wrote to
the grandson who had journeyed across Virginia and north to New
York and New England, hoping to raise funds to save his grandfather's legacy. "She expired about half an hour ago. . . . Heaven seems
to be overwhelming us with every form of misfortune, and I expect
your next will give me the *coup de grâce*."

The death of Anne Randolph Bankhead marked the third generation of Jefferson women to die from childbirth: Thomas Jefferson's
wife, Martha Wayles Skelton Jefferson; his daughter, Mary Jefferson Eppes; and now his eldest granddaughter. Martha had died in
her bedroom, in the first version of Jefferson's great house. Polly had
given birth at Edgehill, to the east, and been carried up the mountain
to die. Anne had died at Carlton, on the western flank of Jefferson's
mountain, at the place her grandfather had taken from her husband
and put aside for her security. The three women's deaths inscribed a
fatal circle around the life of Monticello and the breaking heart of its
master. Every twenty years, it seemed, the Jefferson family tree was
watered with the blood of mothers.

29

When We Think How We Liv'd but to Love Them

A HEAVY PALL descended on Monticello. In the wake of Anne's death, a sober Charles Bankhead had come to seek reconciliation with the family, and to ask them to care for his and Anne's two youngest children, Ellen and the infant William. Patsy could not bear to look at the puny, ailing baby boy "with any feeling but sorrow." But her "beloved and sick father" had made the journey to Carlton, determined to reconcile with the man they called a monster, the man they believed had driven Anne into an early grave. Patsy resolved that she would find forbearance, in memory of "our lost saint, for so in truth I may call her." No one at Monticello could escape the feeling of responsibility for Anne Randolph Bankhead's tragedy. "To all that she has left behind her, and loved," Patsy told Ellen, "I pledge my self to shew that kindness which it was my misfortune not to have had it in my power to shew to herself."

Childbirth was always an occasion for dread in Virginia households. Patsy had lost a mother, a sister, and a daughter that way, and at the moment of Anne's demise, two more of her daughters were expecting. Virginia was wretchedly pregnant at Monticello, while Ellen was nearing her due date in Boston. The terrified Ellen begged to have Cornelia come to be with her. With four young children and the aging Thomas Jefferson to care for, Cornelia was desperately needed at home, and Patsy fretted about the expense of sending her north. But Cornelia needed the break from unrelenting gloom. She insisted that the trip wouldn't cost much. "Now that I am in black," she pointed out, her traveling wardrobe would be "very smal[l] & soon made." The Coolidges finally prevailed on Patsy to spend the money. Jeff was headed north again, in search of loans or gifts to help his grandfather, and he could escort his sister on the five-hundred-mile journey to Massachusetts.

Patsy and her daughters belittled the eccentricities that came with their Randolph heritage, but they relied on the Randolph propensity for producing strong women. When it came to childbearing, Ellen and Virginia were lucky to inherit the Randolph gift for breeding without dying. This was the most valuable legacy that their great-great-grandmother, Jane Rogers Randolph, and their great-grandmother, Jane Randolph Jefferson, handed down to their own mother, Patsy Jefferson Randolph. Given her sister Anne's fatal ordeal, however, Ellen was surprised, and not a little smug, at her easy labor and delivery. "I do not attempt to deceive you as to the pain," she wrote to Virginia, "but upon the whole you get through with it infinitely better than you could possibly conceive without having experienced the strength & support that is granted to a woman even in the hardest part of the operation." Virginia in turn came through the process in good shape. "The baby received the name of Martha Jefferson at her birth," Mary reported, "mama of course opposing it."

THOMAS JEFFERSON LIVED out the final months of his life in a house full of overburdened women and small, demanding children. That

he remained at Monticello at all, given the rising clamor of his creditors, was a matter of immense relief to the family. Patsy poured her
heart out to Ellen in a long and remarkable letter, detailing the ruin
of Thomas Mann Randolph and the approaching disaster at Monticello. Jeff Randolph, now desperately trying to salvage any shred
of his grandfather's legacy, understood that time had run out. They
would have to sell Monticello "and as many negroes as would pay
the debts," and move immediately to Poplar Forest. He could barely
bring himself to propose the scheme to his grandfather, but if they
delayed, they would lose everything. Patsy had never seen her son
"so much agitated as he was, and the situation of the rest of the family
even down to the little children was really as if a recent death had
taken place."

One night as Thomas Jefferson lay awake in pain and worry, he
had a brainstorm. He conceived the idea of a lottery to sell some of his
property at fair value. Under the scheme, Jefferson would offer up particular parcels (for instance, the Shadwell mill), and winning-ticket
holders would get their choice of his offerings. If the Virginia legislature would authorize such a scheme, Jefferson believed, he might not
only pay his debts, educate the youngest Randolph sons, and provide
a home for Patsy and the children, but most of all, he could remain at
Monticello for the waning days of his life. Jeff Randolph agreed that a
lottery might save the day and said he would take the plan to the legislature. Patsy hoped that her son's success would prolong the life of
"my dearest dearest father who . . . would have had his heart broken
by his difficulties and ourselves reduced to abject want."

After considerable arm-twisting, Jeff managed to convince the state
legislature to authorize the lottery. To his great disappointment, and
that of his grandfather, the legislators insisted that the house at Monticello be included in the list of property to be sold, though not immediately. Still, Thomas Jefferson found strength in hope, and in the

assurance that as long as he lived he would be able to stay in his home. He was in near-constant pain and had been taking ever-increasing doses of laudanum, tincture of opium, which doctors prescribed for everything from diarrhea to cardiac disease. After the lottery bill had passed, he seemed to be rallying: "He is diminishing his quantity of laudanum at night which he never ventures to do unless he thinks himself getting better," Mary wrote to Ellen. Unfortunately, once relieved of the immediate burden of worry, Jefferson went back to his old hospitable, profligate ways. "To our great annoyance," Mary told Ellen, "he has resumed the practice . . . of inviting students to dinner on sunday and we are to have to day a company of school boy guests who for any pleasure or profit we expect from their society are not worth the additional trouble their presence gives."

Even as the lottery provided Thomas Jefferson a reprieve, it sealed the ruin of his daughter and her dependents. Patsy contemplated the certainty of being turned out of the home she loved, once her father died. She had no idea where she would go or how she would survive.

Her father, meanwhile, put his affairs in order. On March 16 he made his will. He left Poplar Forest to Francis Eppes, preserving the line of male inheritance he had long held as a self-evident truth. But Jefferson had to face the fact that he could no longer safeguard the women he loved by sequestering them behind a sheltering wall of male provision and protection. If he failed to make special arrangements for Patsy, and simply left the remainder of his property to her, she would be at the mercy of the law. At the moment of his death, everything he left to his daughter would pass to her husband, the bankrupt Thomas Mann Randolph. Everything would be lost to Randolph's many insistent creditors. Patsy, her spinster daughters Cornelia and Mary, her younger children, and even her Bankhead grandchildren would be destitute.

All his life, Thomas Jefferson had insisted that women belonged at home. Their happiness lay in confining themselves strictly to the tender and tranquil amusements of domestic life, and trusting to men to take care of business. Now he was forced to lay aside those articles of faith, in the interest of the women he loved. On March 17, he added a codicil to his will declaring his daughter's "independance." Martha Jefferson Randolph had borne and raised twelve children, run multiple plantations, cared for, supervised, and denied a shadow family of enslaved relations, held rock steady through fifty-four turbulent years. But she had never had the power to make a contract, control her own property, or even take custody of her children. Now, far too late, her dying father designated her as "a femme sole," a single woman whose lawful power to dispose of land and people and possessions, to control her own affairs, was the equivalent of that of a free man.

JEFFERSON ALSO MADE arrangements for another woman he loved. The codicil to his will bestowed freedom on five men, all of them members of the Hemings family, two of them his and Sally Hemings's sons. Madison and Eston Hemings were to serve as apprentices to their uncle John Hemings until they turned twenty-one, at which point they would be free. Since Virginia law at the time required freed slaves to leave the state, Jefferson asked the legislature to grant permission for all five men to remain "where their families and connections are, as an additional instance of the favor, of which I have received so many other manifestations, in the course of my life, and for which I now give them my last, solemn, and dutiful thanks." In such an oblique fashion did Jefferson acknowledge his love and gratitude not only to the men he freed, but to Sally Hemings, the woman who had stood by him nearly forty years, whose name he could not even now bring himself to write. He maintained the public silence with which he had met rumor and scandal, certainly to spare Patsy the embarrassment of further talk, but perhaps also to protect Sally herself from malicious gossip. If it was his wish that she eventually go free, he left that choice in the hands of Martha Jefferson Randolph: Sally's niece, her children's half-sister, her master's daughter.

ON THE FIFTIETH anniversary of the Declaration of Independence, two of the greatest of the Founding Fathers lay dying. American schoolchildren know the story. At the end, John Adams found solace in believing that "Jefferson still lives." Jefferson, his mind on the history he and his old friend had made, asked "Is it the Fourth?" Their near-simultaneous passing and their famous last words have been enshrined as emblems of the moment when a nation lost its greatest leaders and lost its way, left to the inept devices of mediocrities stumbling toward discord, disunion, and the cataclysm of civil war.

Thomas Jefferson believed he had lived too long. From the time he had lost his beloved Martha, and again when Polly died, he had spoken of his death as a release. But now, during the last months of life, he had come to anticipate dying as a reality, as "a person going on a necessary journey," as Jefferson Randolph recalled. By the middle of June, said his grandson, "he gradually declined, but would only have his servants sleeping near him." One of those servants was undoubtedly Burwell Colbert, Monticello's longtime butler and Jefferson's personal servant. It is not clear who else Jefferson kept close by at the end, but the vagueness of the reference raises the likelihood that Sally Hemings was among those near at hand. Many friends and neighbors wanted to visit, but Jefferson would permit only the family, his doctor, and his slaves to visit him in his closing days.

Three men left eyewitness accounts of Thomas Jefferson's final hours: his doctor, Robley Dunglinson, his grandson-in-law, Nicholas Trist, and his grandson, Thomas Jefferson Randolph. They were with him the evening of July 3 when he inquired whether it was the Fourth, and they watched the clock as it neared midnight, hoping that the old man would live long enough to mark the anniversary, as he did. Thomas Jefferson's greatest biographer, Dumas Malone, has given us a version of these last weary hours that preserved the privacy Jefferson had so long cherished. There are no women, no children, no slaves in Malone's brief, moving rendition of the deathbed scene, no extra utterances to append an anticlimactic coda to the poetry of commemoration.

But there is, of course, more to the story. Jeff Randolph remembered that after his grandfather asked the date, the doctor offered his patient his usual dose of laudanum. The dying man refused: "No doctor, nothing more." Thomas Jefferson fell into a restless, delirious state, sitting up in his sleep and going "through all the forms of writing," calling out that the Committee of Safety must be warned. "At four a.m. he called the servants in attendance, with a strong and clear voice, perfectly conscious of his wants. He did not speak again." We do not know who among Thomas Jefferson's slaves were at his bedside, or what he told them at this last lucid moment. Surely Sally Hemings was there at some point to say good-bye. In the morning, Jefferson did communicate again, wordlessly. His longtime "attached servant," Burwell Colbert, knew him so intimately that when Jefferson silently expressed discomfort, it was Colbert who understood that Thomas Jefferson usually slept sitting up. The old man was slumped too far down in his bed. Colbert adjusted his pillows and raised his head, and Jeff Randolph recalled that Jefferson "seemed satisfied."

Martha Jefferson Randolph had sat with her father during the weeks of his decline. On this day of death, it seems she kept away. Here was the moment she had dreaded most in her life. Perhaps she could not bring herself to watch as he slipped into unconsciousness, as he fell in and out of delirium, as he saved his last words for the unnamed servants. So she kept her death vigil in another room, with her daughters, Mary and Virginia, close by her side.

On the morning of the Fourth, Nicholas Trist sat by Jefferson's bed, writing a letter to Ellen's husband, who he hoped was on his way from Boston with Ellen and Cornelia. Trist knew they would be too late for Thomas Jefferson, but not for Patsy. "The presence of E_____ and C_____ is of *inexpressible* importance to mother," wrote Trist. "I need not say more, nor attempt to depict her situation. They (mother and the girls) are fully aware of his condition, and have been told to consider him as already gone." Thomas Jefferson survived until fifty minutes after noon. When the old man had breathed his last, his beloved grandson, Jeff Randolph, closed his eyes.

AT THE END, Thomas Jefferson was surrounded by people he loved: Jeff Randolph and Nicholas Trist, members of the Hemings family, Patsy and Mary and Virginia and the younger Randolph and Bankhead children. Though his body grew weaker by the hour, his mind was clear, nearly to the end. It was summer in Virginia, hot and humid. Other families treated illness by closing all the doors and windows, but the Jeffersons and Randolphs believed in fresh air. The sash windows of his bedroom and cabinet admitted cooling breezes to the alcove bed where he lay. To give him peace and quiet, Patsy might have sent her youngest children, twelve-year-old Septimia and eight-year-old George, along with young Ellen Bankhead, outside to play. If Thomas Jefferson heard their shouts, rolling a hoop on his lawn, it might have given him a small moment of joy.

In the hushed house, sounds would carry to his ears: the murmured reminders of the home he had created, slipping in and out as Patsy or the older daughters tried to maintain routine. From the upstairs a baby cried and was nursed into silent contentment by a slave woman. From Patsy's sitting room came the sounds of children, practicing their reading or their sums. In his own room, rustlings marked the hushed path of Sally Hemings, sweeping, dusting, tidying, smoothing his covers. A cooling hand was laid on his forehead, a damp sponge held to his lips. Strong arms raised him up on his pillows. Silent, loving eyes looked into his own.

Patsy Randolph left no written account of those days. Henry Randall, the man Jefferson's grandchildren trusted with the job of writing his biography, worried about violating Patsy's confidence by saying too much about the details of her grief. Patsy, he said, "shrunk from their exposure, except to the eye of the most intimate friendship. . . . It seemed to her a drawing aside of the veil from domestic scenes, from which delicacy should exclude the observation of all strangers."

Still, Randall was a biographer. He felt compelled to reveal, as far as his own "sense of propriety" permitted, some intimate moments. On July 2, Thomas Jefferson had given his daughter "a little casket" with a message inside. A lover of literature and drama to the end, Jefferson reenacted the scene from the deathbed of his beloved wife, in which Martha had tried to copy out those lines from *Tristram Shandy*, preserved on a scrap of paper he kept all his life. Now, he copied out, in Latin, some lines from a William Shenstone epitaph: *Heu quanto minus est cum reliquis versari quam tui meminisse* ("Ah, how much less all living loves to me / Than that one rapture of remembering thee"). He found the strength, too, to copy at least part of an "Irish Melody" by Thomas Moore, the very man who had written the verse about Thomas Jefferson dreaming of freedom in his slave's embrace. But Jefferson had laughed off that bit of satire. He developed a taste for Moore's poetry, in the form of ballads the family might have sung around the pianoforte, including "It Is Not the Tear at This Moment Shed."

> *It is not the tear at this moment shed,*
> *When the cold turf has just been laid o'er him,*
> *That can tell how belov'd was the friend that's fled,*

Or how deep in our hearts we deplore him.
'Tis the tear, thro' many a long day wept,
'Tis life's whole path o'ershaded;
'Tis the one remembrance, fondly kept,
When all lighter griefs have faded.
Thus his memory, like some holy light,
Kept alive in our hearts, will improve them,
For worth shall look fairer, and truth more bright,
When we think how we liv'd but to love them!
And, as fresher flowers the sod perfume,
Where buried saints are lying,
So our hearts shall borrow a sweet'ning bloom
From the image he left there in dying!

Less poetical, perhaps, but just as heartfelt, Jefferson had also written a tribute to Patsy. He declared that as he went "to his fathers . . . the last pang of life" was in parting from her. He recalled her mother and sister. "Two seraphs," he said, "long shrouded in death," awaited him. He would "bear them her love."

MARTHA JEFFERSON RANDOLPH and Sally Hemings were no strangers to grief. Separated by only a year in age, they were now in their mid-fifties. Each had lived through two revolutions, had seen babies die, had lost adult children, one to death and two to exile. They had survived the deaths of loved ones, standing virtually side by side, separated by the yawning gulf of race and slavery. Thomas Jefferson had been the bright star, the gravitational force that bent the path of their lifetime orbits, day by day, year by year. Now they must live without him.

They were far luckier than most of the people whose lives depended on Jefferson's fortunes. Six months after his death, on five frigid days in January, the first lots of his possession went, as Patsy had once put it, under the hammer. The auctioneer got good prices for Jefferson's horses and cattle, his carriages and his plows. Jeff Randolph had also advertised 126 enslaved people as "the most valuable for their number ever offered at one time in the state of Virginia," and they too sold at above market value. Thomas Jefferson's grandson bought back as many of the slaves as he could afford, but many could not be saved and were sold away from their families and friends. Over the next five years, sale after sale was held, as nearly everything Jefferson had possessed was sold to pay his creditors. Finally, in 1831, his beloved Monticello went the way of everything else.

Thomas Jefferson had lived in luxury and left his family in penury, as his enemies quickly pointed out. But Ellen Randolph Coolidge leapt to defend her grandfather. Not long after his death, a New York publisher approached Ellen for an account of the true state of Jefferson's finances. She offered a description of Monticello as she had known it, or at least as she imagined might appeal to a northern public disdainful of the degradations of slavery. "Much has been said of the elegance of Mr. Jefferson's establishment at Monticello," she wrote, "but there is no person of candour who has ever visited there who could not testify to the contrary of all this. the house has been fifty six years building and is still unfinished. a great deal of the work has been done by Mr Jefferson's own slaves amongst whom there were many tradesmen. there was but little furniture in it & that of no value, and many of the articles made by the negro workmen."

To vindicate her grandfather, Ellen had no problem denigrating the elegant artistry of John Hemings, the master craftsman who had built everything from the "siesta chair" that so comforted Thomas Jefferson's aching bones, to the domed roof over his head at Poplar Forest. Hemings had made a particularly lovely writing desk as a wedding gift to Ellen herself, a treasure that had been lost at sea when the boat carrying all her belongings northward sank off the coast. When he learned of the fate of his special present, John Hemings wept. Thomas Jefferson compensated by sending to Boston the portable desk on which he had written the Declaration of Independence, not to Ellen, but to her husband.

Ellen Randolph Coolidge would make a career of promoting her grandfather's memory, partly by demeaning and erasing the shadow family with whom she had grown up. The Hemingses provided the daily services, small and large, that Ellen had relied on all her life in Virginia, the hot water and clean sheets, the fresh figs and steaming muffins, the knitted stockings and fancy sewing. She had known them from birth, and may even have been the Jefferson grandchild who taught Madison Hemings to read. She missed those things badly in the north, as she found endless occasions to complain about the incompetent, insubordinate, stubbornly free servants of Boston.

But nothing the Hemingses had ever been to her or done for her mattered when the time came to defend Thomas Jefferson against the charge that he had taken a slave concubine and fathered "yellow children." Patsy Randolph had endorsed the denial of Jefferson's paternity of the Hemingses in her father's fashion, pursuing a course of public silence. Ellen, however, took action to combat the rumors. She insisted that her grandfather would never in his life have done such a thing as take Sally Hemings to his bed, precisely because he had loved his white daughters and his grandchildren. "Some of the children currently reported to be Mr. Jefferson's were about the age of his own grandchildren," she wrote her husband while on a visit to Virginia in 1858.

Of course he must have been carrying on his intrigues in the midst of his daughters family and insulting the sanctity of home by his profligacy. But he had a large family of grandchildren of all ages, older & younger. Young men and young girls. He lived, whenever he was at Monticello, and entirely for the last seventeen years of his life, in the midst of these young people, surrounded by them—his intercourse with them of the freest and most affectionate kind. How comes it that his immoralities were never suspected by his own family—that his daughter and her children rejected with horror and contempt the charges brought against him? . . . I would put it to any fair mind to decide if a man so admirable in his domestic character as Mr. Jefferson, so devoted to his daughters and their children, so fond of their society, so tender, considerate, refined in his intercourse with them, so watchful over them in all respects, would be likely to rear a race of half-breeds under their eyes and carry on his low amours in the circle of his family.

Ellen granted that there were mixed-race children at Monticello but insisted that they must have been the offspring of "Irish workmen" or of "dissipated young men in the neighborhood who sought the society of the mulatresses." As for Sally Hemings, Ellen insisted that she was "pretty notoriously the mistress of a married man, a near relation of Mr. Jefferson's," though she admitted that Sally's children were "all fair and all set free at my grandfather's death, or had been suffered to absent themselves permanently before he died." Ellen identified Jefferson's nephew, Samuel Carr, as that near relation, and took pains not only to denigrate that relative, but to smear Sally Hemings in language reminiscent of James T. Callender. "There is a general impression that the four children of Sally Hemmings were *all* the children of Col. Carr, the most notorious good-natured Turk that ever was master of a black seraglio kept at other men's expence. His deeds are as well known as his name." Randolph descendants would stubbornly cling to that myth until DNA evidence proved it false, though some have not stopped looking for alternative explanations of the paternity of Sally Hemings's children.

For Ellen, the very presence of Jefferson's white daughters was proof enough of her case. Sally, she pointed out, "had accompanied Mr. Jefferson's younger daughter to Paris and was lady's maid to both sisters. Again I ask is it likely that so fond, so anxious a father, whose letters to his daughters are replete with tenderness and with good counsels for their conduct, should (when there were so many other objects upon whom to fix his illicit attentions) have selected the female attendant of his own pure children to become his paramour! The thing will not bear telling. There are such things, after all, as moral impossibilities."

Ellen Wayles Randolph Coolidge was either disingenuous or willfully ignorant. Certainly she did what she could to draw a proper Victorian veil over activities that earlier generations regarded in a far different light. Her grandmother, Martha Wayles Skelton Jefferson, had been the much-loved daughter of John Wayles, a man who had taken a slave concubine and fathered six enslaved children alongside his four free daughters. That slave woman, Elizabeth Hemings, had raised Martha and her sisters, and Martha had brought her father's concubine and her slave half-siblings to live with her at Monticello. She had installed Hemingses in positions of respect and authority in her household and relied on them through the chaos of war, in sickness and in health. Her daughters, Patsy and Polly, had stood at their mother's deathbed, side by side with the women of their shadow family. They had heard their father swear never to remarry, in the presence of a beloved wife who had preferred her father's slave mistress to her white stepmothers.

If Thomas Jefferson followed John Wayles's example and took a mistress who was both his daughters' half-aunt and his slave, there was little Patsy or Polly could do except learn to live with their father's choice. Polly's widowed husband, Jack Eppes, may have repeated the pattern for a third generation. In Jefferson's world, liaisons between white masters and slave women may not have been strictly moral, but they were anything but impossible. They were a family tradition.

PATSY RANDOLPH HAD been spared the sight of Jefferson's slaves up on the auctioneer's block. At the time she was far away from Monticello, visiting Ellen in Boston. But she was all too familiar with the sight of human beings sold like cattle. She had lived through the forced sale of her husband's human property. She did not have much sympathy for Ellen's nostalgia for the slaveholder's easy authority, the slave's compulsory obedience, and she had little patience for complaints about the insolence of Boston servants. "The discomfort of slavery I have borne all my life," she had written Ellen at the moment when Thomas Mann Randolph's slaves were sold, "but it's sorrows in all their bitterness I had never before conceived. . . . The country is over run with those trafickers in human blood the negro . . . buyers. . . . how much trouble and distress y[ou] have been spared My beloved Ellen by your removal, for nothing can prosper under such a system of injustice."

Patsy's family had not prospered. "My life of late years has been such a tissue of privations and disappointments that it is impossible for me to believe that any of my wishes will be gratified, or if they are, not to fear some hidden mischief flowing even from their success," Patsy wearily confessed. She would never recover from her father's death. Heartbroken and penniless, she shuttled among her children's homes in Boston and Philadelphia and Virginia. Her poverty was scandalous; she became something of a southern martyr. In 1827, the state legislature of South Carolina voted to give her a ten-thousand-dollar pension, much to the relief of her indigent children. The state of Louisiana would shortly follow suit. Patsy at first insisted that the money be used to pay her father's debts rather than her own living expenses.

But in the end, Patsy Randolph was fortunate to have raised children who loved her, who could provide her comfort and support in those last hard years. As she drifted from place to place, she left behind in Virginia the last vestiges of her father's legacy: the few people she still nominally owned. Among those individuals was Sally Hemings. After Thomas Jefferson had gone to his final rest, next to his wife and younger daughter in the cemetery on the mountainside, Sally Hemings too was lucky enough to be able to depend on her children. She moved to Charlottesville, into a house owned by her sons, Madison and Eston Hemings. The three were listed in the 1833 parish censuses as "free people of color," though Sally had never formally been freed.

Sally Hemings died in Charlottesville in 1835, believing that she had been free, informally, since 1826. She was buried in an unknown grave. Martha Jefferson Randolph followed her half-aunt a year later. She would be buried with her father and mother and sister, at Monticello. Patsy had written a will in 1834, requesting that her heirs give Sally her "time," a way of recognizing Sally's freedom without forcing her to leave the state. In doing so, Patsy redeemed a promise she had made to her father, a last tacit bargain between survivors, a partial, poignant fulfillment between two women who could not begin to speak all the intimacy and experience, all the delight and grief, all the tension and anger, all the courage and cowardice that lay between them.

From the mother whose memory haunted his immortal Declaration, to the wife he tried to keep safe behind brick walls, to the enslaved woman and free daughters and granddaughters who gave him their lives, Thomas Jefferson had lived in a world of women. His love for them informed his greatest achievements and glowed at the heart of his vision of life, liberty, and the pursuit of happiness. He made them promises that he too often failed to keep: noble and self-serving, idealistic and self-deluding, generous and flawed promises. That he spent a lifetime trying to fulfill those promises, and that they returned the effort, testified to the presence of love among them, in all its protean, problematic, potent forms. The women Jefferson loved knew that love itself was no guarantee of prosperity or security, or even bodily safety. It was not the answer to anything. It was not one thing. It was contradictory, costly, complicated, and sometimes deadly. Love could heal, and it could and did hurt. But it was as necessary to him, and to them, as blood and bone, as omnipresent, and sometimes as invisible, as air.

Acknowledgments

THIS BOOK IS the product of a lifelong fascination with Thomas Jefferson, and a long-standing commitment to telling women's stories. I've been reading and thinking about this book, on and off, since I was a graduate student, but only recently have I been able to commit my time and mind to writing it. Over the past four years, I've had the luxury of research fellowships from multiple institutions; the invaluable professional assistance of librarians, archivists, museum curators, and fellow historians; and the amazing support of family and friends. It hardly seems enough to mention all of you by name.

The University of New Mexico gave me a sabbatical year to commence my research, a Research Allocations Grant to travel to Lodi, Italy, on the trail of Maria Cosway, and made it possible for me to spend a year on special assignment at Yale University. Thanks to Patricia Risso, Charlie Steen, Yolanda Martinez, Dana Ellison, Helen Ferguson, and Barbara Wafer in the Department of History, Dean Brenda Claiborne in the College of Arts and Sciences, and the UNM Research Allocations Committee. I want to thank the Women and Gender Study Group in the Department of History for allowing me to present an early version of the first section of this book, and for making absolutely critical suggestions that have shaped the whole project. Thanks, too, to Cathleen Cahill, Barbara Reyes, Elaine Nelson, Rebecca Vanucci, and especially the amazing Sarah Payne, for keeping the UNM Center for the Southwest going and growing over these years. Since coming to New Mexico, I have been privileged to watch a great group of scholars earn their Ph.D.s: Andy Kirk, Abbe Karmen, Pablo Mitchell, John Herron, Michael Anne Sullivan, Judy Morley, Catherine Kleiner, Jeff Sanders, Amy Scott, and Erik Loomis. I also owe a real debt of gratitude to the lively and thoughtful students in my graduate seminar "Sally Hemings, Thomas Jefferson, and the Cultural Politics of History": Heather Baures, Adam Blahut, Kent Blansett, Heather Dahl, Kate Meyers, Allison Paskett, and Rebecca Vanucci.

The Huntington Library awarded me a Mellon Fellowship, and I spent a remarkably productive four months using their rich collections and enjoying the incredible community of Huntington Fellows. Thanks to Roy Ritchie, W. M. Keck director of research, Laura Stalker and the library staff, and Susi Krasnoo, for all they did to assist me. For amazing conversations over lunches at the Rose Garden and food and beverages in other places, I thank Jared Farmer, Jonathan Earle, Leslie Tuttle, Karen Halttunen, Deborah Harkness, Mae Ngai, Terri Snyder, Hal Barron, Mac Rohrbaugh, Sarah Hanley, David Igler, Bill Deverell, Peter Mancall, and Lisa Bitel. I was also privileged to present a portion of this work at the Huntington's wonderful "Past Tense" seminar, and for that I thank conveners Thomas Andrews, Laura Mitchell, and Jenny Price, and everyone who contributed to a great discussion.

My time in Los Angeles was immeasurably enriched by my work as Women of the West chair at the Autry National Center of the American West. I am so grateful to my friends and great thinking partners there, foremost among them Carolyn Brucken, Stephen Aron, Amy Green, and John Gray. Steve and Amy, and their sons Daniel and Jack, have opened their home to me and made me a part of their family over the years I've been traveling to Los Angeles. I've had the enormous pleasure of collaborating with Carolyn, one of the most insightful, intellectually generous, funny, and warmhearted people I've ever known. John's visionary leadership has inspired me and helped me to grow into the job. And all of them made it possible for me to fulfill my commitments to the Autry while also moving to the East Coast for a year. Knowing them, and being part of the Autry, has been one of the great joys of my life.

I would not have been able to write this book without the unparalleled people and resources of the International Center for Jefferson Studies, at Monticello. And I cannot imagine a better place to spend a month in residence than the Roosevelt Cottage at the ICJS. Everyone made me welcome, answered endless queries, offered indispensable advice, assistance, and information, and opened every door for me. It was a privilege to present my Fellows' lecture to a standing-room-only gathering of people who know more about Thomas Jefferson than any group of humans anywhere else on the planet. Boundless thanks to Saunders director Andrew O'Shaughnessy, Joan Hairfield, Cinder Stanton, Gaye Wilson, Leni Sorensen, Derek Wheeler, Jack Robertson, Anna Berkes, Eric Johnson, Leah Stearns, Carrie Taylor, Wayne Mogielnicki, Lisa Francavilla, and Marjorie Webb, at the ICJS, and Susan Stein, Elizabeth Chew, and Diane Ehrenpreis at Monticello for so generously sharing your knowledge, time, help, and encouragement. At the Albert and Shirley Smalls Special Collections Library at the University of Virginia, I want to thank all the librarians and archivists who helped me, particularly Margaret Raby, and Kristy Haney and Jeanne Pardee for their assistance with digital images. Susan Kern and Carl Lounsbury gave me the gift of their vast knowledge of Virginia history, architecture, and culture, and Reuben and Sue Rainey made me welcome in Charlottesville. Brian Truzzie, history specialist at the Chesterfield County Parks and Recreation Department, took me on an amazing visit to Eppington.

Virginia Woolf said that women must have money and a room of their own in order to write. Yale University gave me far more than that. During my year as Beinecke senior research fellow in the Lamar Center for Frontiers and Borders at Yale, I lived the scholar's and writer's dream. Friends have been telling me for years what a happy privilege it is to know Howard and Shirley Lamar, and now I know what they mean. Johnny Faragher and Michelle Hoffnung, George and Nancy Miles, and Jay Gitlin and Ginny Bales made me so very welcome at the Lamar Center and the Beinecke, and I thank them along with Edith Rotkopf and Priscilla Holmes. I can't overestimate the generosity of colleagues including David Blight, John Demos, Paul Sabin, Beverly Gage, Alyssa Mt. Pleasant, Taylor Spence, Honor Sachs, Catherine McNeur, Christine DeLucia, Paul Shin, Ryan Hall, and all the folks at the Wednesday Lamar Center lunches. I must also mention my Lamar Center lecture, accompanied by a never-to-be-forgotten Derby Party and the vocal stylings of, well, everyone. Thanks, too, to the Writing History Group, a source of so many great conversations and ideas. Jonathan Holloway invited me to become a Calhoun College Fellow for the year and gave me the opportunity to present a Fellows' lecture. Dr. Ruth Westheimer offered enthusiasm and excellent advice about Jefferson, women, and being the mother of the groom. And I really appreciate the pleasure of connecting with old friends who made me feel right at home on the East Coast: hosts par excellence Geof and Mary Ann Bonenberger, Craig Pinto, Chris Romney, Tom Jacobson, Nomi and John Stadler, Michael Davis, and Donna Fish.

I am grateful to Carrie Supple and Elaine Grublin, of the Massachusetts Historical Society, Joellen ElBashir, of the Moorland-Spingarn Research Center at Howard University, and Emily Howie and Julie Miller, at the Library of Congress, for assistance with their essential Jefferson collections, and to Andrea Ashby at Independence National Historical Park and Dan Barkley at Zimmerman Library at UNM for his help. Marco Sioli, distinguished historian of early America at the University of Milan, not only arranged for me to visit the Maria Cosway archive at the Fondazione Maria Cosway in Lodi, but also drove me there and translated for me. And have I mentioned that he is a terrific cook, too? In Lodi, thanks to Giovanni Sacchi, secretary of the Fondazione Maria Cosway, and Tino Gipponi, the Cosways' biographer.

In a sense, this book originated over lunch with my literary agent, Elaine Koster, who asked me the question few writers dare ask themselves: "Tell me what book you burn to write." I have been the beneficiary of more than ten years of Elaine's wisdom, encouragement, knowledge, and advocacy. Carolyn Marino acquired the project for HarperCollins and has believed in me and helped me become a better writer for a decade. I am lucky now to be in the hands of my gifted editor at HarperCollins, Gail Winston, who has nurtured and shaped this book. Jason Sack has patiently answered myriad questions. Thomas F. Pitoniak provided expert copyediting. I am genuinely thrilled that Nick Springer, of Springer Cartographics, created the elegant map of the territory these women knew, traveled, and inhabited, which serves as the endpapers of this volume.

Over the years, many friends have watched this project develop from a thought, to a dream, to a reality. Katherine Jensen, Audie Blevins, Jean Owens Schaefer, David Robson, Bob Righter, Sherry Smith, Karen and Kent Anderson, and William H. Sewell, Jr., encouraged me in the early stages. Bill DeBuys, Dan Flores, Patricia Limerick, Elliott West, and Richard White have challenged and cheered me for longer than any of us cares to remember. Beverly Seckinger, Harriet Moss, Ernesto Sanchez, Laura Timothy, Greg Nottage, Mim

Aretsky, Skip Gladney, Katie Curtiss, Hal Corbett, Colin Keeney, Beth Bailey, and David Farber have been more than patient, and have given me unstinting support and helpful suggestions. Dora Wang, my fellow author and delightful friend, has provided unending good counsel. Sally Denton, historian and writer extraordinaire, insisted, reasonably enough, that every American historian should kick off her or his research at the Library of Congress. Sally put me up in Washington, D.C., drove me to Monticello, made me laugh until I fell over, and continues to inspire me with her passion for history and her zest for life. Jon George, Carolina Gómez, María González, and Shannon Vigil often kept the wheels from flying off. Wendy and John Schmidt, and their wonderful children, Tom, Mike, and Allie, are the most delightful, stimulating family I have ever known. Wendy has been one of my closest friends for more than thirty-five years, and during my year at Yale, they showed me more love, hospitality, and joy than I can measure.

I could not ask for better colleagues and friends than the ones I have in the Department of History at the University of New Mexico. Linda Hall first urged me to write a book about Jefferson and women in 1997, and I've been grateful ever since. Melissa Bokovoy, Andrew Sandoval-Strausz, Cathleen Cahill, Tim Moy, Rebecca Ullrich, and Paul Hutton have been dear friends and intellectual companions on this journey. For more than twenty years now, Jane Slaughter and I have had occasionally "energetic" and yes, enlightening discussions about women's history, in a variety of places on two continents. I thank her for the unifying concept of this book and look forward to more spirited conversation, as much of it as possible in Italy.

I am lucky to have a family that has supported me in every way. Vi, Henry, and Sue Levkoff have given me a home away from home in New York, and I treasure my time with them. My brothers and sisters, especially Patty and Steve Bort, have cheered this project on.

Kate Swift has been a mentor and a model as a writer, a feminist, and a person. Peter Swift has been a wonderful father to our two children, Sam and Annie Swift, now well embarked on adventures of their own and making us incredibly proud. I am excited to welcome Jessica Trujillo, a remarkable young woman, to our family.

A number of stalwart souls read all or part of the book manuscript and offered comments as scholars, and as the kind of readers every writer hopes to reach. Susan Kern provided invaluable insight into Jefferson's early life. Joshua Rothman offered suggestions regarding public knowledge of interracial intimacy in Jefferson's Virginia. Alfred Bush, Jan Shipps, and Janet and Bruce Brodie shared their deep knowledge of Jefferson's life and their insights into the politics of recent Jefferson scholarship. Amy Green and John Gray served as discerning lay readers. Stephen Aron urged me to state my big arguments more strongly, and to have courage (something he also recommends at the racetrack). Rick Hills contributed invaluable ideas about the connections between Jefferson's private life and public writings. Peter Mancall helped me see the larger historical context of my stories. Annette Gordon-Reed has served as both inspiration and critic, and generously took time from her busy schedule to offer careful comments that have immeasurably improved this book. Likewise, I can hardly express my gratitude for the support of and very detailed, indispensable reading by the foremost Jefferson scholar of our time, Lucia Stanton, Shannon senior historian at the International Center for Jefferson Studies.

Catherine Kurland deserves a special thanks for her meticulous and thoughtful editing of an early draft of this book. She became a real partner in the enterprise, and even better, a good friend. I look forward to many good times with her and John Serkin.

Three people have stood by my side every step of this journey, and if I could buy them all tickets to Paris, I would. My dear friends Marni

Sandweiss and Maria Montoya read multiple drafts of this manuscript, were available for endless conversations by phone and e-mail and over dinner, hosted me and feasted me, lived and breathed this book with me, and talked me off more than one ledge. I could not have written it without them. Chris Wilson, my partner, not only provided love and support, but read the book with the close and incisive eye of a brilliant historian, worked with me on the map, genealogical table, and images in this book, traveled with me to Virginia, Paris, and London, took photographs, looked after Benny the schnauzer, and kept the home fires burning while I was away. I cannot begin to thank him for all he's done. But now I have time to make a start.

Dramatis Personae

Thomas Jefferson's Grandparents, Parents, Uncles and Aunts, Cousins, Siblings and Their Spouses

CAPTAIN ISHAM RANDOLPH: Father of Jane Randolph Jefferson, maternal grandfather of Thomas Jefferson, sea captain, merchant, planter.

JANE LILBURNE ROGERS RANDOLPH: Mother of Jane Randolph Jefferson, maternal grandmother of Thomas Jefferson, b. Shadwell, England, about 1697; d. Virginia, 1761.

PETER JEFFERSON: Jane Randolph's husband, father of Thomas Jefferson, b. Virginia, 1708; d. 1757.

JANE RANDOLPH JEFFERSON: Mother of Thomas Jefferson, b. 1721, Shadwell, England; d. 1776, Virginia.

WILLIAM ISHAM and THOMAS ESTON RANDOLPH: Brothers of Jane Randolph Jefferson; William, a Loyalist, moved to England before the American Revolution.

MARY RANDOLPH LEWIS: Sister of Jane Randolph Jefferson.

WILLIAM RANDOLPH: Jane R. Jefferson's cousin, great friend of Peter Jefferson, who "sold" him Shadwell for a bowl of punch; master of Tuckahoe.

THOMAS MANN RANDOLPH, SR.: Eldest son of William Randolph; father of Thomas Mann Randolph, Jr.; father-in-law of Patsy Jefferson Randolph.

JANE JEFFERSON (JANE JR.): Eldest of Jane and Peter Jefferson's children; sister of Thomas Jefferson, b. 1740 at Shadwell; d. 1765.

MARY JEFFERSON BOLLING: Second child of Jane and Peter Jefferson; b. 1741 at Shadwell, married John Bolling, alcoholic brother-in-law of Thomas Jefferson.

THOMAS JEFFERSON: Son of Peter Jefferson and Jane Randolph, married Martha Wayles Skelton, 1772; third president of the United States; b. 1743, d. 1826.

ELIZABETH JEFFERSON: Mentally retarded younger sister of Thomas Jefferson; d. 1771.

MARTHA JEFFERSON CARR: Younger sister of Thomas Jefferson, wife of Dabney Carr, Thomas Jefferson's best friend; b. 1746 at Tuckahoe.

DABNEY CARR: Husband of Martha Jefferson; brother-in-law and best friend of Thomas Jefferson; d. 1773.

PETER, SAMUEL, and DABNEY CARR, JR.: Thomas Jefferson's nephews, sons of Martha Jefferson Carr and Dabney Carr. Thomas Jefferson's grandchildren identified Peter and/or Samuel Carr as the father(s) of Sally Hemings's children.

LUCY JEFFERSON LEWIS: Thomas Jefferson's younger sister; mother of Isham and Lilburne Lewis, who in 1811 murdered a seventeen-year-old enslaved man; b. 1752 at Tuckahoe.

CHARLES LILBURN LEWIS: Husband (and first cousin) of Lucy Jefferson, and son of Thomas Jefferson's aunt Mary Randolph and Charles Lewis.

ANNA SCOTT JEFFERSON ("NANCY") MARKS: Thomas Jefferson's youngest sister, twin, wife of Hastings Marks, b. 1755, Shadwell.

RANDOLPH JEFFERSON: Thomas Jefferson's youngest brother, twin, b. 1755, Shadwell.

JOHN GARLAND JEFFERSON: Grandson of Thomas Jefferson's uncle, involved in 1790 altercation with James Rind and Peter Carr.

The Wayles and Eppes Families

JOHN WAYLES: Planter and lawyer, master of the Forest plantation. Father of Martha Jefferson and three other Wayles daughters, and of Sally Hemings and five other Hemings sons and daughters; b. 1715, Lancaster, England; d. 1773.

MARTHA EPPES WAYLES: Daughter of Francis Eppes IV and Sarah Eppes, mother of Martha Jefferson, died in childbirth. Inherited Elizabeth Hemings and her African mother.

[?] COCKE WAYLES: Second wife of John Wayles; first name unknown; mother of Martha Jefferson's half-sisters, Elizabeth, Anne, and Tabitha.

ELIZABETH LOMAX SKELTON: Third wife of John Wayles, widow of Reuben Skelton. Inherited from her first husband Elk Hill plantation, later residence of Martha Jefferson.

MARTHA WAYLES SKELTON JEFFERSON ("PATTY"): Wife of Thomas Jefferson, daughter of John Wayles and Martha Eppes, widow of Bathurst Skelton, half-sister of Sally Hemings, mother of Patsy and Polly Jefferson; b. 1748, d. 1782.

BATHURST SKELTON: First husband of Martha Jefferson, d. 1768.

JOHN SKELTON, son of Bathurst Skelton and Martha Wayles (Jefferson); b. 1767; d. 1771.

ELIZABETH WAYLES EPPES ("BETSY"): Second daughter of John Wayles, half-sister of Martha Jefferson and Sally Hemings, wife of Francis Eppes V, mother of John Wayles Eppes, and surrogate mother to Polly Jefferson.

ANNE WAYLES SKIPWITH ("NANCY"): Third daughter of John Wayles, half-sister of Martha Jefferson and Sally Hemings, wife of Henry Skipwith.

TABITHA WAYLES SKIPWITH ("TIBBY"): Fourth daughter of John Wayles, half-sister of Martha Jefferson and Sally Hemings, wife of Robert Skipwith; d. before 1773.

FRANCIS EPPES V: Husband of Elizabeth Wayles Eppes, first cousin of Martha Jefferson, master of Eppington, close friend of Thomas Jefferson.

RICHARD HENRY EPPES: Teenage half-brother of Francis Eppes V, murdered in 1766 by fourteen-year-old-slave girl, Sukey.

JOHN WAYLES EPPES ("JACK"): Eldest son of Elizabeth and Francis Eppes, nephew and protégé of Thomas Jefferson, husband of Polly Jefferson.

MARTHA JONES EPPES: Second wife of Jack Eppes.

Children and Grandchildren of Thomas Jefferson and Martha Wayles Skelton Jefferson, and Their Spouses

MARTHA JEFFERSON RANDOLPH ("PATSY"): Eldest daughter of Thomas Jefferson; married Thomas Mann Randolph, Jr.; mother of twelve; mistress of Edgehill and Monticello; b. 1772, d. 1836.

JANE RANDOLPH JEFFERSON: Second daughter of Thomas Jefferson and Martha Wayles Skelton Jefferson; died in infancy.

MARY JEFFERSON EPPES (MARIA, "POLLY"): Second daughter of Thomas Jefferson and Martha Wayles Skelton Jefferson to survive to adulthood; married John Wayles Eppes; mother of Francis Eppes and Maria Eppes; resident of Eppington; b. 1778, d. 1804.

LUCY ELIZABETH JEFFERSON: Daughter of Thomas Jefferson and Martha Wayles Skelton Jefferson; died in infancy.

LUCY ELIZABETH JEFFERSON II: Daughter of Thomas Jefferson and Martha Wayles Skelton Jefferson; d. 1784 at Eppington.

THOMAS MANN RANDOLPH, JR. ("TOM"): Husband of Patsy Jefferson; legislator, congressman, and governor of Virginia; planter.

ANNE CARY RANDOLPH BANKHEAD: Eldest grandchild of Thomas Jefferson; eldest daughter of Patsy and Tom Randolph.

CHARLES BANKHEAD: Husband of Anne Randolph Bankhead.

THOMAS JEFFERSON RANDOLPH ("JEFF"): Eldest son of Patsy and Tom Randolph.

ELLEN RANDOLPH: Daughter of Patsy and Tom Randolph; died in infancy.

ELLEN WAYLES RANDOLPH COOLIDGE: Daughter of Patsy and Tom Randolph; married Joseph Coolidge.

JOSEPH COOLIDGE: Boston merchant and husband of Ellen Randolph.

CORNELIA JEFFERSON RANDOLPH: Daughter of Patsy and Tom Randolph; never married.

VIRGINIA JEFFERSON RANDOLPH: Daughter of Patsy and Tom Randolph; married Nicholas Trist.

NICHOLAS TRIST: Husband of Virginia Randolph, grandson of Thomas Jefferson's friend Eliza House Trist.

MARY JEFFERSON RANDOLPH: Daughter of Patsy and Tom Randolph; never married.

JAMES MADISON RANDOLPH: Son of Patsy and Tom Randolph; born in the White House.

BENJAMIN FRANKLIN RANDOLPH: Son of Patsy and Tom Randolph.

MERIWETHER LEWIS RANDOLPH: Son of Patsy and Tom Randolph.

SEPTIMIA ANNE RANDOLPH MEIKLEHAM: Youngest daughter of Patsy and Tom Randolph; married Dr. David Scott Meikleham.

GEORGE WYTHE RANDOLPH: Youngest son of Patsy and Tom Randolph.

SARAH NICHOLAS RANDOLPH: Daughter of Thomas Jefferson Randolph, great-granddaughter of Thomas Jefferson, author of *The Domestic Life of Thomas Jefferson*.

JOHN RANDOLPH OF ROANOKE: Cousin of Thomas Mann Randolph.

Sally Hemings's Family

CAPTAIN HEMINGS: Grandfather of Sally Hemings, English whaling vessel captain.

"AFRICAN WOMAN": Grandmother of Sally Hemings.

JOHN WAYLES: Father of Sally Hemings; see above.

ELIZABETH HEMINGS ("BETTY"): Mother of Sally Hemings, inherited by Martha Jefferson; housekeeper at the Forest, Elk Hill, Monticello.

MARY HEMINGS: Eldest daughter of Betty Hemings and unknown father; common-law wife of Charlottesville merchant Thomas Bell; mother of four children, including Joseph Fossett (enslaved carpenter freed by Thomas Jefferson, probably son of English carpenter William Fossett) and Betsy Hemmings, who was concubine or close companion to John Wayles Eppes. Never freed.

THOMAS BELL: Charlottesville merchant and friend of Thomas Jefferson; father of Mary Hemings's children, Robert Washington Bell and Sally Jefferson Bell, who were freed in Bell's will and heirs to his property.

MARTIN HEMINGS: Eldest son of Betty Hemings and unknown father.

BETTY BROWN: Daughter of Betty Hemings and unknown father, maid to Martha Jefferson; mother of Wormley Hughes, master gardener at Monticello; mother of Burwell Colbert, Thomas

Jefferson's butler and valet. Burwell Colbert was freed by Thomas Jefferson's will.

NANCE HEMINGS: Daughter of Betty Hemings and unknown father.

ROBERT HEMINGS: Son of Betty Hemings and John Wayles; freed by Thomas Jefferson.

JAMES HEMINGS: Son of Betty Hemings and John Wayles; trained as French chef; freed by Thomas Jefferson.

THENIA HEMINGS: Daughter of Betty Hemings and John Wayles; sold by Thomas Jefferson to James Monroe.

CRITTA HEMINGS: Daughter of Betty Hemings and John Wayles; never freed.

PETER HEMINGS: Son of Betty Hemings and John Wayles; trained in French cuisine by his brother James; listed as free at the end of his life.

SALLY HEMINGS: Youngest daughter of Betty Hemings and John Wayles; concubine of Thomas Jefferson; mother of six children likely fathered by Thomas Jefferson; given "her time" by Patsy Randolph after Thomas Jefferson's death; b. 1773, d. 1835.

JOHN HEMINGS: Also known as John Hemmings. Youngest son of Betty Hemings and unknown father, probably Thomas Jefferson's English carpenter Joseph Neilson.

LUCY HEMINGS: Youngest child of Betty Hemings and unknown father, probably Joseph Neilson.

HARRIET HEMINGS: Oldest child of Thomas Jefferson and Sally Hemings; died at the age of two.

BEVERLY HEMINGS: Oldest son of Thomas Jefferson and Sally Hemings; "ran away" from Monticello in 1822.

HARRIET HEMINGS II: Daughter of Thomas Jefferson and Sally Hemings; "ran away" from Monticello in 1822.

JAMES MADISON HEMINGS: Son of Thomas Jefferson and Sally Hemings; freed in Thomas Jefferson's will.

THOMAS ESTON HEMINGS JEFFERSON: Son of Thomas Jefferson and Sally Hemings; freed in Thomas Jefferson's will.

Other Significant People

JUPITER: Slave at Shadwell and Monticello, Thomas Jefferson's valet and stable master, husband of Suck.

SALL: Enslaved woman at Shadwell; mother of Jupiter, Lucinda, "Little Sall," and Caesar.

MYRTILLA: Enslaved woman at Shadwell, mother of Fanny.

HANNAH: Enslaved woman at Shadwell; sent to Randolph Jefferson's Snowdon plantation; possibly beaten to death.

ISAAC BATES: Overseer at Snowdon who beat a slave named Hannah to death.

REVEREND CHARLES CLAY: Episcopal minister, lifelong friend of Thomas Jefferson.

DR. GEORGE GILMER: Doctor at Shadwell.

REVEREND JAMES MAURY: Thomas Jefferson's tutor.

BENJAMIN SNEAD: Tutor for Jefferson daughters and Randolph Jefferson.

DR. THOMAS WALKER and JOHN HARVIE: Executors of Peter Jefferson's estate.

JOHN MURRAY, FOURTH EARL OF DUNMORE: Royal governor of Virginia who attempted to incite slaves to revolt against rebel masters at the onset of the Revolution.

GEORGE GRANGER ("Great George"): Enslaved overseer at Monticello.

URSULA GRANGER: Enslaved cook, nurse, and slaughterer at Monticello, taken captive by the British.

ISAAC JEFFERSON: Son of Ursula and George Granger, brother of George and Bagwell Granger; taken captive by the British.

BARON and BARONESS VON RIEDESEL: German prisoners of war, friends of Thomas Jefferson and Martha Wayles Skelton Jefferson during Revolution.

JOHN CHISWELL: Indebted planter, client of John Wayles.

ROBERT ROUTLEDGE: Virginia merchant said to have murdered Chiswell.

WILLIAM RIND: Publisher of *Virginia Gazette*'s attacks on John Wayles.

JAMES RIND: Lawyer and duelist; son of William Rind and brother of William Rind; involved in altercation with Peter Carr and John Garland Jefferson; lawyer for James T. Callender.

WILLIAM RIND, JR.: brother of James Rind; publisher of *Virginia Federalist*.

JAMES THOMSON CALLENDER: Republican publisher and scandal-monger who exposed Thomas Jefferson's liaison with Sally Hemings.

ANDREW RAMSAY: Captain of the *Robert,* the ship on which Polly Jefferson and Sally Hemings sailed to London in 1787.

ABIGAIL ADAMS: Wife of John Adams and friend of Thomas Jefferson; hosted Polly Jefferson and Sally Hemings in London.

ANNE WILLING BINGHAM: Daughter and wife of Philadelphia bankers and friend of Thomas Jefferson in Paris.

MARIA HADFIELD COSWAY: Anglo-Italian artist and musician, great friend of Thomas Jefferson.

RICHARD COSWAY: Artist and husband of Maria Cosway.

EDMUND BACON: Thomas Jefferson's overseer at Monticello.

Notes

ABBREVIATIONS

Personal names, manuscript collections, and short titles for works frequently cited are identified by the following:

Bear   James A. Bear, Jr., *Jefferson at Monticello: Recollections of a Monticello Slave and of a Monticello Overseer* (Charlottesville: University Press of Virginia, 1999)

Brodie   Fawn Brodie, *Thomas Jefferson: An Intimate History* (New York: Norton, 1974)

Domestic Life   Randolph, Sarah Nicholas. *The Domestic Life of Thomas Jefferson* (New York: Harper & Brothers, 1871)

Family Letters   Edwin Morris Betts and James Adam Bear, Jr., eds., *The Family Letters of Thomas Jefferson* (Charlottesville: University Press of Virginia, 1995)

Farm Book   Edwin Morris Betts, ed., *Thomas Jefferson's Farm Book* (Charlottesville, Va.: Thomas Jefferson Memorial Foundation, 1999)

FLP   Family Letters Project, Thomas Jefferson Foundation, *The Papers of Thomas Jefferson: Retirement Series*, at www.monticello.org/papers/index.html

Free Some Day   Lucia C. Stanton, *Free Some Day: The African-American Families of Monticello* (Charlottesville, Va.: Thomas Jefferson Foundation, 2000)

Garden Book   Edwin Morris Betts, ed., *Thomas Jefferson's Garden Book* (Philadelphia: American Philosophical Society, 1944)

Hemingses   Annette Gordon-Reed, *The Hemingses of Monticello: An American Family* (New York: Norton, 2008)

ICJS   International Center for Jefferson Studies

Kern   Susan Kern, "The Jeffersons at Shadwell: The Social and Material World of a Virginia Family" (Ph.D. diss., College of William and Mary, 2005)

Life   Henry S. Randall, *The Life of Thomas Jefferson*, 3 vols. (New York: Derby & Jackson, 1858)

LOC   Library of Congress

Malone   Dumas Malone, *Jefferson and His Time*, 6 vols. (Boston: Little, Brown, 1948)

MB   James A. Bear, Jr., and Lucia C. Stanton, eds., *Jefferson's Memorandum Books: Accounts, with Legal Records and Miscellany, 1767–1826*, 2 vols. (Princeton, N.J.: Princeton University Press, 1997)

MJE   Mary Jefferson Eppes

MJR   Martha Jefferson Randolph

MWSJ Account Book   Martha Wayles Skelton Jefferson Account Book, Library of Congress

Papers   Julian Boyd, ed., *The Papers of Thomas Jefferson*, 35 vols. to date (Princeton, N.J.: Princeton University Press, 1950–), vol. 1

Parton   James Parton, *Life of Thomas Jefferson, Third President of the United States* (Boston: James R. Osgood, 1874)

SH   Sally Hemings

SSCL   Albert and Shirley Small Special Collections Library, University of Virginia

TJ   Thomas Jefferson

TJ and SH   Annette Gordon-Reed, *Thomas Jefferson and Sally Hemings: An American Controversy* (Charlottesville: University Press of Virginia, 1997)

TMR   Thomas Mann Randolph, Jr.

INTRODUCTION

xiii   **"We are his children":** Mary Jefferson Randolph to Ellen Randolph Coolidge, November 26, 1826; Cornelia Jefferson Randolph to Ellen Wayles Randolph Coolidge, December 11, 1826, Transcripts of Manuscript, Correspondence of Ellen Wayles Randolph Coolidge, SSCL, University of Virginia, FLP.

xvi   **Writing about the heroic Jefferson:** See Fawn M. Brodie, "Jefferson Biographers and the Psychology of Canonization," *Journal of Interdisciplinary History* 2 (1971), 155–71; Annette Gordon-Reed, *Thomas Jefferson and Sally Hemings: An American Controversy* (Charlottesville: University Press of Virginia, 1997).

xvii   **They have shadowed one another:** The interracial Wayles-Jefferson-Eppes-Hemings family was far from unusual in their place and time, as historian Joshua D. Rothman demonstrated in his masterful study, *Notorious in the Neighborhood: Sex and Families across the Color Line in Virginia, 1787–1861* (Chapel Hill: University of North Carolina Press, 2003).

xvii   **To this day, many who revere:** Brodie; Virginia Scharff, "What's Love Got to Do with It? A New Turner Thesis," *Western Historical Quarterly* 40 (Spring 2009), 5–21.

xvii   **Much has changed since Brodie's time:** *TJ and SH;* Eugene A. Foster et al., "Jefferson Fathered Slave's Last Child," *Nature* 396 (November 1998), 27–28. In addition to the documentary and genetic evidence, see also the statistical argument in Fraser D.

Neiman, "Coincidence or Causal Connection? The Relationship between Thomas Jefferson's Visits to Monticello and Sally Hemings's Conceptions," *Forum: Thomas Jefferson and Sally Hemings Redux, William and Mary Quarterly,* 3d series, vol. 57, no. 1 (January 2000), 198–210; *Hemingses.* For a full listing of resources on the DNA controversy and the Hemings-Jefferson relationship, see http://www.monticello.org/plantation/hemingscontro/hemings_report.html.

xxi **These sources make it possible to know:** MB; Kern; Thomas Jefferson Papers, 1606–1827, http://memory.loc.gov/ammem/collections/jefferson_papers; FLP.

1: THE PLANTER'S DAUGHTER

3 **The Randolph clan:** Jonathan Daniels, *The Randolphs of Virginia* (Garden City, N.Y.: Doubleday, 1971); Arthur Pierce Middleton, *Tobacco Coast: A Maritime History of Chesapeake Bay in the Colonial Era* (Newport News, Va.: Mariners' Museum, 1953), 110.

3 **One such guest:** Daniels, *The Randolphs of Virginia,* 37.

4 **The Randolph family sailed:** "Jefferson Family Bible, 1752–1861," accession 4726, SSCL, University of Virginia. See Peter Jefferson's list of birth dates and birthplaces of Jane Randolph Jefferson and siblings.

4 **In times of war:** Middleton, *Tobacco Coast.*

5 **Even on voyages where stores were abundant:** Ibid.,1–15.

5 **Captain Randolph's English wife:** Kern, 30.

5 **Isham's business interests:** The British slave trade had opened to private merchants in 1712. Stephen A. Flanders, *The Atlas of American Migration* (New York: Facts on File, 1998), 52.

5 **Scarcely sixty years earlier:** Kathleen M. Brown, *Good Wives, Nasty Wenches, and Anxious Patriarchs: Gender, Race, and Power in Colonial Virginia* (Chapel Hill: University of North Carolina Press, 1996), 133–36.

6 **Isham Randolph traded the ocean:** Daniels, *Randolphs of Virginia*; Parton; *Life.*

7 **A portrait of Isham:** www.vahistorical.org/dynasties/IshamRandolph.htm.

7 **His Dungeness estate:** Kern, 20–21.

7 **The household was stocked:** Parton, 5.

7 **When Collinson's friend:** Daniels, *Randolphs of Virginia,* 7.

7 **"One thing I must desire":** Ibid.

8 **Daughter Jane:** Kern, 475, transcribes Peter Jefferson's list of "Births and Deaths of the Sons and Daughter[s] of Isham Randolph by Jane his Wife, with whom he intermarried in Byshopsgate chur[ch?] in London the 25th, July 1717," University of Virginia 4726.

9 **According to family tradition:** Ellen Randolph Coolidge, quoted in Brodie, 681, n. 29.

10 **In 1724:** *Virginia Magazine of History and Biography* 14, no. 3 (January 1907), 226–27; Middleton, *Tobacco Coast,* 48–49.

10 **The rigors of such a life:** Jane Rogers Randolph evidently developed such a capacity for command that Isham Randolph took the extraordinary step of appointing his wife as executor of his estate; Kern, 169.

11 **"approved the sometimes savage punishments":** Daniels, *Randolphs of Virginia,* 53.

12 **A 1722 plot:** Mary Miley Theobald, "Slave Conspiracies in Colonial Virginia," *Colonial Williamsburg Journal* (Winter 2005-6).

12 **Insurrection scares and real plots:** Adele Hast, "Legal Status of the Negro in Virginia," *Journal of Negro History* 54 (July 1969).

13 **In 1730, when Jane was ten:** Theobald, "Slave Conspiracies."

13 **Our glimpses of Isham:** *Virginia Magazine of History and Biography* 14, no. 3, 225.

13 **He was thirteen years older:** Malone, 1:3, 10; Paul Leicester Ford, ed., "Autobiography of Thomas Jefferson," in *Writings of Thomas Jefferson,* 10 vols. (New York: Putnam's, 1892-99); Parton, 9.

13 **As for her temperament:** *Domestic Life,* 21-22.

14 **"an agreeable, intelligent woman":** *Life,* 1:16-17.

14 **"Possibly the Dungeness family":** H. J. Eckenrode, *The Randolphs: The Story of a Virginia Family* (Indianapolis and New York: Bobbs-Merrill, 1946), 145-46.

15 **Her father promised her husband:** *Virginia Magazine of History and Biography,* 14, no. 3, 226.

15 **Whatever Isham Randolph's intentions:** Malone, 1:17.

2: THE PLANTER'S WIFE

16 **Peter did what he could:** On plantation life and landscape, see Rhys Isaac, *The Transformation of Virginia, 1740-1790* (Chapel Hill: University of North Carolina Press, 1999), especially pp. 32-3. On Peter Jefferson's plans, see Malone, 1:10, 17. Arrack was an East Indian liquor made from coconut juice. See MB 1:143 n93.

17 **In eighteenth-century Virginia:** On death in childbirth in eighteenth-century America, see http://www.digitalhistory.uh.edu/historyonline/childbirth.cfm. "Account Book of Peter Jefferson" records a payment on August 27, 1758, of two pounds to Mrs. Jane Jefferson "to pay midwives for 4 Negroe wenches," HM912:26, Huntington Library. Although identified in the Huntington collections as Peter Jefferson's book, this ledger was probably a copy made by executor John Harvie.

18 **The Jeffersons would ultimately have:** Kern brilliantly reconstructs the material culture, daily rhythms, and social structure of the Jeffersons' life on their plantation.

19 **For one thing:** Kern, 88.

19 **His earliest recollection:** *Domestic Life,* 6.

19 **At Tuckahoe:** Malone, 1:20.

20 **This was also the time:** Ibid., 22-25.

20 **Back home at Shadwell:** Kern, 467.

20 **The Jeffersons' newly expanded story-and-a-half house:** Kern, 36–44.

21 **Shadwell was a busy:** *Garden Book*, 4–5.

21 **Jane had grown up in a family:** "Inventory of the Estate of Peter Jefferson," HM 912, Huntington Library; Kern, 110; *Garden Book*, 4–5.

21 **The people at Shadwell:** Kern, 456.

21 **There were sheep:** MB 1:406

22 **Jane's daughters:** Kern, 108, 116, 457.

22 **But Jane also paid:** "Account Book of Peter Jefferson."

22 **Generation after generation:** See, for example, Ellen Wayles Randolph to MJR, September 27, 1816; Ellen Wayles Randolph to Nicholas Trist, March 30, 1824; Cornelia Jefferson Randolph to Ellen Wayles Randolph Coolidge, August 3, 1825, Transcripts of Manuscripts, Correspondence of Ellen Wayles Randolph Coolidge, SSCL, University of Virginia, FLP.

23 **Much later, Jefferson recalled:** Brodie, 54, citing Randall, *Jefferson*, 1:131.

23 **Their literate mother:** Malone, 1:22; "Account Book of Peter Jefferson," 29 facing, 36 facing; Jane and her daughter Jane Jr. were unusual women in that they counted books among their personal property; see Kern, 104.

23 **Peter's "tastes approached to the elegant":** *Life*, 1:14.

24 **Peter was fifty years old:** "Account Book of Peter Jefferson"; Kern, 133–34, 164–66, 194.

26 **"How different is the stake":** Brodie, 529, fn. 9, citing TJ to TMR, June 23, 1806, University of Virginia. Much to TJ's relief, the dual between Thomas Mann Randolph and John Randolph of Roanoke was averted.

27 **Thus Jane was spared the fate:** As would befall Dolley Madison. See Catherine Allgor, *A Perfect Union: Dolley Madison and the Creation of the American Nation* (New York: Henry Holt, 2006), 351–53.

27 **There was money enough:** "Account Book of Peter Jefferson."

3: THE WIDOW JEFFERSON

28 **Jane owned a woman named Sall:** Kern, 129, 293–94.

29 **Thomas was then studying the law:** Malone, 1:49–143.

29 **Thomas Jefferson recorded his delight:** *Garden Book*, 4–5. Regarding the gardening pursuits of Squire and Caesar, see *Twinleaf Journal*, http://www.twinleaf.org/articles/aagardens.html.

30 **Jane's children learned to look to marriage:** Kern, 94, 366–67.

31 **Mary Jefferson Bolling kept in close touch:** Kern, 393, 397.

31 **Henry Randall offered:** *Life*, 1:82–83.

32 **When Thomas Jefferson visited:** Thomas Jefferson to John Page, February 21, 1770, *Papers*, 1:36.

32 **This young woman:** *Life*, 1:40–41.

33 **Young Jane Jefferson:** Kern, 457–58.

33 **In December 1771:** MB 1:246–47, n. 56.

33 **A fourth Jefferson daughter:** Ibid., 144.

34 **Thomas Jefferson and his mother:** Purdie and Dixon, *Virginia Gazette*, February 22, 1770, cited in Malone, 1:126; and TJ to John Page, February 21, 1770; *Papers*, 1:35.

34 **Nobody suggested:** MB 1:158–59, n. 43, citing George Tucker, *The Life of Thomas Jefferson* (Philadelphia, 1837), 1:47.

34 **An enslaved man:** MB 200.

35 **One other longtime member:** Ibid.; Jefferson's MB 81, records a 1768 entry "Gave Harry and Myrtilla order on R. Harvie for goods to 16/6." N. 27: eds. Note that "Harry was a farm laborer inherited from PJ [Peter Jefferson]. He joined the British in 1781." According to historian Steven Hochman, as late as 1774 Thomas Jefferson had only sold one enslaved person: Myrtilla. See Steven Hochman, "Thomas Jefferson: A Personal Financial Biography" (Ph.D. diss., University of Virginia, 1987), 72.

36 **The fire also threatened the security:** Kern, 228.

37 **While the site of the Shadwell house:** Ibid., 470.

37 **Jane and Elizabeth and Anna:** *Life*, 1:58–59.

4: THE REVOLUTIONARY'S MOTHER

38 **On a September day in 1772:** Jefferson Family Bible, 1752–1861. Kern, 459–85, provides a masterful analysis of the significance of Jane Jefferson's Bible.

38 **On the page facing:** Kern, 79–132, 459–91.

39 **Perhaps it was the impending birth:** MB 1:294 n. 82.

39 **Only a month before:** Malone, 1:170–71.

39 **Martha had her baby:** MB 1:341 n. 47. James Parton speculated that Carr had died from "a malignant type of typhoid fever"; Parton, 126–29.

39 **In her later years:** *Domestic Life*, 46; Randall, *Life*, 1:83–84.

40 **The steamy heat of a Virginia summer:** *Garden Book*, 40; MB 341 n. 47.

41 **Jefferson distanced himself:** *Garden Book*, 40.

41 **Here lie the remains:** *Domestic Life*, 47.

42 **Perhaps the death of Dabney Carr:** "Dr. George Gilmer's Feebook, 1767, 1771–1775," Gilmer-Skipwith Papers, University of Virginia, MSS 6145; Kern, 361; MB 1:147, 254, 335, 345, 351, 451 for medical bills, 346 for assumption of debts, 353 for Jane's accounts.

42 **The Reverend Charles Clay:** MB 1:370–71.

42 **On February 21, 1774:** Ibid., 369–70.

42 **On March 1:** Ibid., 370.

43 **Her son eagerly joined:** Malone, 1:170–71.

43 **Lord Dunmore:** Ibid.,180–81, MB 1:376 n. 29.

44 **As he set out for Philadelphia:** MB 1:396.

45 **Certainly she could see the vast differences:** Bernard Mayo, ed., *Thomas Jefferson and His Unknown Brother, Randolph* (Charlottesville: University Press of Virginia,

1942), reproduces all the known letters between these brothers in a slim volume. The birthing of twins was hazardous business in eighteenth-century Virginia. Some historians have speculated that both Randolph and Anna Scott Jefferson suffered brain damage in the birthing process and were forever after affected.

45 **The wrath of the English authorities:** Brodie, 131–32, 167–68.

45 **Thomas Jefferson, then in Philadelphia:** Robert Carter Nicholas to the Virginia Delegates in Congress, Williamsburg, November 25, 1775, *Papers,* 1:266.

46 **The Jefferson family:** On the lives of slaves at Shadwell, see Kern, 189–305.

46 **Jane would not live:** Brodie, 584. See Robert Penn Warren, *Brother to Dragons: A Tale in Verse and Voices* (Baton Rouge: Louisiana State University Press, 1996).

47 **How loyal were the Jefferson family slaves:** MB 81 records a 1768 entry "Gave Harry and Myrtilla order on R. Harvie for goods to 16/6." The editors note that "Harry was a farm laborer inherited from PJ [Peter Jefferson]. He joined the British in 1781."

47 **Jane Jefferson lived out her last months:** MB 1:415, TJ to Thomas Nelson, May 16, 1776; *Papers,* 1:292; TJ to William Randolph, ca. June 1776; *Papers,* 1:408–10.

50 **As the historian Susan Kern has pointed out:** Kern, 120–21.

50 **Those who argue:** Jack McLaughlin, *Jefferson and Monticello: The Biography of a Builder* (New York: Henry Holt, 1988), 46–47; Kenneth A. Lockridge, *On the Sources of Patriarchal Rage: The Commonplace Books of William Byrd and Thomas Jefferson and the Gendering of Power in the Eighteenth Century* (New York: New York University Press, 1992), 70.

50 **They also point to the vicious misogyny:** McLaughlin, *Jefferson and Monticello;* Lockridge, *Patriarchal Rage,* 70. See also Jon Kukla, *Mr. Jefferson's Women* (New York: Knopf, 2007).

50 **We should recall:** Brown, *Good Wives, Nasty Wenches.* See also Paige Raibmon, "Naturalizing Power: Land and Sexual Violence along William Byrd's Dividing Line," in Virginia J. Scharff, ed., *Seeing Nature through Gender* (Lawrence: University Press of Kansas, 2003), 20–39.

51 **Those who have dismissed:** Malone, 1:37; McLaughlin, *Jefferson and Monticello,* 46–47; Lockridge, *Patriarchal Rage,* 48, 70.

51 **In the latter:** Ford, ed., "Autobiography," 1:2.

51 **He had also lived for more than six decades:** See, for instance, Cynthia Kierner, *Scandal at Bizarre: Rumor and Reputation in Jefferson's America* (Charlottesville: University Press of Virginia, 2004); Boynton Merrill, *Jefferson's Nephews: A Frontier Tragedy* (Princeton, N.J.: Princeton University Press, 1976).

52 **When Jane Jefferson wrote her family history:** Kern, 470–75.

52 **So what of the letter:** *Papers,* 1:408.

53 **Jefferson began his letter:** Ibid., 1:408–10.

55 **"These facts have given":** "The Declarations of Jefferson and Congress" in Garry Wills, *Inventing America: Jefferson's Declaration of Independence* (New York: Vintage, 1978), 378.

55 **Historian Joseph Ellis:** Joseph Ellis, *American Sphinx: The Character of Thomas Jefferson* (New York: Vintage, 1998), 62.

56 **On October 7, 1791:** TJ to James Lyle, October 7, 1791, Jefferson Papers, Huntington Library, MSS HM5632; *Papers*, 22:201.

56 **But here we also find the tenderness:** Jefferson never did manage to pay off his mother's debts; see *Papers*, 28:417.

56 **In this effort to finish paying off debts:** TJ to John Bolling, *Papers*, 22:198.

56 **And then, of course, there was her Bible:** "Jefferson Bible," University of Virginia, Accession 4726.

5: THE DEBT COLLECTOR'S DAUGHTER

61 **John Wayles of Virginia:** The most thorough account of John Wayles's origins and life is in *Hemingses,* 57–76.

61 **Yet he perpetually walked the line:** On the emergence of the conflict between British merchants and Virginia planters, see Woody Holton, *Forced Founders: Indians, Debtors, Slaves, and the Making of the American Revolution in Virginia* (Chapel Hill: University of North Carolina Press, 1999), 39–73.

62 **"a species of property":** Quoted in Malone, 1:201.

62 **When John Wayles came to visit:** John M. Hemphill II, ed., "John Wayles Rates His Neighbours," *Virginia Magazine of History and Biography* 66, no. 3 (July 1958), 302–6.

62 **Some offered bonds:** Ibid., 303.

62 **Others used their family connections:** Ibid., 303.

62 **A Mr. Syme:** Ibid., 304.

62 **He was, according to Thomas Jefferson:** Ford, ed., "Autobiography," 1:6.

63 **The first was the widow Martha Eppes Eppes:** "Thomas Jefferson memorandum," Edgehill-Randolph Papers, University of Virginia, photocopy in "Martha Wayles Jefferson" information file, ICJS.

63 **When she married John Wayles:** Wills of Francis Eppes, Francis Eppes and Lewellin Eppes, Jr., transcribed by Diane Ehrenpreis, information file, "People—Martha Wayles Jefferson," ICJS.

63 **She made a somewhat different arrangement:** "Henrico Co. Will and Deed Book, C, 1744–1748," 132–34, transcribed by Diane Ehrenpreis in "Martha Wayles Jefferson File," ICJS. On the Eppeses, see *Hemingses,* 54. On the doctrine of coverture, see Marylynn Salmon, *Women and the Law of Property in Early America* (Chapel Hill: University of North Carolina Press, 1989); Brown, *Good Wives, Nasty Wenches, and Anxious Patriarchs: Gender, Race, and Power in Colonial Virginia* (Chapel Hill: University of North Carolina Press, 1996); Carole Shammas, *A History of Household Government in America* (Charlottesville: University Press of Virginia, 2002).

64 **Seven and a half months after they married:** TJ, Memorandum on births and

deaths of Eppes and Wayles family members, Edgehill-Randolph Papers, University of Virginia, copy in "Martha Wayles Jefferson" information file, ICJS.

64 **She delivered a daughter:** Ibid.

64 **By January 1760:** Ibid.

64 **We know all these things about the Wayles family:** Ibid.

65 **John Wayles, thrice wifeless:** On the concept of concubinage, see *Hemingses*, 106-7.

65 **Elizabeth "Betty" Hemings:** Brodie, 89. See Bear, 4; Gordon-Reed, *Thomas Jefferson and Sally Hemings*.

65 **"grew rich himself":** *Hemingses*, 61.

66 **When Betty Hemings began her liaison:** I follow Gordon-Reed in believing that Martha Wayles Skelton Jefferson must have known about her father's relationship with Elizabeth Hemings; ibid., 448. On John Wayles's bequest to Elizabeth Lomax Skelton Wayles, see "Jefferson Family," *Tyler's Quarterly Historical and Genealogical Magazine* 6, no. 3 (January 1925), 268-70, in information file, "People—John Wayles (Estate)," ICJS.

67 **He observed in 1766:** Hemphill, "John Wayles Rates His Neighbors," 305.

68 **While her slaves performed the hardest and worst jobs:** Martha Wayles Skelton Jefferson, 1772-82, Part B: Household Accounts, Thomas Jefferson Papers Series 7, Miscellaneous Bound Volumes, Library of Congress. On plantation mistresses' labor, see Catherine Clinton, *The Plantation Mistress* (New York: Pantheon, 1984); Brown, *Good Wives, Nasty Wenches;* Shammas, *Household Government.*

68 **According to family tradition:** *Domestic Life*, 43-44; *Life*, 1:63-64. Bear, 5.

69 **She had, it seems, a sparkle:** Robert Skipwith to TJ, September 20, 1771, *Papers*, 1:83-84.

69 **Her granddaughter:** Ellen Randolph Coolidge, cited in *Domestic Life*, 43-44.

69 **This paragon of white southern womanhood:** Ibid., 66.

69 **In the summer of 1766:** Holton, *Forced Founders*, 39-73.

69 **John Wayles found himself to be:** *Hemingses*, 74.

70 **Wayles tried to refute:** Ibid., 74-76.

70 **In the same summer: Martha's first cousin:** *New-York Mercury*, July 21, 1766, in *America's Historical Newspapers*, NewsBank and the American Antiquarian Society, 2004, http://infoweb.newsbank.com.

71 **Local authorities wasted no time:** John Frederick Dorman, *Ancestors and Descendants of Francis Epes I of Virginia* (Society of the Descendants of Francis Epes I of Virginia, 1992), 1:153, 2:397, ICJS.

72 **The killing of Richard Henry Eppes:** Ibid., 2:398.

6: BRIDE AND WIDOW

73 **She married twenty-two-year-old Bathurst Skelton:** TJ Memorandum, Edgehill-Randolph Papers. University of Virginia, ICJS; Inventory of Bathurst Skelton's

estate, Charles City County Will Book, 1766–74, 525–27, copy in Monticello Women's Project files, "Martha Wayles Skelton Jefferson," ICJS; Marie Kimball, *Jefferson: The Road to Glory 1743–1776* (New York: Coward-McCann, 1943), 169–70.

74 **The Skeltons set up housekeeping at Elk Hill:** Elie Weeks, "Thomas Jefferson's Elk-Hill," *Goochland County Historical Society Magazine* 3 (1971), 6–11; information file, "Places—Goochland County—Thomas Jefferson Land," ICJS.

74 **They occupied a bluff-top brick house:** Weeks, "Thomas Jefferson's Elk-Hill," 6–11; MB 1:329–32, 366; Malone, 1:162; Kimball, *Road to Glory*, 170.

74 **Ten months later:** "Jefferson Family," *Tyler's Quarterly*, 268.

75 **Thus Martha, at the age of nineteen:** Skelton left behind a young gentleman's accoutrements—in addition to his books, his horse and saddle, phaeton and harnesses, trunk and pocket instruments and razors—along with the basics of genteel housekeeping, silver flatware and cruets, copper plate warmers and chafing dishes, candlesticks, coffee pots, dishes and wash basins, along with four bottles of "mountain wine." But by far his most valuable inventoried assets were six enslaved adults and two children, valued together at £260, making up more than 80 percent of the value of his portable property. Inventory of Bathurst Skelton's estate, 525–27, ICJS.

75 **Her father was a churchgoing man:** See Rhys Isaac, *The Transformation of Virginia, 1740–1790* (Chapel Hill: University of North Carolina Press, 1982).

75 **He was an active member:** *Hemingses,* 67. As Holton points out, William Byrd III, here identified as a friend of John Wayles, was another chronic debtor who was involved with John Chiswell in a failed mining scheme. Like Chiswell, Byrd took his own life. See Holton, *Forced Founders,* 43.

76 **When Martha returned to the Forest:** *Farm Book,* 26; *Free Some Day,* family tree inside back cover.

76 **The law gave Martha Wayles Skelton a right to own property:** The most thorough treatment of this subject is Brown, *Good Wives, Nasty Wenches.* See also Shammas, *Household Government,* and Jan Lewis, *The Pursuit of Happiness: Family and Values in Jefferson's Virginia* (New York: Cambridge University Press, 1983).

77 **One such admirer:** Jefferson paid the blacksmith at the Forest before heading back to Williamsburg: "Gave smith at Wayles's 1/3." MB 1:209.

77 **Thomas Jefferson was a busy man:** See Malone, 1:129–42.

77 **And he was working frantically:** Jefferson moved to his new home on the mountaintop on October 26, 1770, settled some business in Charlottesville, tended to his cases, and found his way back to the Forest by December 10. He was back again by December 20. MB 1:209, 212–13.

77 **"Mr. Jefferson was generally":** *Life,* 1:33–34.

78 **Martha Skelton and Thomas Jefferson shared:** Ibid., 65; *Domestic Life,* 44.

78 **But they also had similar ideas:** Parton, 101. On the cultures of sentiment and sensibility, see William Reddy, *The Navigation of Feeling: A Framework for the History of Emotions* (Cambridge, England: Cambridge University Press, 2001); Martha Tomhave Blauvelt, *The Work of the Heart: Young Women and Emotion, 1780–1830*

(Charlottesville: University Press of Virginia, 2007); Nicole Eustace, *Passion Is the Gale: Emotion, Power, and the Coming of the American Revolution* (Chapel Hill: University of North Carolina Press, 2008). On TJ and sentiment, see Wills, *Inventing America.*

79 **By the beginning of 1771:** TJ to James Ogilvie, February 20, 1771, *Papers,* 1:62–63.

80 **A Quaker woman he knew from Williamsburg:** Mrs. Drummond to TJ, March 12, 1771, ibid., 66.

80 **And while Jefferson's letter:** Hemphill, "John Wayles Rates His Neighbors," 306.

80 **By the beginning of June:** *Life,* 1:65.

82 **As Jefferson looked forward to setting up housekeeping:** TJ to Thomas Adams, June 1, 1771, *Papers,* 1:71–72.

82 **Music, love, luxury, and indebtedness:** Ibid.

83 **Jefferson, for his part, prepared to take on a wife:** TJ "Fee Book, 1764–74 [other accounts, 1764 to 1794]," HM 836, Huntington Library.

83 **On May 26, a terrible flood:** *Garden Book,* 27; MB 1:256; information file, "People—John Wayles," ICJS; Elizabeth Coleman, "The Great Fresh of 1771," *Virginia Cavalcade* 1 (1951), 20–22.

83 **We don't know if little John Skelton was a sickly child:** TJ memorandum, Edgehill-Randolph Papers, University of Virginia, ICJS; Malone, 1:158, 432.

84 **"Come to the new Rowanty":** TJ to Robert Skipwith, August 3, 1771, *Papers,* 1:78.

84 **"Your invitation to the New Rowanty":** Robert Skipwith to TJ, September 20, 1771, *Papers,* 1:83–84.

85 **The pretty vision they shared:** "Jefferson Family," *Tyler's Quarterly,* 269–70.

7: MR. AND MRS. JEFFERSON

86 **Throughout the fall of 1771:** MB 1:266, 284–85.

86 **Finally, after all the delays:** *Papers,* 1:86–87.

86 **The guest list included:** On Anne Wayles and Henry Skipwith, see MB 1:342. On Francis and Elizabeth Eppes and their home at Eppington, see "Places—Eppington," ICJS vertical file; Mary Miley Theobald, "Eppington," *Colonial Williamsburg* (Summer 1997), 54–60; Betty Woodson Weaver, "Mary Jefferson and Eppington," *Virginia Cavalcade* 19, no. 2 (Autumn 1969), 30–35. I am also grateful to Brian Truzzie, historic sites specialist for Chesterfield County, for materials on Eppington and for a tour of the house on June 20, 2008.

87 **There was music and feasting:** MB 1:285.

87 **Martha Wayles Skelton and Thomas Jefferson made their vows:** Church of England, *Book of Common Prayer, and Administration of the Sacraments and Other Rites and Ceremonies of the Church: Together with the Psalter Or Psalms of David, Pointed as They are to be Sung Or Said in Churches* (London: Joseph Bentham, 1765). Original from the New York Public Library, digitized August 2, 2006, 420 pages, books.google.com/books.

87 **The ceremony began:** Ibid.

88 **By the time Martha and Thomas came together:** Shammas, *Household Government*, 80.

88 **"Gentle and sympathetic people":** Malone, 1:158.

89 **The historian Kathleen Brown:** Brown, *Good Wives, Nasty Wenches*, 342.

89 **The trip would become the stuff of family legend:** *Garden Book*, 33; *Life*, 63–65; Parton, 102–3.

90 **The place was dark, the hearth cold:** *Life*, 1:64–65; Parton, 103.

90 **Linger here a moment:** TJ, Autobiography, *The Thomas Jefferson Papers, Series 1. General Correspondence. 1606–51–1827*, Thomas Jefferson, July 27, 1821, Autobiography Draft Fragment, January 6 through July 27, http://memory.loc.gov/ammem/collections/jefferson_papers/.

90 **Here is a picture of them:** http://en.wikipedia.org/wiki/ossian.

91 **a bed he had recently bought:** MB 1:265.

91 **Both she and Thomas generally traveled:** Bear, 6; *Hemingses*, 114.

92 **By February 2, they had relinquished:** MB 1:286–301. MWSJ kept accounts that year, which TJ copied down. See MB 1:300.

93 **She may have had some trouble:** Ibid., 290.

93 **Martha's book:** MWSJ Account Book, Library of Congress.

94 **As hard as they worked for their masters:** On trade between masters and slaves, see Philip D. Morgan, *Slave Counterpoint: Black Culture in the Eighteenth Century Chesapeake and Low Country* (Chapel Hill: University of North Carolina Press, 1998), 358–61.

94 **In the summer of 1772:** MB 1:300–1.

94 **The Monticello well was unreliable:** Ibid., 291; McLaughlin, *Jefferson and Monticello:* 156–57.

94 **For all the trouble Martha would later have:** MWSJ Account Book.

95 **John Wayles was worried:** John Wayles to TJ, October 20, 1772, *Papers*, 1:95–96. On the voyage of the Prince of Wales, see the Transatlantic Slave Trade Database, http://www.slavevoyages.org/tast/database/search.faces. The clearest exposition of the Prince of Wales matter is in *Hemingses*, 68–69.

95 **He went to a plantation called Maiden's Adventure:** Bear, 3.

96 **But the relationship between the mistress and her slave woman:** MB 1:334; *Free Some Day*, 33–34. On the debt collection, see Hochman, "Thomas Jefferson," 72–73; Bear, 3. On Ursula's storytelling, see Rhys Isaac, "The First Monticello," in Peter Onuf, ed., *Jeffersonian Legacies* (Charlottesville: University Press of Virginia, 1993), 80.

96 **Her sister Elizabeth Eppes:** *Dictionary of American Biography* (New York: Scribner's, 1931); Dorman, *Ancestors and Descendants of Francis Epes I*, 1:399; "People—Jefferson Family—Eppes Family," vertical file, ICJS.

96 **Martha had worries as well as joy:** MWSJ Account Book.

96 **Consequently, the Jeffersons were absent:** MB 1:336–37.

97 **Carr was feeling poorly:** Elizabeth Dabney Coleman, "The Carrs of Albemarle County" (unpublished M.A. thesis: University of Virginia, 1944), cited in "People—General—Carr, Dabney," vertical file, ICJS.

97 **Thomas Jefferson's terrible grief:** TJ to the Reverend Charles Clay, May 21, 1773, *Papers*, 15:571.

97 **Carr's second grave:** Her housekeeping journal lapsed during that time, and we have other reason to think that she and Thomas were often apart during the spring of 1773. Martha Jefferson would prove to be a remarkably fertile woman. The patterns of her childbearing closely reflected the time she and Thomas were able to spend together during the course of their marriage. She did not become pregnant with their second child (her third) until late July or early August, when they were back at Monticello, MB 1:336–346; MWSJ Account Book; Malone, 1:434.

97 **Historian Rhys Isaac:** Isaac, "The First Monticello," 90–93.

98 **He was still looking out for her:** "Jefferson Family," *Tyler's Quarterly*, 269–70.

99 **Wayles, however, made it clear:** Ibid.

99 **Martha chose not to intermingle:** MB 1:329, fn. 13.

8: MARTHA'S PROPERTY

100 **Thomas too was attending to his human property:** MB 1:346, September 29, 1773: TJ takes "an appointmt. Of 11 slaves from my mother, revocable by her last will & paimt. Of all monies she shall owe me." These appear to be slaves from Peter Jefferson's estate and their children. According to footnote 64, "Although his mother's will devised four of the slaves to other children, TJ was never reimbursed for his disbursements of her behalf so that all of the slaves became his absolute property in 1777, one year after her death" (as per Fee Book: Jane Jefferson Account, Personal estate account, Misc. accts.: Jane Jefferson acct.) Huntington Library, HN 5572 FAC.

100 **Now Martha had to make some decisions:** MB 1:342–43; *Free Some Day*, p. 103.

101 **The oldest Hemings sons:** MB 1:342; *Farm Book*, 9. Mary Hemings, Elizabeth's oldest child and the mother of Daniel, was at Wingo's, or Poplar Forest, at this time. She later went to Monticello.

102 **It was only three years since the murder:** See chapter 3.

102 **His brothers-in-law:** MB 1:329, fn. 15.

102 **Jefferson noted his intent:** Ibid., 371.

103 **In 1948, Dumas Malone would write blithely:** Malone, 1:161–62.

105 **Thomas Jefferson admonished Martha:** Ellen Randolph Coolidge letterbook, University of Virginia Library, Accession 9090, 66–67.

106 **She watched closely over the slaughtering:** Jefferson noted his own suspicions of theft at his Bedford plantation: "Stanly [the overseer there] has killed by his own confession 12 hogs, but as Jupiter (one of his negroes who kept a tally of it) sais 16. Stanly told Garth some time ago he had about 50 or 60 lb. of butter to send me, but now he has but about 20 lb. The negroes say he has sold a great deal of corn." MB 1:380.

106 **Jefferson hated violence:** Marie Morgan and Edmund S. Morgan, "Jefferson's Concubine," *New York Review of Books*, October 9, 2008, 15.

106 **The Hemingses did not go all at once:** *Farm Book*, 15–18.

106 **Even though she had not insisted:** MB 1:329, fn. 15: "In the partition Martha received all the lands in Bedford and Amherst counties and the Willis Creek lands and part of the St. James' lands in Cumberland County. In addition to her share in the division of the estate, she came into possession of two properties which Wayles had held as tenant by courtesy: Elk Island, to which she had dower rights from her first husband, and Indian Camp, an entailed estate inherited through her mother. . . .

"TJ and Martha soon sold over half this land in an attempt to pay off their share of the debts of the estate. Henry Skipwith bought the St. James' and Indian Camp lands, giving the Elk Hill plantation as part of the purchase price. The Willis Creek lands were sold in 1790 and in Bedford County TJ retained only the Poplar Forest property." See also MB 1:366, fn. 1. For the three Elk–hill deeds, see MSS 1162, Special Collections, University of Virginia.

107 **Isaac Jefferson, Ursula's son:** Bear, 15–16.

108 **In the wake of John Wayles's death:** MB 1:383; MWSJ Account Book.

108 **February brought the frightening earthquake:** See chapter 3.

108 **As he recovered from that tragedy:** *Garden Book*, 47–50; MB 1:372.

9: HIS WORLD AND HERS

110 **She duly recorded:** MWSJ Account Book; MB 1:374–75; *Garden Book*, 55.

110 **Down in Williamsburg:** Malone, 1:172.

110 **As he looked back later:** TJ to Thomas Cooper, February 10, 1814, cited in Malone, 1:174.

111 **Martha, back at Monticello:** MB 1:374–75; MWSJ Account Book; Malone, 1:179–86.

111 **As historian Fawn Brodie pointed out:** Brodie, 120.

111 **He was on perilous political ground:** *A Summary View of the Rights of British America*, http://books.google.com/books; Thomas Jefferson, John P. Foley, *The Jeffersonian Cyclopedia* (New York: Funk & Wagnalls, 1900), digitized February 23, 2007, 963, 966.

112 **The free man depicted in the *Summary View*:** Ibid., 966.

113 **Jefferson had ordered fourteen:** MB 1:405; Malone, 1:191–93; McLaughlin, *Jefferson and Monticello*, 163–64.

113 **The want of those windows:** MB 1:389–91; MWSJ Account Book.

113 **As Thomas sallied forth:** MB 1:399–403.

114 **One of those terrors became a reality:** Malone, 1:210, 434.

114 **Both women:** Dorman, *Ancestors and Descendants of Francis Epes I*, 1:399.

115 **There was fighting along the coast:** Brodie, 130; chapter 1 herein.

115 **"I wrote to Patty on my arrival":** TJ to Francis Eppes, October 10, 1775, *Papers*, 1:246.

115 **Even in Philadelphia, family tragedy:** TJ to Francis Eppes, October 24, 1775, *Papers*, 249.

116 **"I have never received the scrip of a pen":** TJ to Francis Eppes, November 7, 1775, *Papers*, 252.

116 **"I have written to Patty a proposition":** TJ to Francis Eppes, November 21, 1775, *Papers*, 264.

116 **"The Person of no Man in the Colony is safe":** Robert Carter Nicholas to the Virginia Delegates in Congress, Williamsburg, November 25, 1775, *Papers*, 1:266. For a fuller rendition of this message, see chapter 1.

116 **Still, Jefferson could not go:** MB 1:411.

116 **For her part, Martha was back at Monticello:** MWSJ Account Book.

117 **She may have had her hands full:** TJ to Thomas Nelson, Jr., May 16, 1776, *Papers*, 1:292.

118 **"You must certainly bring Mrs. Jefferson":** Thomas Nelson, Jr., to TJ, February 4, 1776, *Papers*, 1:286.

118 **Whether or not Martha wanted to go:** TJ to Thomas Nelson, Jr., May 16, 1776, *Papers*, 1:292: "I am here in the same uneasy anxious state in which I was the last fall without Mrs. Jefferson who could not come with me."

118 **Fawn Brodie speculated:** Brodie, 149–50.

118 **Before he left, he gave her ten pounds:** MB 1:417, 431.

119 **"I have snatched a few Moments":** John Page to Thomas Jefferson, April 26, 1776, *Papers*, 1:288.

10: DOMESTIC TRANQUILITY

121 **But in a far less celebrated passage:** Wills, *Inventing America*, p. 377. Thanks to Rick Hills for reminding me of this section of Jefferson's draft.

122 **"I am sorry the situation":** TJ to Edmund Pendleton, June 30, 1776, *Papers*, 1:408.

122 **On July 4, 1776:** MB 1:421.

122 **"I have received no letter this week":** TJ to Francis Eppes, July 23, 1776, *Papers*, 1:473.

122 **"For god's sake, for your country's sake":** TJ to Richard Henry Lee, July 29, 1776, *Papers*, 1:477; TJ to John Page, July 30, 1776, *Papers*, 1:483.

123 **"We return'd last Sunday from Elk-Hill":** Francis Eppes to TJ, July 3, 1776, *Papers*, 15:576.

123 **By the end of that month:** TJ to Francis Eppes, August 9, 1776, *Papers* 1:488; Edmund Pendleton to TJ, August 26, 1776; *Papers*, 1:508.

123 **It took Jefferson only six days:** MB 1:425; Malone, 1:245–46.

123 **Despite the perils of war:** MB 1:428–29.

124 **Dunmore had sailed away:** Edmund Pendleton to TJ, May 24, 1776, *Papers*, 1:296–97.

124 **On the way home, he bought five bushels of salt:** MB 1:430–31.

124 **In January, she and Ursula killed sixty-eight hogs:** MWSJ Account Book.

124 **"Could we but get a good Regular Army":** Thomas Nelson, Jr., to TJ, January 2, 1777, *Papers*, 2:3.

125 **But at Monticello, peace reigned:** MWSJ Account Book; MB 1:445–47.

125 **In August, she determined to get control:** MWSJ Account Book. On hog butchering in eighteenth-century Virginia, see http://faroutliers.wordpress.com/2007/10/17/hogs-ham-and-us-history.

126 **"It will not perhaps be disagreeable":** Richard Henry Lee to TJ, August 25, 1777, *Papers*, 2:13.

126 **So she kept busy in the house:** MWSJ Account Book, March 1778.

126 **He planted his vegetable garden:** *Garden Book*, 76.

126 **Their third daughter:** Jefferson would pay Dr. Gilmer "in full £43-12." MB 1:468–69.

127 **He went reluctantly."** MB 1:472–75; Malone, 1:293.

127 **The War for Independence came to Albemarle County:** Malone, 1:293–96.

128 **"Often our lives were in danger":** Baroness von Riedesel, *Baroness von Riedesel and the American Revolution: Journal and Correspondence of a Tour of Duty, 1776–1783*, revised translation with introduction and notes by Marvin L. Brown, Jr., with the assistance of Marta Huth (Chapel Hill: Institute of Early American History and Culture, and University of North Carolina Press, 1965), 79.

129 **The baroness prided herself:** Ibid., 82–83.

129 **"Many of them let the slaves walk about":** Ibid., 86.

130 **"There are, of course, good masters too":** Ibid.

130 **The families did spend time together:** Baron Riedesel to TJ, December 4, 1779, *Papers*, 3:212.

130 **They shared a love of music:** Cited in Malone, 1:296.

130 **The entire time the Jeffersons and Riedesels were together:** Brodie, 171–72.

131 **Thomas Jefferson sold the pianoforte:** MB 1:478–80; John Page to TJ, June 2, 1779, *Papers*, 2:278; TJ to John Page, June 3, 1779, *Papers* 2:279.

11: THE WAR COMES HOME

132 **She started out asking for small sums:** MB 1:488–91.

133 **He recalled much later the impressive procession:** Bear, 4, 6.

133 **"It was cold weather when they moved up":** Ibid., 6.

133 **General Riedesel, then in New York:** General Riedesel to TJ, March 30, 1780, *Papers*, 3:338.

133 **"I sincerely condole with Madame de Riedesel":** TJ to General Riedesel, May 3, 1780, *Papers,* 3:368.

134 **Her letter echoed her pride:** MWSJ to Eleanor Madison, August 8, 1780, *Papers,* 3:532. Diane Ehrenpreis, curatorial art historian at Monticello, has located at least one additional letter sent by Martha Jefferson on behalf of this effort. Personal communication, Diane Ehrenpreis, June 5, 2008.

135 **Martha could not "do more":** Baron Riedesel's October 2 letter to Jefferson offered congratulations on "Mrs. Jeffersons health and recovery." Riedesel to TJ, October 2, 1780, *Papers,* 4:4.

135 **On November 3, Martha gave birth to Lucy Elizabeth:** MB 1:502; Kelly Neff Quattrin, "For the Life of Her: Martha Wayles Jefferson and Diabetes," draft article in information file, "People—Martha Wayles Jefferson," ICJS.

136 **Things went from bad to worse:** Malone, 1:337–39.

136 **The day before Arnold's troops arrived:** Bear, 8.

137 **The British moved on:** Ibid., 10.

138 **The Jefferson slaves remained with the British:** Ibid.

139 **"The day is so very bad":** TJ to David Jameson, April 16, 1781, *Papers,* 5:468.

139 **Martha, Patsy, and Polly fled Richmond:** MB 1:509.

139 **"We receive every day vague reports":** Bolling Stark to TJ, April 30, 1781, *Papers,* 5:579–80.

140 **"Mrs. Jefferson and your little family were very well":** Ibid.

140 **Tarleton arrived on June 4:** *Hemingses,* 119.

141 **But Cornwallis, in Jefferson's words:** TJ to Dr. William Gordon, July 16, 1788, *Papers,* 13:363–64.

142 **Some thirty slaves left with Cornwallis:** *Farm Book,* 29.

142 **In his later recollection:** *Farm Book,* 29, and TJ to William Gordon, *Papers,* 13:363–64.

142 **Jefferson scholars have, until recently, taken an oddly sanguine view:** Malone, 1:391.

12: THE BUTCHER'S BILL

144 **While Cornwallis raged at Elk Hill:** MB 1:511; *Papers,* 4:261, 266, 268.

144 **When they got back to Monticello:** MWSJ Account Book.

145 **Martha's body was scarred and weakened:** MB 1:519.

146 **"Because of this impenetrable silence":** Malone, 1:397.

147 **Jefferson's letter to Monroe:** Thomas Jefferson to James Monroe, May 20, 1782, *Papers,* 6:186.

148 **Some of Jefferson's other friends:** Brodie, 206.

148 **But Monroe was deeply sympathetic:** Monroe to Jefferson, June 28, 1782, *Papers,* 6:192.

148 **Sometime near the end:** *Papers,* 6:196.

149 **"The House servants":** Bear, 99–100. Brodie, 208–9, has speculated on the reasons for Bacon's error regarding the number of living Jefferson children.

150 **"My dear wife died this day":** MB 1:521.

150 **"A moment before the closing scene":** Mary Randolph and Anne Cary, "Reminiscences of Th.J. by MR," *Papers*, 6:199–200.

150 **"He kept his room for three weeks":** Ibid.

151 **"Mrs. Jefferson has at last shaken off her tormenting pains":** Edmund Randolph to James Madison, September 20, 1782, cited in *Papers*, 6:199.

151 **"When at last he left his room":** Randolph and Cary, "Reminiscences of Th.J. by MR," *Papers*, 6:199–200.

151 **Martha Wayles Skelton Jefferson was buried at Monticello:** http://wiki.monticello.org/mediawiki/index.php/Martha_Jefferson_Epitaph.

152 **"This miserable kind of existence":** Thomas Jefferson to Elizabeth Eppes, October 3(?), 1782, *Papers*, 6:198–99.

152 **Even in this private letter:** Ibid.

153 **"Patsy rides with me":** Ibid.

153 **Some historians have seen:** Brodie, 211; *Hemingses*, 147.

153 **If Thomas Jefferson held any truth to be self-evident:** On Jefferson's gender ideology, see Kukla, *Mr. Jefferson's Women*; and Brian Steele, "Thomas Jefferson's Gender Frontier," *Journal of American History* 95, no. 1 (June 2008).

154 **In the shadow of her death:** "I received yesterday your favor of the 9th. inst. And am happy that the sale of Elkhill is at length compleeted." Thomas Jefferson to Daniel Hylton, January 20, 1783, *Papers*, 6:220.

154 **"Old Master had a small brick house":** Bear, 17.

154 **Jefferson scholar James A. Bear, Jr.:** Ibid., 127, n. 62.

155 **Yet he could describe the place with precision:** "Jefferson's Advertisement for Sale of Elk Hill," October 5, 1790, *Papers*, 17:567–69; MSS 4009, Special Collections, University of Virginia.

155 **Dumas Malone wrote:** Malone, 1:397.

13: STORIES AND SHADOW FAMILIES

159 **"I never knew of but one white man":** "Life Among the Lowly, No. 1," *Pike County (Ohio) Republican*, March 13, 1873, reprinted as "Reminiscences of Madison Hemings," in Brodie, 637–38.

160 **"Capt. Hemings happened to be":** Ibid.; see also Bear, 4; and Life Among the Lowly, No. 3," *Pike County (Ohio) Republican*, December 25, 1873, reprinted as "Memoirs of Israel Jefferson" in Annette Gordon-Reed, *Thomas Jefferson and Sally Hemings: An American Controversy* (Charlottesville: University Press of Virginia, 1997), 252–53.

161 **She was the property of Francis and Sarah Eppes:** The marriage indenture made April 9, 1746, and recorded by Bowler Cocke in Henrico County established that John Wayles would get a life estate in Martha Eppes's inheritance, which included nine enslaved people including "Parthenia, Betty & Ben a Boy together with all their

offspring born and to be born," and that Martha would receive her dower rights as well as her own property in the event of John Wayles's death, "notwithstanding her Coverture." Information file, "People—John Wayles," ICJS, marriage indenture transcribed by Diane Ehrenpreis.

161 **He was careful to note that his great-grandfather:** See Marcus Rediker, *The Slave Ship: A Human History* (New York: Viking, 2007).

164 **"Just as Elizabeth Hemings and her daughters had seen":** *Hemingses*, 148.

164 **In fact, he had to hire a guide:** MB 1:523–54; Malone, 1:399.

165 **And now came months of uncertainty:** Malone, 1:419, 421. 12,

165 **Jefferson left the management of his business affairs:** TJ to Nicholas Lewis, July 11, 1788, *Papers,* 13:343.

165 **Jefferson also made provision for Betty's older sons:** Ibid.; *Hemingses*, 317.

166 **And Sally Hemings, at nine or ten years old:** Malone, 1:39–40.

166 **Elizabeth Eppes was also half-sister:** Bear, 15.

167 **Elizabeth Eppes's life:** John Frederick Dorman, *Ancestors and Descendants of Francis Epes I*, 2:398–99; Information file, "Places—Eppington," ICJS; Bettie Woodson Weaver, "Mary Jefferson and Eppington," *Virginia Cavalcade* 19, no. 2 (Autumn 1969), 30–35; Mary Miley Theobald, "Eppington," *Colonial Williamsburg* (Summer 1997), 54–60.

167 **Francis Eppes, like Thomas Jefferson:** See McLaughlin, *Jefferson and Monticello;* Information File, "Places—Eppington," ICJS.

167 **Eppes had begun to build in about 1770:** Dorman, *Ancestors and Descendants of Francis Epes I*, 2:398–99; Information file, "Places—Eppington," ICJS; Weaver, "Mary Jefferson and Eppington," 30–35; Theobald, "Eppington," 54–60. On the gendered architecture of Monticello, see Elizabeth V. Chew, "Inhabiting the Great Man's House: Women and Space at Monticello," in Joan E. Hartman and Adele Seeff, eds., *Structures and Subjectivities: Attending to Early Modern Women* (Newark: University of Delaware Press, 2007), 223–52.

168 **But for Sally Hemings:** Robert Hemings had also been sent to Eppington with a letter from Thomas Jefferson to Francis Eppes. Francis Eppes to TJ, September 16, 1784, *Papers*, 15:615.

168 **People began to suffer the symptoms of pertussis:** http://en.wikipedia.org/wiki/Pertussis.

169 **"I wish it was in my power":** Francis Eppes to TJ, September 16, 1784, *Papers*, 15:616.

169 **"It is impossible to paint the anguish":** Elizabeth Wayles Eppes, to TJ, October 13, 1784, *Papers*, 7:441.

170 **It took nearly seven months for this letter:** Ibid.; Malone, , 2:xxv.

170 **He had, however, found out about his daughter's death:** James Currie to Thomas Jefferson, November 20, 1784, *Papers*, 6:538–39.

170 **He wrote to Francis Eppes:** TJ to Francis Eppes, May 11, 1785, *Papers*, 8:141.

14: SUMMONED AND SENT

173 **"Dear Papa":** Mary Jefferson to Thomas Jefferson, ca. September 13, 1785, *Papers*, 8:517.

173 **Jefferson acknowledged the problems:** TJ to Francis Eppes, August 30, 1785, *Papers*, 8:451.

174 **"Their dispositions are . . . hostile":** TJ to Eppes, December 11, 1785, *Papers*, 9:91–92.

174 **Jefferson was so worried about pirates:** TJ to Eppes, January 7, 1786, *Papers*, 9:159.

174 **Jefferson had begun by proposing the idea:** TJ to Eppes, May 11, 1785, *Papers*, 8:141.

174 **"With respect to the person":** TJ to Eppes, August 30, 1785, *Papers*, 8:451.

175 **"She would be in the best hands possible":** TJ to Eppes, December 11, 1785, *Papers*, 9:91–92.

175 **"I know that Mrs. Eppes's goodness":** TJ to Eppes, January 24, 1786, *Papers*, 9:211–12.

176 **In the end, Francis Eppes decided:** Eppes to TJ, April 14, 1787, *Papers*, 15:636.

177 **Francis Eppes set about pursuing:** Eppes to TJ, August 31, 1786, *Papers*, 15:631.

177 **In the meantime, Isabel returned to Monticello:** *Free Some Day*, 39.

177 **The child was so distraught:** Malone, 2:134–35.

179 **She was, according to the few descriptions we have:** Bear, 4; "Life Among the Lowly, No. 3," *Pike County (Ohio) Republican*, December 25, 1873, reprinted as "Memoirs of Israel Jefferson," in Annette Gordon-Reed, *Thomas Jefferson and Sally Hemings: An American Controversy* (Charlottesville: University Press of Virginia, 1997), 252–53.

179 **He would eventually marry his first cousin:** See http://wiki.monticello.org/mediawiki/index.php/Betsy_Hemmings; http://www.monticello.org/gettingword/betsyhemmingsfamily.html; http://www.buckinghamhemmings.com/.

181 **She would cling to Andrew Ramsay:** Andrew Ramsay to Thomas Jefferson, July 6, 1787, *Papers*, 11:556.

181 **They even worried Patsy Jefferson:** Martha Jefferson to TJ, May 3, 1787, *Papers*, 11:334.

182 **"They returned to virginia":** Ibid.

182 **He had written in December:** TJ to Abigail Adams, December 21, 1786, *Papers*, 10:621; TJ to Francis Eppes, July 2, 1787, *Papers*, 11:524.

182 **Adams had a terrible time prying Polly loose:** Abigail Adams to TJ, June 26, 1787, *Papers*, 11:502.

183 **Adams, who had found Polly in such ragged condition:** Abigail Adams to TJ, June 27, 1787, *Papers*, 11:503.

183 **Abigail Adams had considerable knowledge:** David McCullough, *John Adams* (New York: Simon & Schuster, 2001), 67; Abigail Adams to TJ, July 6, 1787, *Papers*, 11:551.

183   **Instead of coming to get Polly himself:** TJ to Abigail Adams, July 1, 1787, *Papers*, 11:514.

183   **Polly, disappointed and betrayed once again:** Abigail Adams to TJ, July 6, 1787, *Papers*, 11:551.

184   **Dumas Malone took from Adams's remark:** Malone, 2:135.

184   **Malone, one of the people who most vehemently denied:** Fawn M. Brodie, "Jefferson Biographers and the Psychology of Canonization," *Journal of Interdisciplinary History* 2 (1971), 157–58 and 160–61.

185   **Polly Jefferson was educated:** Francis Eppes to TJ, August 31, 1786, *Papers*, 15:631.

185   **Polly was also a hearty eater:** Elizabeth Eppes to TJ, July 30, 1786, *Papers*, 15:628.

185   **If the two girls arrived in London:** Abigail Adams to TJ, July 10, 1787, *Papers*, 11:572–74.

186   **Andrew Ramsay may have offered:** Andrew Ramsay to TJ, July 6, 1787, *Papers*, 11:556.

187   **Gordon-Reed reminds us:** *Hemingses*, 200.

187   **In the end, Sally Hemings found her way to Paris:** *Free Some Day*, 108.

15: PARIS

188   **The fourteen-year-old girl:** *Hemingses*, 166.

189   **In addition to his mundane duties:** TJ to André Limozin, September 9, 1787, *Papers*, 12:110; TJ to Zachariah Loreilhe, September 9, 1787, *Papers*, 12: 111.

189   **Polly "had totally forgotten her sister":** TJ to Abigail Adams, July 16, 1787, *Papers*, 11:592.

189   **Her reaction was understandable:** TJ to Elizabeth Eppes, July 28, 1787, *Papers*, 11:634.

189   **Madison Hemings:** "Reminiscences of Madison Hemings," in Brodie, 639–40.

189   **Abigail Adams, on the other hand:** Abigail Adams to TJ, June 27, 1787, *Papers*, 11:503.

190   **As the hired coach turned off the Champs-Elysées:** McLaughlin, *Jefferson and Monticello*, 169–71.

191   **The Hôtel de Langeac:** Ibid., 211–12.

191   **Within a week of her arrival:** TJ to Mary Jefferson Bolling, July 23, 1787, *Papers*, 11:612.

191   **He was just finishing up his apprenticeship:** MB 1:673, 681.

192   **In addition to Petit:** MB 1:603. William Howard Adams, *The Paris Years of Thomas Jefferson* (New Haven, Conn.: Yale University Press, 1997), 19–20.

192   **As soon as he could, Jefferson sent her off:** MB 1:685; *Hemingses*, 213–23.

192   **For more than two years, Sally Hemings lived in Paris:** "Reminiscences of Madison Hemings," in Brodie, 639–40.

192   **Polly and Patsy were also studying and speaking French:** *Free Some Day*, 110; Martha Jefferson to TJ, May 29, 1787, *Papers*, 11:381.

193 **Just as he made certain that Sally was secure:** *Hemingses*, 224–27.

193 **She ate what the other servants did:** Papers of Trist and Burke Family Members, MSS 5385-f, Special Collections, University of Virginia.

193 **Patsy began to go out more:** MB 1:729, 734; *Free Some Day*, 110.

193 **Just as he began to pay James Hemings:** MB 1:690, 718, 721, 722, 725.

194 **She learned to care for the fine fabrics:** *Hemingses*, 236–39.

194 **The working women of Paris:** On women and the French Revolution, see Joan B. Landes, *Women and the Public Sphere in the Age of the French Revolution* (Ithaca, N.Y.: Cornell University Press, 1988); Dominique Godineau, *The Women of Paris and Their French Revolution* (Berkeley: University of California Press, 1998).

195 **"I observe women and children carrying heavy burthens":** TJ, "Notes on a Tour through Southern France and Italy," *Papers*, 11:415.

196 **As he thought about how women lived:** Steele, "Thomas Jefferson's Gender Frontier," 17–42.

196 **"Can we wonder if such of them as have a little beauty":** *Papers*, 11:446.

197 **"While one considers them as useful and rational companions":** TJ, "Notes of a Tour through Holland and the Rhine Valley, 1788," *Papers*, 13:27.

16: AMAZONS VERSUS ANGELS

199 **He spent time with flamboyant women:** On his later avoidance of female company, see Catherine Allgor, *Parlor Politics: In Which the Ladies of Washington Help Build a City and a Government* (Charlottesville: University Press of Virginia, 2000).

199 **"atheists, deists and libertines":** Adams, *The Paris Years*, 75.

199 **Some of them were especially aggressive:** William Stephens Smith to William Short, July 30, 1787, quoted in MB 1:611.

200 **Years earlier, he had decided not to hire:** TJ to James Madison, February 14, 1783, *Papers*, 6:241.

201 **As the Binghams made their way back to America:** TJ to Madison, January 20, 1787, *Papers*, 11:95.

201 **"At eleven o'clock it is day chez Madame":** TJ to Anne Willing Bingham, February 7, 1787, *Papers*, 11:122–24.

202 **"Thus the days of life are consumed":** Ibid.

202 **"In America, on the other hand":** Ibid.

202 **Jefferson closed his letter:** Ibid.

203 **"This is my plan Madam":** TJ to Madame de Tessé, March 20, 1787, *Papers*, 11:227.

203 **Her outraged response:** Abigail Adams to TJ, January 29, 1787, *Papers*, 11:86; TJ to Abigail Adams, February 22, 1787, *Papers*, 11:174.

204 **He paid for wine and art:** MB 1:680–85.

204 **"May your days and nights be many":** TJ to William Stephens Smith, July 9, 1786, *Papers*, 10:116–17.

204 **He concluded another letter:** TJ to Smith, October 22, 1786, *Papers,* 10:479.

204 **The object of Jefferson's passion:** On the life and career of Maria Cosway, see Gerald Barnet, *Richard and Maria Cosway: A Biography* (Cambridge, England: Lutterworth, 1995); Helen Duprey Bullock, *My Head and My Heart: A Little History of Thomas Jefferson and Maria Cosway* (New York: Putnam's, 1945); George C. Williamson, *Richard Cosway, R.A.* (London: George Bell, 1905); and Ellen C. Clayton, *English Female Artists*, 2 vols. (London: Tinsley Brothers, 1876), vol. 1.

207 **That night, he sat down to write to Maria Cosway:** TJ to Maria Cosway, October 12, 1786, *Papers,* 10:443–55.

207 **That summer, he traveled in northern Italy:** TJ to Maria Cosway, July 1, 1787, *Papers,* 11:519–20.

208 **"I leave you with very melancholy ideas":** Maria Cosway to TJ, December 7, 1787, *Papers,* 12:403.

209 **"Society is spoilt by it":** TJ to the Marquise de Bréhan, May 9, 1788, *Papers,* 13:150.

209 **"the civil dissensions":** TJ to Maria Cosway, July 27, 1788, *Papers,* 13:424.

209 **Anne Willing Bingham had replied:** Anne Willing Bingham to TJ, June 1, 1787, *Papers,* 11:392–94.

210 **"The women of France interfere":** Ibid.

210 **"We have now need of something to make us laugh":** TJ to Bingham, May 11, 1788, *Papers* 13:151–52.

210 **"You too have had your political fever":** Ibid.

212 **After she died, that bell:** Susan Stein, *The Worlds of Thomas Jefferson at Monticello* (New York: Harry N. Abrams, 1993), 16.

213 **Who could more perfectly fulfill:** For an extended discussion of the "amazons and angels" comparison with regard to Sally Hemings, see *Hemingses*, 275–80.

17: SALLY'S CHOICE

214 **"When Mr. Jefferson went to France":** "Reminiscences of Madison Hemings," in Brodie, 639–40.

215 **"We are here experiencing a Siberian degree of cold":** TJ to Francis Eppes, December 15, 1788, *Papers*,14:357–59; TJ to the Marquise de Bréhan, March 14, 1789, *Papers,* 14:656.

216 **"I have for two months past had a very sick family":** TJ to Maria Cosway, January 14, 1789, *Papers,* 14:446.

216 **"kiss Polly for me":** Marie Jacinthe de Botidoux to Martha Jefferson, November 4, 1789, Special Collections, University of Virginia, MSS 5385-a.a.

216 **The daughters of the French nobility:** Ibid.

217 **"Surely it was never so cold before":** TJ to Maria Cosway, January 14, 1789, *Papers,* 14:446. Fawn Brodie interpreted this letter as significant evidence that Jefferson had begun his affair with Hemings. See Brodie, 299.

217 **Jefferson paid Dupré:** *Hemingses*, 244–46; MB 1:731; TJ to Francis Eppes, December 15, 1788, *Papers*, 14:357–59; MB 1:729, 730–31, 734.

218 **Of course, as a slave:** Annette Gordon-Reed offers a brilliant analysis of the differences between Sally Hemings's status and choices and that of her half-sister, Martha Jefferson, in *Hemingses*, 353–76.

219 **Madison may have been in error about this pregnancy:** Eugene A. Foster et al., "Jefferson Fathered Slave's Last Child," *Nature* 396 (November 1998), 27–28.

219 **Generations of Jefferson scholars have denied:** Ibid.; *TJ and SH*. In addition to the documentary and genetic evidence, see also the statistical argument in Fraser D. Neiman, "Coincidence or Causal Connection? The Relationship between Thomas Jefferson's Visits to Monticello and Sally Hemings's Conceptions," *Forum: Thomas Jefferson and Sally Hemings Redux, William and Mary Quarterly,* 3d series, vol. 57, no. 1 (January 2000), 198–210. For a full listing of resources on the DNA controversy and the Hemings-Jefferson relationship, see http://www.monticello.org/plantation/hemingscontro/hemings_report.html.

221 **Jefferson had expressed his views:** Thomas Jefferson, *Notes on the State of Virginia* (New York: Harper Torchbooks, 1964), 132–39.

221 **Jefferson was, as Joseph Ellis has so eloquently explained:** Joseph Ellis, *American Sphinx: The Character of Thomas Jefferson* (New York: Vintage, 1998).

222 **Sally was not the first woman of her family:** *Free Some Day; Hemingses.*

18: COMING HOME

226 **"your creditors are very pressing":** Francis Eppes to TJ, September 16, 1784, *Papers*, 15:616; Francis Eppes to TJ, October 23, 1786, *Papers*, 10:483.

226 **When Francis Eppes spoke of selling:** TJ to Nicholas Lewis, July 11, 1788, *Papers*, 13:339–44; TJ to Alexander McCaul, July 12, 1788, *Papers*, 13:349.

227 **"Mine is a journey of duty and affection":** TJ to Maria Cosway, September 26, 1788, *Papers*, 13:639.

227 **Meanwhile, he let the folks back home know:** TJ to Elizabeth Eppes, December 15, 1788, *Papers*, 14:355–56; TJ to Francis Eppes, December 15, 1788, *Papers*, 14:357–59.

228 **And then there was all that baggage:** MB 1:744; "Jefferson's Instructions for Procuring Household Goods," *Papers*, 16:321–24.

228 **Jefferson hoped to embark:** TJ to Nicholas Lewis, December 16, 1788, *Papers*, 14:362; MB 1:716.

228 **To his frustration:** TJ to Angelica Schuyler Church, February 15, 1789, *Papers*, 228:554.

229 **He rode in his carriage past the king's foreign mercenaries:** See Malone, 2:215–27; MB 1:738.

230 **Jefferson bought a shepherd dog:** MB 1:745.

230 **Dumas Malone imagined:** Malone, 2:236.

230 **On October 5, a crowd of some six thousand women:** On the women's march to Versailles, see Darline Gay Levy, *Women in Revolutionary Paris, 1789–1795* (Champaign: University of Illinois Press, 1981).

230 **Malone envisioned the voyage as a placid one:** Malone, 2:243, 241.

232 **"After beating about three days":** *Domestic Life*, 151.

234 **Wormley Hughes, Sally Hemings's nephew:** *Life*, 1:552–53. On the condition of the Three-Notched Road, see TJ to Henry Skipwith, December 26, 1789, *Papers*, 16:51–52.

234 **They had reason to be happy:** Parton, 1:286.

235 **Jefferson was quickly consumed:** On the Peter Jefferson estate matters, see, for example, TJ to Thomas Walker, January 18, 1790, *Papers*, 16:112–14; Walker to TJ, January 19, 1790, *Papers*, 16:114–15; TJ to John Nicholas, Sr., January 20, 1790, *Papers*, 16:115–16; TJ to Walker, January 25, 1790, *Papers*, 16:127–29; TJ to John Bolling, March 6, 1790, *Papers*, 16:207–8. On the moldboard plow, see TMR to TJ, April 23, 1790, *Papers*, 16:370–71; On Martha Jefferson's betrothal, see Thomas Mann Randolph, Sr., to TJ, January 30, 1790, *Papers*, 16:135–36; and TJ to Thomas Mann Randolph, Sr., February 4, 1790, *Papers*, 16:154–55.

235 **Patsy and Tom Randolph were married:** "Marriage Settlement for Martha Jefferson," *Papers*, 16:189–91.

235 **He was concerned about the volatile situation:** TJ to Madame de Corny, April 2, 1790, *Papers*, 16:289–90.

236 **Still, he was glad to be home:** TJ to Francis Willis, Jr., April 18, 1790, *Papers*, 16:353.

236 **Sally Hemings's mother:** Family trees of the Jefferson and Hemings families, *Free Some Day*, insert inside back cover; see also chapter 3 herein.

19: PATSY AND POLLY

239 **He told George Washington that:** TJ to George Washington, December 15, 1789, *Papers*, 16:34.

240 **Thomas Mann Randolph, Jr.:** TMR to TJ, August 16, 1786, *Papers*, 9:260.

240 **Young Randolph had corresponded:** TJ to Thomas Mann Randolph, Sr., August 11, 1787, *Papers*, 12:22.

241 **As wedding presents:** "Marriage Settlement for Martha Jefferson," February 21, 1790, *Papers*, 16:189.

241 **"Having had yourself and dear Poll":** TJ to MJR, April 4, 1790, *Papers*, 16:300.

241 **"Lead and even steel":** William H. Gaines, Jr., *Thomas Mann Randolph: Jefferson's Son-in-Law* (Baton Rouge: Louisiana State University Press, 1966), vi.

242 **"Your new condition will call for abundance of little sacrifices":** TJ to MJR, April 4, 1790, *Papers*, 16:300.

242 **"The more you learn the more I love you":** TJ to MJR, March 6, 1786, *Family Letters*, 30.

242 **Jefferson expected a lot from Patsy:** TJ to Barbe de Marbois, December 5, 1783, *Papers,* 6:374.

243 **"from 8. to 10 o'clock practice music":** TJ to MJR, November 28, 1783, *Family Letters,* 19.

243 **"I expect you will write to me by every post":** Ibid.

244 **"Be you from the moment you rise till you go to bed":** TJ to MJR, December 22, 1783, *Family Letters,* 22.

244 **"never do or say a bad thing":** TJ to MJR, December 11, 1783, *Family Letters,* 21.

244 **"Being disappointed in my expectation":** MRJ to TJ, March 8, 1787, *Family Letters,* 32.

245 **At Panthémont, she practiced the pianoforte:** MJR to TJ, May 27, 1787, *Family Letters,* 42.

245 **"I am not so industrious as you or I would wish":** MJR to TJ, April 9, 1787, *Family Letters,* 37.

245 **"My expectations for you are high":** TJ to MJR, March 28, 1787, *Family Letters,* 35.

245 **Patsy loved Panthémont:** *Papers,* 14:356n. Biographer Fawn Brodie surmised that Patsy's religious zeal was an expression of her jealousy of Maria Cosway; see Brodie, 305.

246 **But she did not know the first thing:** TJ to Elizabeth Eppes, July 28, 1787, *Papers,* 11:634.

246 **Biographer Fawn Brodie saw in this hasty marriage:** Brodie, 325.

246 **Jefferson continued to hope:** Thomas Mann Randolph, Sr., to TJ, January 30, 1790, *Papers,* 16:135; TJ to Thomas Mann Randolph, Sr., February 4, 1790, *Papers* 16:154–55; TMR to TJ, April 23, 1790, *Papers* 16:370; TJ to MJR, April 26, 1790, *Papers,* 16:386; TMR to TJ, May 25, 1790, *Papers,* 16:441–42.

247 **It was, moreover, so hot there:** TMR to TJ, May 25, 1790, *Papers,* 16:441–42; TJ to Elizabeth Wayles Eppes, July 25, 1790, *Papers,* 17:264.

247 **Patsy, who had reveled in the female world:** TJ to Elizabeth Wayles Eppes, July 25, 1790, *Papers,* 17:266.

247 **The property at Varina had been run into the ground:** TMR to TJ, May 25, 1790, *Papers,* 16:441.

247 **"I am sensible of your goodness":** TJ to Elizabeth Wayles Eppes, June 13, 1790, *Papers,* 17:489.

248 **"I have written you, my dear Maria":** TJ to MJE, July 4, 1790, *Papers,* 16:599.

248 **"She is a Sweet Girl":** Martha Jefferson Carr to TJ, May 22, 1786, *Papers,* 27:755–56.

248 **She had used every weapon:** Martha Jefferson Carr to TJ, January 2, 1787, *Papers,* 15:633; Mary Jefferson Bolling to TJ, May 3, 1787, *Papers,* 27:758.

248 **So she learned to resist passively:** TJ to MJE, July 25, 1790, *Papers,* 17:271–72.

249 **Polly returned the favor:** MJE to TJ, July 20, 1790, *Papers,* 17:239.

249 **He continued to promote the Randolphs' plan:** TJ to Thomas Mann Randolph, Sr., July 25, 1790, *Papers,* 17:274–76.

250 **Both she and her husband hoped to find:** TMR to TJ, March 5, 1791, *Papers*, 18:420.

250 **Jefferson was sympathetic to Randolph Sr.'s annoyance:** TJ to Thomas Mann Randolph, Sr., October 22, 1790, *Papers*, 17:624.

250 **Meanwhile, it suited him:** TJ to Mary Jefferson Bolling, October 31, 1790, *Papers*, 17:655.

251 **"the solitude she will be in":** TJ to Elizabeth Wayles Eppes, October 31, 1790, *Papers*, 17:658.

251 **Eighteen-year-old Jack Eppes:** TJ to Elizabeth Wayles Eppes, *Papers*, 20:413.

252 **"Mr. Randolph and my daughters":** TJ to Nicholas Lewis, ca. November 7, 1790, *Papers*, 18:29.

20: TROUBLE IN THE NEIGHBORHOOD

253 **Garland Jefferson and Peter Carr made the mistake:** The elder Rind had criticized John Wayles's conduct in the Chiswell affair; see chapter 5.

253 **"That you may have no uneasiness":** TJ to Martha Jefferson Carr, November 7, 1790, *Papers*, 18:26.

254 **Jefferson asked his sister:** Ibid.

254 **The two, accordingly, wrote a letter:** John Garland Jefferson to TJ, November 12, 1790, *Papers*, 18:43–44.

255 **When John Garland Jefferson got to Goochland County:** Ibid.

256 **At the time of James Rind's altercation:** See *TJ and SH*.

256 **As historian Joshua Rothman has pointed out:** Joshua D. Rothman, *Notorious in the Neighborhood: Sex and Families across the Color Line in Virginia, 1787–1861* (Chapel Hill: University of North Carolina Press, 2003), 30, 53–56.

256 **But this 1790 episode was also only one:** Ibid.

256 **"I hope that this affair will never more be thought of":** TJ to John Garland Jefferson, February 5, 1791, *Papers*, 19:252.

256. **He continued to pay Garland Jefferson's bills:** Thomas Bell to TJ, June 12, 1793, *Papers*, 26:258–59.

257 **"Martin has left us":** MJR to TJ, January 16, 1791, *Papers*, 18:499.

258 **Polly too came under Patsy's eagle eye:** Ibid.

259 **Patsy came through the birth of her first child:** Mary Walker Lewis to TJ, January 23, 1791, *Papers*, 18:594; TMR to TJ, February 2, 1791, *Papers*, 19:239–40; TMR to TJ, February 8, 1791, *Papers*, 19:259; MJE to TJ, February 13, 1791, *Papers*, 19:271.

259 **The new parents asked Thomas Jefferson:** TJ to MJR, February 9, 1791, *Papers*, 19:264; TJ to TMR, March 17, 1791, *Papers*, 19:582.

260 **In 1792, Jefferson sold Mary Hemings:** TJ to Nicholas Lewis, April 12, 1792, *Papers*, 23:408; *Free Some Day*, 132.

260 **Thenia Hemings was sold:** James Monroe to TJ, June 17, 1794, *Papers*, 28:100.

260 **Martin Hemings, who had served as majordomo:** *Hemingses*, 486.

261 **On Christmas Eve, 1794:** "Deed of Manumission for Robert Hemings," December 24, 1794, *Papers*, 28:222; TJ toTMR, December 26, 1794, *Papers*, 28:225.

261 **The wrenching separation between Thomas Jefferson and Robert Hemings:** MJR to TJ, January 15, 1795, *Papers*, 28:246.

261 **In 1793, Jefferson wrote up an agreement:** "Agreement with James Hemings," *Papers*, 27:119–20.

262 **Jefferson resigned himself to selling human beings:** TJ to Bowling Clark, September 21, 1792, *Papers*, 24:408.

262 **"I heartily congratulate you":** TJ to Francis Eppes, March 14, 1791, *Papers*, 19:554; TJ to Francis Eppes, January 20, 1791, *Papers*, 18:578; Francis Eppes to TJ, April 5, 1791, *Papers*, 20:151; Henry Skipwith to TJ, April 7, 1791, *Papers*, 20:166; Francis Eppes to TJ, April 27, 1791, *Papers*, 20:313; TJ to Henry Skipwith, May 6, 1791, *Papers*, 20:373–76.

263 **He could only bring himself to speak bluntly:** TJ to John Bolling, October 7, 1791, *Papers*, 22:198.

263 **When the sales finally occurred:** TJ to TMR, March 1, 1792, *Papers*, 23:253.

263 **Patsy Randolph could not have been ignorant:** Thomas Bell to TJ, June 12, 1797, *Papers*, 29:427.

263 **Surely it occurred to Patsy:** *TJ and SH*, 80–81.

264 **He made the point, in a letter to Patsy:** TJ to MJR, December 4, 1791, *Papers*, 22:376.

265 **When there was some kind of unspecified friction:** TJ to MJR, March 19, 1793, *Papers*, 25:353; TJ to MJR, March 18, 1793, *Papers*, 25:404.

266 **In the fall of 1792:** See Cynthia Kierner, *Scandal at Bizarre: Rumor and Reputation in Jefferson's America* (Charlottesville: University Press of Virginia, 2004).

266 **The rumors spread all the way to Philadelphia:** TJ to MJR, April 28, 1793, *Papers*, 25:621.

267 **Patsy replied that she was standing by Nancy Randolph:** MJR to TJ, May 16, 1793, *Papers*, 26:53.

268 **Thomas Jefferson was very worried about his son-in-law:** TJ to TMR, August 7, 1794, *Papers*, 28:111.

269 **That summer of 1795:** TJ to TMR, August 18, 1795, *Papers*, 28:438; TJ to TMR, August 20, 1795, *Papers*, 28:439; TJ to MJR, July 31, 1795, *Papers*, 28:429.

269 **Jefferson sent James Hemings:** TJ to TMR, July 26, 1795, *Papers*, 28:419; MB 2:930.

269 **But the parents did not return:** MJR to TJ, January 1, 1796, *Papers*, 28:569.

21: DOMESTIC TRANQUILITY, REVISITED

270 **As the terrible summer of 1795 slipped into autumn:** TJ to Angelica Schuyler Church, September 8, 1795, *Papers*, 28:454.

270 **He wrote Maria Cosway:** TJ to Maria Cosway, September 8, 1795, *Papers*, 28:455.

270 **He told Eliza House Trist:** TJ to Eliza House Trist, September 23, 1795, *Papers*, 28:455.

270 **On October 5, 1795:** Fraser D. Neiman, "Coincidence or Causal Connection? The Relationship between Thomas Jefferson's Visits to Monticello and Sally Hemings's Conceptions," *William and Mary Quarterly*, 3rd series, vol. 57, no. 1 (January 2000), 205.

271 **"There is vast alarm here about corn":** TJ to TMR, February 7, 1796, *Papers*, 28:608.

271 **In 1796, James Hemings made an inventory:** "Deed of Manumission for James Hemings," February 5, 1796, *Papers*, 28:605; "James Hemings's Inventory of Kitchen Utensils at Monticello," February 20, 1796, *Papers*, 28:610.

271 **The public business of buying and selling:** TJ to TMR, April 11, 1796, *Papers*, 29:63; TJ to James Lyle, May 12, 1796, *Papers*, 29:96; TMR to TJ, February 26, 1798, *Papers*, 30:145.

272 **On October 12, 1797:** TJ to MJR, June 8, 1797, *Papers*, 29:424.

272 **"This event in compleating the circle":** TJ to MJE, June 14, 1797, *Papers*, 29:430.

273 **He was so depressed:** TMR to TJ, November 6, 1797, *Papers*, 29:568.

273 **Polly and Jack Eppes gravitated to Eppington:** John Wayles Eppes to TJ, September 25, 1796, *Papers*, 29:186; TJ to MJR, June 8, 1797, *Papers*, 29:424; TJ to Francis Eppes, September 24, 1797, *Papers*, 29:532; Elizabeth Wayles Eppes to TJ, October 10, 1797, *Papers*, 29:546; "Marriage Settlement for John Wayles Eppes," October 12, 1797, *Papers*, 29:547-50.

273 **Jefferson insisted that he had no appetite for public life:** TJ to TMR, November 28, 1796, *Papers*, 29:211; TJ to TMR, January 9, 1797, *Papers*, 29:260; TJ to TMR, January 22, 1797, *Papers*, 29:273-74; TJ to Benjamin Rush, January 22, 1797, *Papers*, 29:275; TJ to TMR, March 23, 1797, *Papers*, 29:322.

274 **In the cold, wet winter of 1798:** TMR to TJ, January 13, 1798, *Papers*, 30:28; MJR to TJ, January 22, 1798, *Papers*, 30:43.

275 **"Yours of the 13th":** TJ to TMR, January 25, 1798, *Papers*, 30:55.

275 **"I feel every day more strongly the impossibility":** MJR to TJ, January 22, 1798, *Papers*, 30:44.

276 **"What an economist, what a manager she is become":** MJE to TJ, February 27, 1796, *Papers*, 29:308.

276 **Even after she had married Jack Eppes:** MJE to TJ, February 1, 1798, *Papers*, 30:69.

276 **He, in turn, frequently reminded his daughters:** TJ to MJE, March 11, 1797, *Papers*, 29:314.

276 **"My uncle Bolling is much as usual":** MJE to TJ, December 8, 1797, *Papers*, 29:579.

276 **"Mr. B.'s habitual intoxication":** TJ to MJE, January 7, 1798, *Papers*, 30:15.

22: DANGER

280 **Callender was a Scotsman:** See Brodie, 416–28; *TJ and SH*.

281 **Callender kept Jefferson posted:** James Thomson Callender to TJ, March 21, 1798, *Papers*, 30:188.

281 **"You should know the rancorous passions":** TJ to MJR, May 17, 1798, *Papers*, 30:355.

281 **By 1800, the Adams administration:** TJ to Callender, October 6, 1799, *Papers*, 31:200; Callender to TJ, February 15, 1800, *Papers*, 31:376; "Pardon for James Thomson Callender," March 16, 1801, *Papers*, 33:309–10; Brodie, 424.

282 **Twenty-first-century readers:** TJ to Martha Jefferson Carr, April 21, 1800, *Papers*, 31:525.

282 **Jefferson believed, however, that he had insulated:** TJ to Thomas Bell, May 18, 1797, *Papers*, 29:371; Thomas Bell to TJ, June 12, 1797, *Papers*, 29:427.

283 **As president he dined mostly with men:** See Allgor, *Parlor Politics*, 4–47.

284 **He had far more trouble with his debts, his crops:** TMR to TJ, February 26, 1798, *Papers*, 30:145.

284 **Construction supervisors pulled down in sections:** TMR to TJ, January 3, 1801, *Papers*, 32:390. On the failure to number the column pieces, see McLaughlin, *Jefferson and Monticello*, p. 287.

284 **Patsy announced that she looked forward to his return:** MJR to TJ, June 23, 1798, *Papers*, 30:424.

284 **Nonetheless, when Sally gave birth to her third child:** TJ to John Wayles Eppes, December 21, 1799, *Papers*, 31:274.

286 **It is not clear what sort of illness:** MJR to TJ, January 30, 1800, *Papers*, 31:347–48; TMR to TJ, ca. April 19, 1800, *Papers*, 31:523.

287 **Jefferson still hoped that he could induce Polly and Jack:** TJ to MJE, April 13, 1799, *Papers*, 31:90; MJE to TJ, June 26, 1799, *Papers*, 31:139.

287 **"Promises must not be forgotten":** TJ to John Wayles Eppes, July 4, 1799, *Papers*, 31:146.

288 **Maria Jefferson Eppes bore a daughter:** TJ to MJR, January 21, 1800, *Papers*, 31:331; MJR to TJ, January 31, 1800, *Papers*, 31:347; John Wayles Eppes to TJ, February 7, 1800, *Papers*, 31:362; TJ to MJR, February 11, 1800, *Papers*, 31:366.

288 **"Mr. Eppes's last letter informed me":** TJ to MJE, February 12, 1800, *Papers*, 31:368.

289 **"politics are such a torment":** TJ to MJR, February 11, 1800, *Papers*, 31:366.

289 **The moment they learned of Polly's predicament:** TMR to TJ, February 22, 1800, *Papers*, 31:389; TJ to TMR, March 4, 1800, *Papers*, 31:415; John Wayles Eppes to TJ, March 16, 1800, *Papers*, 31:440.

23: SCANDAL

291 **Old hatreds festered:** Brodie, 427.

292 **"There seemed to be some special necessity in him":** Ibid., 417.

292 **When Jefferson was at home:** MJR to TJ, January 31, 1801, *Papers,* 32:527.

292 **Jefferson offered sympathy:** TJ to MJR, February 5, 1801, *Papers,* 32:556.

293 **They may, indeed, have resented:** Brodie, 432–34.

293 **Jefferson was indignant:** Ibid., 458–60.

293 **While Jefferson tried to deal with Callender:** Malone, 4:xxvi; MB 2:1051, 1053; *Farm Book,* 130; TJ to MJE, October 26, 1801, in *Family Letters,* 211; Rothman, *Notorious in the Neighborhood,* 30.

294 **James wanted to go to Washington:** *Free Some Day,* 128–29; *Hemingses,* 544–51.

294 **James Hemings returned to Baltimore:** Ibid.

295 **The news was a terrible blow:** MJE to TJ, November 6, 1801, *Family Letters,* 211; MJR to TJ, November 18, 1801, *Family Letters,* 212–13.

295 **Those trials alone were enough:** MJE to TJ, November 6, 1801, *Family Letters,* 211; MJE to TJ, April 21, 1802, *Family Letters,* 224.

295 **"With how much regret have I look'd back":** MJE to TJ, January 24, 1802, *Family Letters,* 217.

296 **On September 1, 1802, he went public:** *Richmond Recorder,* September 1, 1802, cited in Brodie, 464.

296 **The Republican *Richmond Examiner* quickly moved:** *Richmond Examiner,* September 25, 1802, cited in Brodie, 465.

297 **"Jefferson before the eyes of his two daughters":** *Richmond Recorder,* September 22, 1802; September 29, 1802; December 1, 1802, cited in Brodie, 468–69.

297 **Their information was off the mark in some cases:** For a full listing of resources on the DNA controversy and the Hemings–Jefferson relationship, see http://www.monticello.org/plantation/hemingscontro/hemings_report.html.

297 **The *Frederick-Town Herald* assured readers:** *Frederick-Town Herald,* reprinted in the *Richmond Recorder,* December 8, 1802, cited in Brodie, 469.

298 **"These daughters, who should have been the principal object":** Lynchburg *Virginia Gazette,* reprinted in the *Richmond Recorder,* November 3, 1802, cited in Brodie, 470.

298 **His son, Madison Hemings, told an Ohio newspaper editor:** "Reminiscences of Madison Hemings," Brodie, Appendix I, 641–42.

299 **Callender continued his attacks:** See Michael Durey, *With the Hammer of Truth: James Thomson Callender and America's Early National Heroes* (Charlottesville: University Press of Virginia, 1990), 165.

299 **Jefferson's onetime mouthpiece:** On Jefferson's interest in Elizabeth Walker, see Kukla, *Mr. Jefferson's Women,* 41–62.

300 **He pushed them to make a visit to Washington:** TJ to MJE, March 3, 1802, *Family Letters,* 219; MJE to TJ, April 21, 1802, *Family Letters,* 224; TJ to MJR, May 1, 1802, *Family Letters,* 225; TJ to MJE, May 1, 1802, *Family Letters,* 225–26; TJ to MJR, June 3, 1802, *Family Letters,* 226–28.

300 **"I think I discover in you a willingness to withdraw":** TJ to MJE, March 3, 1802, *Family Letters,* 219.

301 **Polly resisted his pleas:** TJ to MJR, October 7, 1802, *Family Letters*, 236; TJ to MJE, October 7, 1802, *Family Letters*, 236–37; TJ to MJR, October 18, 1802, *Family Letters*, 237; TJ to MJE, October 18, 1802, *Family Letters*, 237; MJR to TJ, October 29, 1802, *Family Letters*, 238; TJ to MJR, November 2, 1802, *Family Letters*, 238–39.

302 **Traveling the rugged roads:** MJE to TJ, November 5, 1802, *Family Letters*, 239; MJR to TJ, November 9, 1802, *Family Letters*, 239.

303 **Jefferson's daughters made their way to Washington:** MJE to TJ, January 11, 1803, *Family Letters*, 240.

303 **But Thomas Jefferson turned a blind eye to his own distresses:** TJ to MJE, January 18, 1802, *Family Letters*, 241.

24: MOTHERHOOD AND MORTALITY

306 **"Take care of yourself":** TJ to MJE, November 27, 1803, *Family Letters*, 249.

306 **"Some friend of your Mama's":** TJ to MJE, December 26, 1803, *Family Letters*, 250.

306 **"I write amid the noises and confusion":** MJR to TJ, January 14, 1804, *Family Letters*, 252–53.

307 **Thomas Jefferson was determined to cheer up his daughters:** TJ to MJR, January 23, 1804, *Family Letters*, 254–55.

307 **"Let us all see that you have within yourself":** TJ to MJE, January 29, 1804, *Family Letters*, 256.

308 **In a letter to her father:** MJE to TJ, February 10, 1804, *Family Letters*, 256.

308 **Patsy's daughter Ellen remembered:** *Domestic Life*, 300.

308 **"This morning between 8. & 9. aclock":** MB 2:1125.

308 **Thomas Jefferson had now outlived:** *Domestic Life*, 300; *Garden Book*, Plate X, facing p. 94.

309 **"It has been some time since I conceived that any event":** Abigail Adams to TJ, quoted in *Domestic Life*, 304–5.

310 **"Others may lose of their abundance":** TJ to John Page, June 25, 1804, cited in *Domestic Life*, 302–3.

311 **"The scene passing here":** TJ to MJE, February 15, 1801, *Papers*, 32:593.

25: DOMESTIC DIVERSIFICATION

315 **"I do not hesitate to declare":** MJR to TJ, May 31, 1804, *Family Letters*, 260.

316 **"We are as usual well here":** Ibid., 261.

316 **Patsy had a history of digestive disorders:** Ibid.; for her history of complaints, see MJR to TJ, January 31, 1801, *Family Letters*, 192.

317 **"In endeavoring to spare my feelings":** TJ to MJR, January 21, 1805, *Family Letters*, 266.

317 **"Had not Congress been sitting":** Ibid.

317 **She finally admitted:** MJR to TJ, February 28, 1805, *Family Letters*, 268; Ellen Wayles Randolph to TJ, July 4, 1805, *Family Letters*, 275.

318 **"When Heaven has taken from us":** TJ to Maria Cosway, October 12, 1786, *Papers*, 10:443-55.

318 **Within a month of Polly's death:** Neiman, "Coincidence or Causal Connection?" 205; *Hemingses*, 590.

318 **In the fall of 1805:** MJR to TJ, October 26, 1805, *Family Letters*, 280.

320 **As Madison Hemings recalled:** "Reminiscences of Madison Hemings," in Brodie, 641.

320 **Sally Hemings would bear Thomas Jefferson yet one more child:** E. A. Foster et al., "Jefferson Fathered Slave's Last Child," *Nature* 396 (November 1998), 27-28; Neiman, "Coincidence or Causal Connection?"; "Report of the Research Committee on Thomas Jefferson and Sally Hemings," Thomas Jefferson Foundation, 2000, http://www.monticello.org/plantation/hemingscontro/hemings_report.html.

321 **Once he had laid claim to Sally Hemings:** *Hemingses; TJ and SH;* Neiman, "Coincidence or Causal Connection?": "Report of the Research Committee on Thomas Jefferson and Sally Hemings," Thomas Jefferson Foundation, 2000, http://www.monticello.org/plantation/hemingscontro/hemings_report.html.

322 **Randolph alternately raged and despaired:** Letters from TJ to MJR, March 1, 2, 6, 9, 11, 20, 23, 27, 30, 1807; MJR to TJ, March 20, 1807, *Family Letters*, 296-306.

324 **Patsy raised her children to compete:** MJR to TJ, January 31, 1801, *Family Letters*, 193. TJ referred to "Elleanoroon" in letter to MJR, December 27, 1798, *Papers*, 30:605.

324 **He eagerly encouraged them:** TJ to MJR, February 5, 1801, *Family Letters*, 195.

325 **On the family's annual summer visit:** Anne Cary Randolph, 1805-1808, Household Accounts, Thomas Jefferson Papers, Series 7, Miscellaneous Bound Volumes, Library of Congress; Malone, 5:611-12.

326 **Anne Randolph was a gentle girl:** TJ to Anne Cary Randolph, May 20, 1803, *Family Letters*, 245-46; Anne Cary Randolph to TJ, December 12, 1806, *Family Letters*, 292.

326 **By the summer of 1807, Jefferson was treating Anne:** Anne Cary Randolph to TJ, November 9, 1807, *Family Letters*, 314.

326 **"The tulips and Hyacinths":** Ibid.

326 **The person who did the planting:** Lucia C. Stanton, "Wormley Hughes (1781-1858)," http://www.monticello.org/plantation/lives/wormley.html.

326 **By the time she had reached the age of five:** MJR to TJ, April 16, 1802, *Family Letters*, 223.

327 **Ellen would prove:** Thomas Jefferson Randolph to TJ, February 24, 1803, *Family Letters*, 243.

327 **By that time, Patsy had reached the conclusion:** MJR to TJ, July 12, 1803, *Family Letters*, 246-47.

328 **By the age of nine, Ellen was engaging Jefferson:** Ellen Wayles Randolph to TJ,

July 4, 1805, *Family Letters*, 274; TJ to Ellen Wayles Randolph, July 10, 1805, *Family Letters*, 276; TJ to Ellen Wayles Randolph, November 30, 1806, *Family Letters*, 291; Ellen Wayles Randolph to TJ, December 12, 1806, *Family Letters*, 293.

328 **Jefferson urged Ellen:** TJ to Ellen Wayles Randolph, June 7, 1807, *Family Letters*, 309–10.

329 **With this offhand bit of interpretive animal husbandry:** TJ to Francis C. Gray, March 4, 1815, Thomas Jefferson Papers, Series 1, General Correspondence, 1651–1827, Library of Congress. See Fawn Brodie's discussion of Jefferson's letter to Francis C. Gray on the mathematics of miscegenation, Brodie, 586–87.

329 **As he reminded Ellen of her responsibility:** Ibid.

26: THE PURSUIT OF HAPPINESS

331 **For Thomas Jefferson, the end to government service:** Malone, vol. 5, *Jefferson the President: Second Term, 1805–1809* (Boston: Little, Brown, 1974), xi.

331 **His grandchildren could hardly wait:** Ellen Wayles Randolph to TJ, January 15, 1808, *Family Letters*, 321; Anne Cary Randolph to TJ, January 22, 1808, *Family Letters*, 324.

332 *"The weary statesman":* On Moore's verses, see Lucia C. Stanton, "Looking for Liberty: Thomas Jefferson and the British Lions," *Eighteenth-Century Studies* 26, no. 4 (Summer 1993), 651.

333 **Toward the end of the renovation:** McLaughlin, *Jefferson and Monticello*, 323–28.

333 **Thomas Jefferson had taken a page:** Chew, "Inhabiting the Great Man's House: Women and Space at Monticello," 223–52.

334 **For Patsy's growing daughters:** Ibid., 232.

335 **Sally Hemings may have lived:** *Free Some Day*, 112–13; Bear, 46.

335 **"We were free from the dread":** "Reminiscences of Madison Hemings," in Brodie, 641–43; Bear, 102.

336 **Monticello remained a musical place:** *Free Some Day*, 101.

337 **But Jefferson had his way of coping:** S. Allen Chambers, *Poplar Forest and Thomas Jefferson* (Forest, Va.: Corporation for Jefferson's Poplar Forest, 1993), 21–34.

338 **"You may consider your journey to Bedford":** Ellen Wayles Randolph to MJR, September 27, 1816, Transcript of Manuscript, Correspondence of Ellen Wayles Randolph Coolidge, SSCL, University of Virginia, FLP.

338 **"Ellen and Cornelia are the severest students":** TJ to MJR, August 31, 1817, *Family Letters*, 419.

339 **On a visit in July 1819:** Ellen Wayles Randolph to MJR, July 18, 1819, Correspondence of Ellen Wayles Randolph Coolidge, SSCL, FLP.

339 **"I have often thought that the life of a student":** Ibid.

340 **"The ruin of the family is still extending itself":** MJR to TJ, January 2, 1808, *Family Letters*, 318.

340 **"I have now the gloomy prospect":** TJ to MJR, January 5, 1808, *Family Letters*, 319.

341 **"Your last letter has cast a gloom":** MJR to TJ, January 16, 1808, *Family Letters*, 322–3.

27: THE PERILS OF MATRIMONY

342 **As he settled into retirement at home:** Malone, vol. 6, *The Sage of Monticello* (Boston: Little, Brown, 1981), 275–82.

342 **None of his grandsons were serious scholars:** Ibid., 389–90, 464–69.

343 **"I think this is the most extraordinary collection of talent":** American Presidency Project, http://www.presidency.ucsb.edu/ws/index.php?pid=8623.

344 **Jefferson's eldest granddaughter was the first:** *Family Letters*, 357n.

344 **Two months after the wedding:** MJR to TJ, November 18, 1808, *Family Letters*, 360.

344 **But Anne's bridal anguish turned out to be prescient:** MB 2:1270; Malone, 6:159. MJR to Elizabeth House Trist, May 31, 1815, Transcript of Manuscript, Elizabeth House Trist Papers, Virginia Historical Society, FLP.

345 **Anne Randolph Bankhead's marriage was a living hell:** TJ to MJE, January 7, 1798, *Family Letters*, 151–53; Bear, 94.

345 **Anne's husband became so uncontrollable:** MJR to TJ, November 20, 1816, *Family Letters*, 417.

346 **Anne, much to everyone's dismay:** Wilson Cary Nicholas to TJ, February 28, 1819, and TJ to Wilson Cary Nicholas, March 8, 1819, Thomas Jefferson Papers, Library of Congress, cited in Alan Pell Crawford, *Twilight at Monticello: The Final Years of Thomas Jefferson* (New York: Random House, 2008), 170–71.

346 **Charles Bankhead, for his part:** Malone, 6:299–30. On court day, see Rhys Isaac, *The Transformation of Virginia, 1740–1790* (Chapel Hill: University of North Carolina Press, 1982), 88–90.

347 **Even after Charles Bankhead had stabbed her brother:** MJR to TJ, August 7, 1819, *Family Letters*, 430; Cornelia Jefferson Randolph to Virginia Randolph Trist, August 11, 1819, Transcript of Manuscript, Nicholas Philip Trist Papers, Southern Historical Collection, University of North Carolina, FLP.

347 **"Ellen fulfills the promises":** MJR to Elizabeth House Trist, May 31, 1815, Transcript of Manuscript, Elizabeth House Trist Papers, Virginia Historical Society, FLP.

348 **"Really, my dear Nicholas":** Ellen Wayles Randolph to Nicholas Philip Trist, March 30, 1824, Transcript of Manuscript, Nicholas Philip Trist Papers, Library of Congress; FLP.

350 **Cornelia mocked a pretty girl:** Cornelia Jefferson Randolph to Virginia Randolph Trist, August 11, 1819, Nicholas Philip Trist Papers, Southern Historical Collection, FLP.

350 **Ellen and Cornelia amused each other:** Ellen Wayles Randolph to MJR, April 14, 1818, Correspondence of Ellen Wayles Randolph Coolidge, SSCL, FLP.

350 **The Randolph girls made an inside joke:** MJR to Virginia Jefferson Randolph Trist, January 10, 1822, Nicholas Philip Trist Papers, Southern Historical Collection, FLP.

351 **On a visit to Richmond, Cornelia could barely endure:** Cornelia Jefferson Randolph to Virginia Jefferson Randolph Trist, December 14, 1817, Nicholas Philip Trist Papers, Southern Historical Collection, FLP.

352 **She was at first appalled by the cost of fashion:** Ellen Wayles Randolph to MJR, March 2, 1814, Correspondence of Ellen Wayles Randolph Coolidge, SSCL, FLP.

352 **But even as she began to visit in town:** Ellen Wayles Randolph to MJR, April 14, 1818, Correspondence of Ellen Wayles Randolph Coolidge, SSCL, University of Virginia, FLP.

353 **"I have already been held to the world":** Ellen Wayles Randolph to MJR, 21 December 1818, Correspondence of Ellen Wayles Randolph Coolidge, SSCL, FLP.

353 **Still single three years later:** Ellen Wayles Randolph to MJR, April 3, 1822, Correspondence of Ellen Wayles Randolph Coolidge, SSCL, FLP.

353 **She was still single and nearly ready to give up trying:** Malone, 6:456–59.

354 **Her mother and sisters rejoiced at her rescue from their ruin:** Mary Jefferson Randolph to Ellen Wayles Randolph Coolidge, October 23, 1825, Correspondence of Ellen Wayles Randolph Coolidge, SSCL, FLP.

355 **"I know I wish I could do something":** Cornelia Jefferson Randolph to Ellen Wayles Randolph Coolidge, November 24, 1825, Correspondence of Ellen Wayles Randolph Coolidge, SSCL, FLP.

28: THE CAPRICIOUSNESS OF FORTUNE

356 **In 1819, the first great financial panic:** Herbert E. Sloan, *Principle and Interest: Thomas Jefferson and the Problem of Debt* (New York: Oxford University Press, 1995). On salad oil, see TJ to TJR, April 16, 1810, *Family Letters*, 396. Even as late as 1822, TJ purchased marble busts of James Madison and James Monroe; see MB 2:1383.

357 **But the bonds of friendship and kinship dragged him down:** Ellen Wayles Randolph to MJR, August 11, 1819, Transcript of Manuscript, Correspondence of Ellen Wayles Randolph Coolidge, SSCL, FLP.

358 **When John Wayles Eppes married Polly Jefferson:** Francis Wayles Eppes to TJ, May 13, 1822, *Family Letters*, 445; Francis Wayles Eppes to TJ, April 23, 1824, *Family Letters*, 449.

358 **Betsy Hemmings, the niece of Sally Hemings:** Descendants of Betsy Hemmings (the Buckingham County spelling of the family name) offer their version of the doubled history of their branch of the Wayles-Hemings-Eppes family at http://www.buckinghamhemmings.com/.

359 **Out of generosity to Polly's only surviving child:** Malone, 6:287. Polly's baby daughter, Maria, lived only to the age of three. See *Free Some Day*, Jefferson Family genealogical chart.

359 **Thomas Mann Randolph was never able to escape:** TMR to Thomas Taylor, May 19, 1819, Robert Alonzo Brock Collection, Box 8, Folder 14, Huntington Library.

359 **"The negroes, all of which I part from":** TMR to Taylor, November 17, 1815, Robert Alonzo Brock Collection.

360 **"This momentous question, like a fire bell in the night":** TJ to John Holmes, April 22, 1820, Transcript of Manuscript, Thomas Jefferson Papers, Series 1, General Correspondence, 1651–1827, Library of Congress, http://www.loc.gov/exhibits/jefferson/159.html.

361 **"I regret that I am now to die in the belief":** Ibid.

362 **According to Jefferson's beliefs:** Thomas Jefferson to Francis C. Gray, March 4, 1815, Thomas Jefferson Papers, Series 1, General Correspondence, 1651–1827, Library of Congress. TJ to Ellen Wayles Randolph, June 7, 1807, *Family Letters*, 309–10. See Fawn Brodie's discussion of Jefferson's letter to Francis C. Gray on the mathematics of miscegenation, Brodie, 586–87.

362 **Though the enslavement of Sally Hemings:** Gordon-Reed, in *Hemingses,* 596–98, offers the definitive discussion of the Hemings children's understanding of their racial and legal status.

362 **By the time he was twelve years old:** *Farm Book*, 128.

363 **When Jefferson inventoried his slaves:** Ibid.

363 **Their brother Madison reported:** Brodie, 640.

363 **Harriet Hemings made a lifelong impression:** Bear, 102.

364 **By the summer of 1825:** MJR to Anne Cary Randolph Morris, August 8, 1825(?), Houston-Morris-Ogden Family Papers, FLP; MJR to Anne Cary Randolph Morris, January 22, 1826, Smith-Houston-Morris-Ogden Family Papers, FLP.

365 **"My dear father wrote most kindly":** Ibid.

365 **"Mama and myself were so peculiarly unfortunate":** Mary J. Randolph and Virginia J. Randolph Trist to Ellen W. Randolph Coolidge, September 11, 1825, Correspondence of Ellen Wayles Randolph Coolidge, SSCL, FLP.

366 **"Nothing new has happened":** TJ to Anne Randolph Bankhead, May 26, 1811, *Family Letters*, 400.

366 **Sometime after the new year of 1826:** Cornelia Jefferson Randolph to Ellen Wayles Randolph Coolidge, February 23, 1826, Correspondence of Ellen Wayles Randolph Coolidge, SSCL, FLP.

367 **Thomas Jefferson had been too ill:** Eyewitness account by Dr. Robley Dunglinson, in *Life*, 3:549; TJ to Thomas Jefferson Randolph, February 11, 1826, *Family Letters*, 470.

29: WHEN WE THINK HOW WE LIV'D BUT TO LOVE THEM

368 **A heavy pall descended on Monticello:** MJR to Ellen Randolph Coolidge, March 1, 1826, Correspondence of Ellen Wayles Randolph Coolidge, SSCL, FLP.

368 **Childbirth was always an occasion for dread:** Joseph Coolidge and Ellen Randolph

Coolidge to MJR, February 8, 1826; Ellen Randolph Coolidge to MJR, March 23, 1826, Correspondence of Ellen Wayles Randolph Coolidge, SSCL, FLP.

369 **Patsy and her daughters belittled the eccentricities:** Cornelia Jefferson Randolph to Ellen Randolph Coolidge, February 23, 1826, Correspondence of Ellen Wayles Randolph Coolidge, SSCL, FLP; Ellen Randolph Coolidge to Virginia Randolph Trist, May 6, 1826, Mary Jefferson Randolph to Ellen Randolph Coolidge, April 16 and May 12, 1826, Transcripts of Manuscript, Correspondence of Ellen Wayles Randolph Coolidge, SSCL, FLP.

369 **Thomas Jefferson lived out the final months of his life:** MJR and Nicholas Trist to Ellen Randolph Coolidge, April 5, 1826, Transcript of Manuscript, Correspondence of Ellen Wayles Randolph Coolidge, SSCL, FLP.

370 **One night as Thomas Jefferson lay awake in pain and worry:** MJR and Nicholas Trist to Ellen Randolph Coolidge, April 5, 1826, Correspondence of Ellen Wayles Randolph Coolidge, SSCL, FLP.

370 **After considerable arm-twisting:** Mary Jefferson Randolph to Ellen Randolph Coolidge, April 16, 1826, Correspondence of Ellen Wayles Randolph Coolidge, SSCL, FLP.

371 **Her father, meanwhile, put his affairs in order:** Transcript, http://wiki.monticello.org/mediawiki/index.php/Jefferson%27s_Will; Albemarle County Will Book, 8:248–50.

373 **On the fiftieth anniversary of the Declaration of Independence:** *Life*, 3:543–44.

373 **Three men left eyewitness accounts:** http://wiki.monticello.org/mediawiki/index.php/Jefferson%27s_Last_Words.

374 **There are no women, no children, no slaves:** Malone, 6:497.

374 **Jeff Randolph remembered:** *Life*, 3:544.

374 **Martha Jefferson Randolph had sat with her father:** Ibid., 3:547.

376 **Henry Randall, the man Jefferson's grandchildren trusted:** Ibid., 3:545; Stanton, "Looking for Liberty," 655–56; 666–68.

377 **Less poetical, perhaps, but just as heartfelt:** 3:545.

377 **They were far luckier than most of the people:** *Free Some Day*, 141–42.

378 **Thomas Jefferson had lived in luxury and left his family in penury:** Ellen Randolph Coolidge to Nicholas Trist, September 27, 1826; Ellen Randolph Coolidge, "Essay on Thomas Jefferson's Finances," 1826, Correspondence of Ellen Wayles Randolph Coolidge, SSCL, FLP.

378 **To vindicate her grandfather:** TJ to Ellen Randolph Coolidge, November 14, 1825, *Family Letters*, 461.

379 **She missed those things badly in the north:** As she commented in 1826, "The curse of domestic life in New England is the insolence & insubordination of the servants & the difficulty of getting any that do not give more trouble than they save." See Ellen Randolph Coolidge to Virginia Randolph Trist, May 29, 1826, Correspondence of Ellen Wayles Randolph Coolidge, SSCL, FLP.

379 **Patsy Randolph had endorsed the denial:** Patsy did tell Jeff Randolph to defend her father against the charges; *TJ and SH*, 80.

379 **Ellen, however, took action to combat the rumors:** Ellen Wayles Randolph Coolidge to Joseph Coolidge, October 24, 1858, Correspondence of Ellen Wayles Randolph Coolidge, SSCL, FLP.

380 **Ellen granted that there were mixed-race children:** Ibid. For the definitive discussion of Ellen Coolidge and Jefferson Randolph's promotion of the Carr brothers as Hemings progenitors, see *TJ and SH*. For the most recent attempt to pin the paternity of the Hemings children on anyone except Thomas Jefferson, particularly the Carr brothers and now Randolph Jefferson, see William G. Hyland, Jr., *In Defense of Thomas Jefferson: The Sally Hemings Sex Scandal* (New York: St. Martin's, 2009).

381 **For Ellen, the very presence of Jefferson's white daughters:** Ibid.

382 **"The discomfort of slavery I have borne all my life":** MJR to Ellen Randolph Coolidge, August 2, 1825, Correspondence of Ellen Wayles Randolph Coolidge, SSCL, FLP.

382 **"My life of late years has been such a tissue of privations":** MJR to Ann Cary (Nancy) Randolph Morris, January 22, 1826, Smith-Houston-Morris-Ogden Family Papers, FLP.

382 **Her poverty was scandalous:** Mary Jefferson Randolph to Ellen Randolph Coolidge, January 25, 1827, Correspondence of Ellen Wayles Randolph Coolidge, SSCL, FLP; MJR to Ann Cary (Nancy) Randolph Morris, March 22, 1827, Houston-Morris-Ogden Family Papers, FLP; MJR to Ann Cary (Nancy) Randolph Morris, January 22, 1826, Smith-Houston-Morris-Ogden Family Papers, FLP.

383 **Sally Hemings died in Charlottesville:** *Free Some Day*, 143.

Bibliography

BOOKS

Adams, William Howard. *The Paris Years of Thomas Jefferson*. New Haven, Conn.: Yale University Press, 1997.

Allgor, Catherine. *Parlor Politics: In Which the Ladies of Washington Help Build a City and a Government*. Charlottesville: University Press of Virginia, 2000.

———. *A Perfect Union: Dolley Madison and the Creation of the American Nation*. New York: Henry Holt, 2006.

Barnet, Gerald. *Richard and Maria Cosway: A Biography*. Cambridge, England: Lutterworth, 1995.

Bear, James A., Jr. *Jefferson at Monticello: Recollections of a Monticello Slave and of a Monticello Overseer*. Charlottesville: University Press of Virginia, 1999.

Bear, James A., Jr., and Lucia C. Stanton, eds. *Jefferson's Memorandum Books: Accounts, with Legal Records and Miscellany, 1767–1826*. 2 vols. Princeton, N.J.: Princeton University Press, 1997.

Betts, Edwin Morris. *Thomas Jefferson's Farm Book*. Charlottesville: Thomas Jefferson Memorial Foundation, 1999.

———. *Thomas Jefferson's Garden Book*. Philadelphia: American Philosophical Society, 1944.

Betts, Edwin Morris, and James Adam Bear, Jr. *The Family Letters of Thomas Jefferson*. Charlottesville: University Press of Virginia, 1966.

Blauvelt, Martha Tomhave. *The Work of the Heart: Young Women and Emotion, 1780–1830*. Charlottesville: University Press of Virginia, 2007.

Boyd, Julian, ed. *The Papers of Thomas Jefferson*. 35 vols. to date. Princeton: Princeton University Press, 1950–.

Brodie, Fawn. *Thomas Jefferson: An Intimate History*. New York: Norton, 1974.

Brown, Kathleen M. *Good Wives, Nasty Wenches, and Anxious Patriarchs: Gender, Race, and Power in Colonial Virginia*. Chapel Hill: University of North Carolina Press, 1996.

Bullock, Helen Duprey. *My Head and My Heart: A Little History of Thomas Jefferson and Maria Cosway*. New York: Putnam's, 1945.

Chambers, S. Allen. *Poplar Forest and Thomas Jefferson*. Forest, Va.: Corporation for Jefferson's Poplar Forest, 1993.

Church of England. *Book of Common Prayer, and Administration of the Sacraments and Other Rites and Ceremonies of the Church: Together with the Psalter Or Psalms of David, Pointed as They are to be Sung Or Said in Churches*. London: Joseph Bentham, 1765.

Clayton, Ellen C. *English Female Artists*. Vol. 1. London: Tinsley Brothers, 1876.

Clinton, Catherine. *The Plantation Mistress*. New York: Pantheon, 1984.

Crawford, Alan Pell. *Twilight at Monticello: The Final Years of Thomas Jefferson*. New York: Random House, 2008.

Daniels, Jonathan. *The Randolphs of Virginia*. Garden City, N.Y.: Doubleday, 1971.

Dictionary of American Biography. New York: Charles Scribner's, 1931.

Dorman, John Frederick. *Ancestors and Descendants of Francis Epes I of Virginia*. 2 Vols. Society of the Descendants of Francis Epes I of Virginia, 1992.

Durey, Michael. *With the Hammer of Truth: James Thomson Callender and America's Early National Heroes*. Charlottesville: University Press of Virginia, 1990.

Eckenrode, H. J. *The Randolphs: The Story of a Virginia Family*. Indianapolis and New York: Bobbs-Merrill, 1946.

Ellis, Joseph. *American Sphinx: The Character of Thomas Jefferson*. New York: Vintage, 1998.

Eustace, Nicole. *Passion Is the Gale: Emotion, Power, and the Coming of the American Revolution*. Chapel Hill: University of North Carolina Press, 2008.

Flanders, Stephen A. *The Atlas of American Migration*. New York: Facts on File, 1998.

Foley, John P., ed. *The Jeffersonian Cyclopedia*. New York: Funk & Wagnalls, 1900.

Ford, Paul Leicester, ed. "The Autobiography of Thomas Jefferson." In *The Writings of Thomas Jefferson*. 10 vols. New York: Putnam's, 1892–99.

Gaines, William H. Jr. *Thomas Mann Randolph: Jefferson's Son-in-Law*. Baton Rouge: Louisiana State University Press, 1966.

Godineau, Dominique. *The Women of Paris and Their French Revolution*. Berkeley: University of California Press, 1998.

Gordon-Reed, Annette. *The Hemingses of Monticello: An American Family*. New York: Norton, 2008.

———. *Thomas Jefferson and Sally Hemings: An American Controversy*. Charlottesville: University Press of Virginia, 1997.

Holton, Woody. *Forced Founders: Indians, Debtors, Slaves, and the Making of the American Revolution in Virginia*. Chapel Hill: University of North Carolina Press, 1999.

Hyland, William G. *In Defense of Thomas Jefferson: The Sally Hemings Sex Scandal*. New York: St. Martin's, 2009.

Isaac, Rhys. *The Transformation of Virginia, 1740–1790.* Chapel Hill: University of North Carolina Press, 1982.

Jefferson, Thomas. *Notes on the State of Virginia.* New York: Harper Torchbooks, 1964.

Kierner, Cynthia. *Scandal at Bizarre: Rumor and Reputation in Jefferson's America.* Charlottesville: University of Virginia Press, 2004.

Kimball, Marie. *Jefferson: The Road to Glory, 1743–1776.* New York: Coward-McCann, 1943.

Kukla, Jon. *Mr. Jefferson's Women.* New York: Knopf, 2007.

Landes, Joan B. *Women and the Public Sphere in the Age of the French Revolution.* Ithaca, N.Y.: Cornell University Press, 1988.

Levy, Darline Gay. *Women in Revolutionary Paris, 1789–1795.* Champaign: University of Illinois Press, 1981.

Lewis, Jan. *The Pursuit of Happiness: Family and Values in Jefferson's Virginia.* New York: Cambridge University Press, 1983.

Lockridge, Kenneth A. *On the Sources of Patriarchal Rage: The Commonplace Books of William Byrd and Thomas Jefferson and the Gendering of Power in the Eighteenth Century.* New York: New York University Press, 1992.

Malone, Dumas. *Jefferson and His Time.* 6 vols. Boston: Little, Brown, 1948–81.

Mayo, Bernard, ed. *Thomas Jefferson and His Unknown Brother, Randolph.* Charlottesville: University Press of Virginia, 1942.

McCullough, David. *John Adams.* New York: Simon & Schuster, 2001.

McLaughlin, Jack. *Jefferson and Monticello: The Biography of a Builder.* New York: Henry Holt, 1988.

Merrill, Boynton. *Jefferson's Nephews: A Frontier Tragedy.* Princeton, N.J.: Princeton University Press, 1976.

Middleton, Arthur Pierce. *Tobacco Coast: A Maritime History of Chesapeake Bay in the Colonial Era.* Newport News, Va.: Mariners' Museum, 1953.

Morgan, Philip D. *Slave Counterpoint: Black Culture in the Eighteenth Century Chesapeake and Low Country.* Chapel Hill: University of North Carolina Press, 1998.

Parton, James. *Life of Thomas Jefferson, Third President of the United States.* Boston: James R. Osgood, 1874.

Randall, Henry S. *The Life of Thomas Jefferson.* 3 vols. New York: Derby & Jackson, 1858.

Randolph, Sarah Nicholas. *The Domestic Life of Thomas Jefferson, Compiled from Family Letters and Reminiscences by His Great Granddaughter.* 1871. Rept. Scituate, Mass.: Digital Scanning and Publishing, 2001.

Reddy, William. *The Navigation of Feeling: A Framework for the History of Emotions.* Cambridge, England: Cambridge University Press, 2001.

Rediker, Marcus. *The Slave Ship: A Human History.* New York: Viking, 2007.

Riedesel, Baroness von. *Baroness von Riedesel and the American Revolution: Journal and Correspondence of a Tour of Duty, 1776–1783.* A revised translation with Introduction and Notes by Marvin L. Brown, Jr., with the assistance of Marta Huth. Chapel Hill:

Institute of Early American History and Culture, and University of North Carolina Press, 1965.

Rothman, Joshua D. *Notorious in the Neighborhood: Sex and Families across the Color Line in Virginia, 1787–1861*. Chapel Hill: University of North Carolina Press, 2003.

Salmon, Marylynn. *Women and the Law of Property in Early America*. Chapel Hill: University of North Carolina Press, 1989.

Shammas, Carole. *A History of Household Government in America*. Charlottesville: University Press of Virginia, 2002.

Sloan, Herbert E. *Principle and Interest: Thomas Jefferson and the Problem of Debt*. New York: Oxford University Press, 1995.

Stanton, Lucia C. *Free Some Day: The African-American Families of Monticello*. Charlottesville: Thomas Jefferson Foundation, 2000.

Stein, Susan. *The Worlds of Thomas Jefferson at Monticello*. New York: Harry N. Abrams, 1993.

Williamson, George C. *Richard Cosway, R.A.* London: George Bell, 1905.

Wills, Garry. *Inventing America: Jefferson's Declaration of Independence*. New York: Vintage, 1978.

ARTICLES

Brodie, Fawn M. "Jefferson Biographers and the Psychology of Canonization." *Journal of Interdisciplinary History* 2 (1971), 157–58, 160–61.

Chew, Elizabeth V. "Inhabiting the Great Man's House: Women and Space at Monticello." In Joan E. Hartman, and Adele Seeff, eds., *Structures and Subjectivities: Attending to Early Modern Women*. Newark: University of Delaware Press, 2007.

Coleman, Elizabeth. "The Great Fresh of 1771." *Virginia Cavalcade* 1 (1951), 20–22.

Foster, E. A., et al. "Jefferson Fathered Slave's Last Child." *Nature* 396 (November 1998).

Hast, Adele. "Legal Status of the Negro in Virginia." *Journal of Negro History* 54 (July 1969).

Hemphill, John M. II, ed. "John Wayles Rates His Neighbours." *Virginia Magazine of History and Biography* 66, no. 3 (July 1958), 302–6.

Isaac, Rhys. "The First Monticello." In Peter Onuf, ed., *Jeffersonian Legacies*. Charlottesville: University Press of Virginia, 1993.

"Jefferson Family." *Tyler's Quarterly Historical and Genealogical Magazine* 6, no. 3 (January 1925).

Kern, Susan. "Material World of the Jeffersons at Shadwell." *William and Mary Quarterly* (April 2005).

"Life Among the Lowly, No. 1." *Pike County (Ohio) Republican*, March 13, 1873. Reprinted as "Reminiscences of Madison Hemings," in Fawn M. Brodie, *Thomas Jefferson: An Intimate History*. New York: Norton, 1974.

"Life Among the Lowly, No. 3." *Pike County (Ohio) Republican*, December 25, 1873. Reprinted as "Memoirs of Israel Jefferson," in Annette Gordon-Reed, *Thomas Jefferson and Sally Hemings: An American Controversy*. Charlottesville: University Press of Virginia, 1997.

Morgan, Marie, and Edmund S. Morgan. "Jefferson's Concubine." *New York Review of Books*, October 9, 2008.

Neiman, Fraser D. "Coincidence or Causal Connection? The Relationship between Thomas Jefferson's Visits to Monticello and Sally Hemings's Conceptions." *Forum: Thomas Jefferson and Sally Hemings Redux, William and Mary Quarterly*, 3rd Series, vol. 57, no. 1 (January 2000), 198–210.

Raibmon, Paige. "Naturalizing Power: Land and Sexual Violence along William Byrd's Dividing Line." In Virginia J. Scharff, ed., *Seeing Nature through Gender*. Lawrence: University Press of Kansas, 2003.

Randolph, Mary, and Anne Cary. "Reminiscences of Th.J. by MR. " Manuscript copy by University of Virginia Library. In Julian Boyd, ed., *The Papers of Thomas Jefferson*. Princeton: Princeton University Press, 1950, vol. 6.

Stanton, Lucia C. "Looking for Liberty: Thomas Jefferson and the British Lions." *Eighteenth-Century Studies* 26, no. 1 (Summer 1993).

Steele, Brian. "Thomas Jefferson's Gender Frontier." *Journal of American History* 95, no.1 (June 2008).

Theobald, Mary Miley. "Eppington." *Colonial Williamsburg* (Summer 1997).

———. "Slave Conspiracies in Colonial Virginia." *Colonial Williamsburg Journal* (Winter 2005–2006).

Virginia Magazine of Biography and History 14, no. 3 (January 1907), 226–27.

Weaver, Betty Woodson. "Mary Jefferson and Eppington." *Virginia Cavalcade* 19, no. 2 (Autumn 1969).

Weeks, Elie. "Thomas Jefferson's Elk-Hill." *Goochland County Historical Society Magazine* 3 (1971), 6–11.

MANUSCRIPTS, COLLECTIONS

"Account Book of Peter Jefferson," HM912. The Huntington Library.

"Inventory of the Estate of Peter Jefferson." Huntington Library. HM 912.

"Jefferson Family Bible, 1752–1861." University of Virginia Library. Accession 4726.

"Jefferson Papers," Huntington Library. HM5632.

American Philosophical Society. Smith-Houston-Morris-Ogden Family Papers. Family Letters Project. Thomas Jefferson Foundation, at www.monticello.org/papers/index.html.

Anne Cary Randolph, 1805–1808. Household Accounts. Thomas Jefferson Papers. Series 7. Miscellaneous Bound Volumes. Library of Congress.

Coleman, Elizabeth Dabney. "The Carrs of Albemarle County." M.A. thesis, University of Virginia, 1944.

Coolidge, Ellen Randolph. Letterbook, Special Collections. University of Virginia Library. Accession 9090.

Correspondence of Ellen Wayles Randolph Coolidge. Albert and Shirley Small Special Collections Library. University of Virginia. Family Letters Project. Thomas Jefferson Foundation.

Edgehill-Randolph Papers. University of Virginia. "Thomas Jefferson Memorandum."

Elizabeth House Trist Papers. Virginia Historical Society. Family Letters Project. Thomas Jefferson Foundation.

Gilmer-Skipwith Papers. University of Virginia Library. "Dr. George Gilmer's Feebook, 1767, 1771–1775." MSS 6145.

Hochman, Steven. "Thomas Jefferson: A Personal Financial Biography." Ph.D. diss., University of Virginia, 1987.

Kern, Susan. "The Jeffersons at Shadwell: The Social and Material World of a Virginia Family." Ph.D. diss., College of William and Mary, 2005.

Martha Wayles Jefferson. International Center for Jefferson Studies.

Martha Wayles Skelton Jefferson Account Book. Library of Congress.

Martha Wayles Skelton Jefferson, 1772–1782. Part B: Household Accounts.

Nicholas Philip Trist Papers. Southern Historical Collection. University of North Carolina. Family Letters Project. Thomas Jefferson Foundation.

Papers of Trist and Burke Family Members. Special Collections. University of Virginia Library. MSS 5385-f.

Robert Alonzo Brock Collection. Huntington Library.

Thomas Jefferson "Fee Book, 1764–74 [other accounts, 1764 to 1794]." Huntington Library. HM 836.

Thomas Jefferson Papers Series 7. Miscellaneous Bound Volumes. Library of Congress.

Thomas Jefferson Papers, 1606–1827, http://memory.loc.gov/ammem/collections/jefferson_papers.

WEBSITES

American Presidency Project. http://www.presidency.ucsb.edu/ws/index.php?pid=8623.

America's Historical Newspapers. NewsBank and the American Antiquarian Society, 2004. http://infoweb.newsbank.com.

Family Letters Digital Archive. Papers of Thomas Jefferson, Retirement Series, at www.monticello.org/papers/index.html.

http://www.slavevoyages.org/tast/database/search.faces.

"Report of the Research Committee on Thomas Jefferson and Sally Hemings." Thomas Jefferson Foundation, 2000. http://www.monticello.org/plantation/hemingscontro/hemings_report.html.

Stanton, Lucia C. "Wormley Hughes (1781–1858)." http://www.monticello.org/plantation/lives/wormley.html.

Thomas Jefferson Monticello: Thomas Jefferson Encyclopedia. http://wiki.monticello.org/.

Thomas Jefferson Papers, 1606–1827. http://memory.loc.gov/ammem/collections/jefferson_papers.

Twinleaf Journal. African-American Gardens at Monticello. Thomas Jefferson Center for Historic Plants. http://www.twinleaf.org/articles/aagardens.html.

Virginia Historical Society, Online Exhibitions: Virginia's Colonial Dynasties. www.vahistorical.org/dynasties/ishamrandolph.htm.

PERSONAL COMMUNICATION

Personal communication, Diane Ehrenpreis, curatorial art historian, Monticello, June 5, 2008.

Illustration Credits

Grateful acknowledgment is made for permission to reprint the images in the insert:

Page 1: Thomas Jefferson (1791) by Charles Willson Peale (Independence National Historical Park). Page from Martha Wayles Skelton Jefferson Household Accounts (1777) (Martha Wayles Skelton Jefferson, 1772–1782, Part B: Household Accounts. From the Library of Congress "The Thomas Jefferson Papers, 1606-1827, http://memory.loc.gov/cgi-bin/ampage?collId=mtj7&fileName=mtj7page059.db&recNum=26&itemLink=/ammem/collections/jefferson_papers/mtjser7.html&linkText=7&tempFile=./temp/~ammem_OozC&filecode=mtj&next_filecode=mtj&itemnum=1&ndocs=19, accessed January 28, 2010). **Page 2:** Map of Elk Hill Property, drawn from memory by Thomas Jefferson (1793) (Courtesy of the Massachusetts Historical Society). The house at Eppington (Photograph by Chris Wilson). **Page 3:** Maria Cosway, Mezzotint by Valentine Green after Maria Cosway self-portrait (Monticello/photograph by H. Andrew Johnson). The Monticello mansion (Monticello/photograph by Robert Lautman). **Page 4:** Thomas Jefferson's Bedroom and Study (Monticello/photograph by Robert Lautman). Martha Jefferson Randolph, portrait by Thomas Sully (Monticello/photograph by Ed Owen). **Page 5:** Martha Jefferson Randolph's Sitting Room (South Square Room) at Monticello (Monticello/photograph by Robert Lautman). The Monticello staircase (Monticello/photograph by Robert Lautman). **Page 6:** Cook's Room in South Dependency, similar to room in which Sally Hemings may have lived for a time (Monticello/Thomas Jefferson Foundation, Inc.). Ann Cary Randolph Bankhead, portrait by James Ford (Monticello/Thomas Jefferson Foundation, Inc.). **Page 7**: Portrait of Ellen Wayles Randolph Coolidge (Courtesy Ellen Eddy Thorndike). Cornelia Jefferson Randolph, bust by William Coffee (Monticello/photograph by Ed Owen). **Page 8**: Floor plan of Monticello, with estate inventory, by Cornelia Jefferson Randolph (Special Collections, University of Virginia Library). Photograph of Virginia Randolph Trist and Ellen (Eleanora) Wayles Randolph Coolidge (ca. 1850s) (Monticello/Thomas Jefferson Foundation, Inc.). Bell used by Martha Jefferson, given to Sally Hemings (Monticello/Thomas Jefferson Foundation, Inc./Courtesy Moorland-Spingarn Research Center, Howard University).

Index

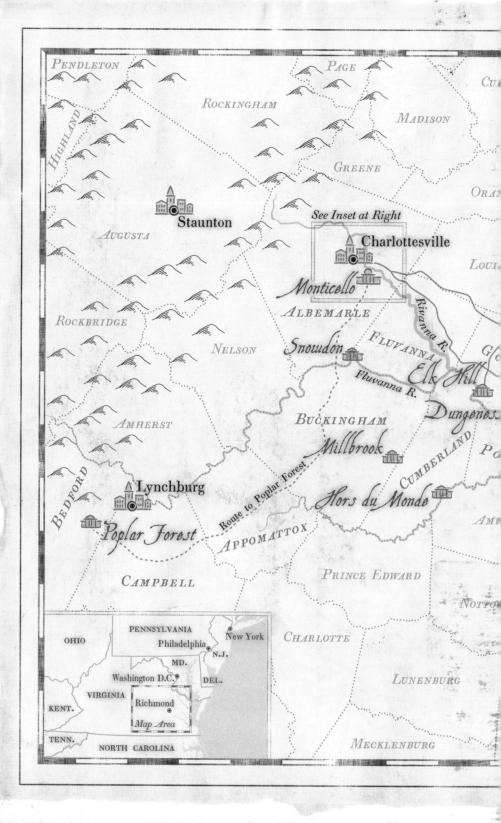